Advanced Strategic Cost Management

Virginia Tech

ACIS 5214

| PEARSON COLLECTIONS |

PEARSON

Cover Art: Courtesy of Photodisc/Getty Images

Attention bookstores: For permission to return any unsold stock, contact us at pe-uscustomreturns@pearson.com

Pearson Learning Solutions, 501 Boylston Street, Suite 900, Boston, MA 02116

A Pearson Education Company
www.pearsoned.com

PEARSON

ISBN 10: 1323717137

ISBN 13: 9781323717134

Printed in the USA
1 17

Table of Contents

Activity-Based Costing and Activity-Based Management

From Chapter 5 of *Horngren's Cost Accounting: A Managerial Emphasis*, Sixteenth Edition. Srikant M. Datar, Madhav V. Rajan.

Activity-Based Costing and Activity-Based Management

LEARNING OBJECTIVES

1 Explain how broad averaging undercosts and overcosts products or services

2 Present three guidelines for refining a costing system

3 Distinguish between simple and activity-based costing systems

4 Describe a four-part cost hierarchy

5 Cost products or services using activity-based costing

6 Evaluate the benefits and costs of implementing activity-based costing systems

7 Explain how managers use activity-based costing systems in activity-based management

8 Compare activity-based costing systems and department costing systems

A good mystery never fails to capture the imagination.

Business and organizations are like a good mystery. Their costing systems are often filled with unresolved questions: Why are we bleeding red ink? Are we pricing our products accurately? Activity-based costing can help unravel the mystery and result in improved operations. General Motors uses activity-based costing to evaluate the cost of its suppliers' products.

GENERAL MOTORS AND ACTIVITY-BASED COSTING[1]

In 2015, General Motors (GM) launched an automotive parts-buying program that forgoes conventional supplier bidding. Under the new program, any automotive parts supplier that wants GM's business agrees to let a team of GM engineers and purchasing managers evaluate the supplier's factories and cost data using activity-based costing. This evaluation assesses material costs, labor, scrap, production cycle times, and other factors that, in turn, help GM attach activity costs to each of the tens of thousands of parts needed to build its lineup of cars, trucks, and SUVs.

This new program allows GM, which spent approximately $85 billion in 2005 on parts and supplies, to develop more realistic cost estimates for its vehicles. Each year, GM can update its activity-based costing analyses to see whether suppliers can cut costs by more efficient production. Suppliers in the program benefit by receiving long-term contracts from GM, who agrees not to seek competing bids from other vendors.

In this chapter, we show how ABC systems help managers make cost-management decisions by improving product designs, processes, and efficiency.

Drive Images/Alamy Stock Photo

[1] *Sources:* David Sedgwick, "GM to Suppliers: Let's See Books, Not Bids," *Automotive News*, May 11, 2015 (http://www.autonews.com/article/20150511/OEM10/305119952/gm-to-suppliers:-lets-see-books-not-bids); General Motors Company, 2015 Annual Report.

Broad Averaging and Its Consequences

LEARNING OBJECTIVE 1

Explain how broad averaging undercosts and overcosts products or services

. . . it does not measure the different resources consumed by different products and services

Historically, companies (such as television and automobile manufacturers) produced a limited variety of products. These companies used few overhead resources to support these simple operations, so indirect (or overhead) costs were a relatively small percentage of total costs. Managers used simple costing systems to allocate overhead costs broadly in an easy, inexpensive, and reasonably accurate way. But as product diversity and indirect costs increased, broad averaging led to inaccurate product costs. That's because simple *peanut-butter costing* (yes, that's what it's called) broadly averages or spreads the cost of resources uniformly to cost objects (such as products or services) when, in fact, the individual products or services use those resources in nonuniform ways.

Undercosting and Overcosting

The following example illustrates how averaging can result in inaccurate and misleading cost data. Consider the cost of a restaurant bill for four colleagues who meet monthly to discuss business developments. Each diner orders separate entrees, desserts, and drinks. The restaurant bill for the most recent meeting is as follows.

	Emma	James	Jessica	Matthew	Total	Average
Entree	$11	$20	$15	$14	$ 60	$15
Dessert	0	8	4	4	16	4
Drinks	4	14	8	6	32	8
Total	$15	$42	$27	$24	$108	$27

If the $108 total restaurant bill is divided evenly, $27 is the average cost per diner. This cost-averaging approach treats each diner the same. When costs are averaged across all four diners, both Emma and Matthew are overcosted (the cost allocated to them is higher than their individual cost), James is undercosted (the cost allocated to him is lower than his individual cost), and Jessica is (by coincidence) accurately costed. Emma, especially, may object to paying the average bill of $27 because her individual bill is only $15.

Broad averaging often leads to undercosting or overcosting of products or services:

- **Product undercosting**—a product is reported to have a low cost per unit but consumes a higher level of resources per unit (James's dinner).
- **Product overcosting**—a product is reported to have a high cost per unit but consumes a lower level of resources per unit (Emma's dinner).

What are the strategic consequences of product undercosting and overcosting? Suppose a manager uses cost information about products to guide pricing decisions. Undercosted products will be underpriced and may even lead to sales that actually result in losses because the sales may bring in less revenue than the cost of resources they use. Overcosted products will lead to overpricing, causing those products to lose market share to competitors producing similar products. But what if prices of products, such as refrigerators, are determined by the market based on consumer demand and competition among companies? Consider a company manufacturing refrigerators with different features and complexities (such as different types of internal compartments, cooling systems, and vents). Suppose the complex refrigerator is undercosted and the simple refrigerator is overcosted. In this case, the complex refrigerator will appear to be more profitable than it actually is while the simple refrigerator will appear to be less profitable than it actually is. Managers may strategically promote the complex undercosted refrigerators thinking they are highly profitable, when in fact these refrigerators consume large amounts of resources and are far less profitable than they appear. They may underinvest in the simple overcosted refrigerator, which shows low profits when in fact the profits from this refrigerator may be considerably better. Alternatively, they may focus on trying to reduce the cost of the simple refrigerator to make it more profitable when, in fact, this refrigerator is reasonably profitable and the opportunities to reduce its costs may be quite limited.

Product-Cost Cross-Subsidization

Product-cost cross-subsidization means that if a company undercosts one of its products, it will overcost at least one of its other products. Similarly, if a company overcosts one of its products, it will undercost at least one of its other products. Product-cost cross-subsidization is very common when a cost is uniformly spread—meaning it is broadly averaged—across multiple products without managers recognizing the amount of resources each product consumes.

In the restaurant-bill example, the amount of cost cross-subsidization of each diner can be readily computed *because all cost items can be traced as direct costs to each diner*. If all diners pay $27, Emma is paying $12 more than her actual cost of $15. She is cross-subsidizing James who is paying $15 less than his actual cost of $42. Calculating the amount of cost cross-subsidization takes more work when there are indirect costs to be considered. Why? Because when two or more diners use the resources represented by indirect costs, we need to find a way to allocate costs to each diner. Consider, for example, a $40 bottle of wine whose cost is shared equally. Each diner would pay $10 ($40 ÷ 4). Suppose Matthew drinks two glasses of wine, while Emma, James, and Jessica drink one glass each for a total of five glasses. Allocating the cost of the bottle of wine on the basis of the glasses of wine that each diner drinks would result in Matthew paying $16 ($40 × 2/5) and each of the others paying $8 ($40 × 1/5). In this case, by sharing the cost equally, Emma, James, and Jessica are each paying $2($10 − $8) more and are cross-subsidizing Matthew who is paying $6($16 − $10) less for his wine for the night.

DECISION POINT

When does product undercosting or overcosting occur?

To see the effects of broad averaging on direct and indirect costs, we next consider Plastim Corporation's costing system.

Simple Costing System at Plastim Corporation

Plastim Corporation manufactures lenses for the rear taillights of automobiles. A lens, made from black, red, orange, or white plastic, is the part of the taillight visible on the automobile's exterior. Lenses are made by injecting molten plastic into a mold, which gives the lens its desired shape. The mold is cooled to allow the molten plastic to solidify, and the lens is removed.

Plastim sells all its lenses to Giovanni Motors, a major automobile manufacturer. Under the contract, Plastim manufactures two types of lenses for Giovanni: a simple lens called S3 and a complex lens called C5. The complex lens is large and has special features, such as multicolor molding (when more than one color is injected into the mold) and a complex shape that wraps around the corner of the car. Manufacturing C5 lenses is complicated because various parts in the mold must align and fit precisely. The S3 lens is simpler to make because it has a single color and few special features.

Design, Manufacturing, and Distribution Processes

Whether lenses are simple or complex, Plastim follows this sequence of steps to design, produce, and distribute them:

- **Design products and processes.** Each year Giovanni Motors specifies details of the simple and complex lenses it needs for its new models of cars. Plastim's design department designs the new molds and specifies the manufacturing process to make the lenses.
- **Manufacture lenses.** The lenses are molded, finished, cleaned, and inspected.
- **Distribute lenses.** Finished lenses are packed and sent to Giovanni Motors' plants.

Plastim is operating at capacity and incurs very low marketing costs. Because of its high-quality products, Plastim has minimal customer-service costs. Plastim competes with several other companies who also manufacture simple lenses. At a recent meeting, Giovanni's purchasing manager informed Plastim's sales manager that Bandix, which makes only simple lenses, is offering to supply the S3 lens to Giovanni at a price of $53, well below the $63 price that Plastim is currently projecting and budgeting for 2017. Unless Plastim can lower its selling price, it will lose the Giovanni business for the simple lens for the upcoming model year. Fortunately, the same competitive pressures do not exist for the complex lens, which Plastim currently sells to Giovanni at $137 per lens.

Plastim's managers have two primary options:

- Give up the Giovanni business in simple lenses if selling them is unprofitable. Bandix makes only simple lenses and perhaps, therefore, uses simpler technology and processes than Plastim. The simpler operations may give Bandix a cost advantage that Plastim cannot match. If so, it is better for Plastim to not supply the S3 lens to Giovanni.
- Reduce the price of the simple lens and either accept a lower margin or aggressively seek to reduce costs.

To make these long-run strategic decisions, managers first need to understand the costs to design, make, and distribute the S3 and C5 lenses.

Bandix makes only simple lenses and can fairly accurately calculate the cost of a lens by dividing total costs by the number of simple lenses produced. Plastim's costing environment is more challenging because the manufacturing overhead costs support the production of both simple and complex lenses. Plastim's managers and management accountants need to find a way to allocate overhead costs to each type of lens.

In computing costs, Plastim assigns both variable costs and costs that are fixed in the short run to the S3 and C5 lenses. Managers cost products and services to guide long-run strategic decisions, such as what mix of products and services to produce and sell and what prices to charge for them. In the long run, managers have the ability to influence all costs. The firm will only survive in the long run if revenues exceed total costs, regardless of whether these costs are variable or fixed in the short run.

To guide pricing and cost-management decisions, Plastim's managers need to consider all costs and therefore assign both manufacturing and nonmanufacturing costs to the S3 and C5 lenses. If managers had wanted to calculate the cost of inventory, Plastim's management accountants would have assigned only manufacturing costs to the lenses, as required by Generally Accepted Accounting Principles. Surveys of company practice across the globe indicate that the vast majority of companies use costing systems not just for inventory costing but also for strategic purposes, such as pricing and product-mix decisions and decisions about cost reduction, process improvement, design, and planning and budgeting. Managers of these companies assign all costs to products and services. Even merchandising-sector companies (for whom inventory costing is straightforward) and service-sector companies (who have no inventory) expend considerable resources in designing and operating their costing systems to allocate costs for strategic purposes.

Simple Costing System Using a Single Indirect-Cost Pool

Plastim currently has a simple costing system that allocates indirect costs using a single indirect-cost rate. Exhibit 1 shows an overview of Plastim's simple costing system. Use this exhibit as a guide as you study the following steps, each of which is marked in Exhibit 1.

Step 1: Identify the Products That Are the Chosen Cost Objects. The cost objects are the 60,000 simple S3 lenses and the 15,000 complex C5 lenses that Plastim will produce in 2017. Plastim's management accountants first calculate the total costs and then the unit cost of designing, manufacturing, and distributing lenses.

Step 2: Identify the Direct Costs of the Products. The direct costs are direct materials and direct manufacturing labor. Exhibit 2 shows the direct and indirect costs for the S3 and the C5 lenses using the simple costing system. The direct-cost calculations appear on lines 5, 6, and 7 in Exhibit 2. Plastim's simple costing system classifies all costs other than direct materials and direct manufacturing labor as indirect costs.

Step 3: Select the Cost-Allocation Bases to Use for Allocating Indirect (or Overhead) Costs to the Products. A majority of the indirect costs consists of salaries paid to supervisors, engineers, manufacturing support, and maintenance staff that support direct manufacturing labor. Plastim's managers use direct manufacturing labor-hours as the only

EXHIBIT 1

Overview of Plastim's Simple Costing System

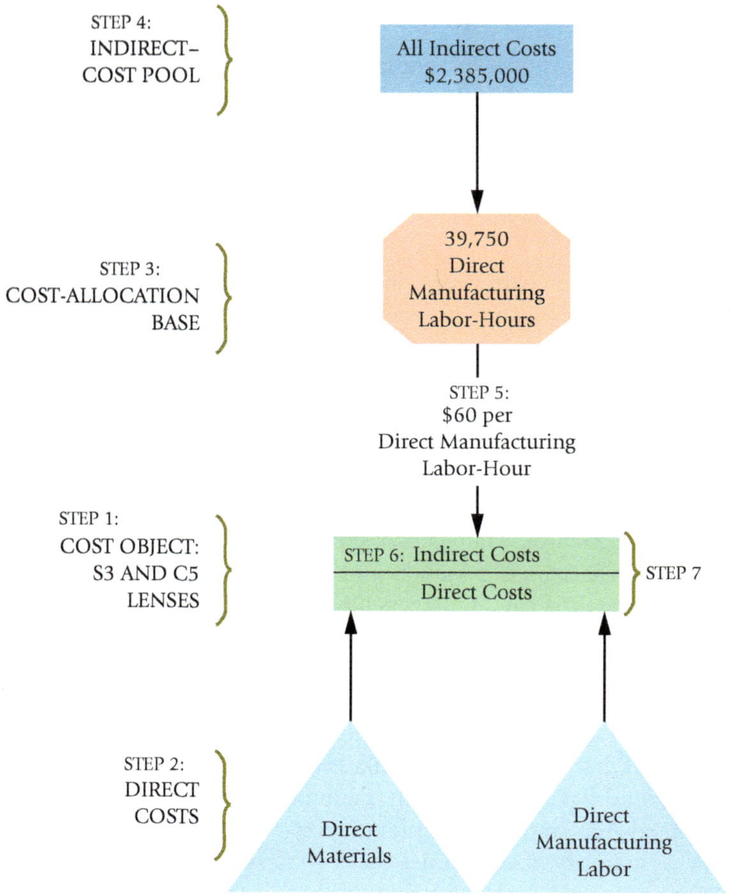

allocation base to allocate all manufacturing and nonmanufacturing indirect costs to S3 and C5. Historically, many companies used such simple costing systems because overhead costs were only a small component of costs and because a single cost driver accurately reflected how overhead resources were used. In 2017, Plastim's managers budget 39,750 direct manufacturing labor-hours.

Step 4: Identify the Indirect Costs Associated with Each Cost-Allocation Base. Because Plastim uses only a single cost-allocation base, Plastim's management accountants group all budgeted indirect costs of $2,385,000 for 2017 into a single overhead cost pool.

EXHIBIT 2 Plastim's Product Costs Using the Simple Costing System

	A	B	C	D	E	F	G
1		60,000			15,000		
2		Simple Lenses (S3)			Complex Lenses (C5)		
3		Total	per Unit		Total	per Unit	Total
4		(1)	(2) = (1) ÷ 60,000		(3)	(4) = (3) ÷ 15,000	(5) = (1) + (3)
5	Direct materials	$1,125,000	$18.75		$ 675,000	$45.00	$1,800,000
6	Direct manufacturing labor	600,000	10.00		195,000	13.00	795,000
7	Total direct costs (Step 2)	1,725,000	28.75		870,000	58.00	2,595,000
8	Indirect costs allocated (Step 6)	1,800,000	30.00		585,000	39.00	2,385,000
9	Total costs (Step 7)	$3,525,000	$58.75		$1,455,000	$97.00	$4,980,000
10							

Step 5: Compute the Rate per Unit of Each Cost-Allocation Base.

$$\text{Budgeted indirect-cost rate} = \frac{\text{Budgeted total costs in indirect-cost pool}}{\text{Budgeted total quantity of cost-allocation base}}$$

$$= \frac{\$2{,}385{,}000}{39{,}750 \text{ direct manufacturing labor-hours}}$$

$$= \$60 \text{ per direct manufacturing labor-hour}$$

Step 6: Compute the Indirect Costs Allocated to the Products. Plastim's managers budget 30,000 total direct manufacturing labor-hours to make the 60,000 S3 lenses and 9,750 total direct manufacturing labor-hours to make the 15,000 C5 lenses. Exhibit 2 shows indirect costs of $1,800,000 ($60 per direct manufacturing labor-hour × 30,000 direct manufacturing labor-hours) allocated to the simple lens and $585,000 ($60 per direct manufacturing labor-hour × 9,750 direct manufacturing labor-hours) allocated to the complex lens.

Step 7: Compute the Total Cost of the Products by Adding All Direct and Indirect Costs Assigned to the Products. Exhibit 2 presents the product costs for the simple and complex lenses. The direct costs are calculated in Step 2 and the indirect costs in Step 6. Be sure you see the parallel between the simple costing system overview diagram (Exhibit 1) and the costs calculated in Step 7. Exhibit 1 shows two direct-cost categories and one indirect-cost category. Therefore, the budgeted cost of each type of lens in Step 7 (Exhibit 2) has three line items: two for direct costs and one for allocated indirect costs. It is very helpful to draw overview diagrams to see the big picture of costing systems before getting into the detailed costing of products and services. The budgeted cost per S3 lens is $58.75, well above the $53 selling price quoted by Bandix. The budgeted cost per C5 lens is $97.

TRY IT! 1

Amherst Metal Works produces two types of metal lamps. Amherst manufactures 20,000 basic lamps and 5,000 designer lamps. Its simple costing system uses a single indirect-cost pool and allocates costs to the two lamps on the basis of direct manufacturing labor-hours. It provides the following budgeted cost information:

	Basic Lamps	Designer Lamps	Total
Direct materials per lamp	$ 9	$15	
Direct manufacturing labor per lamp	0.5 hours	0.6 hours	
Direct manufacturing labor rate per hour	$20	$20	
Indirect manufacturing costs			$234,000

Calculate the total budgeted costs of the basic and designer lamps using Amherst's simple costing system.

Applying the Five-Step Decision-Making Process at Plastim

To decide how it should respond to the threat that Bandix poses to its S3 lens business, Plastim's managers work through the five-step decision-making process.

Step 1: Identify the Problem and Uncertainties. The problem is clear: If Plastim wants to retain the Giovanni business for S3 lenses and make a profit, it must find a way to reduce the price and costs of the S3 lens. The two major uncertainties Plastim faces are (1) whether its technology and processes for the S3 lens are competitive with Bandix's and (2) whether Plastim's S3 lens is overcosted by the simple costing system.

Step 2: Obtain Information. Senior management asks a team of design and process engineers to analyze and evaluate the design, manufacturing, and distribution operations for the S3 lens. The team is very confident that the technology and processes for the S3 lens are not inferior to those of Bandix and other competitors because Plastim has many years of experience in manufacturing and distributing the S3 lens with a history and culture of continuous process improvements. The team is less certain about Plastim's capabilities in manufacturing and distributing complex lenses because it only recently started making this type of lens. Given these doubts, senior management is happy that Giovanni Motors considers the price of the C5 lens to be competitive. Plastim's managers are puzzled, though, by how, at the currently budgeted prices, Plastim is expected to earn a very large profit margin percentage (operating income ÷ revenues) on the C5 lenses and a small profit margin on the S3 lenses:

	60,000 Simple Lenses (S3)		15,000 Complex Lenses (C5)		
	Total (1)	per Unit (2) = (1) ÷ 60,000	Total (3)	per Unit (4) = (3) ÷ 15,000	Total (5) = (1)+(3)
Revenues	$3,780,000	$63.00	$2,055,000	$137.00	$5,835,000
Total costs	3,525,000	58.75	1,455,000	97.00	4,980,000
Operating income	$ 255,000	$ 4.25	$ 600,000	$ 40.00	$ 855,000
Profit margin percentage		6.75%		29.20%	

As they continue to gather information, Plastim's managers begin to ponder why the profit margins are under so much pressure for the S3 lens, where the company has strong capabilities, but not on the newer, less-established C5 lens. Plastim is not deliberately charging a low price for S3, so managers begin to evaluate the costing system. Plastim's simple costing system may be overcosting the simple S3 lens (assigning too much cost to it) and undercosting the complex C5 lens (assigning too little cost to it).

Step 3: Make Predictions About the Future. Plastim's key challenge is to get a better estimate of what it will cost to design, make, and distribute the S3 and C5 lenses. Managers are fairly confident about the direct material and direct manufacturing labor cost of each lens because these costs are easily traced to the lenses. Of greater concern is how accurately the simple costing system measures the indirect resources used by each type of lens. The managers believe the costing system can be substantially improved.

Even as they come to this conclusion, managers want to avoid biased thinking. In particular, they want to be careful that the desire to be competitive on the S3 lens does not lead to assumptions that bias them in favor of lowering costs of the S3 lens.

Step 4: Make Decisions by Choosing Among Alternatives. On the basis of predicted costs and taking into account how Bandix might respond, Plastim's managers must decide whether they should bid for Giovanni Motors' S3 lens business and, if they do bid, what price they should offer.

Step 5: Implement the Decision, Evaluate Performance, and Learn. If Plastim bids and wins Giovanni's S3 lens business, it must compare actual costs as it makes and ships the S3 lenses to predicted costs and learn why actual costs deviate from predicted costs. Such evaluation and learning form the basis for future improvements.

The next few sections focus on Steps 3, 4, and 5: (3) how Plastim improves the allocation of indirect costs to the S3 and C5 lenses, (4) how it uses these predictions to bid for the S3 lens business, and (5) how it evaluates performance, makes product design and process improvements, and learns using the new system.

LEARNING OBJECTIVE 2

Present three guidelines for refining a costing system

. . . classify more costs as direct costs, expand the number of indirect-cost pools, and identify cost drivers

Refining a Costing System

A **refined costing system** reduces the use of broad averages for assigning the cost of resources to cost objects (such as jobs, products, and services) and provides better measurement of the costs of indirect resources used by different cost objects, no matter how differently various cost objects use indirect resources. Refining a costing system helps managers make better decisions about how to allocate resources and which products to produce.

Reasons for Refining a Costing System

Three principal reasons have accelerated the demand for refinements to the costing system.

1. **Increase in product diversity.** The growing demand for customized products has led managers to increase the variety of products and services their companies offer. Kanthal, a Swedish manufacturer of heating elements, for example, produces more than 10,000 different types of electrical heating wires and thermostats. Banks, such as Barclays Bank in the United Kingdom, offer many different types of accounts and services: special passbook accounts, ATMs, credit cards, and electronic banking products. Producing these products places different demands on resources because of differences in volume, process, technology, and complexity. For example, the computer and network resources needed to support electronic banking products are much greater than the computer and network resources needed to support a passbook savings account. The use of broad averages fails to capture these differences in demand and leads to distorted and inaccurate cost information.
2. **Increase in indirect costs with different cost drivers.** The use of product and process technology such as computer-integrated manufacturing (CIM) and flexible manufacturing systems (FMS) has led to an increase in indirect costs and a decrease in direct costs, particularly direct manufacturing labor costs. In CIM and FMS, computers on the manufacturing floor instruct equipment to set up and run quickly and automatically. The computers accurately measure hundreds of production parameters and directly control the manufacturing processes to achieve high-quality output. Managing complex technology and producing diverse products also require additional support function resources for activities such as production scheduling, product and process design, and engineering. Because direct manufacturing labor is not a cost driver of these costs, allocating indirect costs on the basis of direct manufacturing labor (as in Plastim's simple costing system) does not accurately measure how resources are being used by different products.
3. **Competition in product markets.** As markets have become more competitive, managers have felt the need to obtain more accurate cost information to help them make important strategic decisions, such as how to price products and which products to sell. Making correct decisions about pricing and product mix is critical in competitive markets because competitors quickly capitalize on a manager's mistakes. For example, if Plastim overcosts the S3 lens and charges a higher price, a competitor aware of the true costs of making the lens could charge a lower price and gain the S3 business as Bandix is attempting to do.

The preceding factors explain why managers want to refine cost systems. Refining costing systems requires gathering, validating, analyzing, and storing vast quantities of data. Advances in information technology have drastically reduced the costs of performing these activities.

Guidelines for Refining a Costing System

There are three main guidelines for refining a costing system:

1. **Direct-cost tracing.** Identify as many direct costs as is economically feasible. This guideline aims to reduce the amount of costs classified as indirect, thereby minimizing the extent to which costs have to be allocated rather than traced.
2. **Indirect-cost pools.** Expand the number of indirect-cost pools until each pool is more homogeneous. All costs in a *homogeneous cost pool* have the same or a similar cause-and-effect (or benefits-received) relationship with a single cost driver that is used as the cost-allocation base. Consider, for example, a single indirect-cost pool containing both indirect machining costs and indirect distribution costs that are allocated to products using machine-hours. This pool is not homogeneous because machine-hours are a cost driver of machining costs but not of distribution costs, which has a different cost driver, cubic feet of product delivered. If, instead, machining costs and distribution costs are separated into two indirect-cost pools, with machine-hours as the cost-allocation base for the machining cost pool and cubic feet of product delivered as the cost-allocation base for the distribution cost pool, each indirect-cost pool would become homogeneous.

DECISION POINT

How do managers refine a costing system?

3. **Cost-allocation bases.** As we describe later in the chapter, whenever possible, managers should use the cost driver (the cause of indirect costs) as the cost-allocation base for each homogeneous indirect-cost pool (the effect).

Activity-Based Costing Systems

LEARNING OBJECTIVE 3

Distinguish between simple and activity-based costing systems

...unlike simple systems, activity-based costing systems calculate costs of individual activities to cost products

One of the best tools for refining a costing system is *activity-based costing*. **Activity-based costing (ABC)** refines a costing system by identifying individual activities as the fundamental cost objects. An **activity** is an event, task, or unit of work with a specified purpose—for example, designing products, setting up machines, operating machines, or distributing products. More informally, activities are verbs; they are things that a firm does. To help make strategic decisions, ABC systems identify activities in all functions of the value chain, calculate costs of individual activities, and assign costs to cost objects such as products and services on the basis of the mix of activities needed to produce each product or service.[2]

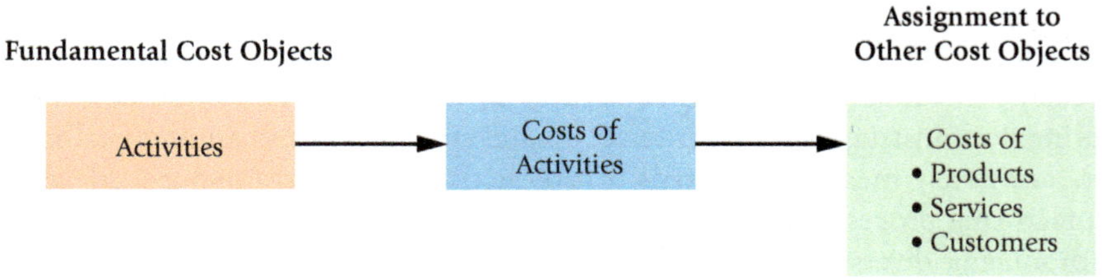

Plastim's ABC System

After reviewing its simple costing system and the potential miscosting of product costs, Plastim's managers decide to implement an ABC system. Direct material costs and direct manufacturing labor costs can be traced to products easily, so the ABC system focuses on refining the assignment of indirect costs to departments, processes, products, or other cost objects. To identify activities, Plastim organizes a team of managers from design, manufacturing, distribution, accounting, and administration. Plastim's ABC system then uses activities to break down its current single indirect-cost pool into finer pools of costs related to the various activities.

Defining activities is difficult. The team evaluates hundreds of tasks performed at Plastim. It must decide which tasks should be classified as separate activities and which should be combined. For example, should maintenance of molding machines, operations of molding machines, and process control be regarded as separate activities or combined into a single activity? An activity-based costing system with many activities becomes overly detailed and unwieldy to operate. An activity-based costing system with too few activities may not be refined enough to measure cause-and-effect relationships between cost drivers and various indirect costs. To achieve an effective balance, Plastim's team focuses on activities that account for a sizable fraction of indirect costs and combines activities that have the same cost driver into a single activity. For example, the team decides to combine maintenance of molding machines, operations of molding machines, and process control into a single activity—molding machine operations—because all these activities have the same cost driver: molding machine-hours.

The team identifies the following seven activities based on the steps and processes needed to design, manufacture, and distribute S3 and C5 lenses.

a. Design products and processes
b. Set up molding machines to ensure that the molds are properly held in place and parts are properly aligned before manufacturing starts

[2] For more details on ABC systems, see R. Cooper and R. S. Kaplan, *The Design of Cost Management Systems* (Upper Saddle River, NJ: Prentice Hall, 1999); G. Cokins, *Activity-Based Cost Management: An Executive's Guide* (Hoboken, NJ: John Wiley & Sons, 2001); and R. S. Kaplan and S. Anderson, *Time-Driven Activity-Based Costing: A Simpler and More Powerful Path to Higher Profits* (Boston: Harvard Business School Press, 2007).

c. Operate molding machines to manufacture lenses
d. Clean and maintain the molds after lenses are manufactured
e. Prepare batches of finished lenses for shipment
f. Distribute lenses to customers
g. Administer and manage all processes at Plastim

These activity descriptions (or *activity list* or *activity dictionary*) form the basis of the activity-based costing system. Compiling the list of tasks, however, is only the first step in implementing activity-based costing systems. Plastim must also identify the cost of each activity and the related cost driver by using the three guidelines for refining a costing system.

1. **Direct-cost tracing.** Plastim's ABC system subdivides the single indirect-cost pool into seven smaller cost pools related to the different activities. The costs in the cleaning and maintenance activity cost pool (item d) consist of salaries and wages paid to workers who clean the mold. These costs are direct costs because they can be economically traced to a specific mold and lens.
2. **Indirect-cost pools.** The remaining six activity cost pools are indirect-cost pools. Unlike the single indirect-cost pool of Plastim's simple costing system, each of the activity-related cost pools is homogeneous. That is, each activity cost pool includes only those narrow and focused sets of costs that have the same cost driver. Consider, for example, distribution costs. Managers identify cubic feet of packages delivered as the only cost driver of distribution costs because all distribution costs (such as wages of truck drivers) vary with the cubic feet of packages delivered. In the simple costing system, Plastim pooled all indirect costs together and used a single cost-allocation base, direct manufacturing labor-hours, which was not a cost driver of all indirect costs. Managers were therefore unable to measure how different cost objects (the S3 and C5 lenses) used resources.

   To determine the costs of activity pools, managers assign costs accumulated in various account classifications (such as salaries, wages, maintenance, and electricity) to each of the activity cost pools. This process is commonly called *first-stage allocation*. For example, as we will see later in the chapter, of the $2,385,000 in the total indirect-cost pool, Plastim identifies setup costs of $300,000. Setup costs include depreciation and maintenance costs of setup equipment, wages of setup workers, and allocated salaries of design engineers, process engineers, and supervisors. We focus here on the *second-stage allocation*, the allocation of costs of activity cost pools to products.
3. **Cost-allocation bases.** For each activity cost pool, Plastim uses the cost driver (whenever possible) as the cost-allocation base. To identify cost drivers, Plastim's managers consider various alternatives and use their knowledge of operations to choose among them. For example, Plastim's managers choose setup-hours rather than the number of setups as the cost driver of setup costs because Plastim's managers believe that the more complex setups of C5 lenses take more time and are more costly. Over time, Plastim's managers can use data to test their beliefs.

The logic of ABC systems is twofold. First, when managers structure activity cost pools more finely, using cost drivers for each activity cost pool as the cost-allocation base, it leads to more accurate costing of activities. Second, allocating these costs to products by measuring the cost-allocation bases of different activities used by different products leads to more accurate product costs. We illustrate this logic by focusing on the setup activity at Plastim.

Setting up molding machines frequently entails trial runs, fine-tuning, and adjustments. Improper setups cause quality problems such as scratches on the surface of the lens. The resources needed for each setup depend on the complexity of the manufacturing operation. Complex lenses require more setup resources (setup-hours) per setup than simple lenses. Furthermore, complex lenses can be produced only in small batches because the molds for complex lenses need to be cleaned more often than molds for simple lenses. Relative to simple lenses, complex lenses therefore not only use more setup-hours per setup, but also require more frequent setups.

Setup data for the simple S3 lens and the complex C5 lens are as follows.

		Simple S3 Lens	Complex C5 Lens	Total
1	Quantity of lenses produced	60,000	15,000	
2	Number of lenses produced per batch	240	50	
3 = (1) ÷ (2)	Number of batches	250	300	
4	Setup time per batch	2 hours	5 hours	
5 = (3) × (4)	Total setup-hours	500 hours	1,500 hours	2,000 hours

Recall that in its simple costing system, Plastim uses direct manufacturing labor-hours to allocate all $2,385,000 of indirect costs (which includes $300,000 of indirect setup costs) to products. The following table compares how setup costs allocated to simple and complex lenses will be different if Plastim allocates setup costs to lenses based on setup-hours rather than direct manufacturing labor-hours. Of the $60 total rate per direct manufacturing labor-hour, the setup cost per direct manufacturing labor-hour amounts to $7.54717 ($300,000 ÷ 39,750 total direct manufacturing labor-hours). The setup cost per setup-hour equals $150 ($300,000 ÷ 2,000 total setup-hours).

	Simple S3 Lens	Complex C5 Lens	Total
Setup cost allocated using direct manufacturing labor-hours:			
$7.54717 × 30,000; $7.54717 × 9,750	$226,415	$ 73,585	$300,000
Setup cost allocated using setup-hours:			
$150 × 500; $150 × 1,500	$ 75,000	$225,000	$300,000

ABC systems that use available time (setup-hours in our example) to calculate the cost of a resource and to allocate costs to cost objects are sometimes called *time-driven activity-based costing (TDABC) systems.* Following guidelines 2 and 3, Plastim should use setup hours, the cost driver of set up costs, and not direct manufacturing labor hours, to allocate setup costs to products. The C5 lens uses substantially more setup-hours than the S3 lens (1,500 hours ÷ 2,000 hours = 75% of the total setup-hours) because the C5 requires a greater number of setups (batches) and each setup is more challenging and requires more setup-hours.

DECISION POINT

What is the difference between the design of a simple costing system and an activity-based costing (ABC) system?

The ABC system therefore allocates significantly more setup costs to C5 than to S3. When direct manufacturing labor-hours rather than setup-hours are used to allocate setup costs in the simple costing system, the S3 lens is allocated a very large share of the setup costs because the S3 lens uses a larger proportion of direct manufacturing labor-hours (30,000 ÷ 39,750 = 75.47%). As a result, the simple costing system overcosts the S3 lens with regard to setup costs.

As we will see later in the chapter, ABC systems provide valuable information to managers beyond more accurate product costs. For example, identifying setup-hours as the cost driver correctly orients managers' cost reduction efforts on reducing setup-hours and cost per setup-hour. Note that setup-hours are related to batches (or groups) of lenses made, not the number of individual lenses. Activity-based costing attempts to identify the most relevant cause-and-effect relationship for each activity pool without restricting the cost driver to be units of output or variables related to units of output (such as direct manufacturing labor-hours). As our discussion of setups illustrates, limiting cost-allocation bases to only units of output weakens the cause-and-effect relationship between the cost-allocation base and the costs in a cost pool. Broadening cost drivers to batches (or groups) of lenses, not just individual lenses, leads us to *cost hierarchies.*

LEARNING OBJECTIVE 4

Describe a four-part cost hierarchy

. . . a four-part cost hierarchy is used to categorize costs based on different types of cost drivers—for example, costs that vary with each unit of a product versus costs that vary with each batch of products

Cost Hierarchies

A **cost hierarchy** categorizes various activity cost pools on the basis of the different types of cost drivers, cost-allocation bases, or different degrees of difficulty in determining cause-and-effect (or benefits-received) relationships. ABC systems commonly use a cost hierarchy with four levels to identify cost-allocation bases that are cost drivers of the activity cost pools: (1) output unit–level costs, (2) batch-level costs, (3) product-sustaining costs, and (4) facility-sustaining costs.

Output unit–level costs are the costs of activities performed on each individual unit of a product or service. Machine operations costs (such as the cost of energy, machine depreciation, and repair) related to the activity of running the automated molding machines are output unit–level costs because, over time, the cost of this activity increases with additional units of output produced (or machine-hours used). Plastim's ABC system uses molding machine-hours, an output unit–level cost-allocation base, to allocate machine operations costs to products.

Batch-level costs are the costs of activities related to a group of units of a product or service rather than each individual unit of product or service. In the Plastim example, setup costs are batch-level costs because, over time, the cost of this setup activity varies with the setup-hours needed to produce batches (groups) of lenses regardless of the total number of lenses produced. For example, if Plastim produces 20% fewer lenses using the same number of setup hours, would setup costs change? No, because setup hours not the number of lenses produced drive setup costs.

As described in the table, the S3 lens requires 500 setup-hours (2 setup-hours per batch × 250 batches). The C5 lens requires 1,500 setup-hours (5 setup-hours per batch × 300 batches). The total setup costs allocated to S3 and C5 depend on the total setup-hours required by each type of lens, not on the number of lenses of S3 and C5 produced. Plastim's ABC system uses setup-hours, a batch-level cost-allocation base, to allocate setup costs to products. Other examples of batch-level costs are material-handling and quality-inspection costs associated with batches (not the quantities) of products produced and costs of placing purchase orders, receiving materials, and paying invoices related to the number of purchase orders placed rather than the quantity or value of materials purchased.

Product-sustaining costs (service-sustaining costs) are the costs of activities undertaken to support individual products or services regardless of the number of units or batches in which the units are produced or services provided. In the Plastim example, design costs are product-sustaining costs. Over time, design costs depend largely on the time designers spend on designing and modifying the product, mold, and process, not on the number of lenses subsequently produced or the number of batches in which the lenses are produced using the mold. These design costs are a function of the complexity of the mold, measured by the number of parts in the mold multiplied by the area (in square feet) over which the molten plastic must flow (12 parts × 2.5 square feet, or 30 parts-square feet for the S3 lens; and 14 parts × 5 square feet, or 70 parts-square feet for the C5 lens). Plastim's ABC system uses parts-square feet, a product-sustaining cost-allocation base, to allocate design costs to products. Other examples of product-sustaining costs are product research and development costs, costs of making engineering changes, and marketing costs to launch new products.

Facility-sustaining costs are the costs of activities that managers cannot trace to individual products or services but that support the organization as a whole. In the Plastim example and at companies such as Volvo, Samsung, and General Electric, the general administration costs (including top management compensation, rent, and building security) are facility-sustaining costs. It is usually difficult to find a good cause-and-effect relationship between these costs and the cost-allocation base, so some companies deduct facility-sustaining costs as a separate lump-sum amount from operating income rather than allocate these costs to products. Managers who follow this approach need to keep in mind that when making decisions based on costs (such as pricing), some lump-sum costs have not been allocated. They must set prices that are much greater than the allocated costs to recover some of the unallocated facility-sustaining costs. Other companies, such as Plastim, allocate facility-sustaining costs to products on some basis—for example, direct manufacturing labor-hours—because management believes all costs should be allocated to products even if it's done in a somewhat arbitrary way. Allocating all costs to products or services ensures that managers take into account all costs when making decisions based on costs. So long as managers are aware of the nature of facility-sustaining costs and the pros and cons of allocating them, which method a manager chooses is a matter of personal preference.

DECISION POINT

What is a cost hierarchy?

Implementing Activity-Based Costing

LEARNING OBJECTIVE 5

Cost products or services using activity-based costing

. . . use cost rates for different activities to compute indirect costs of a product

Now that you understand the basic concepts of ABC, let's see how Plastim's managers refine the simple costing system, evaluate the two systems, and identify the factors to consider when deciding whether to develop the ABC system.

Implementing ABC at Plastim

To implement ABC, Plastim's managers follow the seven-step approach to costing and the three guidelines for refining costing systems (increase direct-cost tracing, create homogeneous indirect-cost pools, and identify cost-allocation bases that have cause-and-effect relationships with costs in the cost pool). Exhibit 3 shows an overview of Plastim's ABC system. Use this exhibit as a guide as you study the following steps, each of which is marked in Exhibit 3.

Step 1: Identify the Products That Are the Chosen Cost Objects. The cost objects are the 60,000 S3 and the 15,000 C5 lenses that Plastim will produce in 2017. Plastim's managers want to determine the total costs and then the per-unit cost of designing, manufacturing, and distributing these lenses.

Step 2: Identify the Direct Costs of the Products. The managers identify the following direct costs of the lenses because these costs can be economically traced to a specific mold and lens: direct material costs, direct manufacturing labor costs, and mold cleaning and maintenance costs.

Exhibit 5 shows the direct and indirect costs for the S3 and C5 lenses using the ABC system. The direct costs calculations appear on lines 6, 7, 8, and 9 in Exhibit 5. Plastim's managers classify all other costs as indirect costs, as we will see in Exhibit 4.

Step 3: Select the Activities and Cost-Allocation Bases to Use for Allocating Indirect Costs to the Products. Following guideline 2 (subdivide into homogeneous cost pools) and guideline

EXHIBIT 3 Overview of Plastim's Activity-Based Costing System

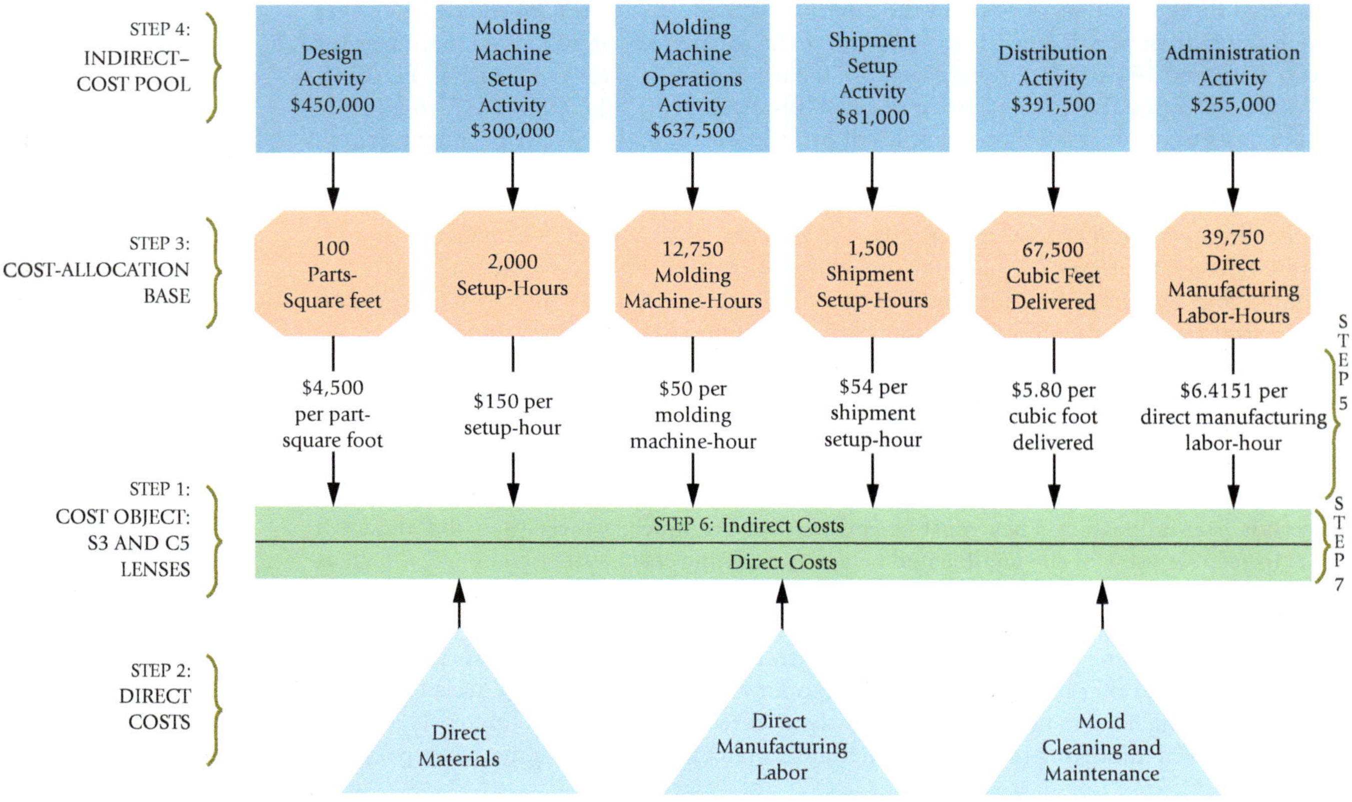

EXHIBIT 4 Activity-Cost Rates for Indirect-Cost Pools

Home Insert Page Layout Formulas Data Review View

	A	B	C	D	E	F	G	H
1			(Step 4)	(Step 3)		(Step 5)		
2	Activity	Cost Hierarchy Category	Total Budgeted Indirect Costs	Budgeted Quantity of Cost-Allocation Base		Budgeted Indirect Cost Rate		Cause-and-Effect Relationship Between Allocation Base and Activity Cost
3	(1)	(2)	(3)	(4)		(5) = (3) ÷ (4)		(6)
4	Design	Product-sustaining	$450,000	100	parts-square feet	$ 4,500	per part-square foot	Design Department indirect costs increase with more complex molds (more parts, larger surface area).
5	Molding machine setup	Batch-level	$300,000	2,000	setup-hours	$ 150	per setup-hour	Indirect setup costs increase with setup-hours.
6	Machine operations	Output unit-level	$637,500	12,750	molding machine-hours	$ 50	per molding machine-hour	Indirect costs of operating molding machines increases with molding machine-hours.
7	Shipment setup	Batch-level	$ 81,000	1,500	shipment setup-hours	$ 54	per shipment setup-hour	Shipping costs incurred to prepare batches for shipment increase with the number of shipment setup-hours.
8	Distribution	Output-unit-level	$391,500	67,500	cubic feet delivered	$ 5.80	per cubic foot delivered	Distribution costs increase with the cubic feet of packages delivered.
9	Administration	Facility sustaining	$255,000	39,750	direct manuf. labor-hours	$6.4151	per direct manuf. labor-hour	The demand for administrative resources increases with direct manufacturing labor-hours.

3 (identify relevant cost-allocation bases) for refining a costing system, Plastim's managers identify six activities for allocating indirect costs to products: (a) design, (b) molding machine setup, (c) machine operations, (d) shipment setup, (e) distribution, and (f) administration. Exhibit 4, column 2, shows the cost hierarchy category, and column 4 shows the cost-allocation base and the budgeted quantity of the cost-allocation base for each activity described in column 1.

Identifying the cost-allocation bases defines the number of activity pools into which costs must be grouped in an ABC system. For example, rather than define the design activities of product design, process design, and prototyping as separate activities, Plastim's managers define these three activities together as a combined "design" activity and form a homogeneous design cost pool. Why? Because the same cost driver—the complexity of the mold—drives the costs of each design activity. A second consideration for choosing a cost-allocation base is the availability of reliable data and measures. For example, in its ABC system, Plastim's managers measure mold complexity in terms of the number of parts in the mold and the surface area of the mold (parts-square feet). If these data are difficult to obtain or measure, Plastim's managers may be forced to use some other measure of complexity, such as the amount of material flowing through the mold that may only be weakly related to the cost of the design activity.

Step 4: Identify the Indirect Costs Associated with Each Cost-Allocation Base. In this step, Plastim's managers try to assign budgeted indirect costs for 2017 to activities (see Exhibit 4, column 3) on the basis of a cause-and-effect relationship between the cost-allocation base for an activity and the cost. For example, all costs that have a cause-and-effect relationship to cubic feet of packages moved are assigned to the distribution cost pool. Of course, the strength of the cause-and-effect relationship between the cost-allocation base and the cost of an activity varies across cost pools. For example, the cause-and-effect relationship between direct manufacturing labor-hours and administration activity costs, which is somewhat arbitrary, is not as strong as the relationship between setup-hours and setup activity costs, where setup-hours is the cost driver of setup costs.

Some costs can be directly identified with a particular activity. For example, salaries paid to design engineers and depreciation of equipment used in the design department are directly identified with the design activity. Other costs need to be allocated across activities. For example, on the basis of interviews or time records, manufacturing engineers and supervisors estimate the time they will spend on design, molding machine setup, and molding machine operations. If a manufacturing engineer spends 15% of her time on design, 45% of her time managing molding machine setups, and 40% of her time on molding operations, the company will allocate the manufacturing engineer's salary to each of these activities in proportion to the time spent. Still other costs are allocated to activity-cost pools using allocation bases that measure how these costs support different activities. For example, rent costs are allocated to activity-cost pools on the basis of square-feet area used by different activities.

As you can see, most costs do not fit neatly into activity categories. Often, costs may first need to be allocated to activities (Stage 1 of the two-stage cost-allocation model) before the costs of the activities can be allocated to products (Stage 2).

The following table shows the assignment of costs to the seven activities identified earlier. Recall that Plastim's management accountants reclassify mold cleaning costs as a direct cost because these costs can be easily traced to a specific mold and lens.

	Design	Molding Machine Setups	Molding Operations	Mold Cleaning	Shipment Setup	Distribution	Administration	Total
Salaries (supervisors, design engineers, process engineers)	$320,000	$105,000	$137,500	$ 0	$21,000	$ 61,500	$165,000	$ 810,000
Wages of support staff	65,000	115,000	70,000	234,000	34,000	125,000	40,000	683,000
Depreciation	24,000	30,000	290,000	18,000	11,000	140,000	15,000	528,000
Maintenance	13,000	16,000	45,000	12,000	6,000	25,000	5,000	122,000
Power and fuel	18,000	20,000	35,000	6,000	5,000	30,000	10,000	124,000
Rent	10,000	14,000	60,000	0	4,000	10,000	20,000	118,000
Total	$450,000	$300,000	$637,500	$270,000	$81,000	$391,500	$255,000	$2,385,000

Step 5: Compute the Rate per Unit of Each Cost-Allocation Base. Exhibit 4, column 5, summarizes the calculation of the budgeted indirect-cost rates using the budgeted quantity of the cost-allocation base from Step 3 and the total budgeted indirect costs of each activity from Step 4.

Step 6: Compute the Indirect Costs Allocated to the Products. Exhibit 5 shows total budgeted indirect costs of $1,153,953 allocated to the simple lens and $961,047 allocated to the complex lens. Follow the budgeted indirect-cost calculations for each lens in Exhibit 5. For each activity, Plastim's operations personnel indicate the total quantity of the cost-allocation base that will be used by each type of lens (recall that Plastim operates at capacity). For example, lines 15 and 16 in Exhibit 5 show that of the 2,000 total setup-hours, the S3 lens is budgeted to use 500 hours and the C5 lens 1,500 hours. The budgeted indirect-cost rate is $150 per setup-hour (Exhibit 4, column 5, line 5). Therefore, the total budgeted cost of the setup activity allocated to the S3 lens is $75,000 (500 setup-hours × $150 per setup-hour) and to the C5 lens is $225,000 (1,500 setup-hours × $150 per setup-hour). Budgeted setup cost per unit equals $1.25 ($75,000 ÷ 60,000 units) for the S3 lens and $15 ($225,000 ÷ 15,000 units) for the C5 lens.

Next consider shipment setup costs. Plastim supplies its S3 and C5 lenses to two different Giovanni plants. One of these is an international plant in Mexico. Preparing for these

EXHIBIT 5 Plastim's Product Costs Using Activity-Based Costing System

Home Insert Page Layout Formulas Data Review View

	A	B	C	D	E	F	G
1		60,000			15,000		
2		Simple Lenses (S3)			Complex Lenses (C5)		
3		Total	per Unit		Total	per Unit	Total
4	**Cost Description**	(1)	(2) = (1) ÷ 60,000		(3)	(4) = (3) ÷ 15,000	(5) = (1) + (3)
5	Direct costs						
6	Direct materials	$1,125,000	$18.75		$ 675,000	$ 45.00	$1,800,000
7	Direct manufacturing labor	600,000	10.00		195,000	13.00	795,000
8	Direct mold cleaning and maintenance costs	120,000	2.00		150,000	10.00	270,000
9	Total direct costs (Step 2)	1,845,000	30.75		1,020,000	68.00	2,865,000
10	Indirect Costs of Activities						
11	Design						
12	S3, 30 parts-sq.ft. × $4,500	135,000	2.25				} 450,000
13	C5, 70 parts-sq.ft. × $4,500				315,000	21.00	
14	Setup of molding machines						
15	S3, 500 setup-hours × $150	75,000	1.25				} 300,000
16	C5, 1,500 setup-hours × $150				225,000	15.00	
17	Machine operations						
18	S3, 9,000 molding machine-hours × $50	450,000	7.50				} 637,500
19	C5, 3,750 molding machine-hours × $50				187,500	12.50	
20	Shipment setup						
21	S3, 750 shipment setup hours × $54	40,500	0.67				} 81,000
22	C5, 750 shipment setup hours × $54				40,500	2.70	
23	Distribution						
24	S3, 45,000 cubic feet delivered × $5.80	261,000	4.35				} 391,500
25	C5, 22,500 cubic feet delivered × $5.80				130,500	8.70	
26	Administration						
27	S3, 30,000 dir. manuf. labor-hours × $6.4151	192,453	3.21				} 255,000
28	C5, 9,750 dir. manuf. labor-hours × $6.4151				62,547	4.17	
29	Total indirect costs allocated (Step 6)	1,153,953	19.23		961,047	64.07	2,115,000
30	Total Costs (Step 7)	$2,998,953	$49.98		$1,981,047	$132.07	$4,980,000
31							

shipments is more time consuming than preparing shipments to the local plant in Indiana because of additional documents related to customs, taxes, and insurance. The following table shows the budgeted number of shipments of S3 and C5 lenses to each plant.

	Mexico Plant Shipments	Indiana Plant Shipments	Total Shipments
Simple S3 lens shipments	10	100	110
Complex C5 lens shipments	30	60	90
			200

Each shipment to the Mexico plant requires 12.5 hours of the shipment department personnel's time while each shipment to the Indiana plant requires half that time, 6.25 hours. The following table indicates the budgeted shipping setup-hours for the S3 and C5 lenses.

	Shipment Setup-Hours for Mexico Plant	Shipment Setup-Hours for Indiana Plant	Total Shipment Setup-Hours
Simple S3 lens shipment setup-hours (12.5 hours × 10; 6.25 hours × 100)	125	625	750
Complex C5 lens shipment setup-hours (12.5 hours × 30; 6.25 hours × 60)	375	375	750
			1,500

The budgeted indirect-cost rate is \$54 per shipment setup-hour (Exhibit 4, column 5, line 7). Therefore, lines 21 and 22 in Exhibit 5 show that the total budgeted cost of the shipment setup activity allocated to the S3 lens is \$40,500 (750 shipment setup-hours × \$54 per shipment setup-hour) and to the C5 lens is \$40,500 (750 shipment setup-hours × \$54 per shipment setup-hour). Budgeted setup cost per unit equals \$0.67 (\$40,500 ÷ 60,000 units) for the S3 lens and \$2.70 (\$40,500 ÷ 15,000 units) for the C5 lens.

Costing for shipment setups using shipment setup-hours as the cost driver is another example of time-driven activity-based costing (TDABC) because it leverages the time taken for different activities within a cost pool. TDABC allows Plastim's managers to account for different complexities of shipments of S3 and C5 lenses. Notice that if Plastim had ignored the complexity of different shipments and allocated costs to lenses based only on the number of shipments, it would have calculated a budgeted indirect-cost rate of \$405 per shipment in Exhibit 4 (\$81,000 ÷ 200 shipments). Using this rate the total budgeted cost of the shipment setup activity allocated to the S3 lens is \$44,550 (110 shipments × \$405 per shipment) and to the C5 lens is \$36,450 (90 shipments × \$54 per shipment). The budgeted setup cost per unit equals \$0.74 (\$44,550 ÷ 60,000 units) for the S3 lens and \$2.43 (\$36,450 ÷ 15,000 units) for the C5 lens. Using the number of shipments, rather than shipment setup-hours, as the cost driver would overcost the simple S3 lens and undercost the complex C5 lens.

Step 7: Compute the Total Cost of the Products by Adding All Direct and Indirect Costs Assigned to the Products. Exhibit 5 presents the product costs for the simple and complex lenses. The direct costs are calculated in Step 2, and the indirect costs are calculated in Step 6. The ABC system overview in Exhibit 3 shows three direct-cost categories and six indirect-cost categories. The budgeted cost of each lens type in Exhibit 5 has nine line items, three for direct costs and six for indirect costs. The differences between the ABC product costs of S3 and C5 calculated in Exhibit 5 highlight how each of these products uses different amounts of direct and indirect costs in each activity area.

TRY IT! **2**

Amherst Metal Works produces two types of metal lamps. Amherst manufactures 20,000 basic lamps and 5,000 designer lamps. Its activity-based costing system uses two indirect-cost pools. One cost pool is for setup costs and the other for general manufacturing overhead. Amherst allocates setup costs to the two lamps based on setup labor-hours and general manufacturing overhead costs on the basis of direct manufacturing labor-hours. It provides the following budgeted cost information:

	Basic Lamps	Designer Lamps	Total
Direct materials per lamp	\$9	\$15	
Direct manufacturing labor-hours per lamp	0.5 hours	0.6 hours	
Direct manufacturing labor rate per hour	\$20	\$20	
Setup costs			\$114,000
Lamps produced per batch	250	50	
Setup-hours per batch	1 hour	3 hours	
General manufacturing overhead costs			\$120,000

Calculate the total budgeted costs of the basic and designer lamps using Amherst's activity-based costing system.

We emphasize two features of ABC systems. First, these systems identify all costs used by products, whether the costs are variable or fixed in the short run. When making long-run strategic decisions using ABC information, managers want revenues to exceed total costs. Otherwise, a company will make losses and will be unable to continue in business. Second, recognizing the hierarchy of costs is critical when allocating costs to products. Management accountants use the cost hierarchy to first calculate the total costs of each product. They then derive per-unit costs by dividing total costs by the number of units produced.

DECISION POINT

How do managers cost products or services using ABC systems?

Comparing Alternative Costing Systems

Exhibit 6 compares the simple costing system using a single indirect-cost pool (Exhibits 1 and 2) that Plastim had been using and the ABC system (Exhibits 3 and 5). Note three points in Exhibit 6, consistent with the guidelines for refining a costing system: (1) ABC systems trace more costs as direct costs; (2) ABC systems create homogeneous cost pools linked to different activities; and (3) for each activity-cost pool, ABC systems seek a cost-allocation base that has a cause-and-effect relationship with costs in the cost pool.

The homogeneous cost pools and the choice of cost-allocation bases, tied to the cost hierarchy, give Plastim's managers greater confidence in the activity and product cost numbers from the ABC system. The bottom part of Exhibit 6 shows that allocating costs to lenses

EXHIBIT 6 Comparing Alternative Costing Systems

	Simple Costing System Using a Single Indirect-Cost Pool (1)	ABC System (2)	Difference (3) = (2) − (1)
Direct-cost categories	2	3	1
	Direct materials Direct manufacturing labor	Direct materials Direct manufacturing labor Direct mold cleaning and maintenance labor	
Total direct costs	$2,595,000	$2,865,000	$270,000
Indirect-cost pools	1	6	5
	Single indirect-cost pool allocated using direct manufacturing labor-hours	Design (parts-square feet)[1] Molding machine setup (setup-hours) Machine operations (molding machine-hours) Shipment setup (shipment setup-hours) Distribution (cubic feet delivered) Administration (direct manufacturing labor-hours)	
Total indirect costs	$2,385,000	$2,115,000	($270,000)
Total costs assigned to simple (S3) lens	$3,525,000	$2,998,953	($526,047)
Cost per unit of simple (S3) lens	$58.75	$49.98	($8.77)
Total costs assigned to complex (C5) lens	$1,455,000	$1,981,047	$526,047
Cost per unit of complex (C5) lens	$97.00	$132.07	$35.07

[1]Cost drivers for the various indirect-cost pools are shown in parentheses.

using only an output unit–level allocation base—direct manufacturing labor-hours, as in the single indirect-cost pool system used prior to ABC—overcosts the simple S3 lens by $8.77 per unit and undercosts the complex C5 lens by $35.07 per unit. The C5 lens uses a disproportionately larger amount of output unit–level, batch-level, and product-sustaining costs than is represented by the direct manufacturing labor-hour cost-allocation base. The S3 lens uses a disproportionately smaller amount of these costs.

The benefit of an ABC system is that it provides information to make better decisions. But managers must weigh this benefit against the measurement and implementation costs of an ABC system.

Considerations in Implementing Activity-Based Costing Systems

LEARNING OBJECTIVE 6

Evaluate the benefits and costs of implementing activity-based costing systems

...more accurate costs that aid in decision making when products make diverse demands on indirect resources versus measurement difficulties

Managers choose the level of detail to use in a costing system by evaluating the expected costs of the system against the expected benefits that result from better decisions.

Benefits and Costs of Activity-Based Costing Systems

Here are some of the telltale signs when an ABC system is likely to provide the most benefits:

- Significant amounts of indirect costs are allocated using only one or two cost pools.
- All or most indirect costs are identified as output unit–level costs (few indirect costs are described as batch-level costs, product-sustaining costs, or facility-sustaining costs).
- Products make diverse demands on resources because of differences in volume, process steps, batch size, or complexity.
- Products that a company is well suited to make and sell show small profits; whereas products that a company is less suited to make and sell show large profits.
- Operations staff has substantial disagreement with the reported costs of manufacturing and marketing products and services.

When managers decide to implement ABC, they must make important choices about the level of detail to use. Should managers choose many finely specified activities, cost drivers, and cost pools, or would a few suffice? For example, Plastim's managers could identify a different molding machine-hour rate for each different type of molding machine. In making such choices, managers weigh the benefits against the costs and limitations of implementing a more detailed costing system.

The main costs and limitations of an ABC system are the measurements necessary to implement it. ABC systems require managers to estimate costs of activity pools and to identify and measure cost drivers for these pools to serve as cost-allocation bases. Even basic ABC systems require many calculations to determine costs of products and services. These measurements are costly. Activity-cost rates also need to be updated regularly.

As ABC systems get very detailed and more cost pools are created, more allocations are necessary to calculate activity costs for each cost pool, which increases the chances of misidentifying the costs of different activity cost pools. For example, supervisors are more prone to incorrectly identify the time they spend on different activities if they have to allocate their time over five activities rather than only two activities.

Occasionally, managers are also forced to use allocation bases for which data are readily available rather than allocation bases they would have liked to use. For example, a manager might be forced to use the number of loads moved, instead of the degree of difficulty and distance of different loads moved, as the allocation base for material-handling costs because data on degree of difficulty and distance of moves are difficult to obtain. When incorrect cost-allocation bases are used, activity-cost information can be misleading. For example, if the cost per load moved decreases, a company may conclude that it has become more efficient in its materials-handling operations. In fact, the lower cost per load moved may have resulted solely from moving many lighter loads over shorter distances.

Many companies, such as Kanthal, a Swedish heating elements manufacturer, have found the strategic and operational benefits of a less-detailed ABC system to be good enough to not warrant incurring the costs and challenges of operating a more detailed system. Other organizations, such as Hewlett-Packard, have implemented ABC in only certain divisions (such as the Roseville Networks Division, which manufactures printed circuit boards) or functions (such as procurement and production). As improvements in information technology and accompanying declines in measurement costs continue, more detailed ABC systems have become a practical alternative in many companies. As these advancements become more widespread, more detailed ABC systems will be better able to pass the cost–benefit test.

Global surveys of company practice suggest that ABC implementation varies among companies. Nevertheless, its framework and ideas provide a standard for judging whether any simple costing system is good enough for a particular management's purposes. ABC thinking can help managers improve any simple costing system.

Behavioral Issues in Implementing Activity-Based Costing Systems

Successfully implementing ABC systems requires more than an understanding of the technical details. ABC implementation often represents a significant change in the costing system and, as the chapter indicates, requires a manager to choose how to define activities and the level of detail. What then are some of the behavioral issues to which managers and management accountants must be sensitive?

1. **Gaining support of top management and creating a sense of urgency for the ABC effort.** This requires managers and management accountants to clearly communicate the strategic benefits of ABC, such as improvements in product and process design. For example, at USAA Federal Savings Bank, managers calculated the cost of individual activities such as opening and closing accounts and demonstrated how the information gained from ABC provided insights into ways of improving the efficiency of bank operations that were previously unavailable.
2. **Creating a guiding coalition of managers throughout the value chain for the ABC effort.** ABC systems measure how the resources of an organization are used. Managers responsible for these resources have the best knowledge about activities and cost drivers. Getting managers to cooperate and take the initiative for implementing ABC is essential for gaining the required expertise, the proper credibility, greater commitment, valuable coordination, and the necessary leadership.
3. **Educating and training employees in ABC as a basis for employee empowerment.** Management accountants must disseminate information about ABC throughout the organization to enable employees in all areas of a business to use their knowledge of ABC to make improvements. For example, WS Industries, an Indian manufacturer of insulators, not only shared ABC information with its workers but also established an incentive plan that gave them a percentage of the cost savings. The results were dramatic because employees were empowered and motivated to implement numerous cost-saving projects.
4. **Seeking small short-run successes as proof that the ABC implementation is yielding results.** Too often, managers and management accountants seek big results and major changes far too quickly. In many situations, achieving a significant change overnight is difficult. However, showing how ABC information has helped improve a process and save costs, even if only in small ways, motivates the team to stay on course and build momentum. The credibility gained from small victories leads to additional and bigger improvements involving larger numbers of people and different parts of the organization. Eventually ABC becomes rooted in the culture of the organization. Sharing short-term successes also helps motivate employees to be innovative. At USAA Federal Savings Bank, managers created a "process improvement" mailbox in Microsoft Outlook to facilitate the sharing of process improvement ideas.

DECISION POINT

What should managers consider when deciding to implement ABC systems?

5. **Recognizing that ABC information is not perfect because it balances the need for better information against the costs of creating a complex system that few managers and employees can understand.** The management accountant must help managers recognize both the value and the limitations of ABC and not oversell it. Open and honest communication about ABC ensures that managers use ABC thoughtfully to make good decisions. Managers can then make critical judgments without being adversarial and can ask tough questions to help drive better decisions about the system.

Activity-Based Management

LEARNING OBJECTIVE 7

Explain how managers use activity-based costing systems in activity-based management

...such as pricing decisions, product-mix decisions, and cost reduction

The emphasis of this chapter so far has been on the role of ABC systems in obtaining better product costs. However, Plastim's managers must now use this information to make decisions (Step 4 of the five-step decision process) and to implement the decision, evaluate performance, and learn (Step 5). **Activity-based management (ABM)** is a method of management decision making that uses activity-based costing information to improve customer satisfaction and profitability. We define ABM broadly to include decisions about pricing and product mix, cost reduction, process improvement, and product and process design.

Pricing and Product-Mix Decisions

An ABC system gives managers information about the costs of making and selling diverse products. With this information, managers can make pricing and product-mix decisions. For example, the ABC system indicates that Plastim can match its competitor's price of $53 for the S3 lens and still make a profit because the ABC cost of S3 is $49.98 (see Exhibit 5).

Plastim's managers offer Giovanni Motors a price of $52 for the S3 lens. Plastim's managers are confident that they can use the deeper understanding of costs that the ABC system provides to improve efficiency and further reduce the cost of the S3 lens. Without information from the ABC system, Plastim managers might have erroneously concluded that they would incur an operating loss on the S3 lens at a price of $53. This incorrect conclusion would have probably caused Plastim to reduce or exit its business in simple lenses and focus instead on complex lenses, where its single indirect-cost-pool system indicated it is very profitable.

Focusing on complex lenses would have been a mistake. The ABC system indicates that the cost of making the complex lens is much higher—$132.07 versus $97 indicated by the direct manufacturing labor-hour-based costing system Plastim had been using. As Plastim's operations staff had thought all along, Plastim has no competitive advantage in making C5 lenses. At a price of $137 per lens for C5, the profit margin is very small ($137.00 − $132.07 = $4.93). As Plastim reduces its prices on simple lenses, it would need to negotiate a higher price for complex lenses while also reducing costs.

Cost Reduction and Process Improvement Decisions

Managers use ABC systems to focus on how and where to reduce costs. They set cost reduction targets for the cost per unit of the cost-allocation base in different activity areas. For example, the supervisor of the distribution activity area at Plastim could have a performance target of decreasing distribution cost per cubic foot of products delivered from $5.80 to $5.40 by reducing distribution labor and warehouse rental costs. The goal is to reduce these costs by improving the way work is done without compromising customer service or the actual or perceived value (usefulness) customers obtain from the product or service. That is, the supervisor will attempt to take out only those costs that are *nonvalue added*.

Controlling cost drivers, such as setup-hours or cubic feet delivered, is another fundamental way that operating personnel manage costs. For example, the distribution department can decrease distribution costs by packing the lenses in a way that reduces the bulkiness of the packages delivered.

The following table shows the reduction in distribution costs of the S3 and C5 lenses as a result of actions that lower cost per cubic foot delivered (from \$5.80 to \$5.40) and total cubic feet of deliveries (from 45,000 to 40,000 for S3 and 22,500 to 20,000 for C5).

	60,000 (S3) Lenses		15,000 (C5) Lenses	
	Total (1)	per Unit (2) = (1) ÷ 60,000	Total (3)	per Unit (4) = (3) ÷ 15,000
Distribution costs (from Exhibit 5)				
S3: 45,000 cubic feet × \$5.80/cubic feet	\$261,000	\$4.35		
C5: 22,500 cubic feet × \$5.80/cubic feet			\$130,500	\$8.70
Distribution costs as a result of process improvements				
S3: 40,000 cubic feet × \$5.40/cubic feet	216,000	3.60		
C5: 20,000 cubic feet × \$5.40/cubic feet			108,000	7.20
Savings in distribution costs from process improvements	\$ 45,000	\$0.75	\$ 22,500	\$1.50

In the long run, total distribution costs will decrease from \$391,500 (\$261,000 + \$130,500) to \$324,000 (\$216,000 + \$108,000). In the short run, however, distribution costs may be fixed and may not decrease. Suppose all \$391,500 of distribution costs are fixed costs in the short run. The efficiency improvements (using less distribution labor and space) mean that the same \$391,500 of distribution costs can now be used to distribute 72,500 $\left(= \frac{\$391{,}500}{\$5.40 \text{ per cubic feet}}\right)$ cubic feet of lenses compared to the 67,500 cubic feet of lenses it currently distributes (see Exhibit 4). In this case, how should costs be allocated to the S3 and C5 lenses?

ABC systems distinguish costs incurred from resources used to design, manufacture, and deliver products and services. For the distribution activity, after process improvements,

Costs incurred = \$391,500
Resources used = \$216,000 (for S3 lens) + \$108,000 (for C5 lens) = \$324,000

On the basis of the resources used by each product, Plastim's ABC system allocates \$216,000 to S3 and \$108,000 to C5 for a total of \$324,000. The difference of \$67,500 (\$391,500 − \$324,000) is shown as costs of unused but available distribution capacity. Plastim's ABC system does not allocate the costs of unused capacity to products so as not to burden the product costs of S3 and C5 with the cost of resources not used by these products. Instead, the system highlights the amount of unused capacity as a separate line item to alert managers to reduce these costs, such as by redeploying labor to other uses or laying off workers.

Design Decisions

ABC systems help managers to evaluate the effect of current product and process designs on activities and costs and to identify new designs to reduce costs. For example, design decisions that decrease the complexity of the mold reduce costs of design, but also materials, labor, machine setups, machine operations, and mold cleaning and maintenance because a less-complex design reduces scrap and the time for setups and operations of the molding machine. Plastim's customers may be willing to give up some features of the lens in exchange for a lower price. Note that Plastim's previous costing system, which used direct manufacturing labor-hours as the cost-allocation base for all indirect costs, would have mistakenly signaled that Plastim choose designs that most reduce direct manufacturing labor-hours. In fact, there is a weak cause-and-effect relationship between direct manufacturing labor-hours and indirect costs.

Planning and Managing Activities

DECISION POINT

How can ABC systems be used to manage better?

Most managers implementing ABC systems for the first time start by analyzing actual costs to identify activity-cost pools and activity-cost rates. Managers then calculate a budgeted rate (as in the Plastim example) that they use for planning, making decisions, and managing activities. At year-end, managers compare budgeted costs and actual costs to evaluate how well activities were managed. Management accountants make adjustments for underallocated or overallocated indirect costs for each activity. As activities and processes change, managers calculate new activity-cost rates.

Activity-Based Costing and Department Costing Systems

LEARNING OBJECTIVE 8

Compare activity-based costing systems and department costing systems

...activity-based costing systems refine department costing systems into more-focused and homogenous cost pools

Companies often use costing systems that have features of ABC systems—such as multiple cost pools and multiple cost-allocation bases—but that do not emphasize individual activities. Many companies have evolved their costing systems from using a single indirect cost rate system to using separate indirect cost rates for each department (such as design, manufacturing, and distribution) or each subdepartment (such as machining and assembly departments within manufacturing) that often represent broad tasks. ABC systems, with their focus on specific activities, are a further refinement of department costing systems. In this section, we compare ABC systems and department costing systems.

Plastim uses the design department indirect cost rate to cost its design activity. To do so Plastim calculates the design activity rate by dividing total design department costs by total parts-square feet, a measure of the complexity of the mold and the driver of design department costs. Plastim does not find it worthwhile to calculate separate activity rates within the design department for the different design activities, such as designing products, making temporary molds, and designing processes. The complexity of a mold is an appropriate cost-allocation base for costs incurred in each design activity because design department costs are homogeneous with respect to this cost-allocation base.

In contrast, the manufacturing department identifies two activity cost pools—a setup cost pool and a machine operations cost pool—instead of a single manufacturing department overhead cost pool. It identifies these activity-cost pools for two reasons. First, each of these activities within manufacturing incurs significant costs and has a different cost driver, setup-hours for the setup cost pool and machine-hours for the machine operations cost pool. Second, the S3 and C5 lenses do not use resources from these two activity areas in the same proportion. For example, C5 uses 75% (1,500 ÷ 2,000) of the setup-hours but only 29.4% (3,750 ÷ 12,750) of the machine-hours. Using only machine-hours, say, to allocate all manufacturing department costs at Plastim would result in C5 being undercosted because it would not be charged for the significant amounts of setup resources it actually uses.

For the reasons we just explained, using department indirect-cost rates to allocate costs to products results in similar information as activity cost rates if (1) a single activity accounts for a sizable proportion of the department's costs; or (2) significant costs are incurred on different activities within a department, but each activity has the same cost driver and therefore cost-allocation base (as was the case in Plastim's design department). From a purely product costing standpoint, department and activity indirect-cost rates will also result in the same product costs if (1) significant costs are incurred for different activities with different cost-allocation bases within a department but (2) different products use resources from the different activity areas in the same proportions (for example, if C5 had used 65%, say, of the setup-hours and 65% of the machine-hours). In this case, though, not identifying activities and cost drivers within departments conceals activity cost information that would help managers manage costs and improve design and processes.

We close this section with a note of caution: Do not assume that because department costing systems require the creation of multiple indirect-cost pools that they properly recognize the drivers of costs within departments as well as how resources are used by products. As we have indicated, in many situations, department costing systems can be refined using ABC. Emphasizing activities leads to more-focused and homogeneous cost pools, aids in identifying cost-allocation bases for activities that have a better cause-and-effect relationship with the costs in activity-cost pools, and leads to better design and process decisions. But these benefits of an ABC system would need to be balanced against its costs and limitations.

DECISION POINT

When can department costing systems be used instead of ABC systems?

ABC in Service and Merchandising Companies

Although many early examples of ABC originated in manufacturing, managers also use ABC in service and merchandising companies. For instance, the Plastim example includes the application of ABC to a service activity—design—and to a merchandising activity—distribution. Companies such as USAA Federal Savings Bank, Braintree Hospital, BCTel in the telecommunications industry, and Union Pacific in the railroad industry have implemented some form of ABC system to identify profitable product mixes, improve efficiency, and satisfy customers. Similarly, many retail and wholesale companies—for example, Supervalu, a retailer and distributor of grocery store products, and Owens and Minor, a medical supplies distributor—have used ABC systems. A large number of financial services companies (as well as other companies) employ variations of ABC systems to analyze and improve the profitability of their customer interactions.

The widespread use of ABC systems in service and merchandising companies reinforces the idea that ABC systems are used by managers for strategic decisions rather than for inventory valuation. (Inventory valuation is fairly straightforward in merchandising companies and not needed in service companies.) Service companies, in particular, find great value from ABC because a vast majority of their cost structure is composed of indirect costs. After all, there are few direct costs when a bank makes a loan or when a representative answers a phone call at a call center. As we have seen, a major benefit of ABC is its ability to assign indirect costs to cost objects by identifying activities and cost drivers. As a result, ABC systems provide greater insight than traditional systems into the management of these indirect costs. The general approach to ABC in service and merchandising companies is similar to the ABC approach in manufacturing.

USAA Federal Savings Bank followed the approach described in this chapter when it implemented ABC in its banking operations. Managers calculated the cost rates of various activities, such as performing ATM transactions, opening and closing accounts, administering mortgages, and processing Visa transactions by dividing the cost of these activities by the time available to do them. Managers used these time-based rates to cost individual products, such as checking accounts, mortgages, and Visa cards, and to calculate the costs of supporting different types of customers. Information from this time-driven activity-based costing system helped USAA Federal Savings Bank to improve its processes and to identify profitable products and customer segments. Concepts in Action: Mayo Clinic Uses Time-Driven Activity-Based Costing to Reduce Costs and Improve Care describes how the Mayo Clinic has similarly benefited from ABC analysis.

Activity-based costing raises some interesting issues when it is applied to a public service institution, such as the U.S. Postal Service. The costs of delivering mail to remote locations are far greater than the costs of delivering mail within urban areas. However, for fairness and community-building reasons, the Postal Service does not charge higher prices to customers in remote areas. In this case, activity-based costing is valuable for understanding, managing, and reducing costs but not for pricing decisions.

CONCEPTS IN ACTION

Mayo Clinic Uses Time-Driven Activity-Based Costing to Reduce Costs and Improve Care

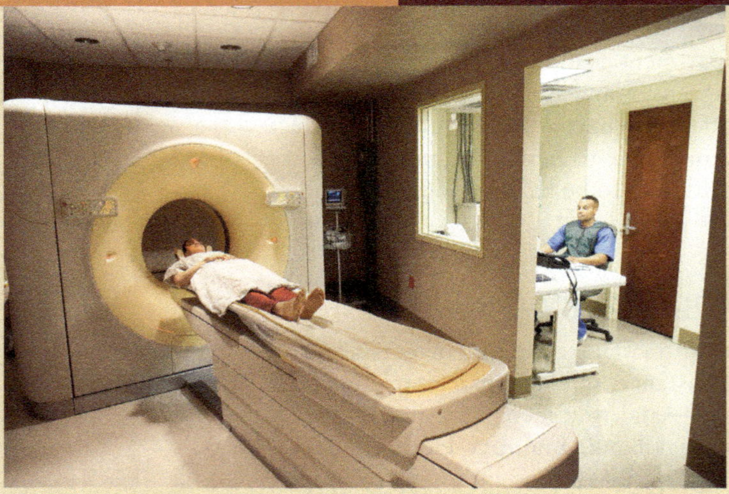

Fuse/Corbis/Getty Images

By 2024, $1 of every $5 spent in the United States will be on health care. Several medical centers, such as the Mayo Clinic in Rochester, Minnesota, are using time-driven activity-based costing (TDABC) to help bring accurate cost and value measurement practices into the health care delivery system.

TDABC assigns all of the organization's resource costs to cost objects using a framework that requires two sets of estimates. TDABC first calculates the cost of supplying resource capacity, such as a doctor's time. The total cost of resources—including personnel, supervision, insurance, space occupancy, technology, and supplies—is divided by the available capacity—the time available for doctors to do their work—to obtain the capacity cost rate. Next, TDABC uses the capacity cost rate to drive resource costs to cost objects, such as the number of patients seen, by estimating the demand for resource capacity (time) that the cost object requires.

Medical centers implementing TDABC have succeeded in reducing costs. For orthopedic procedures at the Mayo Clinic, the TDABC-modified process resulted in shorter stays for patients, a 24% decrease in patients discharged to expensive skilled nursing facilities, and a 15% decrease in cost. Follow-on improvements have included obtaining patient-reported outcomes from tablets and smartphones and eliminating major variations in the cost of prostheses and other supplies.

More broadly, health care providers implementing TDABC have found that better outcomes for patients often go hand in hand with lower total costs. For example, spending more on early detection and better diagnosis of disease reduces patient suffering and often leads to less-complex and less-expensive care. With the insights from TDABC, health care providers can utilize medical staff, equipment, facilities, and administrative resources far more efficiently; streamline the path of patients through the system; and select treatment approaches that improve outcomes while eliminating services that do not.

Sources: Derek A. Haas, Richard A. Helmers, March Rucci, Meredith Brady, and Robert S. Kaplan, "The Mayo Clinic Model for Running a Value-Improvement Program," HBR.org, October 22, 2015 (https://hbr.org/2015/10/the-mayo-clinic-model-for-running-a-value-improvement-program); Dan Mangan, "$1 of Every $5 Spent in US Will Be on Health Care," CNBC, July 28, 2015 (http://www.cnbc.com/2015/07/28/1-of-every-5-spent-in-us-will-be-on-health-care.html); Robert S. Kaplan and Michael E. Porter, "How to Solve the Cost Crisis in Health Care," *Harvard Business Review*, September 2011 (https://hbr.org/2011/09/how-to-solve-the-cost-crisis-in-health-care); Robert S. Kaplan and Steven R. Anderson, "The Innovation of Time-Driven Activity-Based Costing," *Journal of Cost Management*, 21, no. 2 (March-April 2007): 5–15.

PROBLEM FOR SELF-STUDY

Family Supermarkets (FS) has decided to increase the size of its Memphis store. It wants information about the profitability of individual product lines: soft drinks, fresh produce, and packaged food. FS provides the following data for 2017 for each product line:

	Soft Drinks	Fresh Produce	Packaged Food
Revenues	$317,400	$840,240	$483,960
Cost of goods sold	$240,000	$600,000	$360,000
Cost of bottles returned	$ 4,800	$ 0	$ 0
Number of purchase orders placed	144	336	144
Number of deliveries received	120	876	264
Hours of shelf-stocking time	216	2,160	1,080
Items sold	50,400	441,600	122,400

FS also provides the following information for 2017:

Activity (1)	Description of Activity (2)	Total Support Costs (3)	Cost-Allocation Base (4)
1. Bottle returns	Returning of empty bottles to store	$ 4,800	Direct tracing to soft-drink line
2. Ordering	Placing of orders for purchases	$ 62,400	624 purchase orders
3. Delivery	Physical delivery and receipt of merchandise	$100,800	1,260 deliveries
4. Shelf-stocking	Stocking of merchandise on store shelves and ongoing restocking	$ 69,120	3,456 hours of shelf-stocking time
5. Customer support	Assistance provided to customers, including checkout and bagging	$122,880	614,400 items sold
Total		$360,000	

Required

1. Family Supermarkets currently allocates store support costs (all costs other than cost of goods sold) to product lines on the basis of cost of goods sold of each product line. Calculate the operating income and operating income as a percentage of revenues for each product line.
2. If Family Supermarkets allocates store support costs (all costs other than cost of goods sold) to product lines using an ABC system, calculate the operating income and operating income as a percentage of revenues for each product line.
3. Comment on your answers in requirements 1 and 2.

Solution

1. The following table shows the operating income and operating income as a percentage of revenues for each product line. All store support costs (all costs other than cost of goods sold) are allocated to product lines using cost of goods sold of each product line as the cost-allocation base. Total store support costs equal $360,000 (cost of bottles returned, $4,800 + cost of purchase orders, $62,400 + cost of deliveries, $100,800 + cost of shelf-stocking, $69,120 + cost of customer support, $122,880). The allocation rate for store support costs = $360,000 ÷ $1,200,000 (soft drinks $240,000 + fresh produce $600,000 + packaged food, $360,000) = 30% of cost of goods sold. To allocate support costs to each product line, FS multiplies the cost of goods sold of each product line by 0.30.

	Soft Drinks	Fresh Produce	Packaged Food	Total
Revenues	$317,400	$840,240	$483,960	$1,641,600
Cost of goods sold	240,000	600,000	360,000	1,200,000
Store support cost				
($240,000; $600,000; $360,000) × 0.30	72,000	180,000	108,000	360,000
Total costs	312,000	780,000	468,000	1,560,000
Operating income	$ 5,400	$ 60,240	$ 15,960	$ 81,600
Operating income ÷ Revenues	1.70%	7.17%	3.30%	4.97%

2. The ABC system identifies bottle-return costs as a direct cost because these costs can be traced to the soft-drink product line. FS then calculates cost-allocation rates for each activity area (as in Step 5 of the seven-step costing system). The activity rates are as follows.

Activity (1)	Cost Hierarchy (2)	Total Costs (3)	Quantity of Cost-Allocation Base (4)	Overhead Allocation Rate (5) = (3) ÷ (4)
Ordering	Batch-level	$ 62,400	624 purchase orders	$100 per purchase order
Delivery	Batch-level	$100,800	1,260 deliveries	$80 per delivery
Shelf-stocking	Output unit–level	$ 69,120	3,456 shelf-stocking hours	$20 per stocking-hour
Customer support	Output unit–level	$122,880	614,400 items sold	$0.20 per item sold

Store support costs for each product line by activity are obtained by multiplying the total quantity of the cost-allocation base for each product line by the activity-cost rate. Operating income and operating income as a percentage of revenues for each product line are as follows:

	Soft Drinks	Fresh Produce	Packaged Food	Total
Revenues	$317,400	$840,240	$483,960	$1,641,600
Cost of goods sold	240,000	600,000	360,000	1,200,000
Bottle-return costs	4,800	0	0	4,800
Ordering costs (144; 336; 144) purchase orders × $100	14,400	33,600	14,400	62,400
Delivery costs (120; 876; 264) deliveries × $80	9,600	70,080	21,120	100,800
Shelf-stocking costs (216; 2,160; 1,080) stocking-hours × $20	4,320	43,200	21,600	69,120
Customer-support costs (50,400; 441,600; 122,400) items sold × $0.20	10,080	88,320	24,480	122,880
Total costs	283,200	835,200	441,600	1,560,000
Operating income	$ 34,200	$ 5,040	$ 42,360	$ 81,600
Operating income ÷ Revenues	10.78%	0.60%	8.75%	4.97%

3. Managers believe the ABC system is more credible than the simple costing system. The ABC system distinguishes the different types of activities at FS more precisely. It also tracks more accurately how individual product lines use resources. Rankings of relative profitability—operating income as a percentage of revenues—of the three product lines under the simple costing system and under the ABC system are as follows.

Simple Costing System		ABC System	
1. Fresh produce	7.17%	1. Soft drinks	10.78%
2. Packaged food	3.30%	2. Packaged food	8.75%
3. Soft drinks	1.70%	3. Fresh produce	0.60%

The percentage of revenues, cost of goods sold, and activity costs for each product line are as follows.

	Soft Drinks	Fresh Produce	Packaged Food
Revenues	19.34%	51.18%	29.48%
Cost of goods sold	20.00	50.00	30.00
Bottle returns	100.00	0	0
Activity areas:			
Ordering	23.08	53.84	23.08
Delivery	9.53	69.52	20.95
Shelf-stocking	6.25	62.50	31.25
Customer support	8.20	71.88	19.92

Soft drinks have fewer deliveries and require less shelf-stocking time and customer support than either fresh produce or packaged food. Most major soft-drink suppliers deliver merchandise to the store shelves and stock the shelves themselves. In contrast, the fresh produce area has the most deliveries and consumes a large percentage of shelf-stocking time. It also has the highest number of individual sales items and so requires the most customer support. The simple costing system assumed that each product line used the resources in each activity area in the same ratio as their respective individual cost of goods sold to total cost of goods sold. Clearly, this assumption is incorrect. Relative to cost of goods sold, soft drinks and packaged food use fewer resources while fresh produce uses more resources. As a result, the ABC system reduces the costs assigned to soft drinks and packaged food and increases the costs assigned to fresh produce. The simple costing system is an example of averaging that is too broad.

FS managers can use the ABC information to guide decisions such as how to allocate a planned increase in floor space. An increase in the percentage of space allocated to soft drinks is warranted. Note, however, that ABC information is only one input into decisions about shelf-space allocation. In many situations, companies cannot make product decisions in isolation but must consider the effect that dropping or de-emphasizing a product might have on customer demand for other products. For example, FS will have a minimum limit on the shelf space allocated to fresh produce because reducing the choice of fresh produce will lead to customers not shopping at FS, resulting in loss of sales of other, more profitable products.

Pricing decisions can also be made in a more informed way with ABC information. For example, suppose a competitor announces a 5% reduction in soft-drink prices. Given the 10.78% margin FS currently earns on its soft-drink product line, it has flexibility to reduce prices and still make a profit on this product line. In contrast, the simple costing system erroneously implied that soft drinks only had a 1.70% margin, leaving little room to counter a competitor's pricing initiatives.

DECISION **POINTS**

The following question-and-answer format summarizes the chapter's learning objectives. Each decision presents a key question related to a learning objective. The guidelines are the answer to that question.

Decision	Guidelines
1. When does product undercosting or overcosting occur?	Product undercosting (overcosting) occurs when a product or service is reported to have a low (high) cost but consumes a high (low) level of resources. Broad averaging, or peanut-butter costing, a common cause of undercosting or overcosting, is the result of using broad averages that uniformly assign, or spread, the cost of resources to products when the individual products use those resources in a nonuniform way. Product-cost cross-subsidization exists when one undercosted (overcosted) product results in at least one other product being overcosted (undercosted).
2. How do managers refine a costing system?	Refining a costing system means making changes that result in cost numbers better measuring the way different cost objects, such as products, use different amounts of resources of the company. These changes can require additional direct-cost tracing, the choice of more-homogeneous indirect-cost pools, or the use of cost drivers as cost-allocation bases.
3. What is the difference between the design of a simple costing system and an activity-based costing (ABC) system?	The ABC system differs from the simple system by its fundamental focus on activities. The ABC system typically has more homogeneous indirect-cost pools than the simple system, and more cost drivers are used as cost-allocation bases.
4. What is a cost hierarchy?	A cost hierarchy categorizes costs into different cost pools on the basis of the different types of cost-allocation bases or different degrees of difficulty in determining cause-and-effect (or benefits-received) relationships. A four-part hierarchy to cost products consists of output unit–level costs, batch-level costs, product-sustaining or service-sustaining costs, and facility-sustaining costs.
5. How do managers cost products or services using ABC systems?	In ABC, costs of activities are used to assign costs to other cost objects such as products or services based on the activities the products or services consume.

Decision	Guidelines
6. What should managers consider when deciding to implement ABC systems?	ABC systems are likely to yield the most decision-making benefits when indirect costs are a high percentage of total costs or when products and services make diverse demands on indirect resources. The main costs of ABC systems are the difficulties of the measurements necessary to implement and update the systems.
7. How can ABC systems be used to manage better?	Activity-based management (ABM) is a management method of decision making that uses ABC information to satisfy customers and improve profits. ABC systems are used for such management decisions as pricing, product-mix, cost reduction, process improvement, product and process redesign, and planning and managing activities.
8. When can department costing systems be used instead of ABC systems?	Activity-based costing systems are a refinement of department costing systems into more-focused and homogeneous cost pools. Cost information in department costing systems approximates cost information in ABC systems only when each department has a single activity (or a single activity accounts for a significant proportion of department costs) or a single cost driver for different activities or when different products use the different activities of the department in the same proportions.

TERMS TO LEARN

This chapter and the Glossary at the end of this chapter contain definitions of the following important terms:

activity
activity-based costing (ABC)
activity-based management (ABM)
batch-level costs
cost hierarchy
facility-sustaining costs
output unit–level costs
product-cost cross-subsidization
product overcosting
product-sustaining costs
product undercosting
refined costing system
service-sustaining costs

ASSIGNMENT MATERIAL

MyAccountingLab

Questions

1 What is broad averaging, and what consequences can it have on costs?
2 Why should managers worry about product overcosting or undercosting?
3 What is costing system refinement? Describe three guidelines for refinement.
4 What is an activity-based approach to designing a costing system?
5 Describe four levels of a cost hierarchy.
6 Why is it important to classify costs into a cost hierarchy?
7 What are the key reasons for product cost differences between simple costing systems and ABC systems?
8 Describe four decisions for which ABC information is useful.
9 "Department indirect-cost rates are never activity-cost rates." Do you agree? Explain.
10 Describe four signs that help indicate when ABC systems are likely to provide the most benefits.
11 What are the main costs and limitations of implementing ABC systems?
12 "ABC systems only apply to manufacturing companies." Do you agree? Explain.
13 "Activity-based costing is the wave of the present and the future. All companies should adopt it." Do you agree? Explain.
14 "Increasing the number of indirect-cost pools is guaranteed to sizably increase the accuracy of product or service costs." Do you agree? Why?

15 The controller of a retail company has just had a $50,000 request to implement an ABC system quickly turned down. A senior vice president, in rejecting the request, noted, "Given a choice, I will always prefer a $50,000 investment in improving things a customer sees or experiences, such as our shelves or our store layout. How does a customer benefit by our spending $50,000 on a supposedly better accounting system?" How should the controller respond?

Multiple-Choice Questions

MyAccountingLab

In partnership with:

BECKER PROFESSIONAL EDUCATION®

16 Conroe Company is reviewing the data provided by its management accounting system. Which of the following statements is/are correct?

I. A cost driver is a causal factor that increases the total cost of a cost object.
II. Cost drivers may be volume based or activity based.
III. Cost drivers are normally the largest cost in the manufacturing process.

1. I, II, and III are correct.
2. I and II only are correct.
3. I only is correct.
4. II and III only are correct.

17 Nobis Company uses an ABC system. Which of the following statements is/are correct with respect to ABC?

I. Departmental costing systems are a refinement of ABC systems.
II. ABC systems are useful in manufacturing, but not in merchandising or service industries.
III. ABC systems can eliminate cost distortions because ABC develops cost drivers that have a cause-and-effect relationship with the activities performed.

1. I, II, and III are correct.
2. II and III only are correct.
3. III only is correct.
4. None of the listed choices is correct.

Exercises

18 **Cost hierarchy.** Roberta, Inc., manufactures elliptical machines for several well-known companies. The machines differ significantly in their complexity and their manufacturing batch sizes. The following costs were incurred in 2017:

a. Indirect manufacturing labor costs such as supervision that supports direct manufacturing labor, $935,000
b. Procurement costs of placing purchase orders, receiving materials, and paying suppliers related to the number of purchase orders placed, $650,000
c. Cost of indirect materials, $234,000
d. Costs incurred to set up machines each time a different product needs to be manufactured, $392,000
e. Designing processes, drawing process charts, and making engineering process changes for products, $236,900
f. Machine-related overhead costs such as depreciation, maintenance, and production engineering, $865,000 (These resources relate to the activity of running the machines.)
g. Plant management, plant rent, and plant insurance, $498,000

Required

1. Classify each of the preceding costs as output unit–level, batch-level, product-sustaining, or facility-sustaining. Explain each answer.
2. Consider two types of elliptical machines made by Roberta, Inc. One machine, designed for professional use, is complex to make and is produced in many batches. The other machine, designed for home use, is simple to make and is produced in few batches. Suppose that Roberta needs the same number of machine-hours to make each type of elliptical machine and that Roberta allocates all overhead costs using machine-hours as the only allocation base. How, if at all, would the machines be miscosted? Briefly explain why.
3. How is the cost hierarchy helpful to Roberta in managing its business?

19 ABC, cost hierarchy, service. (CMA, adapted) Vineyard Test Laboratories does heat testing (HT) and stress testing (ST) on materials and operates at capacity. Under its current simple costing system, Vineyard aggregates all operating costs of $1,190,000 into a single overhead cost pool. Vineyard calculates a rate per test-hour of $17 ($1,190,000 ÷ 70,000 total test-hours). HT uses 40,000 test-hours, and ST uses 30,000 test-hours. Gary Celeste, Vineyard's controller, believes that there is enough variation in test procedures and cost structures to establish separate costing and billing rates for HT and ST. The market for test services is becoming competitive. Without this information, any miscosting and mispricing of its services could cause Vineyard to lose business. Celeste divides Vineyard's costs into four activity-cost categories.

a. Direct-labor costs, $146,000. These costs can be directly traced to HT, $100,000, and ST, $46,000.
b. Equipment-related costs (rent, maintenance, energy, and so on), $350,000. These costs are allocated to HT and ST on the basis of test-hours.
c. Setup costs, $430,000. These costs are allocated to HT and ST on the basis of the number of setup-hours required. HT requires 13,600 setup-hours, and ST requires 3,600 setup-hours.
d. Costs of designing tests, $264,000. These costs are allocated to HT and ST on the basis of the time required for designing the tests. HT requires 3,000 hours, and ST requires 1,400 hours.

Required

1. Classify each activity cost as output unit–level, batch-level, product- or service-sustaining, or facility-sustaining. Explain each answer.
2. Calculate the cost per test-hour for HT and ST. Explain briefly the reasons why these numbers differ from the $17 per test-hour that Vineyard calculated using its simple costing system.
3. Explain the accuracy of the product costs calculated using the simple costing system and the ABC system. How might Vineyard's management use the cost hierarchy and ABC information to better manage its business?

20 Alternative allocation bases for a professional services firm. The Walliston Group (WG) provides tax advice to multinational firms. WG charges clients for (a) direct professional time (at an hourly rate) and (b) support services (at 30% of the direct professional costs billed). The three professionals in WG and their rates per professional hour are as follows:

Professional	Billing Rate per Hour
Max Walliston	$640
Alexa Boutin	220
Jacob Abbington	100

WG has just prepared the May 2017 bills for two clients. The hours of professional time spent on each client are as follows:

	Hours per Client	
Professional	**San Antonio Dominion**	**Amsterdam Enterprises**
Walliston	26	4
Boutin	5	14
Abbington	39	52
Total	70	70

Required

1. What amounts did WG bill to San Antonio Dominion and Amsterdam Enterprises for May 2017?
2. Suppose support services were billed at $75 per professional labor-hour (instead of 30% of professional labor costs). How would this change affect the amounts WG billed to the two clients for May 2017? Comment on the differences between the amounts billed in requirements 1 and 2.
3. How would you determine whether professional labor costs or professional labor-hours is the more appropriate allocation base for WG's support services?

21 Plant-wide, department, and ABC indirect cost rates. Roadster Company (RC) designs and produces automotive parts. In 2017, actual variable manufacturing overhead is $280,000. RC's simple costing system allocates variable manufacturing overhead to its three customers based on machine-hours and prices its contracts based on full costs. One of its customers has regularly complained of being charged noncompetitive prices, so RC's controller Matthew Draper realizes that it is time to examine the consumption of overhead resources more closely. He knows that there are three main departments that consume overhead resources: design, production, and engineering. Interviews with the department personnel and examination of time records yield the following detailed information:

Home Insert Page Layout Formulas Data Review View

	A	B	C	D	E	F
1				Usage of Cost Drivers by Customer Contract		
2	Department	Cost Driver	Manufacturing Overhead in 2017	Southern Motors	Caesar Motors	Jupiter Auto
3	Design	CAD–design-hours	$ 35,000	150	250	100
4	Production	Engineering–hours	25,000	130	100	270
5	Engineering	Machine–hours	220,000	300	3,700	1,000
6	Total		$280,000			

Required

1. Compute the manufacturing overhead allocated to each customer in 2017 using the simple costing system that uses machine-hours as the allocation base.
2. Compute the manufacturing overhead allocated to each customer in 2017 using department-based manufacturing overhead rates.
3. Comment on your answers in requirements 1 and 2. Which customer do you think was complaining about being overcharged in the simple system? If the new department-based rates are used to price contracts, which customer(s) will be unhappy? How would you respond to these concerns?
4. How else might RC use the information available from its department-by-department analysis of manufacturing overhead costs?
5. RC's managers are wondering if they should further refine the department-by-department costing system into an ABC system by identifying different activities within each department. Under what conditions would it not be worthwhile to further refine the department costing system into an ABC system?

22 **Plant-wide, department, and activity-cost rates.** Acclaim Inc. makes two styles of trophies, basic and deluxe, and operates at capacity. Acclaim does large custom orders. Acclaim budgets to produce 10,000 basic trophies and 5,000 deluxe trophies. Manufacturing takes place in two production departments: forming and assembly. In the forming department, indirect manufacturing costs are accumulated in two cost pools, setup and general overhead. In the assembly department, all indirect manufacturing costs are accumulated in one general overhead cost pool. The basic trophies are formed in batches of 200 but because of the more intricate detail of the deluxe trophies, they are formed in batches of 50.

The controller has asked you to compare plant-wide, department, and activity-based cost allocation.

Acclaim Budgeted Information for the Year Ended November 30, 2017

Forming Department	**Basic**	**Deluxe**	**Total**
Direct materials	$60,000	$35,000	$95,000
Direct manufacturing labor	30,000	20,000	50,000
Overhead costs			
Setup			48,000
General overhead			32,000
Assembly Department	**Basic**	**Deluxe**	**Total**
Direct materials	$ 5,000	$10,000	$15,000
Direct manufacturing labor	15,000	25,000	40,000
Overhead costs			
General overhead			40,000

Required

1. Calculate the budgeted unit cost of basic and deluxe trophies based on a single plant-wide overhead rate, if total overhead is allocated based on total direct costs. (Don't forget to include direct material and direct manufacturing labor cost in your unit cost calculation.)
2. Calculate the budgeted unit cost of basic and deluxe trophies based on departmental overhead rates, where forming department overhead costs are allocated based on direct manufacturing labor costs of the forming department and assembly department overhead costs are allocated based on total direct manufacturing labor costs of the assembly department.
3. Calculate the budgeted unit cost of basic and deluxe trophies if Acclaim allocates overhead costs in each department using activity-based costing, where setup costs are allocated based on number of batches and general overhead costs for each department are allocated based on direct manufacturing labor costs of each department.
4. Explain briefly why plant-wide, department, and activity-based costing systems show different costs for the basic and deluxe trophies. Which system would you recommend and why?

23 ABC, process costing. Sander Company produces mathematical and financial calculators and operates at capacity. Data related to the two products are presented here:

	Mathematical	Financial
Annual production in units	45,000	90,000
Direct material costs	$180,000	$360,000
Direct manufacturing labor costs	$ 90,000	$180,000
Direct manufacturing labor-hours	4,500	9,000
Machine-hours	30,000	60,000
Number of production runs	45	45
Inspection hours	1,200	600

Total manufacturing overhead costs are as follows:

	Total
Machining costs	$360,000
Setup costs	108,000
Inspection costs	117,000

Required

1. Choose a cost driver for each overhead cost pool and calculate the manufacturing overhead cost per unit for each product.
2. Compute the manufacturing cost per unit for each product.
3. How might Sander's managers use the new cost information from its activity-based costing system to better manage its business?

24 Department costing, service company. DLN is an architectural firm that designs and builds buildings. It prices each job on a cost plus 20% basis. Overhead costs in 2017 are $8,100,000. DLN's simple costing system allocates overhead costs to its jobs based on number of jobs. There were three jobs in 2017. One customer, Chandler, has complained that the cost and price of its building in Chicago was not competitive. As a result, the controller has initiated a detailed review of the overhead allocation to determine if overhead costs should be charged to jobs in proportion to consumption of overhead resources by jobs. She gathers the following information:

			Quantity of Cost Drivers Used by Each Project		
Department	Cost Driver	Overhead Costs in 2017	Chandler	Henry	Manley
Design	Design department hours	$3,000,000	2,000	10,000	8,000
Engineering	Number of engineering hours	1,000,000	4,000	4,000	4,500
Construction	Labor-hours	4,100,000	29,000	27,000	26,000
		$8,100,000			

Required

1. Compute the overhead allocated to each project in 2017 using the simple costing system that allocates overhead costs to jobs based on the number of jobs.
2. Compute the overhead allocated to each project in 2017 using department overhead cost rates.
3. Do you think Chandler had a valid reason for dissatisfaction with the cost and price of its building? How does the allocation based on department rates change costs for each project?
4. What value, if any, would DLN get by allocating costs of each department based on the activities done in that department?

25 Activity-based costing, service company. Speediprint Corporation owns a small printing press that prints leaflets, brochures, and advertising materials. Speediprint classifies its various printing jobs as standard jobs or special jobs. Speediprint's simple job-costing system has two direct-cost categories (direct materials and direct labor) and a single indirect-cost pool. Speediprint operates at capacity and allocates all indirect costs using printing machine-hours as the allocation base.

Speediprint is concerned about the accuracy of the costs assigned to standard and special jobs and therefore is planning to implement an activity-based costing system. Speediprint's ABC system would have the same direct-cost categories as its simple costing system. However, instead of a single indirect-cost pool there would now be six categories for assigning indirect costs: design, purchasing, setup, printing machine operations, marketing, and administration. To see how activity-based costing would affect the costs of standard and special jobs, Speediprint collects the following information for the fiscal year 2017 that just ended.

Home Insert Page Layout Formulas Data Review View

	A	B	C	D	E	F	G	H
1		Standard Job	Special Job	Total	Cause-and-Effect Relationship Between Allocation Base and Activity Cost			
2	Number of printing jobs	400	200					
3	Price per job	$ 600	$ 750					
4	Cost of supplies per job	$ 100	$ 125					
5	Direct labor costs per job	$ 90	$ 100					
6	Printing machine-hours per job	10	10					
7	Cost of printing machine operations			$ 75,000	Indirect costs of operating printing machines			
8					increase with printing machine-hours			
9	Setup-hours per job	4	7					
10	Setup costs			$ 45,000	Indirect setup costs increase with setup-hours			
11	Total number of purchase orders	400	500					
12	Purchase order costs			$ 18,000	Indirect purchase order costs increase with			
13					number of purchase orders			
14	Design costs	$4,000	$16,000	$ 20,000	Design costs are allocated to standard and special			
15					jobs based on a special study of the design department			
16	Marketing costs as a percentage of revenues	5%	5%	$ 19,500				
17	Administration costs			$ 24,000	Demand for administrative resources increases with direct labor costs			

Required

1. Calculate the cost of a standard job and a special job under the simple costing system.
2. Calculate the cost of a standard job and a special job under the activity-based costing system.
3. Compare the costs of a standard job and a special job in requirements 1 and 2. Why do the simple and activity-based costing systems differ in the cost of a standard job and a special job?
4. How might Speediprint use the new cost information from its activity-based costing system to better manage its business?

26 Activity-based costing, manufacturing. Decorative Doors, Inc., produces two types of doors, interior and exterior. The company's simple costing system has two direct-cost categories (materials and labor) and one indirect-cost pool. The simple costing system allocates indirect costs on the basis of machine-hours. Recently, the owners of Decorative Doors have been concerned about a decline in the market share for their interior doors, usually their biggest seller. Information related to Decorative Doors production for the most recent year follows:

	Interior	Exterior
Units sold	3,200	1,800
Selling price	$ 125	$ 200
Direct material cost per unit	$ 30	$ 45
Direct manufacturing labor cost per hour	$ 16	$ 16
Direct manufacturing labor-hours per unit	1.50	2.25
Production runs	40	85
Material moves	72	168
Machine setups	45	155
Machine-hours	5,500	4,500
Number of inspections	250	150

The owners have heard of other companies in the industry that are now using an activity-based costing system and are curious how an ABC system would affect their product costing decisions. After analyzing the indirect-cost pool for Decorative Doors, the owners identify six activities as generating indirect costs: production scheduling, material handling, machine setup, assembly, inspection, and marketing. Decorative Doors collected the following data related to the indirect-cost activities:

Activity	Activity Cost	Activity Cost Driver
Production scheduling	$95,000	Production runs
Material handling	$45,000	Material moves
Machine setup	$25,000	Machine setups
Assembly	$60,000	Machine-hours
Inspection	$ 8,000	Number of inspections

Marketing costs were determined to be 3% of the sales revenue for each type of door.

Required

1. Calculate the cost of an interior door and an exterior door under the existing simple costing system.
2. Calculate the cost of an interior door and an exterior door under an activity-based costing system.
3. Compare the costs of the doors in requirements 1 and 2. Why do the simple and activity-based costing systems differ in the cost of an interior door and an exterior door?
4. How might Decorative Doors, Inc., use the new cost information from its activity-based costing system to address the declining market share for interior doors?

27 ABC, retail product-line profitability. Fitzgerald Supermarkets (FS) operates at capacity and decides to apply ABC analysis to three product lines: baked goods, milk and fruit juice, and frozen foods. It identifies four activities and their activity cost rates as follows:

Ordering	$95 per purchase order
Delivery and receipt of merchandise	$76 per delivery
Shelf-stocking	$19 per hour
Customer support and assistance	$ 0.15 per item sold

The revenues, cost of goods sold, store support costs, activities that account for the store support costs, and activity-area usage of the three product lines are as follows:

	Baked Goods	Milk and Fruit Juice	Frozen Products
Financial data			
Revenues	$60,000	$66,500	$50,500
Cost of goods sold	$41,000	$51,000	$32,000
Store support	$12,300	$15,300	$ 9,600
Activity-area usage (cost-allocation base)			
Ordering (purchase orders)	44	24	14
Delivery (deliveries)	120	60	36
Shelf-stocking (hours)	170	150	20
Customer support (items sold)	15,400	20,200	7,960

Under its simple costing system, FS allocated support costs to products at the rate of 30% of cost of goods sold.

Required

1. Use the simple costing system to prepare a product-line profitability report for FS.
2. Use the ABC system to prepare a product-line profitability report for FS.
3. What new insights does the ABC system in requirement 2 provide to FS managers?

28 ABC, wholesale, customer profitability. Veritek Wholesalers operates at capacity and sells furniture items to four department-store chains (customers). Mr. Veritek commented, "We apply ABC to determine product-line profitability. The same ideas apply to customer profitability, and we should find out our customer profitability as well." Veritek Wholesalers sends catalogs to corporate purchasing departments on a monthly basis. The customers are entitled to return unsold merchandise within a six-month period from the purchase date and receive a full purchase price refund. The following data were collected from last year's operations:

	Customer			
	1	2	3	4
Gross sales	$40,000	$20,000	$110,000	$95,000
Sales returns:				
Number of items	96	24	64	32
Amount	$ 8,000	$ 3,000	$ 7,700	$ 9,000
Number of orders:				
Regular	30	140	55	100
Rush	8	46	12	45

Veritek has calculated the following activity rates:

Activity	Cost-Driver Rate
Regular order processing	$30 per regular order
Rush order processing	$150 per rush order
Returned items processing	$15 per item
Catalogs and customer support	$1,200 per customer

Customers pay the transportation costs. The cost of goods sold averages 75% of sales.

Required

Determine the contribution to profit from each customer last year. Comment on your solution.

29 Activity-based costing. The job-costing system at Melody's Custom Framing has five indirect cost pools (purchasing, material handling, machine maintenance, product inspection, and packaging). The company is in the process of bidding on two jobs: Job 220, an order of 17 intricate personalized frames, and Job 330, an order of 5 standard personalized frames. The controller wants you to compare overhead allocated under the current simple job-costing system and a newly designed activity-based job-costing system. Total budgeted costs in each indirect-cost pool and the budgeted quantity of activity driver are as follows.

	Budgeted Overhead	Activity Driver	Budgeted Quantity of Activity Driver
Purchasing	$ 28,500	Purchase orders processed	1,500
Material handling	47,700	Material moves	5,300
Machine maintenance	100,000	Machine-hours	10,000
Product inspection	6,800	Inspections	1,700
Packaging	13,200	Units produced	3,300
	$196,200		

Information related to Job 220 and Job 330 follows. Job 220 incurs more batch-level costs because it uses more types of materials that need to be purchased, moved, and inspected relative to Job 330.

	Job 220	Job 330
Number of purchase orders	21	9
Number of material moves	18	6
Machine-hours	30	70
Number of inspections	10	2
Units produced	17	5

Required

1. Compute the total overhead allocated to each job under a simple costing system, where overhead is allocated based on machine-hours.
2. Compute the total overhead allocated to each job under an activity-based costing system using the appropriate activity drivers.
3. Explain why Melody's Custom Framing might favor the ABC job-costing system over the simple job-costing system, especially in its bidding process.

30 ABC, product costing at banks, cross-subsidization. United Savings Bank (USB) is examining the profitability of its Premier Account, a combined savings and checking account. Depositors receive a 2% annual interest rate on their average deposit. USB earns an interest rate spread of 3% (the difference between the rate at which it lends money and the rate it pays depositors) by lending money for home-loan purposes at 5%. Thus, USB would gain $60 on the interest spread if a depositor had an average Premier Account balance of $2,000 in 2017 ($\$2{,}000 \times 3\% = \$60$).

The Premier Account allows depositors unlimited use of services such as deposits, withdrawals, checking accounts, and foreign currency drafts. Depositors with Premier Account balances of $1,000 or more receive unlimited free use of services. Depositors with minimum balances of less than $1,000 pay a $22-a-month service fee for their Premier Account.

USB recently conducted an activity-based costing study of its services. It assessed the following costs for six individual services. The use of these services in 2017 by three customers is as follows:

	Activity-Based Cost per "Transaction"	Account Usage		
		Lindell	Welker	Colston
Deposit/withdrawal with teller	$ 2.50	44	49	4
Deposit/withdrawal with automatic teller machine (ATM)	0.80	12	24	13
Deposit/withdrawal on prearranged monthly basis	0.50	0	14	58
Bank checks written	8.20	8	2	3
Foreign currency drafts	12.10	6	1	5
Inquiries about account balance	1.70	7	16	6
Average Premier Account balance for 2017		$1,200	$700	$24,900

Assume Lindell and Colston always maintain a balance above $1,000, whereas Welker always has a balance below $1,000.

Required

1. Compute the 2017 profitability of the Lindell, Welker, and Colston Premier Accounts at USB.
2. Why might USB worry about the profitability of individual customers if the Premier Account product offering is profitable as a whole?
3. What changes would you recommend for USB's Premier Account?

Problems

31 Job costing with single direct-cost category, single indirect-cost pool, law firm. Wharton Associates is a recently formed law partnership. Denise Peyton, the managing partner of Wharton Associates, has just finished a tense phone call with Gus Steger, president of Steger Enterprises. Gus strongly complained about the price Wharton charged for some legal work done for his company.

Peyton also received a phone call from its only other client, Bluestone, Inc., which was very pleased with both the quality of the work and the price charged on its most recent job.

Wharton Associates operates at capacity and uses a cost-based approach to pricing (billing) each job. Currently it uses a simple costing system with a single direct-cost category (professional labor-hours) and a single indirect-cost pool (general support). Indirect costs are allocated to cases on the basis of professional labor-hours per case. The job files show the following:

	Steger Enterprises	Bluestone Inc.
Professional labor	3,000 hours	2,000 hours

Professional labor costs at Bradley Associates are $160 an hour. Indirect costs are allocated to cases at $100 an hour. Total indirect costs in the most recent period were $500,000.

Required

1. Why is it important for Bradley Associates to understand the costs associated with individual jobs?
2. Compute the costs of the Steger Enterprises and Bluestone Inc. jobs using Bradley's simple costing system.

32 Job costing with multiple direct-cost categories, single indirect-cost pool, law firm (continuation of 31). Peyton asks her assistant to collect details on those costs included in the $500,000 indirect-cost pool that can be traced to each individual job. After analysis, Wharton is able to reclassify $300,000 of the $500,000 as direct costs:

Other Direct Costs	Steger Enterprises	Bluestone Inc.
Research support labor	$36,000	$ 77,000
Computer time	8,000	32,000
Travel and allowances	14,000	84,000
Telephones/faxes	5,000	24,000
Photocopying	6,000	14,000
Total	$69,000	$231,000

Peyton decides to calculate the costs of each job as if Wharton had used six direct-cost pools and a single indirect-cost pool. The single indirect-cost pool would have $200,000 of costs and would be allocated to each case using the professional labor-hours base.

Required

1. Calculate the revised indirect-cost allocation rate per professional labor-hour for Wharton Associates when total indirect costs are $200,000.
2. Compute the costs of the Steger Enterprises and Bluestone Inc. jobs if Wharton Associates had used its refined costing system with multiple direct-cost categories and one indirect-cost pool.
3. Compare the costs of Steger Enterprises and Bluestone Inc. jobs in requirement 2 with those in requirement 2 of Problem 31. Comment on the results.

33 Job costing with multiple direct-cost categories, multiple indirect-cost pools, law firm (continuation of 31 and 32). Wharton has two classifications of professional staff: partners and associates. Peyton asks his assistant to examine the relative use of partners and associates on the recent Steger Enterprises and Bluestone Inc. jobs. The Steger Enterprises job used 1,000 partner-hours and 2,000 associate-hours. The Bluestone Inc. job used 1,500 partner-hours and 500 associate-hours. Therefore, totals of the two jobs together were 2,500 partner-hours and 2,500 associate-hours. Peyton decides to examine how using separate direct-cost rates for partners and associates and using separate indirect-cost pools for partners and associates would have affected the costs of the Steger Enterprises and Bluestone Inc. jobs. Indirect costs in each indirect-cost pool would be allocated on the basis of total hours of that category of professional labor. From the total indirect cost-pool of $200,000, $120,000 is attributable to the activities of partners and $80,000 is attributable to the activities of associates.

The rates per category of professional labor are as follows:

Category of Professional Labor	Direct Cost per Hour	Indirect Cost per Hour
Partner	$200	$120,000 ÷ 2,500 hours = $48
Associate	$120	$ 80,000 ÷ 2,500 hours = $32

Required

1. Compute the costs of the Steger Enterprises and Bluestone Inc. jobs using Wharton's further refined system, with multiple direct-cost categories and multiple indirect-cost pools.
2. For what decisions might Wharton Associates find it more useful to use this job-costing approach rather than the approaches in Problem 31 or 32?

34 First-stage allocation, time-driven activity-based costing, manufacturing sector. Marshall Devices manufactures metal products and uses activity-based costing to allocate overhead costs to customer orders for pricing purposes. Many customer orders are won through competitive bidding based on costs. Direct material and direct manufacturing labor costs are traced directly to each order. Marshall's direct manufacturing labor rate is $20 per hour. The company reports the following budgeted yearly overhead costs:

Wages and salaries	$480,000
Depreciation	60,000
Rent	120,000
Other overhead	240,000
Total overhead costs	$900,000

Marshall has established four activity cost pools and the following budgeted activity for each cost pool:

Activity Cost Pool	Activity Measure	Budgeted Total Activity for the Year
Direct manufacturing labor support	Number of direct manufacturing labor-hours	30,000 direct manufacturing labor-hours
Order processing	Number of customer orders	500 orders
Design support	Number of custom design-hours	2,490 custom design-hours
Other	Facility-sustaining costs allocated to orders based on direct manufacturing labor-hours	30,000 direct manufacturing labor-hours

Some customer orders require more complex designs, while others need simple designs. Marshall estimates that it will do 120 complex designs during a year, which will each take 11.75 hours for a total of 1,410 design-hours. It estimates it will do 180 simple designs, which will each take 6 hours for a total of 1,080 design-hours.

Paul Napoli, Marshall's controller, has prepared the following estimates for distribution of the overhead costs across the four activity-cost pools:

	Direct Manufacturing Labor Support	Order Processing	Design Support	Other	Total
Wages and salaries	40%	25%	30%	5%	100%
Depreciation	25%	10%	15%	50%	100%
Rent	30%	25%	10%	35%	100%
Other overhead	20%	30%	35%	15%	100%

Order 277100 consists of four different metal products. Three products require a complex design and one requires a simple design. Order 277100 requires $4,550 of direct materials and 80 direct manufacturing labor-hours.

Required

1. Allocate the overhead costs to each activity cost pool. Calculate the activity rate for each pool.
2. Determine the cost of Order 277100.
3. How does activity-based costing enhance Marshall's ability to price its orders? Suppose Marshall used a simple costing system to allocate all overhead costs to orders on the basis of direct manufacturing labor-hours. How might this have affected Marshall's pricing decision for Order 227100?
4. When designing its activity-based costing system, Marshall uses time-driven activity-based costing system (TDABC) for its design department. What does this approach allow Marshall to do? How would the cost of Order 277100 have been different if Marshall had used the number of customer designs rather than the number of custom design-hours to allocate costs to different customer orders? Which cost driver do you prefer for design support? Why?

35 First-stage allocation, time-driven activity-based costing, service sector. LawnCare USA provides lawn care and landscaping services to commercial clients. LawnCare USA uses activity-based costing to bid on jobs and to evaluate their profitability. LawnCare USA reports the following budgeted annual costs:

Wages and salaries	$360,000
Depreciation	72,000
Supplies	120,000
Other overhead	288,000
Total overhead costs	$840,000

John Gilroy, controller of LawnCare USA, has established four activity cost pools and the following budgeted activity for each cost pool:

Activity Cost Pool	Activity Measure	Total Activity for the Year
Estimating jobs	Number of job estimates	250 estimates
Lawn care	Number of direct labor-hours	10,000 direct labor-hours
Landscape design	Number of design hours	500 design hours
Other	Facility-sustaining costs that are not allocated to jobs	Not applicable

Gilroy estimates that LawnCare USA's costs are distributed to the activity-cost pools as follows:

	Estimating Jobs	Lawn Care	Landscape Design	Other	Total
Wages and salaries	5%	70%	15%	10%	100%
Depreciation	10%	65%	10%	15%	100%
Supplies	0%	100%	0%	0%	100%
Other overhead	15%	50%	20%	15%	100%

Sunset Office Park, a new development in a nearby community, has contacted LawnCare USA to provide an estimate on landscape design and annual lawn maintenance. The job is estimated to require a single landscape design requiring 40 design hours in total and 250 direct labor-hours annually. LawnCare USA has a policy of pricing estimates at 150% of cost.

Required

1. Allocate LawnCare USA's costs to the activity-cost pools and determine the activity rate for each pool.
2. Estimate total cost for the Sunset Office Park job. How much would LawnCare USA bid to perform the job?
3. LawnCare USA does 30 landscape designs for its customers each year. Estimate the total cost for the Sunset Office park job if LawnCare USA allocated costs of the Landscape Design activity based on the number of landscape designs rather than the number of landscape design-hours. How much would LawnCare USA bid to perform the job? Which cost driver do you prefer for the Landscape Design activity? Why?
4. Sunset Office Park asks LawnCare USA to give an estimate for providing its services for a 2-year period. What are the advantages and disadvantages for LawnCare USA to provide a 2-year estimate?

36 Department and activity-cost rates, service sector. Raynham's Radiology Center (RRC) performs X-rays, ultrasounds, computer tomography (CT) scans, and magnetic resonance imaging (MRI). RRC has developed a reputation as a top radiology center in the state. RRC has achieved this status because it constantly reexamines its processes and procedures. RRC has been using a single, facility-wide overhead allocation rate. The vice president of finance believes that RRC can make better process improvements if it uses more disaggregated cost information. She says, "We have state-of-the-art medical imaging technology. Can't we have state-of-the-art accounting technology?"

Raynham's Radiology Center Budgeted Information for the Year Ended May 31, 2017

	X-rays	Ultrasound	CT Scan	MRI	Total
Technician labor	$ 62,000	$101,000	$155,000	$ 103,000	$ 421,000
Depreciation	42,240	256,000	424,960	876,800	1,600,000
Materials	22,600	16,400	23,600	31,500	94,100
Administration					20,000
Maintenance					250,000
Sanitation					252,500
Utilities					151,100
	$ 126,840	$373,400	$603,560	$1,011,300	$2,788,700
Number of procedures	3,842	4,352	2,924	2,482	
Minutes to clean after each procedure	5	5	15	35	
Minutes for each procedure	5	15	25	40	

RRC operates at capacity. The proposed allocation bases for overhead are:

Administration	Number of procedures
Maintenance (including parts)	Capital cost of the equipment (use Depreciation)
Sanitation	Total cleaning minutes
Utilities	Total procedure minutes

Required

1. Calculate the budgeted cost per service for X-rays, ultrasounds, CT scans, and MRI using direct technician labor costs as the allocation basis.
2. Calculate the budgeted cost per service of X-rays, ultrasounds, CT scans, and MRI if RRC allocated overhead costs using activity-based costing.
3. Explain how the disaggregation of information could be helpful to RRC's intention to continuously improve its services.

37 Activity-based costing, merchandising. Pharmahelp, Inc., a distributor of special pharmaceutical products, operates at capacity and has three main market segments:

a. General supermarket chains
b. Drugstore chains
c. Mom-and-pop single-store pharmacies

Rick Flair, the new controller of Pharmahelp, reported the following data for 2017.

Home | Insert | Page Layout | Formulas | Data | Review | View

	A	B	C	D	E
1					
2	**Pharmahelp, 2017**	**General**			
3		**Supermarket**	**Drugstore**	**Mom-and-Pop**	**Total For**
4		**Chains**	**Chains**	**Single Stores**	**Pharmahelp**
5	Revenues	$3,708,000	$3,150,000	$1,980,000	$8,838,000
6	Cost of goods sold	3,600,000	3,000,000	1,800,000	8,400,000
7	Gross margin	$ 108,000	$ 150,000	$ 180,000	438,000
8	Other operating costs				301,080
9	Operating income				$ 136,920

For many years, Pharmahelp has used gross margin percentage [(Revenue − Cost of goods sold) ÷ Revenue] to evaluate the relative profitability of its market segments. But Flair recently attended a seminar on activity-based costing and is considering using it at Pharmahelp to analyze and allocate "other operating costs." He meets with all the key managers and several of his operations and sales staff, and they agree that there are five key activities that drive other operating costs at Pharmahelp:

Activity Area	Cost Driver
Order processing	Number of customer purchase orders
Line-item processing	Number of line items ordered by customers
Delivering to stores	Number of store deliveries
Cartons shipped to store	Number of cartons shipped
Stocking of customer store shelves	Hours of shelf-stocking

Each customer order consists of one or more line items. A line item represents a single product (such as Extra-Strength Tylenol Tablets). Each product line item is delivered in one or more separate cartons. Each store delivery entails the delivery of one or more cartons of products to a customer. Pharmahelp's staff stacks cartons directly onto display shelves in customers' stores. Currently, there is no additional charge to the customer for shelf-stocking and not all customers use Pharmahelp for this activity. The level of each activity in the three market segments and the total cost incurred for each activity in 2017 is as follows:

	A	B	C	D	E
13					
14	**Activity-based Cost Data**		**Activity Level**		
15	**Pharmahelp 2017**	**General**			**Total Cost**
16		**Supermarket**	**Drugstore**	**Mom-and-Pop**	**of Activity**
17	**Activity**	**Chains**	**Chains**	**Single Stores**	**in 2017**
18	Orders processed (number)	140	360	1,500	$ 80,000
19	Line-items ordered (number)	1,960	4,320	15,000	63,840
20	Store deliveries made (number)	120	360	1,000	71,000
21	Cartons shipped to stores (number)	36,000	24,000	16,000	76,000
22	Shelf stocking (hours)	360	180	100	10,240
23					$301,080

Required

1. Compute the 2017 gross-margin percentage for each of Pharmahelp's three market segments.
2. Compute the cost driver rates for each of the five activity areas.
3. Use the activity-based costing information to allocate the $301,080 of "other operating costs" to each of the market segments. Compute the operating income for each market segment.
4. Comment on the results. What new insights are available with the activity-based costing information?

38 **Choosing cost drivers, activity-based costing, activity-based management.** Pastel Bags (PB) is a designer of high-quality backpacks and purses. Each design is made in small batches. Each spring, PB comes out with new designs for the backpack and for the purse. The company uses these designs for a year and then moves on to the next trend. The bags are all made on the same fabrication equipment that is expected to operate at capacity. The equipment must be switched over to a new design and set up to prepare for the production of each new batch of products. When completed, each batch of products is immediately shipped to a wholesaler. Shipping costs vary with the number of shipments. Budgeted information for the year is as follows:

Pastel Bags
Budget for Costs and Activities
For the Year Ended February 28, 2017

Direct materials—purses	$ 319,155
Direct materials—backpacks	454,995
Direct manufacturing labor—purses	99,000
Direct manufacturing labor—backpacks	113,000
Setup	64,000
Shipping	73,000
Design	169,000
Plant utilities and administration	221,000
Total	$1,513,150

Other budget information follows:

	Backpacks	Purses	Total
Number of bags	6,175	3,075	9,250
Hours of production	1,665	2,585	4,250
Number of batches	120	80	200
Number of designs	2	2	4

Required

1. Identify the cost hierarchy level for each cost category.
2. Identify the most appropriate cost driver for each cost category. Explain briefly your choice of cost driver.
3. Calculate the budgeted cost per unit of cost driver for each cost category.
4. Calculate the budgeted total costs and cost per unit for each product line.
5. Explain how you could use the information in requirement 4 to reduce costs.

39 **ABC, health care.** Crosstown Health Center runs two programs: drug addict rehabilitation and aftercare (counseling and support of patients after release from a mental hospital). The center's budget for 2017 follows.

Professional salaries:		
4 physicians × $150,000	$600,000	
12 psychologists × $75,000	900,000	
16 nurses × $30,000	480,000	$1,980,000
Medical supplies		242,000
Rent and clinic maintenance		138,600
Administrative costs to manage patient charts, food, laundry		484,000
Laboratory services		92,400
Total		$2,937,000

Kim Yu, the director of the center, is keen on determining the cost of each program. Yu compiles the following data describing employee allocations to individual programs:

	Drug	Aftercare	Total Employees
Physicians	4		4
Psychologists	4	8	12
Nurses	6	10	16

Yu has recently become aware of activity-based costing as a method to refine costing systems. She asks her accountant, Gus Gates, how she should apply this technique. Gates obtains the following budgeted information for 2017:

	Drug	Aftercare	Total
Square feet of space occupied by each program	9,000	12,000	21,000
Patient-years of service	50	60	110
Number of laboratory tests	1,400	700	2,100

Required

1. a. Selecting cost-allocation bases that you believe are the most appropriate for allocating indirect costs to programs, calculate the budgeted indirect cost rates for medical supplies; rent and clinic maintenance; administrative costs for patient charts, food, and laundry; and laboratory services.
   b. Using an activity-based costing approach to cost analysis, calculate the budgeted cost of each program and the budgeted cost per patient-year of the drug program.
   c. What benefits can Crosstown Health Center obtain by implementing the ABC system?
2. What factors, other than cost, do you think Crosstown Health Center should consider in allocating resources to its programs?

40 **Unused capacity, activity-based costing, activity-based management.** Zarson's Netballs is a manufacturer of high-quality basketballs and volleyballs. Setup costs are driven by the number of setups. Equipment and maintenance costs increase with the number of machine-hours, and lease rent is paid per square foot. Capacity of the facility is 14,000 square feet, and Zarson is using only 80% of this capacity.

Zarson records the cost of unused capacity as a separate line item and not as a product cost. The following is the budgeted information for Zarson:

Zarson's Netballs
Budgeted Costs and Activities
For the Year Ended December 31, 2017

Direct materials—basketballs	$ 168,100
Direct materials—volleyballs	303,280
Direct manufacturing labor—basketballs	111,800
Direct manufacturing labor—volleyballs	100,820
Setup	157,500
Equipment and maintenance costs	115,200
Lease rent	210,000
Total	$1,166,700

Other budget information follows:

	Basketballs	Volleyballs
Number of balls	58,000	85,000
Machine-hours	13,500	10,500
Number of setups	450	300
Square footage of production space used	3,200	8,000

Required

1. Calculate the budgeted cost per unit of cost driver for each indirect cost pool.
2. What is the budgeted cost of unused capacity?
3. What is the budgeted total cost and the cost per unit of resources used to produce (a) basketballs and (b) volleyballs?
4. Why might excess capacity be beneficial for Zarson? What are some of the issues Zarson should consider before increasing production to use the space?

41 Unused capacity, activity-based costing, activity-based management. Archer Pro manufactures two models of sport bows, Basic and Deluxe, using a combination of machining and hand finishing. Machine setup costs are driven by the number of setups. Indirect manufacturing labor costs increase with direct manufacturing labor costs. Equipment and maintenance costs increase with the number of machine-hours, and facility rent is paid per square foot. Capacity of the facility is 10,000 square feet, and Archer Pro is using only 75% of this capacity. Archer Pro records the cost of unused capacity as a separate line item and not as a product cost. For the current year, Archer Pro has budgeted the following:

Archer Pro Budgeted
Costs and Activities for the
Year Ended December 31, 2017

Direct materials—Basic bows	$ 450,000
Direct materials—Deluxe bows	320,000
Direct manufacturing labor—Basic bows	155,000
Direct manufacturing labor—Deluxe bows	195,000
Indirect manufacturing labor costs	105,000
Machine setup costs	60,000
Equipment and maintenance costs	264,000
Facility rent	250,000
Total	$1799,000

Other budget information follows:

	Basic	Deluxe
Number of bows	10,000	5,000
Machine-hours	15,000	18,000
Number of setups	500	300
Square footage of production space used	4,000	3,500

Required

1. Calculate the cost per unit of each cost-allocation base.
2. What is the budgeted cost of unused capacity?

3. Calculate the budgeted total cost and the cost per unit for each model.
4. Why might excess capacity be beneficial for Archer Pro? What are some of the issues Archer Pro should consider before increasing production to use the space?

42 ABC, implementation, ethics. (CMA, adapted) Plum Electronics, a division of Berry Corporation, manufactures two large-screen television models: the Mammoth, which has been produced since 2013 and sells for $990, and the Maximum, a newer model introduced in early 2015 that sells for $1,254. Based on the following income statement for the year ended November 30, 2017, senior management at Berry have decided to concentrate Plum's marketing resources on the Maximum model and to begin to phase out the Mammoth model because Maximum generates a much bigger operating income per unit.

Plum Electronics
Income Statement for the
Fiscal Year Ended November 30, 2017

	Mammoth	Maximum	Total
Revenues	$21,780,000	$5,016,000	$26,796,000
Cost of goods sold	13,794,000	3,511,200	17,305,200
Gross margin	7,986,000	1,504,800	9,490,800
Selling and administrative expense	6,413,000	1,075,800	7,488,800
Operating income	$ 1,573,000	$ 429,000	$ 2,002,000
Units produced and sold	22,000	4,000	
Operating income per unit sold	$ 71.50	$ 107.25	

Details for cost of goods sold for Mammoth and Maximum are as follows:

	Mammoth		Maximum	
	Total	Per Unit	Total	Per Unit
Direct materials	$ 5,033,600	$ 228.80	$2,569,600	$642.40
Direct manufacturing labor[a]	435,600	19.80	184,800	46.20
Machine costs[b]	3,484,800	158.40	316,800	79.20
Total direct costs	$ 8,954,000	$ 407.00	$3,071,200	$767.80
Manufacturing overhead costs[c]	$ 4,840,000	$ 220.00	$ 440,000	$110.00
Total cost of goods sold	$13,794,000	$ 627.00	$3,511,200	$877.80

[a] Mammoth requires 1.5 hours per unit and Maximum requires 3.5 hours per unit. The direct manufacturing labor cost is $13.20 per hour.

[b] Machine costs include lease costs of the machine, repairs, and maintenance. Mammoth requires 8 machine-hours per unit and Maximum requires 4 machine-hours per unit. The machine-hour rate is $19.80 per hour.

[c] Manufacturing overhead costs are allocated to products based on machine-hours at the rate of $27.50 per hour.

Plum's controller, Steve Jacobs, is advocating the use of activity-based costing and activity-based management and has gathered the following information about the company's manufacturing overhead costs for the year ended November 30, 2017.

		Units of the Cost-Allocation Base		
Activity Center (Cost-Allocation Base)	**Total Activity Costs**	**Mammoth**	**Maximum**	**Total**
Soldering (number of solder points)	$1,036,200	1,185,000	385,000	1,570,000
Shipments (number of shipments)	946,000	16,200	3,800	20,000
Quality control (number of inspections)	1,364,000	56,200	21,300	77,500
Purchase orders (number of orders)	1,045,440	80,100	109,980	190,080
Machine power (machine-hours)	63,360	176,000	16,000	192,000
Machine setups (number of setups)	825,000	16,000	14,000	30,000
Total manufacturing overhead	$5,280,000			

After completing his analysis, Jacobs shows the results to Charles Clark, the Plum division president. Clark does not like what he sees. "If you show headquarters this analysis, they are going to ask us to phase out the Maximum line, which we have just introduced. This whole costing stuff has been a major problem for us. First Mammoth was not profitable and now Maximum.

"Looking at the ABC analysis, I see two problems. First, we do many more activities than the ones you have listed. If you had included all activities, maybe your conclusions would be different. Second, you used number of setups and number of inspections as allocation bases. The numbers would be different had you used setup-hours and inspection-hours instead. I know that measurement problems precluded you from using these other cost-allocation bases, but I believe you ought to make some adjustments to our current numbers to compensate for these issues. I know you can do better. We can't afford to phase out either product."

Jacobs knows that his numbers are fairly accurate. As a quick check, he calculates the profitability of Maximum and Mammoth using more and different allocation bases. The set of activities and activity rates he had used results in numbers that closely approximate those based on more detailed analyses. He is confident that headquarters, knowing that Maximum was introduced only recently, will not ask Plum to phase it out. He is also aware that a sizable portion of Clark's bonus is based on division revenues. Phasing out either product would adversely affect his bonus. Still, he feels some pressure from Clark to do something.

Required

1. Using activity-based costing, calculate the gross margin per unit of the Maximum and Mammoth models.
2. Explain briefly why these numbers differ from the gross margin per unit of the Maximum and Mammoth models calculated using Plum's existing simple costing system.
3. Comment on Clark's concerns about the accuracy and limitations of ABC.
4. How might Plum find the ABC information helpful in managing its business?
5. What should Steve Jacobs do in response to Clark's comments?

43 **Activity-based costing, activity-based management, merchandising.** Mountain Outfitters operates a large outdoor clothing and equipment store with three main product lines: clothing, equipment, and shoes. Mountain Outfitters operates at capacity and allocates selling, general, and administration (S, G & A) costs to each product line using the cost of merchandise of each product line. The company wants to optimize the pricing and cost management of each product line and is wondering if its accounting system is providing it with the best information for making such decisions. Store manager Aaron Budd gathers the following information regarding the three product lines:

Mountain Outfitters Budgeted
Product-Line Information
For the Year Ended December 31, 2017

	Clothing	Equipment	Shoes	Total
Revenues	$1,440,000	$1,840,000	$720,000	$4,000,000
Cost of merchandise	$ 850,000	$1,250,000	$400,000	$2,500,000
Number of purchase orders placed	200	125	175	500
Number of boxes received	450	200	350	1,000
Square feet of store space	4,500	10,000	1,500	16,000

For 2017, Mountain Outfitters budgets the following selling, general, and administration costs:

Mountain Outfitters Selling,
General, and Administration (S, G & A)
Costs For the Year Ended December 31, 2017

Purchasing department expense	$ 320,000
Receiving department expense	210,000
Customer support expense (cashiers and floor employees)	250,000
Rent	240,000
General store advertising	100,000
Store manager's salary	125,000
	$1,245,000

Required

1. Suppose Mountain Outfitters uses cost of merchandise to allocate all S, G & A costs. Prepare budgeted product-line and total company income statements.
2. Identify an improved method for allocating costs to the three product lines. Explain. Use the method for allocating S, G & A costs that you propose to prepare new budgeted product-line and total company income statements. Compare your results to the results in requirement 1.
3. Write a memo to Mountain Outfitters management describing how the improved system might be useful for managing the store.

GLOSSARY

Activity. An event, task, or unit of work with a specified purpose.

Activity-based costing (ABC). Approach to costing that focuses on individual activities as the fundamental cost objects. It uses the costs of these activities as the basis for assigning costs to other cost objects such as products or services.

Activity-based management (ABM). Method of management decision-making that uses activity-based costing information to improve customer satisfaction and profitability.

Batch-level costs. The costs of activities related to a group of units of products or services rather than to each individual unit of product or service.

Cost hierarchy. Categorization of indirect costs into different cost pools on the basis of the different types of cost drivers, or cost-allocation bases, or different degrees of difficulty in determining cause-and-effect (or benefits received) relationships.

Facility-sustaining costs. The costs of activities that cannot be traced to individual products or services but support the organization as a whole.

Output unit–level costs. The costs of activities performed on each individual unit of a product or service.

Product-cost cross-subsidization. Costing outcome where one undercosted (overcosted) product results in at least one other product being overcosted (undercosted).

Product overcosting. A product consumes a low level of resources but is reported to have a high cost per unit.

Product-sustaining costs. The costs of activities undertaken to support individual products regardless of the number of units or batches in which the units are produced.

Product undercosting. A product consumes a high level of resources but is reported to have a low cost per unit.

Refined costing system. Costing system that reduces the use of broad averages for assigning the cost of resources to cost objects (jobs, products, services) and provides better measurement of the costs of indirect resources used by different cost objects, no matter how differently various cost objects use indirect resources.

Service-sustaining costs. The costs of activities undertaken to support individual services regardless of the number of units or batches in which services are provided.

Master Budget and Responsibility Accounting

No one likes to run out of cash.

To manage their spending, businesses, like individuals, need budgets. Budgets help managers and their employees know whether they're on target for their growth and spending goals. Budgets are important for all types of companies: large financial institutions, such as Citigroup, which suffered big financial losses after the housing bubble burst in the mid-2000s; large retailers, such as Home Depot, whose profit margins are thin; profitable computer companies, such as Apple, which sell high dollar-value goods; and luxury hotels, such as the Ritz-Carlton, which sell high dollar-value services.

LEARNING OBJECTIVES

1. Describe the master budget and explain its benefits
2. Describe the advantages of budgets
3. Prepare the operating budget and its supporting schedules
4. Use computer-based financial planning models for sensitivity analysis
5. Describe responsibility centers and responsibility accounting
6. Recognize the human aspects of budgeting
7. Appreciate the special challenges of budgeting in multinational companies

"SCRIMPING" AT THE RITZ: MASTER BUDGETS

"Ladies and gentlemen serving ladies and gentlemen." That's the motto of the Ritz-Carlton. However, the aura of the chain's old-world elegance stands in contrast to its emphasis—behind the scenes, of course—on cost control and budgets. A Ritz hotel's performance is the responsibility of its general manager and controller at each location. Local forecasts and budgets are prepared annually and are the basis of subsequent performance evaluations for the hotel and people who work there. The budget comprises revenue forecasts and standard costs for hotel rooms, conventions, weddings, meeting facilities, merchandise, and food and beverages. Managers monitor the revenue budget daily, review occupancy rates and adjust prices if necessary. Corporate headquarters monitors actual performance each month against the approved budget and other Ritz hotels. Any ideas for boosting revenues and reducing costs are regularly shared among hotels.

Why do successful companies budget? Because, as the Ritz-Carlton example illustrates, budgeting is a critical function in an organization's decision-making process. Southwest Airlines, for example, uses budgets to monitor and manage fluctuating fuel costs. Walmart depends on its budget to maintain razor-thin margins as it competes with Target. Gillette uses budgets to plan marketing campaigns for its razors and blades.

Even though budgeting is essential for businesses, many managers are often frustrated by the budgeting process. They find it difficult to predict the future and dislike superiors challenging them to improve the performance of their departments. They also dislike being personally evaluated on targets that are challenging and prefer to develop budgets that they can beat. We discuss these issues and the ways thoughtful managers deal with them later in this chapter. For now, we highlight some of the benefits managers get from budgeting.

Suzanne Porter/Rough Guides/Dorling Kindersley, Ltd.

From Chapter 6 of *Horngren's Cost Accounting: A Managerial Emphasis*, Sixteenth Edition. Srikant M. Datar, Madhav V. Rajan.

Budgets help managers:

1. Communicate directions and goals to different departments of a company to help them coordinate the actions they must pursue to satisfy customers and succeed in the marketplace.
2. Judge performance by measuring financial results against planned objectives, activities, and timelines and learn about potential problems.
3. Motivate employees to achieve their goals.

Interestingly, even when it comes to entrepreneurial activities, research shows that business planning increases a new venture's probability of survival, as well as its product development and venture-organizing activities.[1] As the old adage goes: "If you fail to plan, you plan to fail."

In this chapter, you will see that a budget is based on an organization's strategy and expresses its operating and financial plans. Most importantly, you will see that budgeting is a human activity that requires judgment and wise interpretation.

Budgets and the Budgeting Cycle

LEARNING OBJECTIVE 1

Describe the master budget

. . . the master budget is the initial budget prepared before the start of a period

and explain its benefits

. . . benefits include planning, coordination, and control

A *budget* is (a) the quantitative expression of a proposed plan of action by management for a specified period and (b) an aid to coordinate what needs to be done to implement that plan. The budget generally includes both the plan's financial and nonfinancial aspects and serves as a road map for the company to follow in an upcoming period. A financial budget quantifies managers' expectations regarding a company's income, cash flows, and financial position. Just as financial statements are prepared for past periods, financial statements can be prepared for future periods—for example, a budgeted income statement, a budgeted statement of cash flows, or a budgeted balance sheet. Managers develop financial budgets using supporting information from nonfinancial budgets for, say, units manufactured or sold, number of employees, and number of new products being introduced to the marketplace.

Strategic Plans and Operating Plans

Budgeting is most useful when it is integrated with a company's strategy. *Strategy* specifies how an organization matches its capabilities with the opportunities in the marketplace to accomplish its objectives. To develop successful strategies, managers must consider questions such as the following:

- What are our objectives?
- How do we create value for our customers while distinguishing ourselves from our competitors?
- Are the markets for our products local, regional, national, or global? What trends affect our markets? How do the economy, our industry, and our competitors affect us?
- What organizational and financial structures serve us best?
- What are the risks and opportunities of alternative strategies, and what are our contingency plans if our preferred plan fails?

A company, such as Home Depot, can have a strategy of providing quality products or services at a low price. Another company, such as Porsche or the Ritz-Carlton, can have a strategy of providing a unique product or service that is priced higher than the products or services of competitors. Exhibit 1 shows that strategic plans are expressed through long-run budgets and operating plans are expressed via short-run budgets. But there is more to the story! The exhibit shows arrows pointing backward as well as forward. The backward arrows show that budgets can lead to changes in plans and strategies. Budgets help managers assess strategic risks and opportunities by providing them with feedback about the likely effects of their strategies and plans. Sometimes that feedback prompts managers to revise their plans and possibly their strategies.

[1] For more details, see Frederic Delmar and Scott Shane, "Does Business Planning Facilitate the Development of New Ventures?" *Strategic Management Journal* (December 2003).

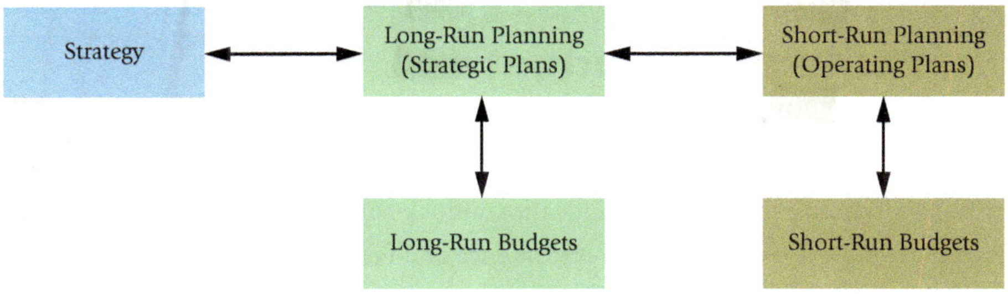

EXHIBIT 1

Strategy, Planning, and Budgets

Boeing's experience with the 747-8 program illustrates how budgets can help managers rework their operating plans. Boeing believed that utilizing some of the design concepts it was implementing in its 787 Dreamliner program would be a relatively inexpensive way to reconfigure its 747-8 jet. However, continued cost overruns and delays undermined that strategy: In early 2012, the 747-8 program was already $2 billion over budget and a year behind schedule. As a result, the company expected to earn no profit on any of the more than 100 orders for 747-8 planes it had on its books. And with the budget revealing higher-than-expected costs in design, rework, and production, Boeing postponed production plans for the 747-8 program. The problems with the 747-8 continue. Boeing plans to manufacture less than ten 747-8 aircraft each year.

Budgeting Cycle and Master Budget

Well-managed companies usually cycle through the following steps during the course of the fiscal year:

1. Before the start of the fiscal year, managers at all levels take into account the company's past performance, market feedback, and anticipated future changes to initiate plans for the next period. For example, an anticipated economic recovery from a recession may cause managers to plan for sales increases, higher production, and greater promotion expenses. Managers and management accountants work together to develop plans for the company as a whole and the performance of its subunits, such as departments or divisions.
2. At the beginning of the fiscal year, senior managers give subordinate managers a frame of reference, a set of specific financial or nonfinancial expectations against which they will compare actual results.
3. During the course of the year, management accountants help managers investigate any deviations from the plans, such as an unexpected decline in sales. If necessary, corrective action follows—changes in a product's features, a reduction in prices to boost sales, or cutting of costs to maintain profitability.

The preceding three steps describe the ongoing budget-related processes. The working document at the core of this process is called the *master budget*. The **master budget** expresses management's operating and financial plans for a specified period, usually a fiscal year, and it includes a set of budgeted financial statements. The master budget is the initial plan of what the company intends to accomplish in the period and evolves from both the operating and financing decisions managers make as they prepare the budget.

- Operating decisions deal with how to best use the limited resources of an organization.
- Financing decisions deal with how to obtain the funds to acquire those resources.

The terminology used to describe budgets varies among companies. For example, budgeted financial statements are sometimes called **pro forma statements**. Some companies, such as Hewlett-Packard, refer to budgeting as *targeting*. And many companies, such as Nissan Motor Company and Owens Corning, refer to the budget as a *profit plan*. Microsoft refers to goals as *commitments* and distributes firm-level goals across the company, connecting them to organizational, team, and—ultimately—individual commitments.

This chapter focuses on how management accounting helps managers make operating decisions, which is why operating budgets are emphasized here. Managers spend a significant part of their time preparing and analyzing budgets because budgeting yields many advantages.

DECISION POINT

What is the master budget and why is it useful?

Advantages and Challenges of Implementing Budgets

LEARNING OBJECTIVE 2

Describe the advantages of budgets

. . . advantages include coordination, communication, performance evaluation, and managerial motivation

Budgets are an integral part of management control systems. As we have discussed at the start of this chapter, when administered thoughtfully by managers, budgets do the following:

- Promote coordination and communication among subunits within the company
- Provide a framework for judging performance and facilitating learning
- Motivate managers and other employees

Promoting Coordination and Communication

Coordination is meshing and balancing all aspects of production or service and all departments in a company in the best way for the company to meet its goals. *Communication* is making sure all employees understand those goals. Coordination forces executives to think about the relationships among individual departments within the company, as well as between the company and its supply-chain partners.

Consider budgeting at Pace, a United Kingdom–based manufacturer of electronic products. A key product is Pace's digital set-top box for decoding satellite broadcasts. The production manager can achieve more timely production by coordinating and communicating with the company's marketing team to understand when set-top boxes need to be shipped to customers. In turn, the marketing team can make better predictions of future demand for set-top boxes by coordinating and communicating with Pace's customers.

Suppose BSkyB, one of Pace's largest customers, is planning to launch a new high-definition personal video recorder service. If Pace's marketing group is able to obtain information about the launch date for the service, it can share this information with Pace's manufacturing group. The manufacturing group must then coordinate and communicate with Pace's materials-procurement group, and so on. The point to understand is that Pace is more likely to have personal video recorders in the quantities customers demand if Pace coordinates and communicates both within its business functions and with its customers and suppliers during the budgeting and production processes.

Providing a Framework for Judging Performance and Facilitating Learning

Budgets enable a company's managers to measure actual performance against predicted performance. Budgets can overcome two limitations of using past performance as a basis for judging actual results. One limitation is that past results often incorporate past miscues and substandard performance. Suppose the cellular telephone company Mobile Communications is examining the current-year (2017) performance of its sales force. The sales force's 2016 performance incorporated the efforts of an unusually high number of salespeople who have since left the company because they did not have a good understanding of the marketplace. The president of Mobile said of those salespeople, "They could not sell ice cream in a heat wave." Using the sales record of those departed employees would set the performance bar for 2017 much too low.

The other limitation of using past performance is that future conditions can be expected to differ from the past. Suppose, in 2017, Mobile had a 20% revenue increase, compared with a 10% revenue increase in 2016. Does this increase indicate outstanding sales performance? Not if the forecasted and actual 2017 industry growth rate was 40%. In this case, Mobile's 20% actual revenue gain in 2017 doesn't look so good, even though it exceeded the 2016 actual growth rate of 10%. Using the 40% budgeted growth rate for the industry provides Mobile Communications with a better benchmark against which to evaluate its 2017 sales performance than using the 2016 actual growth rate of 10%. This is why many companies also evaluate their performance relative to their peers. Using only the budget to evaluate performance creates an incentive for subordinates to set targets that are relatively easy to achieve.[2] Of course, managers at all levels recognize this incentive and therefore work to make the budget more challenging to achieve for the individuals who report to them. Still, the budget is the end product of negotiations among senior and subordinate managers. At the end of the year, senior managers gain information about the performance of competitors and external market conditions. This is valuable information that they can use to judge the performance of subordinate managers.

One of the most valuable benefits of budgeting is that it helps managers gather information for improving future performance. When actual outcomes fall short of budgeted or planned results, it prompts thoughtful senior managers to ask questions about what happened and why and how this knowledge can be used to ensure that such shortfalls do not occur again. This probing and learning is one of the most important reasons why budgeting helps improve performance.

Motivating Managers and Other Employees

Research shows that the performance of employees improves when they receive a challenging budget. Why? Because they view not meeting it as a failure. Most employees are motivated to work more intensely to avoid failure than to achieve success (they are loss-averse). As employees get closer to a goal, they work harder to achieve it. Creating a little anxiety improves performance. However, overly ambitious and unachievable budgets can actually de-motivate employees because they see little chance of avoiding failure. As a result, many executives like to set demanding, but achievable, goals for their subordinate managers and employees.[3] General Electric's former CEO Jack Welch describes challenging, yet achievable, budgets as energizing, motivating, and satisfying for managers and other employees and capable of unleashing out-of-the-box and creative thinking. We will return to the topic of setting difficult-to-achieve targets and how it affects employees later in the chapter.

Challenges in Administering Budgets

The budgeting process involves all levels of management. Top managers want lower-level managers to participate in the budgeting process because they have more specialized knowledge and firsthand experience with the day-to-day aspects of running the business. Participation also creates greater commitment and accountability toward the budget among lower-level managers. This is the bottom-up aspect of the budgeting process. This is counterbalanced by the top-down feature of budgeting where senior managers probe and debate the budgets submitted by subordinates with the goal of setting demanding, but achievable, budget targets.

The budgeting process, however, is time-consuming. Estimates suggest that senior managers spend about 10–20% of their time on budgeting, and financial planning departments spend as much as 50% of their time on it.[4] For most organizations, the annual budget process is a months-long exercise that consumes a tremendous amount of resources.

The widespread use of budgets in companies ranging from major multinational corporations to small local businesses indicates that the advantages of budgeting systems outweigh the costs. To gain the benefits of budgeting, however, management at all levels of a company, particularly senior managers, should understand and support the budget and all aspects of the management control system. Lower-level managers who feel that top managers do not "believe" in budgets are unlikely to be active participants in the formulation and successful administration of budgets.

Budgets should not be administered rigidly. Attaining the budget is not an end in itself, especially when conditions change dramatically. A manager may commit to a budget, but if a situation arises in which some unplanned repairs or an unplanned advertising program would serve the long-run interests of the company, the manager should undertake the additional spending. For example, Chipotle, devastated by food-safety issues that sickened about 500 diners in the

[2] For several examples, see Jeremy Hope and Robin Fraser, *Beyond Budgeting* (Boston: Harvard Business School Press, 2003). The authors also criticize the tendency for managers to administer budgets rigidly even when changing market conditions have rendered the budgets obsolete.

[3] For a detailed discussion and several examples of the merits of setting specific hard goals, see Gary P. Latham, "The Motivational Benefits of Goal-Setting," *Academy of Management Executive* 18, no. 4 (2004).

[4] See Peter Horvath and Ralf Sauter, "Why Budgeting Fails: One Management System Is Not Enough," *Balanced Scorecard Report* (September 2004).

second half of 2015 and resulted in a halving of its stock price, has responded with a new marketing campaign and the largest media buy in its history in an effort to woo customers back. On the flip side, the dramatic decline in consumer demand during the 2007–2009 recession led designers such as Gucci to slash their ad budgets and put on hold planned new boutiques. Macy's and other retailers, stuck with shelves of merchandise ordered before the financial crisis, had no recourse but to slash prices and cut their workforces. J. C. Penney eventually missed its sales projections for 2009 by $2 billion. However, its aggressive actions during the year enabled it to survive the recession. Unfortunately, in 2012, J. C. Penney suffered steep declines in sales as a result of changing its strategy away from offering discounts and deals to everyday low pricing.

DECISION POINT

When should a company prepare budgets? What are the advantages of preparing budgets?

Developing an Operating Budget

LEARNING OBJECTIVE 3

Prepare the operating budget

...the budgeted income statement

and its supporting schedules

...such as cost of goods sold and nonmanufacturing costs

Budgets are typically developed for a set period, such as a month, quarter, or year, which can be then broken into subperiods. For example, a 12-month cash budget may be broken into 12 monthly periods so that cash inflows and outflows can be better coordinated.

Time Coverage of Budgets

The motive for creating a budget should guide a manager in choosing the period for the budget. For example, consider budgeting for a new Harley-Davidson 500-cc motorcycle. If the purpose is to budget for the total profitability of this new model, a 5-year period (or more) may be suitable and long enough to cover the product from design to manufacturing, sales, and after-sales support. In contrast, consider budgeting for a seasonal theater production, which is expected to run for a few months. If the purpose is to estimate all cash outlays, a 6-month period from the planning stage to the final performance should suffice.

The most frequently used budget period is 1 year, which is often subdivided into quarters and months. The budgeted data for a year are frequently revised as the year goes on. At the end of the second quarter, management may change the budget for the next two quarters in light of new information obtained during the first 6 months. For example, with the decline in the value of the pound against the euro following Britain's vote to exit the European Union, sales of Opel's Corsa and Insignia models have been sluggish in Britain. In order to reduce its cost of operations by around $400 million to deal with the sudden turn of events, General Motors recently decided to reduce work hours and production in its Opel plants in Germany.

Businesses are increasingly using *rolling budgets*. A **rolling budget**, also called a **continuous budget** or **rolling forecast**, is a budget that is always available for a specified future period. It is created by continually adding a month, quarter, or year to the period that just ended. Consider Electrolux, a global appliance company, which has a 3- to 5-year strategic plan and a 4-quarter rolling budget. A 4-quarter rolling budget for the April 2016 to March 2017 period is superseded in the next quarter—that is, in June 2016—by a 4-quarter rolling budget for July 2016 to June 2017, and so on. There is always a 12-month budget (for the next year) in place. Rolling budgets constantly force Electrolux's management to think about the forthcoming 12 months, regardless of the quarter at hand. Some companies, such as Borealis, Europe's leading polyolefin plastics manufacturer; Millipore, a life sciences research and manufacturing firm headquartered in Massachusetts; and Nordea, the largest financial services group in the Nordic and Baltic Sea region, prepare rolling financial forecasts that look ahead five quarters. Other companies, such as EMC Corporation, the information infrastructure giant, employ a 6-quarter rolling-forecast process so that budget allocations can be constantly adjusted to meet changing market conditions.

Steps in Preparing an Operating Budget

The best way to learn how to prepare an operating budget is by walking through the steps a company would take to develop it. Consider Stylistic Furniture, a company that makes two types of granite-top coffee tables: Casual and Deluxe. It is late 2016 and Stylistic's CEO, Rex Jordan, is very concerned about how to respond to the board of directors' mandate to increase profits by 10% in the coming year. Jordan goes through the five-step decision-making process.

1. **Identify the Problem and Uncertainties.** The problem is to identify a strategy and to build a budget to achieve 10% profit growth. There are several uncertainties. Can Stylistic dramatically increase the sales of its more profitable Deluxe tables? What price pressures are Stylistic likely to face? Will the cost of materials increase? Can Stylistic reduce costs through efficiency improvements?
2. **Obtain Information.** Stylistic's managers gather information about sales of tables in the current year. They are delighted to learn that sales of Deluxe tables have been stronger than expected. Moreover, one of the key competitors in Stylistic's Casual tables' line has had quality problems that are unlikely to be resolved until 2017. Unfortunately, Stylistic's managers also discover that the prices of direct materials have increased slightly during 2016 when compared to 2015.
3. **Make Predictions About the Future.** Stylistic's managers feel confident that with a little more marketing, they will be able to grow the Deluxe tables' business in 2017 and even increase prices moderately relative to 2016. They also do not expect significant price pressures on Casual tables during the year because of the quality problems faced by a key competitor.

   The purchasing manager anticipates that prices of direct materials will be about the same in 2017 as it was in 2016. The manufacturing manager believes that efficiency improvements would allow the costs of manufacturing the tables to be maintained at 2016 costs despite an increase in the prices of other inputs. Achieving these efficiency improvements is important if Stylistic is to maintain its 12% operating margin (that is, operating income ÷ sales = 12%) and to grow sales and operating income.
4. **Make Decisions by Choosing Among Alternatives.** Jordan and his managers feel confident about their strategy to increase the sales of Deluxe tables. This decision has some risks, but is the best option available for Stylistic to increase its profits by 10%.
5. **Implement the Decision, Evaluate Performance, and Learn.** Managers compare a company's actual performance to its predicted performance to learn why things turned out the way they did and how to do better. Stylistic's managers would want to know whether their predictions about the prices of Casual and Deluxe tables were correct. Did the prices of inputs increase more or less than anticipated? Did efficiency improvements occur? Such learning would be helpful in building budgets in subsequent years.

Stylistic's managers begin their work on the 2017 budget. Exhibit 2 shows the various parts of the master budget, which is composed of the financial projections for Stylistic's operating and financial budgets for 2017. The light, medium, and dark green boxes in Exhibit 2 show the budgeted income statement and its supporting budget schedules, which together are called the **operating budget**.

We show the revenues budget box in light green to indicate that it is often the starting point of the operating budget. The supporting schedules—shown in medium green—quantify the budgets for various business functions of the value chain, from research and development to distribution costs. These schedules build up to the budgeted income statement—the key summary statement in the operating budget—shown in dark green.

The orange and purple boxes in the exhibit are the **financial budget**, which is that part of the master budget made up of the capital expenditures budget, the cash budget, the budgeted balance sheet, and the budgeted statement of cash flows. A financial budget focuses on how operations and planned capital outlays affect cash—shown in orange. Management accountants use the cash budget and the budgeted income statement to prepare two other summary financial statements—the budgeted balance sheet and the budgeted statement of cash flows, which are shown in purple.

Top managers and line managers responsible for various business functions in the value chain finalize the master budget after several rounds of discussions. We next present the steps in preparing an operating budget for Stylistic Furniture for 2017 using Exhibit 2 as a guide. The appendix to this chapter presents Stylistic's cash budget, which is another key component of the master budget. The following details are needed to prepare the budget:

- Stylistic sells two models of granite-top coffee tables: Casual and Deluxe. Revenue unrelated to sales, such as interest income, is zero.
- Work-in-process inventory is negligible and is ignored.

EXHIBIT 2

Overview of the Master Budget for Stylistic Furniture

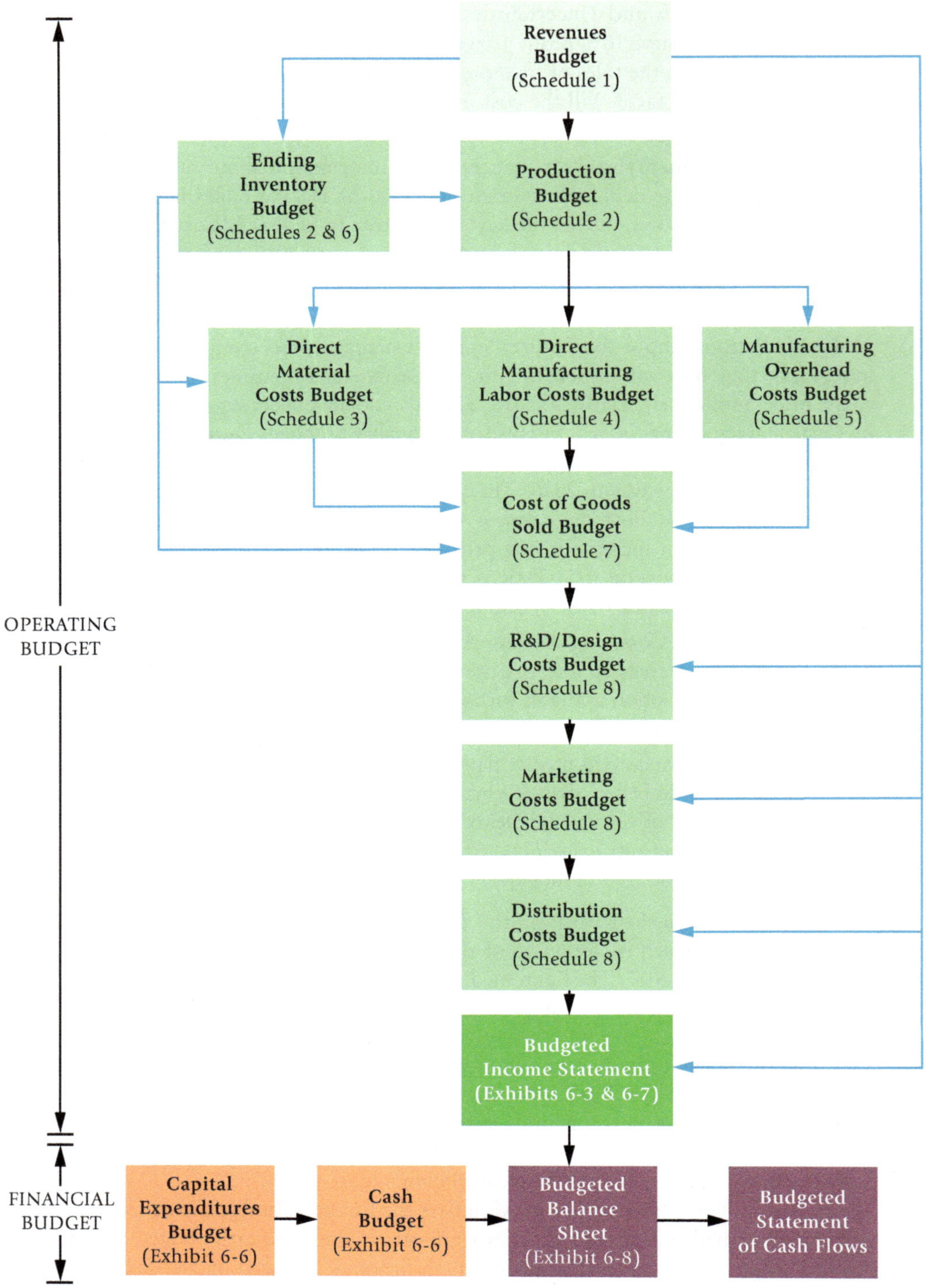

- Direct materials inventory and finished-goods inventory are costed using the first-in, first-out (FIFO) method. The unit costs of direct materials purchased and unit costs of finished-goods sold remain unchanged throughout each budget year, but can change from year to year.
- There are two types of direct materials: red oak (RO) and granite slabs (GS). The direct material costs are variable with respect to units of output—coffee tables.
- Direct manufacturing labor workers are hired on an hourly basis; no overtime is worked.

- There are two cost drivers for manufacturing overhead costs—direct manufacturing labor-hours and setup labor-hours, and two manufacturing overhead cost pools—manufacturing operations overhead and machine setup overhead.
- Direct manufacturing labor-hours is the cost driver for the variable portion of manufacturing operations overhead. The fixed component of manufacturing operations overhead is tied to the manufacturing capacity of 300,000 direct manufacturing labor-hours Stylistic has planned for 2017.
- Setup labor-hours are the cost driver for the variable portion of machine setup overhead. The fixed component of machine setup overhead is tied to the setup capacity of 15,000 setup labor-hours Stylistic has planned for 2017.
- For computing inventoriable costs, Stylistic allocates all (variable and fixed) manufacturing operations overhead costs using direct manufacturing labor-hours and machine setup overhead costs using setup labor-hours.
- Nonmanufacturing costs consist of product design, marketing, and distribution costs. All product design costs are fixed costs for 2017. The variable component of marketing costs is the 6.5% sales commission on revenues paid to salespeople. The variable portion of distribution costs varies with cubic feet of tables sold and shipped.

The following data are available for the 2017 budget:

Direct materials	
Red oak	$ 7 per board foot (b.f.) (same as in 2016)
Granite	$10 per square foot (sq. ft.) (same as in 2016)
Direct manufacturing labor	$20 per hour

	Content of Each Product Unit	
	Casual Granite Table	Deluxe Granite Table
Red oak	12 board feet	12 board feet
Granite	6 square feet	8 square feet
Direct manufacturing labor	4 hours	6 hours

	Product	
	Casual Granite Table	Deluxe Granite Table
Expected sales in units	50,000	10,000
Selling price	$ 600	$ 800
Target ending inventory in units	11,000	500
Beginning inventory in units	1,000	500
Beginning inventory in dollars	$384,000	$262,000

	Direct Materials	
	Red oak	Granite
Beginning inventory	70,000 b.f.	60,000 sq. ft.
Target ending inventory	80,000 b.f.	20,000 sq. ft.

Stylistic bases its budgeted cost information on the costs predicted to support its revenues budget, taking into account the efficiency improvements it expects to make in 2017. Recall from Step 3 of the decision-making process that efficiency improvements are critical to offset the anticipated increases in the cost of inputs and to maintain Stylistic's 12% operating margin.

Most companies have a budget manual that contains a company's particular instructions and information for preparing its budgets. Although the details differ among companies, the following basic steps are common for developing the operating budget for a manufacturing company. Beginning with the revenues budget, each of the other budgets follows step by step in logical fashion. As you go through the details for preparing a budget, think about two things: (1) the information needed to prepare each budget and (2) the actions managers can plan to take to improve the company's performance.

Step 1: Prepare the Revenues Budget. Stylistic's managers plan to continue to sell two models of granite-top coffee tables: Casual and Deluxe. The revenues budget accounts for the quantities and prices of Casual and Deluxe tables that Stylistic expects to sell in 2017.

A revenues budget is the usual starting point for the operating budget. Why? Because the forecasted level of unit sales or revenues has a major impact on the production capacity and the inventory levels planned for 2017—and therefore, manufacturing and nonmanufacturing costs. Many factors affect the sales forecast, including the sales volume in recent periods, general economic and industry conditions, market research studies, pricing policies, advertising and sales promotions, competition, and regulatory policies. The key to Stylistic achieving its goal of growing its profits by 10% is to grow its sales of Deluxe tables from 8,000 tables in 2016 to 10,000 tables in 2017.

Managers use customer relationship management (CRM) or sales management systems to gather information. Statistical approaches such as regression and trend analysis based on indicators of economic activity and past sales data help in forecasting future sales. Sales managers and sales representatives debate how best to position, price, and promote Casual and Deluxe tables relative to competitors' products. Together with top management, they consider various actions, such as adding product features, digital advertising, and changing sales incentives, to increase revenues. The costs of these actions are included in the various cost budgets. In the final analysis, the sales forecast represents the collective experience and judgment of managers.

Top managers decide on the budgeted sales quantities and prices shown in the revenues budget in Schedule 1. These are difficult targets designed to motivate the organization to achieve higher levels of performance.

Schedule 1: Revenues Budget
for the Year Ending December 31, 2017

	Units	Selling Price	Total Revenues
Casual	50,000	$600	$30,000,000
Deluxe	10,000	800	8,000,000
Total			$38,000,000

The $38,000,000 is the amount of revenues in the budgeted income statement.

Revenues budgets are usually based on market conditions and expected demand because demand for a company's products is invariably the limiting factor for achieving profit goals. Occasionally, other factors, such as available production capacity (being less than demand) or a manufacturing input in short supply, limit budgeted revenues. In these cases, managers base the revenues budget on the maximum units that can be produced because sales will be limited by the available production.

Step 2: Prepare the Production Budget (in Units). The next step in the budgeting process is to plan the production quantities of Casual and Deluxe tables. The only new information managers need to prepare the production budget is the desired level of finished goods inventory. High inventory levels increase the cost of carrying inventory, the costs of quality, and shrinkage costs. On the flip side, low inventory levels increase setup costs and result in lost sales because of product unavailability. Stylistic's management decides to maintain the inventory level of Deluxe tables and increase the inventory of Casual tables to avoid the effects of supply shortages that the company encountered in 2016.

The manufacturing manager prepares the production budget, shown in Schedule 2. The units of finished goods to be produced depend on budgeted unit sales (calculated in Step 1), the target ending finished-goods inventory, and the beginning finished-goods inventory:

$$\begin{array}{c}\text{Budget}\\\text{production}\\\text{(units)}\end{array} = \begin{array}{c}\text{Budget}\\\text{sales}\\\text{(units)}\end{array} + \begin{array}{c}\text{Target ending}\\\text{finished goods}\\\text{inventory}\\\text{(units)}\end{array} - \begin{array}{c}\text{Beginning}\\\text{finished goods}\\\text{inventory}\\\text{(units)}\end{array}$$

Schedule 2: Production Budget (in Units)
for the Year Ending December 31, 2017

	Product	
	Casual	**Deluxe**
Budgeted sales in units (Schedule 1)	50,000	10,000
Add target ending finished-goods inventory	11,000	500
Total required units	61,000	10,500
Deduct beginning finished-goods inventory	1,000	500
Units of finished goods to be produced	60,000	10,000

The production budget determines budgeted production costs (for example, direct materials, direct manufacturing labor, and manufacturing overhead) after considering efficiency improvements planned for 2017. Costs are also influenced by actions such as product redesign needed to support the revenues budget.

Managers are always looking for opportunities to reduce costs, for example, by improving processes, streamlining manufacturing, and reducing the time it takes to complete various activities, such as setting up machines or transporting materials. Making these changes improves a company's competitiveness, but it also requires investment. The budgeting exercise is an ideal time for managers to evaluate plans and request the needed financial resources.

Jimenez Corporation manufactures and sells two types of decorative lamps, Knox and Ayer. The following data are available for the year 2017.

1 **TRY IT!**

	Product	
	Knox	**Ayer**
Expected sales in units	21,000	10,000
Selling price	$ 25	$ 40
Target ending inventory in units	2,000	1,000
Beginning inventory in units	3,000	1,000

Calculate the revenues budget (label it Schedule 1) and the production budget in units (label it Schedule 2) for year ending December 31, 2017.

Step 3: Prepare the Direct Materials Usage Budget and Direct Materials Purchases Budget. The budgeted production, calculated in Schedule 2, determines the quantities and dollars of direct materials used. The direct material quantities used depends on the efficiency with which workers use materials to produce a table. In determining budgets, managers are constantly anticipating ways to make process improvements that increase quality and reduce waste, thereby reducing direct material usage and costs. Senior managers set budgets that motivate production managers to reduce direct material costs and keep negligible work-in-process inventory. We ignore work-in-process inventory when preparing Stylistic's budgets for 2017.

Like many companies, Stylistic has a *bill of materials* stored in its computer systems that it constantly updates for efficiency improvements. This document identifies how each product is manufactured, specifying all materials (and components), the sequence in which the materials are used, the quantity of materials in each finished unit, and the work centers where the operations are performed. For example, the bill of materials would indicate that 12 board feet of red oak and 6 square feet of granite are needed to produce each Casual coffee table and 12 board feet of red oak and 8 square feet of granite are needed to produce each Deluxe coffee table. Direct materials inventories are costed using the first-in, first-out (FIFO) method. The management accountant uses this information to calculate the direct materials usage budget in Schedule 3A.

Schedule 3A: Direct Materials Usage Budget in Quantity and Dollars for the Year Ending December 31, 2017

	Material		
	Red oak	Granite	Total
Physical Units Budget			
Direct materials required for Casual tables (60,000 units × 12 b.f. and 6 sq. ft.)	720,000 b.f.	360,000 sq. ft.	
Direct materials required for Deluxe tables (10,000 units × 12 b.f. and 8 sq. ft.)	120,000 b.f.	80,000 sq. ft.	
Total quantity of direct materials to be used	840,000 b.f.	440,000 sq. ft.	
Cost Budget			
Available from beginning direct materials inventory (under a FIFO cost-flow assumption) (Given)			
Red oak: 70,000 b.f. × $7 per b.f.	$ 490,000		
Granite: 60,000 sq. ft. × $10 per sq. ft.		$ 600,000	
To be purchased and used this period			
Red oak: (840,000 − 70,000) b.f. × $7 per b.f.	5,390,000		
Granite: (440,000 − 60,000) sq. ft. × $10 per sq. ft.		3,800,000	
Direct materials to be used this period	$5,880,000	$4,400,000	$10,280,000

The only new information needed to prepare the direct materials purchases budget is the desired levels of direct materials inventory. During 2017, Stylistic's managers plan to increase the inventory of red oak, but reduce the inventory of granite to the levels of ending inventory described. The purchasing manager then prepares the budget for direct material purchases, shown in Schedule 3B:

Schedule 3B: Direct Materials Purchases Budget for the Year Ending December 31, 2017

	Material		
	Red oak	Granite	Total
Physical Units Budget			
To be used in production (from Schedule 3A)	840,000 b.f.	440,000 sq. ft.	
Add target ending inventory	80,000 b.f.	20,000 sq. ft.	
Total requirements	920,000 b.f.	460,000 sq. ft.	
Deduct beginning inventory	70,000 b.f.	60,000 sq. ft.	
Purchases to be made	850,000 b.f.	400,000 sq. ft.	
Cost Budget			
Red oak: 850,000 b.f. × $7 per b.f.	$5,950,000		
Granite: 400,000 sq. ft. × $10 per sq. ft.		$4,000,000	
Direct materials to be purchased this period	$5,950,000	$4,000,000	$9,950,000

Step 4: Prepare the Direct Manufacturing Labor Costs Budget. To create the budget for direct manufacturing labor costs, Stylistic's managers estimate wage rates, production methods, process and efficiency improvements, and hiring plans. The company hires direct manufacturing labor workers on an hourly basis. These workers do not work overtime. Manufacturing managers use *labor standards*, the time allowed per unit of output, to calculate the direct manufacturing labor costs budget in Schedule 4 based on the information.

Schedule 4: Direct Manufacturing Labor Costs Budget for the Year Ending December 31, 2017

	Output Units Produced (Schedule 2)	Direct Manufacturing Labor-Hours per Unit	Total Hours	Hourly Wage Rate	Total
Casual	60,000	4	240,000	$20	$4,800,000
Deluxe	10,000	6	60,000	20	1,200,000
Total			300,000		$6,000,000

TRY IT! 2

Jimenez Corporation manufactures and sells two types of decorative lamps, Knox and Ayer. It expects to manufacture 20,000 Knox lamps and 10,000 Ayer lamps in 2017. The following data are available for the year 2017.

Direct materials	
Metal	$ 3 per pound (same as in 2016)
Fabric	$ 4 per yard (same as in 2016)
Direct manufacturing labor	$20 per hour

Content of Each Product Unit

	Product	
	Knox	Ayer
Metal	2 pounds	3 pounds
Fabric	1 yard	1.5 yards
Direct manufacturing labor	0.15 hours	0.2 hours

	Direct Materials	
	Metal	Fabric
Beginning inventory	12,000 pounds	7,000 yards
Target ending inventory	10,000 pounds	5,000 yards

Calculate (a) the direct materials usage budget in quantity and dollars (label it Schedule 3A); (b) the direct materials purchase budget in quantity and dollars (label it Schedule 3B); and (c) the direct manufacturing labor costs budget (label it Schedule 4) for the year ending December 31, 2017.

Step 5: Prepare the Manufacturing Overhead Costs Budget. Stylistic's managers next budget for manufacturing overhead costs such as supervision, depreciation, maintenance, supplies, and power. Managing overhead costs is important but also challenging because it requires managers to understand the various activities needed to manufacture products and the cost drivers of those activities. As we described earlier, Stylistic's managers identify two activities for manufacturing overhead costs in its activity-based costing system: manufacturing operations and machine setups. The following table presents the activities and their cost drivers.

Manufacturing Overhead Costs	Cost Driver of Variable Component of Overhead Costs	Cost Driver of Fixed Component of Overhead Costs	Manufacturing and Setup Capacity in 2017
Manufacturing Operations Overhead Costs	Direct manufacturing labor-hours	Manufacturing capacity	300,000 direct manufacturing labor-hours
Machine Setup Overhead Costs	Setup labor-hours	Setup capacity	15,000 setup labor-hours

The use of activity-based cost drivers gives rise to **activity-based budgeting (ABB)**, a budgeting method that focuses on the budgeted cost of the activities necessary to produce and sell products and services.

In its activity-based costing system, Stylistic's manufacturing managers estimate various line items of overhead costs that comprise manufacturing operations overhead (that is, all costs for which direct manufacturing labor-hours is the cost driver). Managers identify opportunities for process and efficiency improvements, such as reducing defect rates and the time to manufacture a table, and then calculate budgeted manufacturing operations overhead costs in the operating department. They also determine the resources that they will need from the two support departments—kilowatt-hours of energy from the power department and hours of maintenance service from the maintenance department. The support department managers, in turn, plan the costs of personnel and supplies that they will need in order to provide the operating department with the support services it requires. The costs of the support departments are then allocated (first-stage cost allocation) as part of manufacturing operations overhead. The first half of Schedule 5 shows the various line items of costs that constitute manufacturing operations overhead costs—that is, all variable and fixed overhead costs (in the operating and support departments) that are caused by the 300,000 direct manufacturing labor-hours (the cost driver).

Stylistic budgets costs differently for variable and fixed overhead costs. Consider variable overhead costs of supplies: Stylistic's managers use past historical data and their knowledge of operations to estimate the cost of supplies per direct manufacturing labor-hour of \$5. The total budgeted cost of supplies for 2017 is, therefore, \$5 multiplied by the 300,000 budgeted direct manufacturing labor-hours, for a total of \$1,500,000. The total variable manufacturing operations overhead cost equals \$21.60 per direct manufacturing labor-hour multiplied by the 300,000 budgeted direct manufacturing labor-hours, for a total of \$6,480,000.

Stylistic measures manufacturing operations capacity in terms of the direct manufacturing labor-hours that the facility is configured to support. It currently has a capacity of 300,000 direct manufacturing labor-hours. To support this level of capacity, and taking into account potential cost improvements, managers estimate total fixed manufacturing operations overhead costs of \$2,520,000. (Note that, unlike 2017, Stylistic may not operate at full capacity each year, but its fixed manufacturing operations costs will still be \$2,520,000.) Its fixed manufacturing overhead cost is \$2,520,000 ÷ 300,000 = \$8.40 per direct manufacturing labor-hour (regardless of the budgeted direct manufacturing labor-hours, which may be less than 300,000 in a particular year). That is, each direct manufacturing labor-hour will absorb \$21.60 of variable manufacturing operations overhead plus \$8.40 of fixed manufacturing operations overhead for a total of \$30 of manufacturing operations overhead cost per direct manufacturing labor-hour.

Next, Stylistic's managers determine how setups will be done for the Casual and Deluxe line of tables, taking into account past experiences and potential improvements in setup efficiency.

For example, managers consider the following:

- Increasing the number of tables produced per batch so fewer batches (and therefore fewer setups) are needed for the budgeted production of tables
- Decreasing the setup time per batch
- Reducing the supervisory time needed, for example by increasing the skill base of workers

Stylistic's managers forecast the following setup information for the Casual and Deluxe tables:

	Casual Tables	Deluxe Tables	Total
1. Quantity of tables to be produced	60,000 tables	10,000 tables	
2. Number of tables to be produced per batch	50 tables/batch	40 tables/batch	
3. Number of batches (1) ÷ (2)	1,200 batches	250 batches	
4. Setup time per batch	10 hours/batch	12 hours/batch	
5. Total setup-hours (3) × (4)	12,000 hours	3,000 hours	15,000 hours
6. Setup-hours per table (5) ÷ (1)	0.2 hour	0.3 hour	

Using an approach similar to the one described for manufacturing operations overhead costs, Stylistic's managers estimate various line items of costs that comprise variable machine setup overhead costs (supplies, indirect manufacturing labor, power, depreciation, and supervision)—that is, all costs caused by the 15,000 setup labor-hours (the cost driver): The second half of Schedule 5 summarizes (1) total variable machine setup overhead costs per setup labor-hour = $88 ($26 + $56 + $6) × the budgeted 15,000 setup labor-hours = $1,320,000 and (2) fixed machine setup overhead costs of $1,680,000 needed to support the 15,000 setup labor-hours of capacity that Stylistic's managers have planned. (Again, Stylistic may not operate at full capacity each year. However, the fixed machine setup costs will still be $1,680,000.) The fixed machine setup cost is $1,680,000 ÷ 15,000 = $112 per setup labor-hour (regardless of the budgeted setup labor-hours, which may be less than 15,000 in a particular year). That is, each setup labor-hour will absorb $88 of variable machine setup overhead cost plus $112 of fixed machine setup overhead cost for a total of $200 of machine setup overhead cost per setup labor-hour.

Schedule 5: Manufacturing Overhead Costs Budget
for the Year Ending December 31, 2017

Manufacturing Operations Overhead Costs		
Variable costs (for 300,000 direct manufacturing labor-hours)		
Supplies ($5 per direct manufacturing labor-hour)	$1,500,000	
Indirect manufacturing labor ($5.60 per direct manufacturing labor-hour)	1,680,000	
Power (support department costs) ($7 per direct manufacturing labor-hour)	2,100,000	
Maintenance (support department costs) ($4 per direct manufacturing labor-hour)	1,200,000	$6,480,000
Fixed costs (to support capacity of 300,000 direct manufacturing labor-hours)		
Depreciation	1,020,000	
Supervision	390,000	
Power (support department costs)	630,000	
Maintenance (support department costs)	480,000	2,520,000
Total manufacturing operations overhead costs		$9,000,000
Machine Setup Overhead Costs		
Variable costs (for 15,000 setup labor-hours)		
Supplies ($26 per setup labor-hour)	$ 390,000	
Indirect manufacturing labor ($56 per setup labor-hour)	840,000	
Power (support department costs) ($6 per setup labor-hour)	90,000	$ 1,320,000
Fixed costs (to support capacity of 15,000 setup labor-hours)		
Depreciation	603,000	
Supervision	1,050,000	
Power (support department costs)	27,000	1,680,000
Total machine setup overhead costs		$ 3,000,000
Total manufacturing overhead costs		$12,000,000

Note how using activity-based cost drivers provide additional and detailed information that improves decision making compared with budgeting based solely on output-based cost drivers. Of course, managers must always evaluate whether the expected benefit of adding more cost drivers exceeds the expected cost.[5]

Note that Stylistic is scheduled to operate at capacity. Therefore, the budgeted quantity of the cost allocation base/cost driver is the same for variable overhead costs and fixed overhead costs—300,000 direct manufacturing labor-hours for manufacturing operations overhead costs and 15,000 setup labor-hours for machine setup overhead costs. In this case, the budgeted rate for the manufacturing operations overhead cost does not have to be calculated separately for variable costs and for fixed costs as we did earlier. Instead, it can be calculated directly by estimating total budgeted manufacturing operations overhead: $9,000,000 ÷ 300,000 direct

[5] The Stylistic example illustrates ABB using manufacturing operations and setup costs included in Stylistic's manufacturing overhead costs budget. ABB implementations in practice include costs in many parts of the value chain. For an example, see Sofia Borjesson, "A Case Study on Activity-Based Budgeting," *Journal of Cost Management* 10, no. 4 (Winter 1997): 7–18.

manufacturing labor-hours = \$30 per direct manufacturing labor-hour. Similarly, the budgeted rate for machine setup overhead cost can be calculated as total budgeted machine setup overhead: \$3,000,000 ÷ 15,000 budgeted setup hours = \$200 per setup-hour.

TRY IT! 3

Jimenez Corporation manufactures and sells two types of decorative lamps, Knox and Ayer. The following data are available for the year 2017. Machine setup-hours is the only driver of manufacturing overhead costs. Jimenez has a setup capacity of 1,100 hours

	Knox	Ayer
1. Quantity of lamps to be produced	20,000 lamps	10,000 lamps
2. Number of lamps to be produced per batch	100 lamps/batch	80 lamps/batch
3. Setup time per batch	3 hours/batch	4 hours/batch

Variable cost = \$60 per setup-hour
Fixed cost = \$77,000
Calculate the manufacturing overhead costs budget (label it Schedule 5).

Step 6: Prepare the Ending Inventories Budget. Schedule 6A shows the computation of the unit cost of coffee tables started and completed in 2017. These calculations are needed to calculate the ending inventories budget and the budgeted cost of goods sold. In accordance with Generally Accepted Accounting Principles, Stylistic treats both variable and fixed manufacturing overhead as inventoriable (product) costs. Manufacturing operations overhead costs are allocated to finished-goods inventory at the budgeted rate of \$30 per direct manufacturing labor-hour. Machine setup overhead costs are allocated to finished-goods inventory at the budgeted rate of \$200 per setup-hour.

Schedule 6A: Budgeted Unit Costs of Ending Finished-Goods Inventory December 31, 2017

		Product			
		Casual Tables		Deluxe Tables	
	Cost per Unit of Input	Input per Unit of Output	Total	Input per Unit of Output	Total
Red oak	\$ 7	12 b.f.	\$ 84	12 b.f.	\$ 84
Granite	10	6 sq. ft.	60	8 sq. ft.	80
Direct manufacturing labor	20	4 hrs.	80	6 hrs.	120
Manufacturing operations overhead	30	4 hrs.	120	6 hrs.	180
Machine setup overhead	200	0.2 hrs.	40	0.3 hrs.	60
Total			\$384		\$524

Under the FIFO method, managers use this unit cost to calculate the cost of target ending inventories of finished goods in Schedule 6B.

Schedule 6B: Ending Inventories Budget December 31, 2017

	Quantity	Cost per Unit		Total
Direct materials				
Red oak	80,000*	\$7	\$ 560,000	
Granite	20,000*	10	200,000	\$ 760,000
Finished goods				
Casual	11,000**	\$384***	\$4,224,000	
Deluxe	500**	524***	262,000	4,486,000
Total ending inventory				\$5,246,000

*Data are from page 205. **Data are from page 205. ***From Schedule 6A, this is based on 2017 costs of manufacturing finished goods because under the FIFO costing method, the units in finished-goods ending inventory consists of units that are produced during 2017.

4 **TRY IT!**

Jimenez Corporation manufactures and sells two types of decorative lamps, Knox and Ayer. The following data are available for the year 2017.

	Product	
	Knox	Ayer
Target ending inventory in units	2,000	1,000

Direct materials

Metal	$ 3 per pound (same as in 2016)
Fabric	$ 4 per yard (same as in 2016)
Direct manufacturing labor	$ 20 per hour
Machine setup overhead	$130 per hour

	Content of Each Product Unit	
	Knox	Ayer
Metal	2 pounds	3 pounds
Fabric	1 yard	1.5 yards
Direct manufacturing labor	0.15 hours	0.2 hours
Machine setup overhead	0.03 hours	0.05 hours
	Direct Materials	
	Metal	**Fabric**
Target ending inventory	10,000 pounds	5,000 yards

Calculate (1) the budgeted unit costs of ending finished-goods inventory on December 31, 2017 (label it Schedule 6A) and (2) the ending inventories budget on December 31, 2017 (label it Schedule 6B).

Step 7: Prepare the Cost of Goods Sold Budget. The manufacturing and purchase managers, together with the management accountant, use information from Schedules 3–6 to prepare Schedule 7—the cost of goods sold expense budget that will be matched against revenues to calculate Stylistic's budgeted gross margin for 2017.

Schedule 7: Cost of Goods Sold Budget
for the Year Ending December 31, 2017

	From Schedule		Total
Beginning finished-goods inventory, January 1, 2017	Given*		$ 646,000
Direct materials used	3A	$10,280,000	
Direct manufacturing labor	4	6,000,000	
Manufacturing overhead	5	12,000,000	
Cost of goods manufactured			28,280,000
Cost of goods available for sale			28,926,000
Deduct ending finished-goods inventory, December 31, 2017	6B		4,486,000
Cost of goods sold			$24,440,000

*Based on beginning inventory values in 2017 for Casual tables, $384,000, and Deluxe tables, $262,000 (page 205).

Step 8: Prepare the Nonmanufacturing Costs Budget. Schedules 2–7 represent budgets for Stylistic's manufacturing costs. Stylistic also incurs nonmanufacturing costs in other parts of the value chain—product design, marketing, and distribution. Just as in the case of manufacturing costs, the key to managing nonmanufacturing overhead costs is to understand the various activities that will be needed to support the design, marketing, and distribution of Deluxe and Casual tables in 2017 and the cost drivers of those activities. Managers in these functions of the value chain build in process and efficiency improvements and prepare nonmanufacturing cost budgets on the basis of the quantities of cost drivers planned for 2017.

The number of design changes is the cost driver for product design costs. Product design costs of $1,024,000 are fixed costs for 2017 and adjusted at the start of the year based on the number of design changes planned for 2017.

Total revenue is the cost driver for the variable portion of marketing (and sales) costs. The commission paid to salespeople equals 6.5 cents per dollar (or 6.5%) of revenues. Managers budget the fixed component of marketing costs, $1,330,000, at the start of the year based on budgeted revenues for 2017.

Cubic feet of tables sold and shipped (Casual: 18 cubic feet × 50,000 tables + Deluxe: 24 cubic feet × 10,000 tables = 1,140,000 cubic feet) is the cost driver of the variable component of budgeted distribution costs. Variable distribution costs equal $2 per cubic foot. The fixed component of budgeted distribution costs equal to $1,596,000 varies with the company's distribution capacity, which in 2017 is 1,140,000 cubic feet (to support the distribution of 50,000 Casual tables and 10,000 Deluxe tables). For brevity, Schedule 8 shows the product design, marketing, and distribution costs budget for 2017 in a single schedule.

Schedule 8: Nonmanufacturing Costs Budget for the Year Ending December 31, 2017

Business Function	Variable Costs	Fixed Costs	Total Costs
Product design	—	$1,024,000	$1,024,000
Marketing (Variable cost: $38,000,000 × 0.065)	$2,470,000	1,330,000	3,800,000
Distribution (Variable cost: $2 × 1,140,000 cu. ft.)	2,280,000	1,596,000	3,876,000
	$4,750,000	$3,950,000	$8,700,000

The nonmanufacturing costs in our example focused on activities Stylistic needs to undertake to achieve its revenue goals for the year. The innovations in product design were incremental innovations necessary to generate higher revenues in 2017. Sometimes companies need to invest in research and development (R&D) in a particular year that, if successful, will only result in revenues in a subsequent year. When companies engage in radical rather than incremental innovation, R&D costs may have to be incurred for several years before the company sees the benefits of the R&D in the form of revenues. Many critics argue that the short-term costs of engaging in innovation for uncertain long-term benefits result in companies underinvesting in radical or breakthrough innovations.

Companies that engage in breakthrough innovation budget separately for these resources in their annual budgets. In this way, they separate the operational performance for the year from investments in innovation for subsequent years. They ensure that the innovations pursued are closely linked to their intended strategies and develop project milestones, such as expert evaluations, intellectual property creation, patents received, and customer engagement, to monitor progress and value creation of the innovation projects.

Step 9: Prepare the Budgeted Income Statement. The CEO and managers of various business functions, with help from the management accountant, use information in Schedules 1, 7, and 8 to finalize the budgeted income statement, shown in Exhibit 3. The style used in Exhibit 3 is typical, but managers and accountants could include more details in the income statement. As more details are put in the income statement, fewer supporting schedules are needed.

Budgeting is a cross-functional activity. The strategies developed by top managers for achieving a company's revenue and operating income goals affect the costs planned for the different business functions of the value chain. For example, the budgeted increase in sales at Stylistic is based on spending more for marketing and must be matched with higher production costs to ensure there is an adequate supply of tables and with higher distribution costs to ensure the timely delivery of tables to customers. Rex Jordan, the CEO of Stylistic Furniture, is very pleased with the 2017 budget. It calls for a 10% increase in operating income compared with 2016. The keys to achieving a higher operating income are a significant increase in sales

EXHIBIT 3

Budgeted Income Statement for Stylistic Furniture

	A	B	C	D
1	**Budgeted Income Statement for Stylistic Furniture**			
2	**For the Year Ending December 31, 2017**			
3	Revenues	Schedule 1		$38,000,000
4	Cost of goods sold	Schedule 7		24,440,000
5	Gross margin			13,560,000
6	Operating costs			
7	Product design costs	Schedule 8	$1,024,000	
8	Marketing costs	Schedule 8	3,800,000	
9	Distribution costs	Schedule 8	3,876,000	8,700,000
10	Operating income			$ 4,860,000

of Deluxe tables and process improvements and efficiency gains throughout the value chain. As Rex studies the budget more carefully, however, he is struck by two comments appended to the budget: First, to achieve the budgeted number of tables sold, Stylistic may need to reduce its selling prices by 3% to $582 for Casual tables and to $776 for Deluxe tables. Second, a supply shortage in direct materials may result in a 5% increase in the prices of direct materials (red oak and granite) above the material prices anticipated in the 2017 budget. Even if direct materials prices increase, selling prices are anticipated to remain unchanged. He asks Tina Larsen, a management accountant, to use Stylistic's financial planning model to evaluate how these outcomes will affect budgeted operating income.

DECISION POINT

What is the operating budget and what are its components?

TRY IT! 5

Jimenez Corporation manufactures and sells two types of decorative lamps, Knox and Ayer. The following data are available for the year 2017. The numbers below represent the calculations from the previous Try It! examples (1 through 4) together with the relevant schedule numbers from those examples.

Revenues (Schedule 1)	$925,000
Beginning inventory of finished goods (1-1-2017)	76,200
Ending inventory of finished goods, 12-31-2017 (Schedule 6B)	59,300
Direct materials used (Schedule 3A)	350,000
Direct manufacturing labor (Schedule 4)	100,000
Manufacturing overhead (Schedule 5)	143,000
Variable marketing costs (4% of revenues)	
Fixed marketing costs	43,000
Variable distribution costs ($1.50 per cu. ft. for 30,000 cu. ft.)	
Fixed distribution costs	40,000
Fixed administration costs	75,000

Calculate (1) the cost of goods sold budget (label it Schedule 7); (2) the nonmanufacturing costs budget (label it Schedule 8); and (3) the operating income budget for the year ending December 31, 2017.

LEARNING OBJECTIVE 4

Use computer-based financial planning models for sensitivity analysis

. . . for example, understand the effects of changes in selling prices and direct material prices on budgeted income

Financial Planning Models and Sensitivity Analysis

Financial planning models are mathematical representations of the relationships among operating activities, financing activities, and other factors that affect the master budget. Managers use computer-based systems, such as enterprise resource planning (ERP) systems, to manage their businesses and to perform calculations for these planning models. Budgeting tools within ERP systems simplify budgeting, reduce the need to re-input data, and reduce the time required to prepare budgets. ERP systems store vast quantities of information about the materials, machines and equipment, labor, power, maintenance, and setups needed to produce different products. Once managers identify sales quantities for different products, the software can quickly compute the budgeted costs for manufacturing these products. ERP systems also help managers budget for nonmanufacturing costs. Many service companies, such as banks, hospitals, and airlines, also use ERP systems to manage their operations. The Concepts in Action: 24 Hour Fitness and Internet-Based Budgeting is an example of a service company using a software platform to coordinate and manage its budgets across multiple locations.

As they prepare operating budgets, managers do not focus only on what they can achieve. They also identify the risks they face such as a potential decline in demand for the company's products, the entry of a new competitor, or an increase in the prices of different inputs. Sensitivity analysis is a useful tool that helps managers evaluate these risks. *Sensitivity analysis* is a "what-if" technique that examines how a result will change if the original predicted data are not achieved or if an underlying assumption changes. Software packages typically have a sensitivity analysis module that managers can use in their planning and budgeting activities.

To see how sensitivity analysis works, we consider two scenarios identified as possibly affecting Stylistic Furniture's budget model for 2017. Either of the two scenarios could happen, but not both together.

Scenario 1: A 3% decrease in the selling price of the Casual table and a 3% decrease in the selling price of the Deluxe table.

Scenario 2: A 5% increase in the price per board foot of red oak and a 5% increase in the price per square foot of granite.

Exhibit 4 presents the budgeted operating income for the two scenarios.

In the case of Scenario 1, note that a change in the selling price per table affects revenues (Schedule 1) as well as variable marketing costs (sales commissions, Schedule 8). The Problem for Self-Study at the end of the chapter shows the revised schedules for Scenario 1. Similarly, a change in the price of direct materials affects the direct material usage budget (Schedule 3A), the unit cost of ending finished-goods inventory (Schedule 6A), the ending finished-goods inventories budget (Schedule 6B), and the cost of goods sold budget (Schedule 7). Sensitivity analysis is especially useful to managers incorporating these interrelationships into their budgeting decisions.

Exhibit 4 shows that operating income decreases substantially if selling prices decrease by 3%, but declines much less if direct materials prices increase by 5%. The sensitivity analysis prompts Stylistic's managers to put in place contingency plans. For example, if selling prices decline in 2017, Stylistic may need to reduce costs even more than planned. More generally, when the success or viability of a venture is highly dependent on attaining a certain income target, managers should frequently update their budgets as uncertainty is resolved. These updated budgets can help managers adjust expenditure levels as circumstances change.

DECISION POINT

How can managers plan for changes in the assumptions underlying the budget and manage risk?

EXHIBIT 4 Effect of Changes in Budget Assumptions on Budgeted Operating Income for Stylistic Furniture

Home Insert Page Layout Formulas Data Review View

	A	B	C	D	E	F	G	H	I
1	Key Assumptions								
2		Units Sold		Selling Price		Direct Material Cost		Budgeted Operating Income	
3	What-If Scenario	Casual	Deluxe	Casual	Deluxe	Red Oak	Granite	Dollars	Change from Master Budget
4	Master budget	50,000	10,000	$600	$800	$7.00	$10.00	$4,860,000	
5	Scenario 1	50,000	10,000	582	776	$7.00	$10.00	3,794,100	22% decrease
6	Scenario 2	50,000	10,000	600	800	$7.35	$10.50	4,418,000	9% decrease

CONCEPTS IN ACTION

24 Hour Fitness and Internet-Based Budgeting

B Christopher/Alamy Stock Photo

24 Hour Fitness is one of the largest fitness-club chains in the United States, with nearly 4 million members, more than 450 clubs in 16 states and $1.5 billion in annual revenues. The company uses Longview, an Internet-based software platform, to manage its planning and budgeting process.

Using detailed operational statistics including number of members, number of workouts, and hours worked by each category of staff, accounting and finance managers sign on to the platform and develop budgets for each club. Advertising costs are allocated to each club based on the size, age, and traffic of each club. Using Longview at 24 Hour Fitness has resulted in more accurate budgets and forecasts being developed in less time. Managers can also conduct "what if" budget scenario analysis.

The platform also allows each club manager to track very-detailed revenue and expense data covering individual aspects of club activity, including juice bars, personal training sessions, product sales, and credit card membership dues and to take corrective action. It also enables staff to better support senior management decision making by responding more quickly to information requests. Mike Patano, Senior Director of Financial Planning & Analysis, summarized, "Day to day, it's about being able to thoroughly understand our business, benchmark the performance of our clubs, and understand our business drivers much better and quicker."

Sources: Longview Solutions, "Longview Case Study: 24 Hour Fitness," 2014 (http://info.longview.com/CaseStudy-24HourFitness.html); 24 Hour Fitness, "About Us," http://www.24hourfitness.com/company/about_us/, accessed March 2016.

Earlier in this chapter we described a rolling budget as a budget that is always available for a specified future period. Rolling budgets are constantly updated to reflect the latest cost and revenue information and make managers responsive to changing conditions and market needs.

Instructors and students who, at this point, want to explore the cash budget and the budgeted balance sheet for the Stylistic Furniture example can skip ahead to the appendix.

Budgeting and Responsibility Accounting

LEARNING OBJECTIVE 5

Describe responsibility centers

...a part of an organization that a manager is accountable for

and responsibility accounting

...measurement of plans and actual results that a manager is accountable for

To attain the goals described in the master budget, top managers must coordinate the efforts of all of the firm's employees—from senior executives through middle levels of management to every supervised worker. To coordinate the company's efforts, top managers assign a certain amount of responsibility to lower-level managers and then hold them accountable for how they perform. Consequently, how each company structures its organization significantly shapes how it coordinates its actions.

Organization Structure and Responsibility

Organization structure is an arrangement of lines of responsibility within an organization. A company such as Exxon Mobil is organized by business function—refining, marketing, and so on—with the president of each business function having decision-making authority over his or her function. Functional organizations develop strong competencies within each function but are generally less focused on particular markets or customers. To respond to this concern, other companies, such as Procter & Gamble, the household-products giant, are organized primarily by product line or brand. The managers of the individual divisions (toothpaste, soap, and so on) have decision-making authority concerning all the business functions (manufacturing, marketing, and so on) within that division. This results in some inefficiencies as support functions get duplicated in different divisions without sufficient scale or competence. Some companies combine functional and divisional structures, for example leaving marketing within divisions but having manufacturing organized as a business function to supply products to different divisions. There is no perfect organization structure. Companies choose the structure that best meets their needs at that time making the tradeoff between efficiency and end-to-end business authority.

Each manager, regardless of level, is in charge of a responsibility center. A **responsibility center** is a part, segment, or subunit of an organization whose manager is accountable for a specified set of activities. Higher-level managers supervise centers with broader responsibility and larger numbers of subordinates. **Responsibility accounting** is a system that measures the plans, budgets, actions, and actual results of each responsibility center. There are four types of responsibility centers:

1. **Cost center**—the manager is accountable for costs only.
2. **Revenue center**—the manager is accountable for revenues only.
3. **Profit center**—the manager is accountable for revenues and costs.
4. **Investment center**—the manager is accountable for investments, revenues, and costs.

The maintenance department of a Marriott hotel is a cost center because the maintenance manager is responsible only for costs and the budget is based only on costs. The sales department is a revenue center because the sales manager is responsible primarily for revenues, and the department's budget is primarily based on revenues. The hotel manager is in charge of a profit center because the manager is accountable for both revenues and costs, and the hotel's budget is based on revenues and costs. The regional manager responsible for determining the amount to be invested in new hotel projects and for revenues and costs generated from these investments is in charge of an investment center. So, this center's budget is based on revenues, costs, and the investment base.

A responsibility center can be structured to promote better alignment of individual and company goals. For example, until recently, OPD, an office products distributor, operated its sales department solely as a revenue center. Each salesperson received a commission of 3% of the revenues per order, regardless of its size, the cost of processing it, or the cost of delivering the office products. Upon analyzing customer profitability, OPD found that many customers were unprofitable. The main reason was the high ordering and delivery costs of small orders. OPD's managers decided to make the sales department a profit center, accountable for revenues and costs, and to change the incentive system for salespeople to 15% of the monthly profits of their customers. The costs for each customer included the ordering and delivery costs. The effect of this change was immediate. The sales department began charging customers for ordering and delivery, and salespeople at OPD actively encouraged customers to consolidate their purchases into fewer orders. As a result, each order began producing larger revenues. The profitability of customers increased because of a 40% reduction in ordering and delivery costs in 1 year.

Feedback

Budgets coupled with responsibility accounting provide feedback to top managers about the performance relative to the budget of different responsibility center managers.

Differences between actual results and budgeted amounts—called *variances*—can help managers implement strategies and evaluate them in three ways:

1. **Early warning.** Variances alert managers early to events not easily or immediately evident. Managers can then take corrective actions or exploit the available opportunities. For example, after observing a small decline in sales during a period, managers may want to investigate if this is an indication of an even steeper decline to come later in the year.
2. **Performance evaluation.** Variances prompt managers to probe how well the company has implemented its strategies. Were materials and labor used efficiently? Was R&D spending increased as planned? Did product warranty costs decrease as planned?
3. **Evaluating strategy.** Variances sometimes signal to managers that their strategies are ineffective. For example, a company seeking to compete by reducing costs and improving quality may find that it is achieving these goals but that it is having little effect on sales and profits. Top management may then want to reevaluate the strategy.

Responsibility and Controllability

Controllability is the degree of influence a specific manager has over costs, revenues, or related items for which he or she is responsible. A **controllable cost** is any cost primarily subject to the influence of a given *responsibility center manager* for a given *period*. A responsibility accounting system could either exclude all uncontrollable costs from a manager's performance report or segregate such costs from the controllable costs. For example, a machining supervisor's performance report might be confined to direct materials, direct manufacturing labor, power, and machine maintenance costs and might exclude costs such as rent and taxes paid on the plant.

In practice, controllability is difficult to pinpoint for two main reasons:

1. Few costs are clearly under the sole influence of one manager. For example, purchasing managers are able to affect the prices their firms pay for direct materials, but these prices also depend on market conditions beyond the managers' control. Similarly, the decisions production managers make can affect the quantities of direct materials used but also depend on the quality of materials purchased. Moreover, managers often work in teams. Think about how difficult it is to evaluate individual responsibility in a team situation.
2. With a long enough time span, all costs will come under somebody's control. However, most performance reports focus on periods of a year or less. A current manager may benefit from a predecessor's accomplishments or may inherit a predecessor's problems and inefficiencies. For example, managers may have to work with undesirable contracts with suppliers or labor unions negotiated by their predecessors. How can we separate what the current manager actually controls from the results of decisions other managers made? Exactly what is the current manager accountable for? The answers may not be clear-cut.

Executives differ in how they embrace the controllability notion when evaluating people reporting to them. Some CEOs regard the budget as a firm commitment subordinates must meet and that "numbers always tell the story." Failing to meet the budget is viewed unfavorably. An executive once noted, "You can miss your plan once, but you wouldn't want to miss it twice." Such an approach forces managers to learn to perform under adverse circumstances and to deliver consistent results year after year. It removes the need to discuss which costs are controllable and which are uncontrollable because it does not matter whether the performance was due to controllable or uncontrollable factors. The disadvantage of this approach is that it subjects a manager's compensation to greater risk. It also de-motivates managers when uncontrollable factors adversely affect their performance evaluations even though they have performed well in terms of factors they could control.

Other CEOs believe that focusing on making the numbers in a budget puts excessive pressure on managers. These CEOs adjust for uncontrollable factors and evaluate managers only on what they can control, such as their performance relative to competitors. Using relative performance measures takes out the effects of favorable or unfavorable business conditions that are outside the manager's control and affect all competing managers in the same way. The challenge is in finding the correct benchmarks. Relative performance measures, however, reduce the pressure on managers to perform when circumstances are difficult.

Managers should avoid thinking about controllability only in the context of performance evaluation. Responsibility accounting is more far-reaching. It focuses on gaining *information and knowledge*, not only on control. *Responsibility accounting helps managers to first focus on whom they should ask to obtain information and not on whom they should blame.* Comparing the shortfall of actual revenues to budgeted revenues is certainly relevant when evaluating the performance of the sales managers of Ritz-Carlton hotels. But the more fundamental purpose of responsibility accounting is to gather information from the sales managers to enable future improvement. Holding them accountable for sales motivates them to learn about market conditions and dynamics outside of their personal control but which are relevant for deciding the actions the hotels might take to increase future sales. Similarly, purchasing managers may be held accountable for total purchase costs, not because of their ability to control market prices, but because of their ability to predict and respond to uncontrollable prices and understand their causes.

Performance reports for responsibility centers are sometimes designed to change managers' behavior in the direction top managers desire even if the reports decrease controllability.

Consider a manufacturing department. If the department is designated as a cost center, the manufacturing manager may emphasize efficiency and de-emphasize the pleas of sales personnel for faster service and rush orders that reduce efficiency and increase costs. Evaluating the department as a profit center decreases the manufacturing manager's controllability (because the manufacturing manager has limited influence on sales) but it motivates the manager to look more favorably at rush orders that benefit sales. She will weigh the impact of decisions on costs and revenues rather than on costs alone.

Call centers provide another example. If designated as a cost center, the call-center manager will focus on controlling operating costs, for example, by decreasing the time customer representatives spend on each call. If designed as a profit center, the call-center manager will cause customer-service representatives to balance efficiency against better customer service and lead to efforts to upsell and cross-sell other products. Hewlett-Packard, Microsoft, Oracle, and others offer software platforms designed to prompt and help call-center personnel turn their cost centers into profit centers. The new adage is, "Every service call is a sales call."

DECISION POINT

How do companies use responsibility centers? Should performance reports of responsibility center managers include only costs the manager can control?

Human Aspects of Budgeting

LEARNING OBJECTIVE 6

Recognize the human aspects of budgeting

...to engage subordinate managers in the budgeting process

Why did we discuss the master budget and responsibility accounting in the same chapter? Primarily to emphasize that human factors are crucial in budgeting. Too often, budgeting is thought of as a mechanical tool because the budgeting techniques themselves are free of emotion. However, the administration of budgeting requires education, persuasion, and intelligent interpretation.

Budgetary Slack

As we discussed earlier in this chapter, budgeting is most effective when lower-level managers actively participate and meaningfully engage in the budgeting process. Participation adds credibility to the budgeting process and makes employees more committed and accountable for meeting the budget. But participation requires "honest" communication about the business from subordinates and lower-level managers to their bosses.

At times, subordinates may try to "play games" and build in *budgetary slack*. **Budgetary slack** is the practice of underestimating budgeted revenues or overestimating budgeted costs to make budgeted targets easier to achieve. This practice frequently occurs when budget variances (the differences between actual results and budgeted amounts) are used to evaluate the performance of line managers and their subordinates. Line managers are also unlikely to be fully honest in their budget communications if top managers mechanically institute across-the-board cost reductions (say, a 10% reduction in all areas) in the face of projected revenue reductions.

Budgetary slack provides managers with a hedge against unexpected adverse circumstances. But budgetary slack also misleads top managers about the true profit potential of the company, which leads to inefficient resource planning and allocation and poor coordination of activities across different parts of the company.

To avoid the problems of budgetary slack, some companies use budgets primarily for planning and to a lesser extent for performance evaluation. They evaluate the performance of managers using multiple indicators that take into account various factors that become known during the course of the year, such as the prevailing business environment and the performance of their industry or their competitors. Evaluating performance in this way takes time and requires careful judgment.

One approach to dealing with budgetary slack is to obtain good benchmark data when setting the budget. Consider the plant manager of a beverage bottler. Suppose top managers could purchase a consulting firm's study of productivity levels—such as the number of bottles filled per hour—at a number of comparable plants owned by other bottling companies. The managers could then share this independent information with the plant manager and use it to set the operations budget. Using external benchmark performance measures reduces a manager's ability to set budget levels that are easy to achieve.

Rolling budgets are another approach to reducing budgetary slack. As we discussed earlier in the chapter, companies that use rolling budgets always have a budget for a defined period, say 12 months, by adding, at the end of each quarter, a budget for one more quarter to replace the quarter just ended. The continuous updating of budget information and the richer information it provides reduce the opportunity to create budgetary slack relative to when budgeting is done only annually.

Some companies, such as IBM, have designed innovative performance evaluation measures that reward managers based on the subsequent accuracy of the forecasts used in preparing budgets. For example, the *higher and more accurate* the budgeted profit forecasts of division managers, the higher their incentive bonuses.[6] Another approach to reducing budgetary slack is for managers to involve themselves regularly in understanding what their subordinates are doing. Such involvement should not result in managers dictating the decisions and actions of subordinates. Rather, a manager's involvement should take the form of providing support, challenging in a motivational way the assumptions subordinates make, and enhancing mutual learning about the operations. Regular interaction with their subordinates allows managers to become knowledgeable about the operations and diminishes the ability of subordinates to create slack in their budgets. Instead, the subordinates and their superiors have in-depth dialogues about the budgets and performance goals. Managers then evaluate the performance of subordinates using both subjective and objective measures. Of course, using subjective measures requires that subordinates trust their managers to evaluate them fairly.

In addition to developing their organization's strategies, top managers are responsible for defining a company's core values and norms and building employee commitment toward adhering to them. These values and norms describe what constitutes acceptable and unacceptable behavior. For example, Johnson & Johnson (J&J) has a credo that describes its responsibilities to doctors, patients, employees, communities, and shareholders. Employees are trained in the credo to help them understand the behavior that is expected of them. J&J managers are often promoted from within and are therefore very familiar with the work of the employees reporting to them. J&J also has a strong culture of mentoring subordinates. J&J's values and employee practices create an environment where managers know their subordinates well, which helps to reduce budgetary slack.

Stretch Targets

Many of the best performing companies, such as General Electric, Microsoft, and Novartis, set "stretch" targets. Stretch targets are challenging but achievable levels of expected performance, intended to create a little discomfort. Creating some performance anxiety motivates employees to exert extra effort and attain better performance, but setting targets that are very difficult or impossible to achieve hurts performance because employees give up on achieving them. Organizations such as Goldman Sachs also use "horizontal" stretch goal initiatives. The aim is to enhance professional development of employees by asking them to take on significantly different responsibilities or roles outside their comfort zone.

A major rationale for stretch targets is their psychological motivation. Consider the following two compensation arrangements offered to a salesperson:

- In the first arrangement, the salesperson is paid $80,000 for achieving a sales target of $1,000,000 and 8 cents for every dollar of sales above $1,000,000 up to $1,100,000.
- In the second arrangement, the salesperson is paid $88,000 for achieving a sales target of $1,100,000 (a stretch target) with a reduction in compensation of 8 cents for every dollar of sales less than $1,100,000 up to $1,000,000.

For simplicity we assume that sales will be between $1,000,000 and $1,100,000.

The salesperson receives the same level of compensation under the two arrangements for all levels of sales between $1,000,000 and $1,100,000. The question is whether the psychological motivation is the same in the two compensation arrangements. Many executives who favor stretch targets point to the asymmetric way in which salespeople psychologically perceive the two compensation arrangements. In the first arrangement, achieving the sales target of $1,000,000 is seen as good and everything above it as a bonus. In the second arrangement, not reaching the stretch

[6] For an excellent discussion of these issues, see Chapter 14 ("Formal Models in Budgeting and Incentive Contracts") in Robert S. Kaplan and Anthony A. Atkinson, *Advanced Management Accounting,* 3rd ed. (Upper Saddle River, NJ: Prentice Hall, 1998).

sales target of $1,100,000 is seen as a failure. If salespeople are loss averse, that is, they feel the pain of loss more than the joy of success, they will work harder under the second arrangement to achieve sales of $1,100,000 and not fail.

Ethics

At no point should the pressure for performance embedded in stretch targets push employees to engage in illegal or unethical practices. The more a company tries to push performance, the greater the emphasis it must place on training employees to follow its code of conduct to prohibit behavior that is out of bounds (for example, no bribery, side payments, or dishonest dealings) and its norms and values (for example, putting customers first and not compromising on quality).

Some ethical questions are subtle and not clear-cut. Consider, for example, a division manager, faced with the choice of doing maintenance on a machine at the end of 2016 or early in 2017. It is preferable to do the maintenance in 2016 because delaying maintenance increases the probability of the machine breaking down. But doing so would mean that the manager will not reach his 2016 stretch target for operating income and lose some of his bonus. If the risks of a breakdown and loss are substantial, many observers would view delaying maintenance as unethical. If the risk is minimal, there may be more debate as to whether delaying maintenance is unethical.

Kaizen Budgeting

Kaizen budgeting explicitly incorporates continuous improvement anticipated during the budget period into the budget numbers.(Kaizen means continuous improvement in Japanese.) A number of companies that focus on cost reduction, including General Electric in the United States and Toyota in Japan, use Kaizen budgeting to continuously reduce costs. Much of the cost reduction associated with Kaizen budgeting arises from many small improvements rather than "quantum leaps." The improvements tend to come from employee suggestions as a result of managers creating a culture that values, recognizes, and rewards these suggestions. Employees who actually do the job, whether in manufacturing, sales, or distribution, have the best information and knowledge of how the job can be done better.

As an example, throughout our nine budgeting steps for Stylistic Furniture, we assumed 4 hours of direct labor time were required to manufacture each Casual coffee table. A Kaizen budgeting approach would incorporate continuous improvement based on 4.00 direct manufacturing labor-hours per table for the first quarter of 2017, 3.95 hours for the second quarter, 3.90 hours for the third quarter, and so on. The implications of these reductions would be lower direct manufacturing labor costs as well as lower variable manufacturing operations overhead costs because direct manufacturing labor is the driver of these costs. If Stylistic Furniture doesn't meet continuous improvement goals, its managers will explore the reasons behind the failure to meet the goals and either adjust the targets or seek input from employees to implement process improvements. Of course, top managers should also encourage managers and employees at all levels to try to find a way to achieve bigger (if periodic) cost reductions by changing operating processes and supply-chain relationships.

Managers can also apply Kaizen budgeting to activities such as setups with the goal of reducing setup time and setup costs or distribution with the goal of reducing the cost per cubic foot of shipping tables. Kaizen budgeting for specific activities is a key building block of the master budget for companies that use the Kaizen approach.

DECISION POINT
Why are human factors crucial in budgeting?

A growing number of cash-strapped states and agencies in the United States are using Kaizen techniques to bring together government workers, regulators, and end users of government processes to identify ways to reduce inefficiencies and eliminate bureaucratic procedures. Several state environmental agencies, for example, have conducted a Kaizen session or are planning one.[7] The U.S. Postal Service has identified many different programs to reduce its costs. The success of these efforts will depend heavily on human factors such as the commitment and engagement of managers and other employees to make these changes.

---

[7] For details, see "State Governments, Including Ohio's, Embrace Kaizen to Seek Efficiency via Japanese Methods," http://www.cleveland.com (December 12, 2008).

Budgeting for Reducing Carbon Emissions

In response to pressures from consumers, investors, governments, and NGOs, many companies proactively manage and report on environmental performance. Budgeting is a very effective tool to motivate managers to lessen carbon emissions. Several companies, such as British Telecom, Novartis, and Unilever, set science-based carbon reduction goals based on climate models whose goal is to limit increases in average temperatures to no more than 2°C. The methodology allocates the annual global emissions budget to individual sectors of the economy and then calculates each company's share of that total sector activity.

These science-based targets are stretched to spur innovation, prompt the development of new technologies and business models, and prepare companies for future regulatory and policy changes. What is the effect of stretched targets on actual emission reduction? Some recent research shows that companies that set more difficult targets (to be achieved over several years) complete a higher percentage of such targets. This is particularly true for carbon reduction projects in high-polluting industries that require more innovation.[8]

Many managers regard budgets negatively. To them, the word *budget* is about as popular as, say, *downsizing*, *layoff*, or *strike*. Top managers must convince their subordinates that the budget is a tool designed to help them set and reach goals. As with all tools of management, it has its benefits and challenges. Budgets must be used thoughtfully and wisely, but whatever the manager's perspective on budgets—pro or con—they are not remedies for weak management talent, faulty organization, or a poor accounting system.

Budgeting in Multinational Companies

LEARNING OBJECTIVE 7

Appreciate the special challenges of budgeting in multinational companies

. . . exposure to currency fluctuations and to different legal, political, and economic environments

Multinational companies, such as FedEx, Kraft, and Pfizer, have operations in many countries. An international presence has benefits—access to new markets and resources—and drawbacks—operating in less-familiar business environments and exposure to currency fluctuations. Multinational companies earn revenues and incur expenses in many different currencies and must translate their operating performance into a single currency (say, U.S. dollars) for reporting results to their shareholders each quarter. This translation is based on the average exchange rates that prevail during the quarter. As a result, managers of multinational companies budget in different currencies and also budget for foreign exchange rates. This requires managers and management accountants to anticipate potential changes in exchange rates that might occur during the year. To reduce the possible negative impact a company could experience as a result of unfavorable exchange rate movements, finance managers frequently use sophisticated techniques such as forward, future, and option contracts to minimize exposure to foreign currency fluctuations. Besides currency issues, managers at multinational companies need to understand the political, legal, and, in particular, economic environments of the different countries in which they operate when preparing budgets. For example, in countries such as Turkey, Zimbabwe, and Guinea, annual inflation rates are very high, resulting in sharp declines in the value of the local currency. Managers also need to consider differences in tax regimes, especially when the company transfers goods or services across the many countries in which it operates.

When there is considerable business and exchange rate uncertainty related to global operations, a natural question to ask is: "Do the managers of multinational companies find budgeting to be a helpful tool?" The answer is yes. However, in these circumstances the budgeting is not done to evaluate the firm's performance relative to its budgets—which can be meaningless when conditions are so volatile—but to help managers adapt their plans and coordinate their actions as circumstances change. Senior managers evaluate performance more subjectively, based on how well subordinate managers have managed in these constantly shifting and volatile environments.

DECISION POINT

What are the special challenges involved in budgeting at multinational companies?

[8] See Ioannis Ioannou, Shelley Xin Li, and George Serafeim, "The Effect of Target Difficulty on Target Completion: The Case of Reducing Carbon Emissions," *The Accounting Review* (2016).

PROBLEM FOR SELF-STUDY

Consider the Stylistic Furniture example described earlier. Suppose that to maintain its sales quantities, Stylistic needs to decrease selling prices to $582 per Casual table and $776 per Deluxe table, a 3% decrease in the selling prices used in the chapter illustration. All other data are unchanged.

Required

Prepare a budgeted income statement, including all necessary detailed supporting budget schedules that are different from the schedules presented in the chapter. Indicate those schedules that will remain unchanged.

Solution

Schedules 1 and 8 will change. Schedule 1 changes because a change in selling price affects revenues. Schedule 8 changes because revenues are a cost driver of marketing costs (sales commissions). The remaining Schedules 2–7 will not change because a change in selling price has no effect on manufacturing costs. The revised schedules and the new budgeted income statement follow.

Schedule 1: Revenues Budget
for the Year Ending December 31, 2017

	Selling Price	Units	Total Revenues
Casual tables	$582	50,000	$29,100,000
Deluxe tables	776	10,000	7,760,000
Total			$36,860,000

Schedule 8: Nonmanufacturing Costs Budget
for the Year Ending December 31, 2017

Business Function	Variable Costs	Fixed Costs (as in Schedule 8)	Total Costs
Product design		$1,024,000	$1,024,000
Marketing (Variable cost: $36,860,000 × 0.065)	$2,395,900	1,330,000	3,725,900
Distribution (Variable cost: $2 × 1,140,000 cu. ft.)	2,280,000	1,596,000	3,876,000
	$4,675,900	$3,950,000	$8,625,900

Stylistic Furniture Budgeted Income Statement
for the Year Ending December 31, 2017

Revenues	Schedule 1		$36,860,000
Cost of goods sold	Schedule 7		24,440,000
Gross margin			12,420,000
Operating costs			
Product design	Schedule 8	$1,024,000	
Marketing costs	Schedule 8	3,725,900	
Distribution costs	Schedule 8	3,876,000	8,625,900
Operating income			$ 3,794,100

DECISION POINTS

The following question-and-answer format summarizes the chapter's learning objectives. Each decision presents a key question related to a learning objective. The guidelines are the answer to that question.

Decision	Guidelines
1. What is the master budget, and why is it useful?	The master budget summarizes the financial projections of all the company's budgets. It expresses management's operating and financing plans—the formalized outline of the company's financial objectives and how they will be attained. Budgets are tools that, by themselves, are neither good nor bad. Budgets are useful when administered skillfully.
2. When should a company prepare budgets? What are the advantages of preparing budgets?	Budgets should be prepared when their expected benefits exceed their expected costs. There are four key advantages of budgets: (a) they compel strategic analysis and planning, (b) they promote coordination and communication among subunits of the company, (c) they provide a framework for judging performance and facilitating learning, and (d) they motivate managers and other employees.
3. What is the operating budget and what are its components?	The operating budget is the budgeted income statement and its supporting budget schedules. The starting point for the operating budget is generally the revenues budget. The following supporting schedules are derived from the revenues budget and the activities needed to support the revenues budget: production budget, direct materials usage budget, direct materials purchases budget, direct manufacturing labor cost budget, manufacturing overhead costs budget, ending inventories budget, cost of goods sold budget, R&D/product design cost budget, marketing cost budget, distribution cost budget, and customer-service cost budget.
4. How can managers plan for changes in the assumptions underlying the budget and manage risk?	Managers can use financial planning models—mathematical statements of the relationships among operating activities, financing activities, and other factors that affect the budget. These models make it possible for managers to conduct a what-if (sensitivity) analysis of the risks that changes in the original predicted data or changes in underlying assumptions would have on the master budget and to develop plans to respond to changed conditions.
5. How do companies use responsibility centers? Should performance reports of responsibility center managers include only costs the manager can control?	A responsibility center is a part, segment, or subunit of an organization whose manager is accountable for a specified set of activities. Four types of responsibility centers are cost centers, revenue centers, profit centers, and investment centers. Responsibility accounting systems are useful because they measure the plans, budgets, actions, and actual results of each responsibility center. Controllable costs are costs primarily subject to the influence of a given responsibility center manager for a given time period. Performance reports of responsibility center managers often include costs, revenues, and investments that the managers cannot control. Responsibility accounting associates financial items with managers on the basis of which manager has the most knowledge and information about specific items, regardless of the manager's ability to exercise full control.

Decision	Guidelines
6. Why are human factors crucial in budgeting?	The administration of budgets requires education, participation, persuasion, and intelligent interpretation. When wisely administered, budgets create commitment, accountability, and honest communication among employees and can be used as the basis for continuous improvement efforts. When badly managed, budgeting can lead to game-playing and budgetary slack—the practice of making budget targets more easily achievable.
7. What are the special challenges involved in budgeting at multinational companies?	Budgeting is a valuable tool for multinational companies but is challenging because of the uncertainties posed by operating in multiple countries. In addition to budgeting in different currencies, managers in multinational companies also need to budget for foreign exchange rates and consider the political, legal, and economic environments of the different countries in which they operate. In times of high uncertainty, managers use budgets to help the organization learn and adapt to its circumstances rather than to evaluate performance.

APPENDIX

The Cash Budget

The chapter illustrated the operating budget, which is one part of the master budget. The other part is the financial budget, which is composed of the capital expenditures budget, the cash budget, the budgeted balance sheet, and the budgeted statement of cash flows. This appendix focuses on the cash budget and the budgeted balance sheet. The budgeted statement of cash flows is beyond the scope of this chapter and generally is covered in financial accounting and corporate finance courses.

Why should Stylistic's managers want a cash budget in addition to the operating income budget presented in the chapter? Recall that Stylistic's management accountants prepared the operating budget on an accrual accounting basis consistent with how the company reports its actual operating income. But Stylistic's managers also need to plan cash flows to ensure that the company has adequate cash to pay vendors, meet payroll, and pay operating expenses as these payments come due. Stylistic could be very profitable, but the pattern of cash receipts from revenues might be delayed and result in insufficient cash being available to make scheduled payments. Stylistic's managers may then need to initiate a plan to borrow money to finance any shortfall. Building a profitable operating plan does not guarantee that adequate cash will be available, so Stylistic's managers need to prepare a cash budget in addition to an operating income budget.

Exhibit 5 shows Stylistic Furniture's balance sheet for the year ended December 31, 2016. The budgeted cash flows for 2017 are:

	Quarters			
	1	2	3	4
Collections from customers	$9,136,600	$10,122,000	$10,263,200	$8,561,200
Disbursements				
Direct materials	3,031,400	2,636,967	2,167,900	2,242,033
Direct manufacturing labor payroll	1,888,000	1,432,000	1,272,000	1,408,000
Manufacturing overhead costs	3,265,296	2,476,644	2,199,924	2,435,136
Nonmanufacturing costs	2,147,750	2,279,000	2,268,250	2,005,000
Machinery purchase	—	—	758,000	—
Income taxes	725,000	400,000	400,000	400,000

EXHIBIT 5

Balance Sheet for Stylistic Furniture, December 31, 2016

	A	B	C	D
1	**Stylistic Furniture Balance Sheet**			
2	**December 31, 2016**			
3	**Assets**			
4	Current assets			
5	Cash		$ 300,000	
6	Accounts receivable		1,711,000	
7	Direct materials inventory		1,090,000	
8	Finished goods inventory		646,000	$ 3,747,000
9	Property, Plant, and equipment			
10	Land		2,000,000	
11	Building and equipment	$ 22,000,000		
12	Accumulated depreciation	(6,900,000)	15,100,000	17,100,000
13	Total			$20,847,000
14	**Liabilities and Stockholders' Equity**			
15	Current liabilities			
16	Accounts payable		$ 904,000	
17	Income taxes payable		325,000	$ 1,229,000
18	Stockholders' equity			
19	Common stock, no-par 25,000 shares outstanding		3,500,000	
20	Retained earnings		16,118,000	19,618,000
21	Total			$20,847,000

The quarterly data are based on the budgeted cash effects of the operations formulated in Schedules 1–8 in the chapter, but the details of that formulation are not shown here to keep this illustration as brief and as focused as possible.

Stylistic wants to maintain a $320,000 minimum cash balance at the end of each quarter. The company can borrow or repay money at an interest rate of 12% per year. Management does not want to borrow any more short-term cash than is necessary. By special arrangement with the bank, Stylistic pays interest when repaying the principal. Assume, for simplicity, that borrowing takes place at the beginning and repayment at the end of the quarter under consideration (in multiples of $1,000). Interest is computed to the nearest dollar.

Suppose a management accountant at Stylistic receives the preceding data and the other data contained in the budgets in the chapter. Her manager asks her to:

1. Prepare a cash budget for 2017 by quarter. That is, prepare a statement of cash receipts and disbursements by quarter, including details of borrowing, repayment, and interest.
2. Prepare a budgeted income statement for the year ending December 31, 2017. This statement should include interest expense and income taxes (at a rate of 40% of operating income).
3. Prepare a budgeted balance sheet on December 31, 2017.

Preparation of Budgets

1. The **cash budget** is a schedule of expected cash receipts and cash disbursements. It predicts the effects on the cash position at the given level of operations. Exhibit 6 presents the cash budget by quarters to show the impact of cash flow timing on bank loans and their repayment. In practice, monthly—and sometimes weekly or even daily—cash budgets are critical for cash planning and control. Cash budgets help avoid unnecessary idle

EXHIBIT 6 Cash Budget for Stylistic Furniture for the Year Ending December 31, 2017

	A	B	C	D	E	F
1			Stylistic Furniture			
2			Cash Budget			
3			For Year Ending December 31, 2017			
4		Quarter 1	Quarter 2	Quarter 3	Quarter 4	Year as a Whole
5	Cash balance, beginning	$ 300,000	$ 320,154	$ 320,783	$ 324,359	$ 300,000
6	Add receipts					
7	Collections from customers	9,136,600	10,122,000	10,263,200	8,561,200	38,083,000
8	Total cash available for needs (x)	9,436,600	10,442,154	10,583,983	8,885,559	38,383,000
9	Cash disbursements					
10	Direct materials	3,031,400	2,636,967	2,167,900	2,242,033	10,078,300
11	Direct maufacturing labor payroll	1,888,000	1,432,000	1,272,000	1,408,000	6,000,000
12	Manufacturing overhead costs	3,265,296	2,476,644	2,199,924	2,435,136	10,377,000
13	Nonmanufacturing costs	2,147,750	2,279,000	2,268,250	2,005,000	8,700,000
14	Machinery purchase			758,000		758,000
15	Income taxes	725,000	400,000	400,000	400,000	1,925,000
16	Total cash disbursements (y)	11,057,446	9,224,611	9,066,074	8,490,169	37,838,300
17	Minimum cash balance desired	320,000	320,000	320,000	320,000	320,000
18	Total cash needed	11,377,446	9,544,611	9,386,074	8,810,169	38,158,300
19	Cash excess (deficiency)*	$ (1,940,846)	$ 897,543	$ 1,197,909	$ 75,390	$ 224,700
20	Financing					
21	Borrowing (at beginning)	$ 1,941,000	$ 0	$ 0	$ 0	$ 1,941,000
22	Repayment (at end)	0	(846,000)	(1,095,000)	0	(1,941,000)
23	Interest (at 12% per year)**	0	(50,760)	(98,550)	0	(149,310)
24	Total effects of financing (z)	1,941,000	(896,760)	(1,193,550)	0	(149,310)
25	Cash balance, ending***	$ 320,154	$ 320,783	$ 324,359	$ 395,390	$ 395,390
26	*Excess of total cash available − Total cash needed before financing					
27	**Note that the short-term interest payments pertain only to the amount of principal being repaid at the end of a quarter. The specific computations regarding interest are $846,000 × 0.12 × 0.5 = $50,760; $1,095,000 × 0.12 × 0.75 = $98,550. Also note that *depreciation does not require a cash outlay.*					
28	***Ending cash balance = Total cash available for needs (x) − Total disbursements (y) + Total effects of financing (z)					

cash and unexpected cash deficiencies. They thus keep cash balances in line with needs. Ordinarily, the cash budget has these main sections:

a. **Cash available for needs (before any financing).** The beginning cash balance plus cash receipts equals the total cash available for needs before any financing. Cash receipts depend on collections of accounts receivable, cash sales, and miscellaneous recurring sources, such as rental or royalty receipts. Information on the expected collectability of accounts receivable is needed for accurate predictions. Key factors include bad-debt (uncollectible accounts) experience (not an issue in the Stylistic case because Stylistic sells to only a few large wholesalers) and average time lag between sales and collections.

b. **Cash disbursements.** Cash disbursements by Stylistic Furniture include:

   i. *Direct materials purchases.* Suppliers are paid in full in the month after the goods are delivered.

   ii. *Direct manufacturing labor and other wage and salary outlays.* All payroll-related costs are paid in the month in which the labor effort occurs.

iii. *Other costs.* These depend on timing and credit terms. (In the Stylistic case, all other costs are paid in the month in which the cost is incurred.) *Note that depreciation does not require a cash outlay.*

iv. *Other cash disbursements.* These include outlays for property, plant, equipment, and other long-term investments.

v. Income tax payments as shown each quarter.

c. **Financing effects.** Short-term financing requirements depend on how the total cash available for needs [keyed as (*x*) in Exhibit 6] compares with the total cash disbursements [keyed as (*y*)], plus the minimum ending cash balance desired. The financing plans will depend on the relationship between total cash available for needs and total cash needed. If there is a deficiency of cash, Stylistic obtains loans. If there is excess cash, Stylistic repays any outstanding loans.

d. **Ending cash balance.** The cash budget in Exhibit 6 shows the pattern of short-term "self-liquidating" cash loans. In quarter 1, Stylistic budgets a $1,940,846 cash deficiency. The company therefore undertakes short-term borrowing of $1,941,000 that it pays off over the course of the year. Seasonal peaks of production or sales often result in heavy cash disbursements for purchases, payroll, and other operating outlays as the company produces and sells products. Cash receipts from customers typically lag behind sales. The loan is *self-liquidating* in the sense that the company uses the borrowed money to acquire resources that it uses to produce and sell finished goods and uses the proceeds from sales to repay the loan. This self-liquidating cycle is the movement from cash to inventories to receivables and back to cash.

2. The budgeted income statement is presented in Exhibit 7. It is merely the budgeted operating income statement in Exhibit 3 expanded to include interest expense and income taxes.

3. The budgeted balance sheet is presented in Exhibit 8. Each item is projected in light of the details of the business plan as expressed in all the previous budget schedules. For example, the ending balance of accounts receivable of $1,628,000 is computed by adding the budgeted revenues of $38,000,000 (from Schedule 1) to the beginning balance of accounts receivable of $1,711,000 (from Exhibit 5) and subtracting cash receipts of $38,083,000 (from Exhibit 6).

For simplicity, this example explicitly gave the cash receipts and disbursements. Usually, the receipts and disbursements are calculated based on the lags between the items reported on the accrual basis of accounting in an income statement and balance sheet and their related cash receipts and disbursements. Consider accounts receivable.

EXHIBIT 7

Budgeted Income Statement for Stylistic Furniture for the Year Ending December 31, 2017

Home | Insert | Page Layout | Formulas | Data | Review | View

	A	B	C	D
1	**Stylistic Furniture**			
2	**Budgeted Income Statement**			
3	**For the Year Ending December 31, 2017**			
4	Revenues	Schedule 1		$38,000,000
5	COGS	Schedule 7		24,440,000
6	Gross margin			13,560,000
7	Operating costs			
8	Product design costs	Schedule 8	$1,024,000	
9	Marketing costs	Schedule 8	3,800,000	
10	Distribution costs	Schedule 8	3,876,000	8,700,000
11	Operating income			4,860,000
12	Interest expense	Exhibit 6-6		149,310
13	Income before income taxes			4,710,690
14	Income taxes (at 40%)			1,884,276
15	Net income			$ 2,826,414

EXHIBIT 8 Budgeted Balance Sheet for Stylistic Furniture, December 31, 2017

	A	B	C	D
1	**Stylistic Furniture**			
2	**Budgeted Balance Sheet**			
3	**December 31, 2017**			
4	**Assets**			
5	Current assets			
6	Cash (from Exhibit 6-6)		$ 395,390	
7	Accounts receivable (1)		1,628,000	
8	Direct materials inventory (2)		760,000	
9	Finished goods inventory (2)		4,486,000	$ 7,269,390
10	Property, Plant, and equipment			
11	Land (3)		2,000,000	
12	Building and equipment (4)	$22,758,000		
13	Accumulated depreciation (5)	(8,523,000)	14,235,000	16,235,000
14	Total			$23,504,390
15	**Liabilities and Stockholders' Equity**			
16	Current liabilities			
17	Accounts payable (6)		$ 775,700	
18	Income taxes payable (7)		284,276	$ 1,059,976
19	Stockholders' equity			
20	Common stock, no-par, 25,000 shares outstanding (8)		3,500,000	
21	Retained earnings (9)		18,944,414	22,444,414
22	Total			$23,504,390
23				
24	Notes:			
25	Beginning balances are used as the starting point for most of the following computations			
26	(1) $1,711,000 + $38,000,000 revenues − $38,083,000 receipts (Exhibit 6-6) = $1,628,000			
27	(2) From Schedule 6B, p. 212			
28	(3) From opening balance sheet (Exhibit 6-5)			
29	(4) $22,000,000 (Exhibit 6-5) + $758,000 purchases (Exhibit 6-6) = $22,758,000			
30	(5) $6,900,000 (Exhibit 6-5) + $1,020,000 + $603,000 depreciation from Schedule 5, p. 211			
31	(6) $904,000 (Exhibit 6-5) + $9,950,000 (Schedule 3B) − $10,078,300 (Exhibit 6-6) = $775,300			
32	There are no other current liabilities. From Exhibit 6-6: Cash flows for direct manufacturing labor = $6,000,000 from Schedule 4 Cash flows for manufacturing overhead costs = $10,377,000 ($12,000,000 − depreciation $1,623,000) from Schedule 5 Cash flows for nonmanufacturing costs = $8,700,000 from Schedule 8.			
33	(7) $325,000 (Exhibit 6-5) + $1,884,276 (from Exhibit 6-7) − $1,925,000 payment (Exhibit 6-6) = $284,276			
34	(8) From opening balance sheet (Exhibit 6-5)			
35	(9) $16,118,000 (Exhibit 6-5) + net income $2,826,414 (Exhibit 6-7) = $18,944,414			

The budgeted sales for the year are broken down into sales budgets for each month and quarter. For example, Stylistic Furniture budgets sales by quarter of $9,282,000, $10,332,000, $10,246,000, and $8,140,000, which equal 2017 budgeted sales of $38,000,000.

	Quarter 1		Quarter 2		Quarter 3		Quarter 4	
	Casual	**Deluxe**	**Casual**	**Deluxe**	**Casual**	**Deluxe**	**Casual**	**Deluxe**
Budgeted sales in units	12,270	2,400	13,620	2,700	13,610	2,600	10,500	2,300
Selling price	$ 600	$ 800	$ 600	$ 800	$ 600	$ 800	$ 600	$ 800
Budgeted revenues	$7,362,000	$1,920,000	$8,172,000	$2,160,000	$8,166,000	$2,080,000	$6,300,000	$1,840,000
	$9,282,000		$10,332,000		$10,246,000		$8,140,000	

Notice that sales are expected to be higher in the second and third quarters relative to the first and fourth quarters when weather conditions limit the number of customers shopping for furniture.

Once Stylistic's managers determine the sales budget, a management accountant prepares a schedule of cash collections that serves as an input for the preparation of the cash budget. Stylistic estimates that 80% of all sales made in a quarter are collected in the same quarter and 20% are collected in the following quarter. Estimated collections from customers each quarter are calculated in the following table:

Schedule of Cash Collections

	Quarters			
	1	2	3	4
Accounts receivable balance on 1-1-2017 (Fourth-quarter sales from prior year collected in first quarter of 2017)	$1,711,000			
From first-quarter 2017 sales ($9,282,000 × 0.80; $9,282,000 × 0.20)	7,425,600	$ 1,856,400		
From second-quarter 2017 sales ($10,332,000 × 0.80; $10,332,000 × 0.20)		8,265,600	$ 2,066,400	
From third-quarter 2017 sales ($10,246,000 × 0.80; $10,246,000 × 0.20)			8,196,800	$2,049,200
From fourth-quarter 2017 sales ($8,140,000 × 0.80)				6,512,000
Total collections	$9,136,600	$10,122,000	$10,263,200	$8,561,200

Uncollected fourth-quarter 2017 sales of $1,628,000 ($ 8,140,000 × 0.20) appear as accounts receivable in the budgeted balance sheet of December 31, 2017 (see Exhibit 8). Note that the quarterly cash collections from customers calculated in this schedule equal the cash collections by quarter.

TRY IT! 6

Jimenez Corporation manufactures and sells two types of decorative lamps, Knox and Ayer. The following data are available for the year 2017.

Accounts receivable (January 1, 2017)	$ 46,000
Budgeted sales in Quarter 1 (January 1 to March 31, 2017)	230,000
Budgeted sales in Quarter 2 (April 1 to June 30, 2017)	245,000
Budgeted sales in Quarter 3 (July 1 to September 30, 2017)	210,000
Budgeted sales in Quarter 4 (October 1 to December 31, 2017)	240,000

All sales are made on account with 80% of sales made in a quarter collected in the same quarter and 20% collected in the following quarter.
Calculate the cash collected from receivables in each of the 4 quarters of 2017.

Sensitivity Analysis and Cash Flows

Exhibit 4 shows how differing assumptions about selling prices of coffee tables and direct material prices led to differing amounts for budgeted operating income for Stylistic Furniture. A key use of sensitivity analysis is to budget cash flow. Exhibit 9 outlines the short-term borrowing implications of the two combinations examined in Exhibit 4. Scenario 1, with the lower selling prices per table ($582 for the Casual table and $776 for the Deluxe table), requires $2,146,000 of short-term borrowing in quarter 1 that cannot be fully repaid as of December 31, 2017. Scenario 2, with the 5% higher direct material costs, requires $2,048,000 borrowing by Stylistic Furniture that also cannot be repaid by December 31, 2017. Sensitivity analysis helps managers anticipate such outcomes and take steps to minimize the effects of expected reductions in cash flows from operations.

EXHIBIT 9 Sensitivity Analysis: Effects of Key Budget Assumptions in Exhibit 6-4 on 2017 Short-Term Borrowing for Stylistic Furniture

Home Insert Page Layout Formulas Data Review View

	A	B	C	D	E	F	G	H	I	J
1				Direct Material			Short-Term Borrowing and Repayment by Quarter			
2		Selling Price		Purchase Costs		Budgeted		Quarters		
3	Scenario	Casual	Deluxe	Red Oak	Granite	Operating Income	1	2	3	4
4	1	$582	$776	$7.00	$10.00	$3,794,100	$2,146,000	$(579,000)	$(834,000)	$170,000
5	2	$600	$800	7.35	10.50	4,483,800	2,048,000	$(722,000)	$(999,000)	$41,000

TERMS TO LEARN

This chapter and the Glossary at the end of the chapter contain definitions of the following important terms:

activity-based budgeting (ABB)
budgetary slack
cash budget
continuous budget
controllability
controllable cost
cost center
financial budget
financial planning models
investment center
Kaizen budgeting
master budget
operating budget
organization structure
pro forma statements
profit center
responsibility accounting
responsibility center
revenue center
rolling budget
rolling forecast

ASSIGNMENT MATERIAL

MyAccountingLab

Questions

1 What are the four elements of the budgeting cycle?
2 Define master budget.
3 "Strategy, plans, and budgets are unrelated to one another." Do you agree? Explain.
4 "Budgeted performance is a better criterion than past performance for judging managers." Do you agree? Explain.
5 "Production managers and marketing managers are like oil and water. They just don't mix." How can a budget assist in reducing conflicts between these two areas?
6 "Budgets meet the cost–benefit test. They force managers to act differently." Do you agree? Explain.
7 Define rolling budget. Give an example.
8 Outline the steps in preparing an operating budget.
9 "The sales forecast is the cornerstone for budgeting." Why?
10 How can sensitivity analysis be used to increase the benefits of budgeting?
11 Define Kaizen budgeting.
12 Describe how nonoutput-based cost drivers can be incorporated into budgeting.
13 Explain how the choice of the type of responsibility center (cost, revenue, profit, or investment) affects behavior.
14 What are some additional considerations that arise when budgeting in multinational companies?
15 "Cash budgets must be prepared before the operating income budget." Do you agree? Explain.

Multiple-Choice Questions

MyAccountingLab

In partnership with:

BECKER PROFESSIONAL EDUCATION®

16 Master budget. Which of the following statements is correct regarding the components of the master budget?

- **a.** The cash budget is used to create the capital budget.
- **b.** Operating budgets are used to create cash budgets.
- **c.** The manufacturing overhead budget is used to create the production budget.
- **d.** The cost of goods sold budget is used to create the selling and administrative expense budget.

17 Operating and financial budgets. Which of the following statements is correct regarding the drivers of operating and financial budgets?

- **a.** The sales budget will drive the cost of goods sold budget.
- **b.** The cost of goods sold budget will drive the units of production budget.
- **c.** The production budget will drive the selling and administrative expense budget.
- **d.** The cash budget will drive the production and selling and administrative expense budgets.

18 Production budget. Superior Industries sales budget shows quarterly sales for the next year as follows: Quarter 1–10,000; Quarter 2–8,000; Quarter 3–12,000; Quarter 4–14,000. Company policy is to have a target finished-goods inventory at the end of each quarter equal to 20% of the next quarter's sales. Budgeted production for the second quarter of next year would be:

1. 7,200 units; 2. 8,800 units; 3. 12,000 units; 4. 10,400 units

19 Responsibility centers. Elmhurst Corporation is considering changes to its responsibility accounting system. Which of the following statements is/are correct for a responsibility accounting system.

- **i.** In a cost center, managers are responsible for controlling costs but not revenue.
- **ii.** The idea behind responsibility accounting is that a manager should be held responsible for those items that the manager can control to a significant extent.
- **iii.** To be effective, a good responsibility accounting system must help managers to plan and to control.
- **iv.** Costs that are allocated to a responsibility center are normally controllable by the responsibility center manager.

1. I and II only are correct.
2. II and III only are correct.
3. I, II, and III are correct.
4. I, II and IV are correct.

20 Cash budget. Mary Jacobs, the controller of the Jenks Company is working on Jenks' cash budget for year 2. She has information on each of the following items:

- **i.** Wages due to workers accrued as of December 31, year 1.
- **ii.** Limits on a line of credit that may be used to fund Jenks' operations in year 2.
- **iii.** The balance in accounts payable as of December 31, year 1, from credit purchases made in year 1.

Which of the items above should Jacobs take into account when building the cash budget for year 2?

a. I, II **b.** I, III
c. II, III **d.** I, II, III

MyAccountingLab

Exercises

21 Sales budget, service setting. In 2017, Hart & Sons, a small environmental-testing firm, performed 11,400 radon tests for $260 each and 15,000 lead tests for $210 each. Because newer homes are being built with lead-free pipes, lead-testing volume is expected to decrease by 12% next year. However, awareness of radon-related health hazards is expected to result in a 5% increase in radon-test volume each year in the near future. Jim Hart feels that if he lowers his price for lead testing to $200 per test, he will have to face only a 4% decline in lead-test sales in 2018.

Required

1. Prepare a 2018 sales budget for Hart & Sons assuming that Hart holds prices at 2017 levels.
2. Prepare a 2018 sales budget for Hart & Sons assuming that Hart lowers the price of a lead test to $200. Should Hart lower the price of a lead test in 2018 if the company's goal is to maximize sales revenue?

22 Sales and production budget. The Coby Company expects sales in 2018 of 201,000 units of serving trays. Coby's beginning inventory for 2018 is 13,000 trays, and its target ending inventory is 29,000 trays. Compute the number of trays budgeted for production in 2018.

23 Direct material budget. Dawson Co. produces wine. The company expects to produce 2,535,000 two-liter bottles of Chablis in 2018. Dawson purchases empty glass bottles from an outside vendor. Its target ending inventory of such bottles is 77,000; its beginning inventory is 54,000. For simplicity, ignore breakage. Compute the number of bottles to be purchased in 2018.

24 Material purchases budget. The McGrath Company has prepared a sales budget of 42,000 finished units for a 3-month period. The company has an inventory of 13,000 units of finished goods on hand at December 31 and has a target finished-goods inventory of 15,000 units at the end of the succeeding quarter.

It takes 3 gallons of direct materials to make one unit of finished product. The company has an inventory of 61,000 gallons of direct materials at December 31 and has a target ending inventory of 53,000 gallons at the end of the succeeding quarter. How many gallons of direct materials should McGrath Company purchase during the 3 months ending March 31?

25 Revenues, production, and purchases budgets. The Yucatan Co. in Mexico has a division that manufactures bicycles. Its budgeted sales for Model XG in 2018 are 95,000 units. Yucatan's target ending inventory is 7,000 units, and its beginning inventory is 11,000 units. The company's budgeted selling price to its distributors and dealers is 3,500 pesos per bicycle.

Yucatan buys all its wheels from an outside supplier. No defective wheels are accepted. Yucatan's needs for extra wheels for replacement parts are ordered by a separate division of the company. The company's target ending inventory is 14,000 wheels, and its beginning inventory is 16,000 wheels. The budgeted purchase price is 400 pesos per wheel.

Required

1. Compute the budgeted revenues in pesos.
2. Compute the number of bicycles that Yucatan should produce.
3. Compute the budgeted purchases of wheels in units and in pesos.
4. What actions can Yucatan's managers take to reduce budgeted purchasing costs of wheels assuming the same budgeted sales for Model XG?

26 Revenues and production budget. Saphire, Inc., bottles and distributes mineral water from the company's natural springs in northern Oregon. Saphire markets two products: 12-ounce disposable plastic bottles and 1-gallon reusable plastic containers.

Required

1. For 2018, Saphire marketing managers project monthly sales of 500,000 12-ounce bottles and 130,000 1-gallon containers. Average selling prices are estimated at $0.30 per 12-ounce bottle and $1.60 per 1-gallon container. Prepare a revenues budget for Saphire, Inc., for the year ending December 31, 2018.
2. Saphire begins 2018 with 980,000 12-ounce bottles in inventory. The vice president of operations requests that 12-ounce bottles ending inventory on December 31, 2018, be no less than 660,000 bottles. Based on sales projections as budgeted previously, what is the minimum number of 12-ounce bottles Saphire must produce during 2018?
3. The VP of operations requests that ending inventory of 1-gallon containers on December 31, 2018, be 300,000 units. If the production budget calls for Saphire to produce 1,200,000 1-gallon containers during 2018, what is the beginning inventory of 1-gallon containers on January 1, 2018?

27 Budgeting; direct material usage, manufacturing cost, and gross margin. Xander Manufacturing Company manufactures blue rugs, using wool and dye as direct materials. One rug is budgeted to use 36 skeins of wool at a cost of $2 per skein and 0.8 gallons of dye at a cost of $6 per gallon. All other materials are indirect. At the beginning of the year Xander has an inventory of 458,000 skeins of wool at a cost of $961,800 and 4,000 gallons of dye at a cost of $23,680. Target ending inventory of wool and dye is zero. Xander uses the FIFO inventory cost-flow method.

Xander blue rugs are very popular and demand is high, but because of capacity constraints the firm will produce only 200,000 blue rugs per year. The budgeted selling price is $2,000 each. There are no rugs in beginning inventory. Target ending inventory of rugs is also zero.

Xander makes rugs by hand, but uses a machine to dye the wool. Thus, overhead costs are accumulated in two cost pools—one for weaving and the other for dyeing. Weaving overhead is allocated to products based on direct manufacturing labor-hours (DMLH). Dyeing overhead is allocated to products based on machine-hours (MH).

There is no direct manufacturing labor cost for dyeing. Xander budgets 62 direct manufacturing labor-hours to weave a rug at a budgeted rate of $13 per hour. It budgets 0.2 machine-hours to dye each skein in the dyeing process.

The following table presents the budgeted overhead costs for the dyeing and weaving cost pools:

	Dyeing (based on 1,440,000 MH)	Weaving (based on 12,400,000 DMLH)
Variable costs		
Indirect materials	$ 0	$15,400,000
Maintenance	6,560,000	5,540,000
Utilities	7,550,000	2,890,000
Fixed costs		
Indirect labor	347,000	1,700,000
Depreciation	2,100,000	274,000
Other	723,000	5,816,000
Total budgeted costs	$17,280,000	$31,620,000

Required

1. Prepare a direct materials usage budget in both units and dollars.
2. Calculate the budgeted overhead allocation rates for weaving and dyeing.
3. Calculate the budgeted unit cost of a blue rug for the year.
4. Prepare a revenues budget for blue rugs for the year, assuming Xander sells (a) 200,000 or (b) 185,000 blue rugs (that is, at two different sales levels).
5. Calculate the budgeted cost of goods sold for blue rugs under each sales assumption.
6. Find the budgeted gross margin for blue rugs under each sales assumption.
7. What actions might you take as a manager to improve profitability if sales drop to 185,000 blue rugs?
8. How might top management at Xander use the budget developed in requirements 1–6 to better manage the company?

28 Budgeting, service company. Ever Clean Company provides gutter cleaning services to residential clients. The company has enjoyed considerable growth in recent years due to a successful marketing campaign and favorable reviews on service-rating Web sites. Ever Clean owner Joanne Clark makes sales calls herself and quotes on jobs based on length of gutter surface. Ever Clean hires college students to drive the company vans to jobs and clean the gutters. A part-time bookkeeper takes care of billing customers and other office tasks. Overhead is allocated based on direct labor-hours (DLH).

Joanne Clark estimates that her gutter cleaners will work a total of 1,000 jobs during the year. Each job averages 600 feet of gutter surface and requires 12 direct labor-hours. Clark pays her gutter cleaners $15 per hour, inclusive of taxes and benefits. The following table presents the budgeted overhead costs for 2018:

Variable costs	
Supplies ($6.50 per DLH)	$ 78,000
Fixed costs (to support capacity of 12,000 DLH)	
Indirect labor	25,000
Depreciation	17,000
Other	24,000
Total budgeted costs	$144,000

Required

1. Prepare a direct labor budget in both hours and dollars.
2. Calculate the budgeted overhead allocation rate based on the budgeted quantity of the cost drivers.
3. Calculate the budgeted total cost of all jobs for the year and the budgeted cost of an average 600-foot gutter-cleaning job.
4. Prepare a revenues budget for the year, assuming that Ever Clean charges customers $0.60 per square foot.
5. Calculate the budgeted operating income.
6. What actions can Clark take if sales should decline to 900 jobs annually?

29 Budgets for production and direct manufacturing labor. (CMA, adapted) DeWitt Company makes and sells artistic frames for pictures of weddings, graduations, and other special events. Ron Bahar, the controller, is responsible for preparing DeWitt's master budget and has accumulated the following information for 2018:

	2018				
	January	February	March	April	May
Estimated sales in units	12,000	13,000	6,000	11,000	11,000
Selling price	$ 53.00	$ 52.00	$52.00	$ 52.00	$ 52.00
Direct manufacturing labor-hours per unit	3.0	3.0	2.0	2.0	2.0
Wage per direct manufacturing labor-hour	$ 11.00	$ 11.00	$11.00	$ 12.00	$ 12.00

In addition to wages, direct manufacturing labor-related costs include pension contributions of $0.40 per hour, worker's compensation insurance of $0.10 per hour, employee medical insurance of $0.50 per hour, and Social Security taxes. Assume that as of January 1, 2018, the Social Security tax rates are 7.5% for employers and 7.5% for employees. The cost of employee benefits paid by DeWitt on its direct manufacturing employees is treated as a direct manufacturing labor cost.

DeWitt has a labor contract that calls for a wage increase to $12 per hour on April 1, 2018. New labor-saving machinery has been installed and will be fully operational by March 1, 2018. DeWitt expects to have 16,000 frames on hand at December 31, 2017, and it has a policy of carrying an end-of-month inventory of 100% of the following month's sales plus 50% of the second following month's sales.

Required

1. Prepare a production budget and a direct manufacturing labor cost budget for DeWitt Company by month and for the first quarter of 2018. You may combine both budgets in one schedule. The direct manufacturing labor cost budget should include labor-hours and show the details for each labor cost category.
2. What actions has the budget process prompted DeWitt's management to take?
3. How might DeWitt's managers use the budget developed in requirement 1 to better manage the company?

30 **Activity-based budgeting.** The Jerico store of Jiffy Mart, a chain of small neighborhood convenience stores, is preparing its activity-based budget for January 2018. Jiffy Mart has three product categories: soft drinks (35% of cost of goods sold [COGS]), fresh produce (25% of COGS), and packaged food (40% of COGS). The following table shows the four activities that consume indirect resources at the Jerico store, the cost drivers and their rates, and the cost-driver amount budgeted to be consumed by each activity in January 2018.

			January 2018 Budgeted Amount of Cost Driver Used		
Activity	**Cost Driver**	**January 2018 Budgeted Cost-Driver Rate**	**Soft Drinks**	**Fresh Snacks**	**Packaged Food**
Ordering	Number of purchase orders	$ 45	14	24	14
Delivery	Number of deliveries	$ 41	12	62	19
Shelf stocking	Hours of stocking time	$10.50	16	172	94
Customer support	Number of items sold	$ 0.09	4,600	34,200	10,750

Required

1. What is the total budgeted indirect cost at the Jerico store in January 2018? What is the total budgeted cost of each activity at the Jerico store for January 2018? What is the budgeted indirect cost of each product category for January 2018?
2. Which product category has the largest fraction of total budgeted indirect costs?
3. Given your answer in requirement 2, what advantage does Jiffy Mart gain by using an activity-based approach to budgeting over, say, allocating indirect costs to products based on cost of goods sold?

31 **Kaizen approach to activity-based budgeting (continuation of 30).** Jiffy Mart has a Kaizen (continuous improvement) approach to budgeting monthly activity costs for each month of 2018. Each successive month, the budgeted cost-driver rate decreases by 0.4% relative to the preceding month. So, for example, February's budgeted cost-driver rate is 0.996 times January's budgeted cost-driver rate, and March's budgeted cost-driver rate is 0.996 times the budgeted February rate. Jiffy Mart assumes that the budgeted amount of cost-driver usage remains the same each month.

Required

1. What are the total budgeted cost for each activity and the total budgeted indirect cost for March 2018?
2. What are the benefits of using a Kaizen approach to budgeting? What are the limitations of this approach, and how might Jiffy Mart management overcome them?

32 **Responsibility and controllability.** Consider each of the following independent situations for Prestige Fountains. Prestige manufactures and sells decorative fountains for commercial properties. The company also contracts to service both its own and other brands of fountains. Prestige has a manufacturing plant, a supply warehouse that supplies both the manufacturing plant and the service technicians (who often need parts to repair fountains), and 12 service vans. The service technicians drive to customer sites to service the fountains. Prestige owns the vans, pays for the gas, and supplies fountain parts, but the technicians own their own tools.

1. In the manufacturing plant, the production manager is not happy with the motors that the purchasing manager has been purchasing. In May, the production manager stops requesting motors from the supply warehouse and starts purchasing them directly from a different motor manufacturer. Actual materials costs in May are higher than budgeted.
2. Overhead costs in the manufacturing plant for June are much higher than budgeted. Investigation reveals a utility rate hike in effect that was not figured into the budget.

3. Gasoline costs for each van are budgeted based on the service area of the van and the amount of driving expected for the month. The driver of van 3 routinely has monthly gasoline costs exceeding the budget for van 3. After investigating, the service manager finds that the driver has been driving the van for personal use.
4. Regency Mall, one of Prestige's fountain service customers, calls the service people only for emergencies and not for routine maintenance. Thus, the materials and labor costs for these service calls exceeds the monthly budgeted costs for a contract customer.
5. Prestige's service technicians are paid an hourly wage of $22, regardless of experience or time with the company. As a result of an analysis performed last month, the service manager determined that service technicians in their first year of employment worked on average 20% more slowly than other employees. Prestige bills customers per service call, not per hour.
6. The cost of health insurance for service technicians has increased by 40% this year, which caused the actual health insurance costs to greatly exceed the budgeted health insurance costs for the service technicians.

Required

For each situation described, determine where (that is, with whom) (a) responsibility and (b) controllability lie. Suggest ways to solve the problem or to improve the situation.

33 **Responsibility, controllability, and stretch targets.** Consider each of the following independent situations for Sunrise Tours, a company owned by David Bartlett that sells motor coach tours to schools and other groups. Sunshine Tours owns a fleet of 10 motor coaches and employs 12 drivers, 1 maintenance technician, 3 sales representatives, and an office manager. Sunshine Tours pays for all fuel and maintenance on the coaches. Drivers are paid $0.50 per mile while in transit, plus $15 per hour while idle (time spent waiting while tour groups are visiting their destinations). The maintenance technician and office manager are both full-time salaried employees. The sales representatives work on straight commission.

1. When the office manager receives calls from potential customers, she is instructed to handle the contracts herself. Recently, however, the number of contracts written up by the office manager has declined. At the same time, one of the sales representatives has experienced a significant increase in contracts. The other two representatives believe that the office manager has been colluding with the third representative to send him the prospective customers.
2. One of the motor coach drivers seems to be reaching his destinations more quickly than any of the other drivers and is reporting longer idle time.
3. Regular preventive maintenance of the motor coaches has been proven to improve fuel efficiency and reduce overall operating costs by averting costly repairs. During busy months, however, it is difficult for the maintenance technician to complete all of the maintenance tasks within his 40-hour workweek.
4. David Bartlett has read about stretch targets, and he believes that a change in the compensation structure of the sales representatives may improve sales. Rather than a straight commission of 10% of sales, he is considering a system where each representative is given a monthly goal of 50 contracts. If the goal is met, the representative is paid a 12% commission. If the goal is not met, the commission falls to 8%. Currently, each sales representative averages 45 contracts per month.
5. Fuel consumption has increased significantly in recent months. David Bartlett is considering ways to promote improved fuel efficiency and reduce harmful emissions using stretch environmental targets, where drivers and the maintenance mechanic would receive a bonus if fuel consumption falls below 90% of budgeted fuel usage per mile driven.

Required

For situations 1–3, discuss which employee has responsibility for the related costs and the extent to which costs are controllable and by whom. What are the risks or costs to the company? What can be done to solve the problem or improve the situation? For situations 4 and 5, describe the potential benefits and costs of establishing stretch targets.

34 **Cash flow analysis, sensitivity analysis.** HealthMart is a retail store selling home oxygen equipment. HealthMart also services home oxygen equipment, for which the company bills customers monthly. HealthMart has budgeted for increases in service revenue of $200 each month due to a recent advertising campaign. The forecast of sales and service revenue for the March–June 2018 is as follows:

Sales and Service Revenues Budget March–June 2018

Month	Expected Sales Revenue	Expected Service Revenue	Total Revenue
March	$ 6,000	$4,000	$ 10,000
April	8,000	4,200	12,200
May	7,500	4,400	11,900
June	9,000	4,600	13,600

Almost all of the sales revenues of the oxygen equipment are credit card sales; cash sales are negligible. The credit card company deposits 97% of the revenues recorded each day into HealthMart's account overnight. For the servicing of home oxygen equipment, 60% of oxygen services billed each month is collected in the month of the service, and 40% is collected in the month following the service.

Required

1. Calculate the cash that HealthMart expects to collect in April, May, and June 2018 from sales and service revenues. Show calculations for each month.
2. HealthMart has budgeted expenditures for May of \$11,000 and requires a minimum cash balance of \$250 at the end of each month. It has a cash balance on May 1 of \$400.
   a. Given your answer to requirement 1, will HealthMart need to borrow cash to cover its payments for May and maintain a minimum cash balance of \$250 at the end of May?
   b. Assume (independently for each situation) that (1) May total revenues might be 10% lower or that (2) total costs might be 5% higher. Under each of those two scenarios, show the total net cash for May and the amount HealthMart would have to borrow to cover its cash payments for May and maintain a minimum cash balance of \$250 at the end of May. (Again, assume a balance of \$400 on May 1.)
3. Why do HealthMart's managers prepare a cash budget in addition to the revenue, expenses, and operating income budget? Has preparing the cash budget been helpful? Explain briefly.

MyAccountingLab

Problems

35 Budget schedules for a manufacturer. Hale Specialties manufactures, among other things, woolen blankets for the athletic teams of the two local high schools. The company sews the blankets from fabric and sews on a logo patch purchased from the licensed logo store site. The teams are as follows:

- Broncos, with red blankets and the Broncos logo
- Rams, with black blankets and the Rams logo

Also, the black blankets are slightly larger than the red blankets.

The budgeted direct-cost inputs for each product in 2017 are as follows:

	Broncos Blanket	Rams Blanket
Red wool fabric	5 yards	0 yards
Black wool fabric	0	6
Broncos logo patches	1	0
Rams logo patches	0	1
Direct manufacturing labor	4 hours	5 hours

Unit data pertaining to the direct materials for March 2017 are as follows:

Actual Beginning Direct Materials Inventory (3/1/2017)

	Broncos Blanket	Rams Blanket
Red wool fabric	40 yards	0 yards
Black wool fabric	0	20
Broncos logo patches	50	0
Rams logo patches	0	65

Target Ending Direct Materials Inventory (3/31/2017)

	Broncos Blanket	Rams Blanket
Red wool fabric	30 yards	0 yards
Black wool fabric	0	20
Broncos logo patches	30	0
Rams logo patches	0	30

Unit cost data for direct-cost inputs pertaining to February 2017 and March 2017 are as follows:

	February 2017 (actual)	March 2017 (budgeted)
Red wool fabric (per yard)	\$10	\$11
Black wool fabric (per yard)	14	13
Broncos logo patches (per patch)	8	8
Rams logo patches (per patch)	7	9
Manufacturing labor cost per hour	27	28

Manufacturing overhead (both variable and fixed) is allocated to each blanket on the basis of budgeted direct manufacturing labor-hours per blanket. The budgeted variable manufacturing overhead rate for March 2017 is $17 per direct manufacturing labor-hour. The budgeted fixed manufacturing overhead for March 2017 is $14,625. Both variable and fixed manufacturing overhead costs are allocated to each unit of finished goods.

Data relating to finished-goods inventory for March 2017 are as follows:

	Broncos Blankets	Rams Blankets
Beginning inventory in units	14	19
Beginning inventory in dollars (cost)	$1,960	$2,945
Target ending inventory in units	24	29

Budgeted sales for March 2017 are 140 units of the Broncos blankets and 195 units of the Rams blankets. The budgeted selling prices per unit in March 2017 are $305 for the Broncos blankets and $378 for the Rams blankets. Assume the following in your answer:

- Work-in-process inventories are negligible and ignored.
- Direct materials inventory and finished-goods inventory are costed using the FIFO method.
- Unit costs of direct materials purchased and finished goods are constant in March 2017.

Required

1. Prepare the following budgets for March 2017:
   a. Revenues budget
   b. Production budget in units
   c. Direct material usage budget and direct materials purchases budget
   d. Direct manufacturing labor costs budget
   e. Manufacturing overhead costs budget
   f. Ending inventories budget (direct materials and finished goods)
   g. Cost of goods sold budget
2. Suppose Hale Specialties decides to incorporate continuous improvement into its budgeting process. Describe two areas where it could incorporate continuous improvement into the budget schedules in requirement 1.

36 Budgeted costs, Kaizen improvements environmental costs. US Apparel (USA) manufactures plain white and solid-colored T-shirts. Budgeted inputs include the following:

	Price	Quantity	Cost per unit of output
Fabric	$ 8 per yard	0.75 yard per unit	$6 per unit
Labor	$16 per DMLH	0.25 DMLH per unit	$4 per unit
Dye*	$0.50 per ounce	4 ounces per unit	$2 per unit

*For colored T-shirts only

Budgeted sales and selling price per unit are as follows:

	Budgeted Sales	Selling Price per Unit
White T-shirts	10,000 units	$12 per T-shirt
Colored T-shirts	50,000 units	$15 per T-shirt

USA has the opportunity to switch from using the dye it currently uses to using an environmentally friendly dye that costs $1.25 per ounce. The company would still need 4 ounces of dye per shirt. USA is reluctant to change because of the increase in costs (and decrease in profit), but the Environmental Protection Agency has threatened to fine the company $130,000 if it continues to use the harmful but less expensive dye.

Required

1. Given the preceding information, would USA be better off financially by switching to the environmentally friendly dye? (Assume all other costs would remain the same.)
2. Assume USA chooses to be environmentally responsible regardless of cost, and it switches to the new dye. The production manager suggests trying Kaizen costing. If USA can reduce fabric and labor costs each by 1% per month on all the shirts it manufactures, by how much will overall costs decrease at the end of 12 months? (Round to the nearest dollar for calculating cost reductions.)
3. Refer to requirement 2. How could the reduction in material and labor costs be accomplished? Are there any problems with this plan?

37 **Revenue and production budgets.** (CPA, adapted) The Chen Corporation manufactures and sells two products: Thingone and Thingtwo. In July 2016, Chen's budget department gathered the following data to prepare budgets for 2017:

2017 Projected Sales

Product	Units	Price
Thingone	69,000	$160
Thingtwo	44,000	$258

2017 Inventories in Units

	Expected	Target
Product	January 1, 2017	December 31, 2017
Thingone	24,000	29,000
Thingtwo	7,000	8,000

The following direct materials are used in the two products:

		Amount Used per Unit	
Direct Material	Unit	Thingone	Thingtwo
A	pound	6	7
B	pound	4	5
C	each	0	3

Projected data for 2017 for direct materials are:

Direct Material	Anticipated Purchase Price	Expected Inventories January 1, 2017	Target Inventories December 31, 2017
A	$13	36,000 lb.	38,000 lb.
B	8	31,000 lb.	34,000 lb.
C	7	9,000 units	12,000 units

Projected direct manufacturing labor requirements and rates for 2017 are:

Product	Hours per Unit	Rate per Hour
Thingone	4	$13
Thingtwo	5	18

Manufacturing overhead is allocated at the rate of $24 per direct manufacturing labor-hour.

Required

Based on the preceding projections and budget requirements for Thingone and Thingtwo, prepare the following budgets for 2017:

1. Revenues budget (in dollars)
2. What questions might the CEO ask the marketing manager when reviewing the revenues budget? Explain briefly.
3. Production budget (in units)
4. Direct material purchases budget (in quantities)
5. Direct material purchases budget (in dollars)
6. Direct manufacturing labor budget (in dollars)
7. Budgeted finished-goods inventory at December 31, 2017 (in dollars)
8. What questions might the CEO ask the production manager when reviewing the production, direct materials, and direct manufacturing labor budgets?
9. How does preparing a budget help Chen Corporation's top management better manage the company?

38 **Budgeted income statement.** (CMA, adapted) Smart Video Company is a manufacturer of videoconferencing products. Maintaining the videoconferencing equipment is an important area of customer satisfaction. A recent downturn in the computer industry has caused the videoconferencing equipment segment to suffer, leading to a decline in Smart Video's financial performance. The following income statement shows results for 2017:

Smart Video Company Income Statement for the Year Ended December 31, 2017 (in thousands)

Revenues		
Equipment	$8,000	
Maintenance contracts	1,900	
Total revenues		$9,900
Cost of goods sold		4,000
Gross margin		5,900
Operating costs		
Marketing	630	
Distribution	100	
Customer maintenance	1,100	
Administration	920	
Total operating costs		2,750
Operating income		$3,150

Smart Video's management team is preparing the 2018 budget and is studying the following information:

1. Selling prices of equipment are expected to increase by 10% as the economic recovery begins. The selling price of each maintenance contract is expected to remain unchanged from 2017.
2. Equipment sales in units are expected to increase by 6%, with a corresponding 6% growth in units of maintenance contracts.
3. Cost of each unit sold is expected to increase by 5% to pay for the necessary technology and quality improvements.
4. Marketing costs are expected to increase by $290,000, but administration costs are expected to remain at 2017 levels.
5. Distribution costs vary in proportion to the number of units of equipment sold.
6. Two maintenance technicians are to be hired at a total cost of $160,000, which covers wages and related travel costs. The objective is to improve customer service and shorten response time.
7. There is no beginning or ending inventory of equipment.

Required

1. Prepare a budgeted income statement for the year ending December 31, 2018.
2. How well does the budget align with Smart Video's strategy?
3. How does preparing the budget help Smart Video's management team better manage the company?

39 Responsibility in a restaurant. Paula Beane owns a restaurant franchise that is part of a chain of "southern homestyle" restaurants. One of the chain's popular breakfast items is biscuits and gravy. Central Warehouse makes and freezes the biscuit dough, which it then sells to the franchise stores where it is thawed and baked in the individual stores by the cook. Each franchise also has a purchasing agent who orders the biscuits (and other items) based on expected demand. In March 2018, one of the freezers in Central Warehouse breaks down and biscuit production is reduced by 25% for 3 days. During those 3 days, Paula's franchise runs out of biscuits but demand does not slow down. Paula's franchise cook, Betty Baker, sends one of the kitchen helpers to the local grocery store to buy refrigerated ready-to-bake biscuits. Although the customers are kept happy, the refrigerated biscuits cost Paula's franchise three times the cost of the Central Warehouse frozen biscuits, and the franchise loses money on this item for those 3 days. Paula is angry with the purchasing agent for not ordering enough biscuits to avoid running out of stock and with Betty for spending too much money on the replacement biscuits.

Required

Who is responsible for the cost of the biscuits? At what level is the cost controllable? Do you agree that Paula should be angry with the purchasing agent? With Betty? Why or why not?

40 Comprehensive problem with ABC costing. Animal Gear Company makes two pet carriers, the Cat-allac and the Dog-eriffic. They are both made of plastic with metal doors, but the Cat-allac is smaller. Information for the two products for the month of April is given in the following tables:

Input Prices

Direct materials	
Plastic	$ 5 per pound
Metal	$ 4 per pound
Direct manufacturing labor	$10 per direct manufacturing labor-hour

Input Quantities per Unit of Output

	Cat-allac	Dog-eriffic
Direct materials		
Plastic	4 pounds	6 pounds
Metal	0.5 pounds	1 pound
Direct manufacturing labor-hours	3 hours	5 hours
Machine-hours (MH)	11 MH	19 MH

Inventory Information, Direct Materials

	Plastic	Metal
Beginning inventory	290 pounds	70 pounds
Target ending inventory	410 pounds	65 pounds
Cost of beginning inventory	$1,102	$217

Animal Gear accounts for direct materials using a FIFO cost-flow assumption.

Sales and Inventory Information, Finished Goods

	Cat-allac	Dog-eriffic
Expected sales in units	530	225
Selling price	$ 205	$ 310
Target ending inventory in units	30	10
Beginning inventory in units	10	19
Beginning inventory in dollars	$1,000	$4,650

Animal Gear uses a FIFO cost-flow assumption for finished-goods inventory.

Animal Gear uses an activity-based costing system and classifies overhead into three activity pools: Setup, Processing, and Inspection. Activity rates for these activities are $105 per setup-hour, $10 per machine-hour, and $15 per inspection-hour, respectively. Other information follows:

Cost-Driver Information

	Cat-allac	Dog-eriffic
Number of units per batch	25	9
Setup time per batch	1.50 hours	1.75 hours
Inspection time per batch	0.5 hour	0.7 hour

If necessary, round up to calculate number of batches.

Nonmanufacturing fixed costs for March equal $32,000, half of which are salaries. Salaries are expected to increase 5% in April. Other nonmanufacturing fixed costs will remain the same. The only variable nonmanufacturing cost is sales commission, equal to 1% of sales revenue.

Required

Prepare the following for April:

1. Revenues budget
2. Production budget in units
3. Direct material usage budget and direct material purchases budget
4. Direct manufacturing labor cost budget
5. Manufacturing overhead cost budgets for each of the three activities
6. Budgeted unit cost of ending finished-goods inventory and ending inventories budget
7. Cost of goods sold budget
8. Nonmanufacturing costs budget
9. Budgeted income statement (ignore income taxes)
10. How does preparing the budget help Animal Gear's management team better manage the company?

41 **Cash budget (continuation of 40).** Refer to the information in Problem 40.

Assume the following: Animal Gear (AG) does not make any sales on credit. AG sells only to the public and accepts cash and credit cards; 90% of its sales are to customers using credit cards, for which AG gets the cash right away, less a 2% transaction fee.

Purchases of materials are on account. AG pays for half the purchases in the period of the purchase and the other half in the following period. At the end of March, AG owes suppliers $8,000.

AG plans to replace a machine in April at a net cash cost of $13,000.

Labor, other manufacturing costs, and nonmanufacturing costs are paid in cash in the month incurred except of course depreciation, which is not a cash flow. Depreciation is $25,000 of the manufacturing cost and $10,000 of the nonmanufacturing cost for April.

AG currently has a $2,000 loan at an annual interest rate of 12%. The interest is paid at the end of each month. If AG has more than $7,000 cash at the end of April it will pay back the loan. AG owes $5,000 in income taxes that need to be remitted in April. AG has cash of $5,900 on hand at the end of March.

Required

1. Prepare a cash budget for April for Animal Gear.
2. Why do Animal Gear's managers prepare a cash budget in addition to the revenue, expenses, and operating income budget?

42 **Comprehensive operating budget.** Skulas, Inc., manufactures and sells snowboards. Skulas manufactures a single model, the Pipex. In late 2017, Skulas's management accountant gathered the following data to prepare budgets for January 2018:

Materials and Labor Requirements

Direct materials	
Wood	9 board feet (b.f.) per snowboard
Fiberglass	10 yards per snowboard
Direct manufacturing labor	5 hours per snowboard

Skulas's CEO expects to sell 2,900 snowboards during January 2018 at an estimated retail price of $650 per board. Further, the CEO expects 2018 beginning inventory of 500 snowboards and would like to end January 2018 with 200 snowboards in stock.

Direct Materials Inventories

	Beginning Inventory 1/1/2018	Ending Inventory 1/31/2018
Wood	2,040 b.f.	1,540 b.f.
Fiberglass	1,040 yards	2,040 yards

Variable manufacturing overhead is $7 per direct manufacturing labor-hour. There are also $81,000 in fixed manufacturing overhead costs budgeted for January 2018. Skulas combines both variable and fixed manufacturing overhead into a single rate based on direct manufacturing labor-hours. Variable marketing costs are allocated at the rate of $250 per sales visit. The marketing plan calls for 38 sales visits during January 2018. Finally, there are $35,000 in fixed nonmanufacturing costs budgeted for January 2018.

Other data include:

	2017 Unit Price	2018 Unit Price
Wood	$32.00 per b.f.	$34.00 per b.f.
Fiberglass	$ 8.00 per yard	$ 9.00 per yard
Direct manufacturing labor	$28.00 per hour	$29.00 per hour

The inventoriable unit cost for ending finished-goods inventory on December 31, 2017, is $374.80. Assume Skulas uses a FIFO inventory method for both direct materials and finished goods. Ignore work in process in your calculations.

Required

1. Prepare the January 2018 revenues budget (in dollars).
2. Prepare the January 2018 production budget (in units).
3. Prepare the direct material usage and purchases budgets for January 2018.
4. Prepare a direct manufacturing labor costs budget for January 2018.
5. Prepare a manufacturing overhead costs budget for January 2018.
6. What is the budgeted manufacturing overhead rate for January 2018?
7. What is the budgeted manufacturing overhead cost per output unit in January 2018?
8. Calculate the cost of a snowboard manufactured in January 2018.
9. Prepare an ending inventory budget for both direct materials and finished goods for January 2018.
10. Prepare a cost of goods sold budget for January 2018.
11. Prepare the budgeted income statement for Skulas, Inc., for January 2018.
12. What questions might the CEO ask the management team when reviewing the budget? Should the CEO set stretch targets? Explain briefly.
13. How does preparing the budget help Skulas's management team better manage the company?

43 Cash budgeting, budgeted balance sheet. (Continuation of 42) (Appendix)
Refer to the information in Problem 42.
Budgeted balances at January 31, 2018 are as follows:

Cash	?
Accounts receivable	?
Inventory	?
Property, plant and equipment (net)	$1,175,600
Accounts payable	?
Long-term liabilities	182,000
Stockholders' equity	?

Selected budget information for December 2017 follows:

Cash balance, December 31, 2017	$ 124,000
Budgeted sales	1,650,000
Budgeted materials purchases	820,000

Customer invoices are payable within 30 days. From past experience, Skulas's accountant projects 40% of invoices will be collected in the month invoiced, and 60% will be collected in the following month.

Accounts payable relates only to the purchase of direct materials. Direct materials are purchased on credit with 50% of direct materials purchases paid during the month of the purchase, and 50% paid in the month following purchase.

Fixed manufacturing overhead costs include $64,000 of depreciation costs and fixed nonmanufacturing overhead costs include $10,000 of depreciation costs. Direct manufacturing labor and the remaining manufacturing and nonmanufacturing overhead costs are paid monthly.

All property, plant, and equipment acquired during January 2018 were purchased on credit and did not entail any outflow of cash.

There were no borrowings or repayments with respect to long-term liabilities in January 2018.

On December 15, 2017, Skulas's board of directors voted to pay a $160,000 dividend to stockholders on January 31, 2018.

Required

1. Prepare a cash budget for January 2018. Show supporting schedules for the calculation of collection of receivables and payments of accounts payable, and for disbursements for fixed manufacturing and nonmanufacturing overhead.
2. Skulas is interested in maintaining a minimum cash balance of $120,000 at the end of each month. Will Skulas be in a position to pay the $160,000 dividend on January 31?
3. Why do Skulas's managers prepare a cash budget in addition to the revenue, expenses, and operating income budget?
4. Prepare a budgeted balance sheet for January 31, 2018 by calculating the January 31, 2018 balances in (a) cash (b) accounts receivable (c) inventory (d) accounts payable and (e) plugging in the balance for stockholders' equity.

44 Comprehensive problem; ABC manufacturing, two products. Hazlett, Inc., operates at capacity and makes plastic combs and hairbrushes. Although the combs and brushes are a matching set, they are sold individually and so the sales mix is not 1:1. Hazlett's management is planning its annual budget for fiscal year 2018. Here is information for 2018:

Input Prices

Direct materials	
Plastic	$ 0.30 per ounce
Bristles	$ 0.75 per bunch
Direct manufacturing labor	$ 18 per direct manufacturing labor-hour

Input Quantities per Unit of Output

	Combs	Brushes
Direct materials		
Plastic	5 ounces	8 ounces
Bristles	—	16 bunches
Direct manufacturing labor	0.05 hours	0.2 hours
Machine-hours (MH)	0.025 MH	0.1 MH

Inventory Information, Direct Materials

	Plastic	Bristles
Beginning inventory	1,600 ounces	1,820 bunches
Target ending inventory	1,766 ounces	2,272 bunches
Cost of beginning inventory	$456	$1,419

Hazlett accounts for direct materials using a FIFO cost flow.

Sales and Inventory Information, Finished Goods

	Combs	Brushes
Expected sales in units	12,000	14,000
Selling price	$ 9	$ 30
Target ending inventory in units	1,200	1,400
Beginning inventory in units	600	1,200
Beginning inventory in dollars	$ 2,700	$27,180

Hazlett uses a FIFO cost-flow assumption for finished-goods inventory.

Combs are manufactured in batches of 200, and brushes are manufactured in batches of 100. It takes 20 minutes to set up for a batch of combs and 1 hour to set up for a batch of brushes.

Hazlett uses activity-based costing and has classified all overhead costs as shown in the following table. Budgeted fixed overhead costs vary with capacity. Hazlett operates at capacity so budgeted fixed overhead cost per unit equals the budgeted fixed overhead costs divided by the budgeted quantities of the cost allocation base.

Cost Type	Budgeted Variable	Budgeted Fixed	Cost Driver/Allocation Base
Manufacturing			
Materials handling	$17,235	$22,500	Number of ounces of plastic used
Setup	10,245	16,650	Setup-hours
Processing	11,640	30,000	Machine-hours
Inspection	10,500	1,560	Number of units produced
Nonmanufacturing			
Marketing	$21,150	$90,000	Sales revenue
Distribution	0	1,170	Number of deliveries

Delivery trucks transport units sold in delivery sizes of 1,000 combs or 1,000 brushes.

Do the following for the year 2018:

Required

1. Prepare the revenues budget.
2. Use the revenues budget to:
   a. Find the budgeted allocation rate for marketing costs.
   b. Find the budgeted number of deliveries and allocation rate for distribution costs.
3. Prepare the production budget in units.
4. Use the production budget to:
   a. Find the budgeted number of setups and setup-hours and the allocation rate for setup costs.
   b. Find the budgeted total machine-hours and the allocation rate for processing costs.
   c. Find the budgeted total units produced and the allocation rate for inspection costs.
5. Prepare the direct material usage budget and the direct material purchases budget in both units and dollars; round to whole dollars.
6. Use the direct material usage budget to find the budgeted allocation rate for materials-handling costs.
7. Prepare the direct manufacturing labor cost budget.
8. Prepare the manufacturing overhead cost budget for materials handling, setup, processing, and inspection costs.
9. Prepare the budgeted unit cost of ending finished-goods inventory and ending inventories budget.
10. Prepare the cost of goods sold budget.
11. Prepare the nonmanufacturing overhead costs budget for marketing and distribution.
12. Prepare a budgeted income statement (ignore income taxes).
13. How does preparing the budget help Hazlett's management team better manage the company?

45 Cash budget. (Continuation of 44) (Appendix)

Refer to the information in Problem 44.

All purchases made in a given month are paid for in the following month, and direct material purchases make up all of the accounts payable balance and are reflected in the accounts payable balances at the beginning and the end of the year.

Sales are made to customers with terms net 45 days. Fifty percent of a month's sales are collected in the month of the sale, 25% are collected in the month following the sale, and 25% are collected two months after the sale and are reflected in the accounts receivables balances at the beginning and the end of the year.

Direct manufacturing labor, variable manufacturing overhead and variable marketing costs are paid as they are incurred. Fifty percent of fixed manufacturing overhead costs, 60% of fixed marketing costs, and 100% of fixed distribution costs are depreciation expenses. The remaining fixed manufacturing overhead and marketing costs are paid as they are incurred.

Selected balances for December 31, 2017, follow:

Cash	$29,200
Accounts payable	21,450
Accounts receivable	40,900

Selected budget information for December 2018 follows:

Accounts payable	$27,770
Accounts receivable	48,500

Hazlett has budgeted to purchase equipment costing $145,000 for cash during 2018. Hazlett desires a minimum cash balance of $25,000. The company has a line of credit from which it may borrow in increments of $1,000 at an interest rate of 12% per year. By special arrangement, with the bank, Hazlett pays interest when repaying the principal, which only needs to be repaid in 2019.

Required

1. Prepare a cash budget for 2018. If Hazlett must borrow cash to meet its desired ending cash balance, show the amount that must be borrowed.
2. Does the cash budget for 2018 give Hazlett's managers all of the information necessary to manage cash in 2018? How might that be improved?
3. What insight does the cash budget give to Hazlett's managers that the budgeted income statement does not?

46 Budgeting and ethics. Jayzee Company manufactures a variety of products in a variety of departments and evaluates departments and departmental managers by comparing actual cost and output relative to the budget. Departmental managers help create the budgets and usually provide information about input quantities for materials, labor, and overhead costs.

Kurt Jackson is the manager of the department that produces product Z. Kurt has estimated these inputs for product Z:

Input	Budget Quantity per Unit of Output
Direct material	8 pounds
Direct manufacturing labor	30 minutes
Machine time	24 minutes

The department produces about 100 units of product Z each day. Kurt's department always gets excellent evaluations, sometimes exceeding budgeted production quantities. For each 100 units of product Z produced, the company uses, on average, about 48 hours of direct manufacturing labor (eight people working 6 hours each), 790 pounds of material, and 39.5 machine-hours.

Top management of Jayzee Company has decided to implement budget standards that will challenge the workers in each department, and it has asked Kurt to design more challenging input standards for product Z. Kurt provides top management with the following input quantities:

Input	Budget Quantity per Unit of Output
Direct material	7.9 pounds
Direct manufacturing labor	29 minutes
Machine time	23.6 minutes

Required

Discuss the following:

1. Are these budget standards challenging for the department that produces product Z?
2. Why do you suppose Kurt picked these particular standards?
3. What steps can Jayzee Company's top management take to make sure Kurt's standards really meet the goals of the firm?

47 Kaizen budgeting for carbon emissions. Apex Chemical Company currently operates three manufacturing plants in Colorado, Utah, and Arizona. Annual carbon emissions for these plants in the first quarter of 2018 are 125,000 metric tons per quarter (or 500,000 metric tons in 2018). Apex management is investigating improved manufacturing techniques that will reduce annual carbon emissions to below 475,000 metric tons so that the company can meet Environmental Protection Agency guidelines by 2019. Costs and benefits are as follows:

Total cost to reduce carbon emissions	$10 per metric ton reduced in 2019 below 500,000 metric tons
Fine in 2019 if EPA guidelines are not met	$300,000

Apex Management has chosen to use Kaizen budgeting to achieve its goal for carbon emissions.

Required

1. If Apex reduces emissions by 1% each quarter, beginning with the second quarter of 2018, will the company reach its goal of 475,000 metric tons by the end of 2019?
2. What would be the net financial cost or benefit of their plan? Ignore the time value of money.
3. What factors other than cost might weigh into Apex's decision to carry out this plan?

48 Comprehensive budgeting problem; activity-based costing, operating and financial budgets. Tyva makes a very popular undyed cloth sandal in one style, but in Regular and Deluxe. The Regular sandals have cloth soles and the Deluxe sandals have cloth-covered wooden soles. Tyva is preparing its budget for June 2018 and has estimated sales based on past experience.

Other information for the month of June follows:

Input Prices

Direct materials	
Cloth	$5.25 per yard
Wood	$7.50 per board foot
Direct manufacturing labor	$15 per direct manufacturing labor-hour

Input Quantities per Unit of Output (per pair of sandals)

	Regular	Deluxe
Direct materials		
Cloth	1.3 yards	1.5 yards
Wood	0	2 b.f.
Direct manufacturing labor-hours (DMLH)	5 hours	7 hours
Setup-hours per batch	2 hours	3 hours

Inventory Information, Direct Materials

	Cloth	Wood
Beginning inventory	610 yards	800 b.f.
Target ending inventory	386 yards	295 b.f.
Cost of beginning inventory	$3,219	$6,060

Tyva accounts for direct materials using a FIFO cost-flow assumption.

Sales and Inventory Information, Finished Goods

	Regular	Deluxe
Expected sales in units (pairs of sandals)	2,000	3,000
Selling price	$ 120	$ 195
Target ending inventory in units	400	600
Beginning inventory in units	250	650
Beginning inventory in dollars	$23,250	$92,625

Tyva uses a FIFO cost-flow assumption for finished-goods inventory.

All the sandals are made in batches of 50 pairs of sandals. Tyva incurs manufacturing overhead costs, marketing and general administration, and shipping costs. Besides materials and labor, manufacturing costs include setup, processing, and inspection costs. Tyva ships 40 pairs of sandals per shipment. Tyva uses activity-based costing and has classified all overhead costs for the month of June as shown in the following chart:

Cost Type	Denominator Activity	Rate
Manufacturing		
Setup	Setup-hours	$ 18 per setup-hour
Processing	Direct manufacturing labor-hours (DMLH)	$1.80 per DMLH
Inspection	Number of pairs of sandals	$1.35 per pair
Nonmanufacturing		
Marketing and general administration	Sales revenue	8%
Shipping	Number of shipments	$ 15 per shipment

Required

1. Prepare each of the following for June:
   a. Revenues budget
   b. Production budget in units
   c. Direct material usage budget and direct material purchases budget in both units and dollars; round to dollars
   d. Direct manufacturing labor cost budget
   e. Manufacturing overhead cost budgets for setup, processing, and inspection activities
   f. Budgeted unit cost of ending finished-goods inventory and ending inventories budget
   g. Cost of goods sold budget
   h. Marketing and general administration and shipping costs budget
2. Tyva's balance sheet for May 31 follows.

Tyva Balance Sheet as of May 31

Assets		
Cash		$ 9,435
Accounts receivable	$324,000	
Less: Allowance for bad debts	16,200	307,800
Inventories		
Direct materials		9,279
Finished goods		115,875
Fixed assets	$870,000	
Less: Accumulated depreciation	136,335	733,665
Total assets		$1,176,054
Liabilities and Equity		
Accounts payable		$ 15,600
Taxes payable		10,800
Interest payable		750
Long-term debt		150,000
Common stock		300,000
Retained earnings		698,904
Total liabilities and equity		$1,176,054

Use the balance sheet and the following information to prepare a cash budget for Tyva for June. Round to dollars.

- All sales are on account; 60% are collected in the month of the sale, 38% are collected the following month, and 2% are never collected and written off as bad debts.
- All purchases of materials are on account. Tyva pays for 80% of purchases in the month of purchase and 20% in the following month.
- All other costs are paid in the month incurred, including the declaration and payment of a $15,000 cash dividend in June.
- Tyva is making monthly interest payments of 0.5% (6% per year) on a $150,000 long-term loan.
- Tyva plans to pay the $10,800 of taxes owed as of May 31 in the month of June. Income tax expense for June is zero.
- 30% of processing, setup, and inspection costs and 10% of marketing and general administration and shipping costs are depreciation.

3. Prepare a budgeted income statement for June and a budgeted balance sheet for Tyva as of June 30, 2018.

GLOSSARY

Activity-based budgeting (ABB). Budgeting approach that focuses on the budgeted cost of the activities necessary to produce and sell products and services.

Budgetary slack. The practice of underestimating budgeted revenues, or overestimating budgeted costs, to make budgeted targets more easily achievable.

Cash budget. Schedule of expected cash receipts and disbursements.

Continuous budget. See *rolling budget.*

Controllability. Degree of influence that a specific manager has over costs, revenues, or related items for which he or she is responsible.

Controllable cost. Any cost that is primarily subject to the influence of a given responsibility center manager for a given period.

Cost center. Responsibility center where the manager is accountable for costs only.

Financial budget. Part of the master budget that focuses on how operations and planned capital outlays affect cash. It is made up of the capital expenditures budget, the cash budget, the budgeted balance sheet, and the budgeted statement of cash flows.

Financial planning models. Mathematical representations of the relationships among operating activities, financial activities, and other factors that affect the master budget.

Investment center. Responsibility center where the manager is accountable for investments, revenues, and costs.

Kaizen budgeting. Budgetary approach that explicitly incorporates continuous improvement anticipated during the budget period into the budget numbers.

Master budget. Expression of management's operating and financial plans for a specified period (usually a fiscal year) including a set of budgeted financial statements. Also called *pro forma statements.*

Operating budget. Budgeted income statement (for operations) and its supporting budget schedules.

Organization structure. Arrangement of lines of responsibility within the organization.

Pro forma statements. Budgeted financial statements.

Profit center. Responsibility center where the manager is accountable for revenues and costs.

Responsibility accounting. System that measures the plans, budgets, actions, and actual results of each responsibility center.

Responsibility center. Part, segment, or subunit of an organization whose manager is accountable for a specified set of activities.

Revenue center. Responsibility center where the manager is accountable for revenues only.

Rolling budget. Budget or plan that is always available for a specified future period by adding a period (month, quarter, or year) to the period that just ended. Also called *continuous budget or rolling forecast.*

Rolling forecast. See *rolling budget.*

Flexible Budgets, Direct-Cost Variances, and Management Control

Every organization, regardless of its profitability or growth, has to maintain control over its expenses.

And when customers are cautious in their spending choices, the need for managers to use budgeting and variance analysis tools for cost control becomes especially critical. By studying variances, managers can focus on where specific performances have fallen short and make corrective adjustments and achieve significant savings for their companies. The drive to achieve cost reductions might seem at odds with the growing push for organizations to pursue environmentally sound business practices. To the contrary, managers looking to be more efficient with their plants and operations have found that cornerstones of the sustainability movement, such as reducing waste and power usage, offer fresh ways to help them manage risk and control costs, as the following article shows.

LEARNING OBJECTIVES

1 Understand static budgets and static-budget variances

2 Examine the concept of a flexible budget and learn how to develop it

3 Calculate flexible-budget variances and sales-volume variances

4 Explain why standard costs are often used in variance analysis

5 Compute price variances and efficiency variances for direct-cost categories

6 Understand how managers use variances

7 Describe benchmarking and explain its role in cost management

DELL GOES GREEN TO REDUCE STANDARD COSTS FOR PACKAGING[1]

Product packaging can be both costly and a major cause of waste. At information technology-manufacturer Dell, managers found a way to create more sustainable packaging for its laptop and desktop computers while reducing the company's standard costs.

Dell has a goal to create waste-free packaging by 2020. This has encouraged the company to emphasize materials that can be easily recycled or composted after use. In 2013, Dell added wheat straw to its packaging, after already incorporating biowaste from bamboo and mushrooms, to create new, sustainable boxes that can be recycled like cardboard in most places. After three years, Dell eliminated more than 8,900 tons of packaging materials from its supply chain.

This new packaging reduces Dell's environmental footprint, as well as its packaging costs. After three years, the company saved

George Frey/Bloomberg/Getty Images

[1] *Sources:* Maxine Perella, "Why Dell, Coca-Cola and Carlsberg Are Developing Greener Packaging," *The Guardian*, May 14, 2014; "Dell Commits to Waste-Free Packaging Stream by 2020," Dell Inc. press release, Round Rock, TX, June 5, 2013, (http://www.dell.com/learn/us/en/uscorp1/secure/2013-06-05-dell-environment-sustainable-packaging).

more than $18 million from its previous standard costs for cardboard and Styrofoam-based packaging. As Dell becomes more familiar with using eco-friendly materials, the company expects to see its standard costs for packaging decrease further.

"Packaging is often the first part of our products that customers see and touch," said Oliver Campbell, Dell's director of packaging procurement. "From that first interaction, we want to ensure our customers know we're dedicated to operating in an environmentally responsible manner, and we want to make it easier for them to be sustainable as well."

Budgets help managers with their planning functions. We now explain how budgets, specifically flexible budgets, are used to compute variances, which assist managers in their control function. Variance analysis supports the critical final function in the five-step decision-making process by enabling managers to *evaluate performance and learn* after decisions are implemented.

Static Budgets and Variances

LEARNING OBJECTIVE 1

Understand static budgets

...the master budget based on output planned at start of period

and static-budget variances

...the difference between the actual result and the corresponding budgeted amount in the static budget

A **variance** is the difference between actual results and expected performance. The expected performance is also called **budgeted performance**, which is a point of reference for making comparisons.

The Use of Variances

Variances bring together the planning and control functions of management and facilitate management by exception. **Management by exception** is a practice whereby managers focus more closely on areas that are not operating as expected and less closely on areas that are. Consider the scrap and rework costs at a Maytag appliances plant. If the plant's actual costs are much higher than originally budgeted, the variances will prompt managers to find out why and correct the problem so future operations result in less scrap and rework. Sometimes a large positive variance may occur, such as a significant decrease in the manufacturing costs of a product. Managers will try to understand the reasons for the decrease (better operator training or changes in manufacturing methods, for example) so these practices can be continued and implemented by other divisions within the organization.

Variances are also used for evaluating performance and to motivate managers. Production-line managers at Maytag may have quarterly efficiency incentives linked to achieving a budgeted amount of operating costs.

Sometimes variances suggest that the company should consider a change in strategy. For example, large negative variances caused by excessive defect rates for a new product may suggest a flawed product design. Managers may then want to investigate the product design and potentially change the mix of products being offered. Variances also help managers make more informed predictions about the future and thereby improve the quality of the five-step decision-making process.

The benefits of variance analysis are not restricted to companies. In today's difficult economic environment, public officials have realized that the ability to make timely tactical changes based on variance information can result in their having to make fewer draconian adjustments later. For example, the city of Scottsdale, Arizona, monitors its tax and fee performance against expenditures monthly. Why? One of the city's goals is to keep its water usage rates stable. By monitoring the extent to which the city's water revenues are matching its current expenses, Scottsdale can avoid sudden spikes in the rate it charges residents for water as well as finance water-related infrastructure projects.[2]

[2] For an excellent discussion and other related examples from governmental settings, see S. Kavanagh and C. Swanson, "Tactical Financial Management: Cash Flow and Budgetary Variance Analysis," *Government Finance Review* (October 1, 2009).

How important of a decision-making tool is variance analysis? Very! A survey by the United Kingdom's Chartered Institute of Management Accountants found that it was easily the most popular costing tool used by organizations of all sizes.

Static Budgets and Static-Budget Variances

We will take a closer look at variances by examining one company's accounting system. As you study the exhibits in this chapter, note that "level" followed by a number denotes the amount of detail shown by a variance analysis. Level 1 reports the least detail; level 2 offers more information; and so on.

Consider Webb Company, a firm that manufactures and sells jackets. The jackets require tailoring and many other hand operations. Webb sells exclusively to distributors, who in turn sell to independent clothing stores and retail chains. For simplicity, we assume the following:

1. Webb's only costs are in the manufacturing function; Webb incurs no costs in other value-chain functions, such as marketing and distribution.
2. All units manufactured in April 2017 are sold in April 2017.
3. There is no direct materials inventory at either the beginning or the end of the period. No work-in-process or finished-goods inventories exist at either the beginning or the end of the period.

Webb has three variable-cost categories. The budgeted variable cost per jacket for each category is as follows:

Cost Category	Variable Cost per Jacket
Direct materials costs	$60
Direct manufacturing labor costs	16
Variable manufacturing overhead costs	12
Total variable costs	$88

The *number of units manufactured* is the cost driver for direct materials, direct manufacturing labor, and variable manufacturing overhead. The relevant range for the cost driver is from 0 to 12,000 jackets. Budgeted and actual data for April 2017 are:

Budgeted fixed costs for production between 0 and 12,000 jackets	$276,000
Budgeted selling price	$ 120 per jacket
Budgeted production and sales	12,000 jackets
Actual production and sales	10,000 jackets

The **static budget**, or master budget, is based on the level of output planned at the start of the budget period. The master budget is called a static budget because the budget for the period is developed around a single (static) planned output level. Exhibit 1, column 3, presents the static budget for Webb Company for April 2017 that was prepared at the end of 2016. For each line item in the income statement, Exhibit 1, column 1, displays data for the actual April results. For example, actual revenues are $1,250,000, and the actual selling price is $1,250,000 ÷ 10,000 jackets = $125 per jacket—compared with the budgeted selling price of $120 per jacket. Similarly, actual direct materials costs are $621,600, and the direct material cost per jacket is $621,600 ÷ 10,000 = $62.16 per jacket—compared with the budgeted direct material cost per jacket of $60. We describe potential reasons and explanations for these differences as we discuss different variances throughout the chapter.

The **static-budget variance** (see Exhibit 1, column 2) is the difference between the actual result and the corresponding budgeted amount in the static budget.

A **favorable variance**—denoted F throughout —has the effect, when considered in isolation, of increasing operating income relative to the budgeted amount. For revenue items, F means actual revenues exceed budgeted revenues. For cost items, F means actual costs are less than budgeted costs. An **unfavorable variance**—denoted U throughout —has the effect, when viewed in isolation, of decreasing operating income relative to the budgeted amount. Unfavorable variances are also called *adverse variances* in some countries, such as the United Kingdom.

EXHIBIT 1

Static-Budget-Based Variance Analysis for Webb Company for April 2017[a]

Level 1 Analysis

	Actual Results (1)	Static-Budget Variances (2) = (1) − (3)	Static Budget (3)
Units sold	10,000	2,000 U	12,000
Revenues	$1,250,000	$190,000 U	$1,440,000
Variable costs			
Direct materials	621,600	98,400 F	720,000
Direct manufacturing labor	198,000	6,000 U	192,000
Variable manufacturing overhead	130,500	13,500 F	144,000
Total variable costs	950,100	105,900 F	1,056,000
Contribution margin	299,900	84,100 U	384,000
Fixed costs	285,000	9,000 U	276,000
Operating income	$ 14,900	$ 93,100 U	$ 108,000

$ 93,100 U

Static-budget variance

[a]F = favorable effect on operating income; U = unfavorable effect on operating income.

The unfavorable static-budget variance for operating income of $93,100 in Exhibit 1 is calculated by subtracting static-budget operating income of $108,000 from actual operating income of $14,900:

$$\text{Static-budget variance for operating income} = \text{Actual result} - \text{Static-budget amount}$$

$$= \$14{,}900 - \$108{,}000$$

$$= \$93{,}100\text{ U.}$$

The analysis in Exhibit 1 provides managers with additional information on the static-budget variance for operating income of $93,100 U. The more detailed breakdown indicates how the line items that comprise operating income—revenues, individual variable costs, and fixed costs—add up to the static-budget variance of $93,100.

Webb produced and sold only 10,000 jackets, although managers anticipated an output of 12,000 jackets in the static budget. *Managers want to know how much of the static-budget variance is due to Webb inaccurately forecasting what it expected to produce and sell and how much is due to how it actually performed manufacturing and selling 10,000 jackets.* Managers, therefore, create a flexible budget, which enables a more in-depth understanding of deviations from the static budget.

DECISION POINT

What are static budgets and static-budget variances?

TRY IT!

1 Zenefit Corporation sold laser pointers for $11 each in 2017. Its budgeted selling price was $12 per unit. Other information related to its performance is given below:

	Actual	Budgeted
Units made and sold	28,000	27,500
Variable costs	$90,000	$ 3 per unit
Fixed costs	$55,000	$58,000

Calculate Zenefit's static-budget variance for (a) revenues, (b) variable costs, (c) fixed costs, and (d) operating income.

Flexible Budgets

LEARNING OBJECTIVE 2

Examine the concept of a flexible budget

...the budget that is adjusted (flexed) to recognize the actual output level

and learn how to develop it

...proportionately increase variable costs; keep fixed costs the same

A **flexible budget** calculates budgeted revenues and budgeted costs based on *the actual output in the budget period*. The flexible budget is prepared at the end of the period (April 2017 for Webb), after managers know the actual output of 10,000 jackets. The flexible budget is the *hypothetical* budget that Webb would have prepared at the start of the budget period if it had correctly forecast the actual output of 10,000 jackets. In other words, the flexible budget is not the plan Webb initially had in mind for April 2017 (remember Webb planned for an output of 12,000 jackets). Rather, it is the budget Webb *would have* put together for April if it knew in advance that the output for the month would be 10,000 jackets. In preparing the flexible budget, note that:

- The budgeted selling price is the same $120 per jacket used in the static budget.
- The budgeted unit variable cost is the same $88 per jacket used in the static budget.
- The budgeted *total* fixed costs are the same static-budget amount of $276,000. Why? Because the 10,000 jackets produced falls within the relevant range of 0 to 12,000 jackets. Therefore, Webb would have budgeted the same amount of fixed costs, $276,000, whether it anticipated making 10,000 or 12,000 jackets.

The *only* difference between the static budget and the flexible budget is that the static budget is prepared for the planned output of 12,000 jackets, whereas the flexible budget is prepared retroactively based on the actual output of 10,000 jackets. In other words, the static budget is being "flexed," or adjusted, from 12,000 jackets to 10,000 jackets.[3] The flexible budget for 10,000 jackets assumes all costs are either completely variable or completely fixed with respect to the number of jackets produced.

Webb develops its flexible budget in three steps.

Step 1: Identify the Actual Quantity of Output. In April 2017, Webb produced and sold 10,000 jackets.

Step 2: Calculate the Flexible Budget for Revenues Based on the Budgeted Selling Price and Actual Quantity of Output.

$$\text{Flexible-budget revenues} = \$120 \text{ per jacket} \times 10{,}000 \text{ jackets}$$
$$= \$1{,}200{,}000$$

Step 3: Calculate the Flexible Budget for Costs Based on the Budgeted Variable Cost per Output Unit, Actual Quantity of Output, and Budgeted Fixed Costs.

Flexible-budget variable costs	
Direct materials, $60 per jacket × 10,000 jackets	$ 600,000
Direct manufacturing labor, $16 per jacket × 10,000 jackets	160,000
Variable manufacturing overhead, $12 per jacket × 10,000 jackets	120,000
Total flexible-budget variable costs	880,000
Flexible-budget fixed costs	276,000
Flexible-budget total costs	$1,156,000

These three steps enable Webb to prepare a flexible budget, as shown in Exhibit 2, column 3. The flexible budget allows for a more detailed analysis of the $93,100 unfavorable static-budget variance for operating income.

DECISION POINT

How can managers develop a flexible budget and why is it useful to do so?

Consider Zenefit Corporation. With the same information for 2017 as provided in Try It 1, calculate Zenefit's flexible budget for (a) revenues, (b) variable costs, (c) fixed costs, and (d) operating income. 2

TRY IT!

[3] Suppose Webb, when preparing its annual budget for 2017 at the end of 2016, had perfectly anticipated that its output in April 2017 would equal 10,000 jackets. Then the flexible budget for April 2017 would be identical to the static budget.

EXHIBIT 2 Level 2 Flexible-Budget-Based Variance Analysis for Webb Company for April 2017[a]

Level 2 Analysis

	Actual Results (1)	Flexible-Budget Variances (2) = (1) − (3)	Flexible Budget (3)	Sales-Volume Variances (4) = (3) − (5)	Static Budget (5)
Units sold	10,000	0	10,000	2,000 U	12,000
Revenues	$1,250,000	$50,000 F	$1,200,000	$240,000 U	$1,440,000
Variable costs					
Direct materials	621,600	21,600 U	600,000	120,000 F	720,000
Direct manufacturing labor	198,000	38,000 U	160,000	32,000 F	192,000
Variable manufacturing overhead	130,500	10,500 U	120,000	24,000 F	144,000
Total variable costs	950,100	70,100 U	880,000	176,000 F	1,056,000
Contribution margin	299,900	20,100 U	320,000	64,000 U	384,000
Fixed manufacturing costs	285,000	9,000 U	276,000	0	276,000
Operating income	$ 14,900	$29,100 U	$ 44,000	$ 64,000 U	$ 108,000

Level 2: $29,100 U Flexible-budget variance; $ 64,000 U Sales-volume variance

Level 1: $93,100 U Static-budget variance

[a]F = favorable effect on operating income; U = unfavorable effect on operating income.

Flexible-Budget Variances and Sales-Volume Variances

LEARNING OBJECTIVE 3

Calculate flexible-budget variances

...each flexible-budget variance is the difference between an actual result and a flexible-budget amount

and sales-volume variances

...each sales-volume variance is the difference between a flexible-budget amount and a static-budget amount

Exhibit 2 shows the flexible-budget-based variance analysis for Webb, which subdivides the $93,100 unfavorable static-budget variance for operating income into two parts: a flexible-budget variance of $29,100 U and a sales-volume variance of $64,000 U. The **sales-volume variance** is the difference between a flexible-budget amount and the corresponding static-budget amount. The **flexible-budget variance** is the difference between an actual result and the corresponding flexible-budget amount.

Sales-Volume Variances

Keep in mind that the flexible-budget amounts in column 3 of Exhibit 2 and the static-budget amounts in column 5 are both computed using budgeted selling prices, budgeted variable cost per jacket, and budgeted fixed costs. The difference between the static-budget and the flexible-budget amounts is called the sales-volume variance because it arises *solely* from the difference between the 10,000 actual quantity (or volume) of jackets sold and the 12,000 quantity of jackets expected to be sold in the static budget.

$$\text{Sales-volume variance for operating income} = \text{Flexible-budget amount} - \text{Static-budget amount}$$
$$= \$44{,}000 - \$108{,}000$$
$$= \$64{,}000 \text{ U}$$

The sales-volume variance in operating income for Webb measures the change in the budgeted contribution margin because Webb sold only 10,000 jackets rather than the budgeted 12,000.

$$\begin{aligned}
\text{Sales-volume variance for operating income} &= \left(\text{Budgeted contribution margin per unit}\right) \times \left(\text{Actual units sold} - \text{Static-budget units sold}\right) \\
&= \left(\text{Budgeted selling price} - \text{Budgeted variable cost per unit}\right) \times \left(\text{Actual units sold} - \text{Static-budget units sold}\right) \\
&= (\$120 \text{ per jacket} - \$88 \text{ per jacket}) \times (10{,}000 \text{ jackets} - 12{,}000 \text{ jackets}) \\
&= \$32 \text{ per jacket} \times (-2{,}000 \text{ jackets}) \\
&= \$64{,}000\ \text{U}
\end{aligned}$$

Exhibit 2, column 4, shows the components of this overall variance by identifying the sales-volume variance for each of the line items in the income statement. The unfavorable sales-volume variance in operating income arises because of one or more of the following reasons:

1. Failure of Webb's managers to execute the sales plans
2. Weaker than anticipated overall demand for jackets
3. Competitors taking away market share from Webb
4. Unexpected changes in customer tastes and preferences away from Webb's designs
5. Quality problems leading to customer dissatisfaction with Webb's jackets

How Webb responds to the unfavorable sales-volume variance will depend on what its managers believe caused the variance. For example, if Webb's managers believe the unfavorable sales-volume variance was caused by market-related reasons (reasons 1, 2, 3, or 4), the sales manager would be in the best position to explain what happened and suggest corrective actions that may be needed, such as sales promotions, market studies, or changes to advertising plans. If, however, managers believe the unfavorable sales-volume variance was caused by unanticipated quality problems (reason 5), the production manager would be in the best position to analyze the causes and suggest strategies for improvement, such as changes in the manufacturing process or investments in new machines.

The static-budget variances compared actual revenues and costs for 10,000 jackets against budgeted revenues and costs for 12,000 jackets. A portion of this difference, the sales-volume variance, reflects the effects of selling fewer units or inaccurate forecasting of sales. By removing this component from the static-budget variance, managers can compare their firm's revenues earned and costs incurred for April 2017 against the flexible budget—the revenues and costs Webb would have budgeted for the 10,000 jackets actually produced and sold. *Flexible-budget variances are a better measure of sales price and cost performance than static-budget variances because they compare actual revenues to budgeted revenues and actual costs to budgeted costs for the same 10,000 jackets of output.*

Flexible-Budget Variances

The first three columns of Exhibit 2 compare Webb's actual results with its flexible-budget amounts. The flexible-budget variances for each line item in the income statement are shown in column 2:

$$\text{Flexible-budget variance} = \text{Actual result} - \text{Flexible-budget amount}$$

The operating income line in Exhibit 2 shows the flexible-budget variance is \$29,100 U (\$14,900 − \$44,000). The \$29,100 U arises because the actual selling price, actual variable cost per unit, and actual fixed costs differ from their budgeted amounts. The actual results and budgeted amounts for the selling price and variable cost per unit are as follows:

	Actual Result	Budgeted Amount
Selling price	\$125.00 (\$1,250,000 ÷ 10,000 jackets)	\$120.00 (\$1,200,000 ÷ 10,000 jackets)
Variable cost per jacket	\$ 95.01 (\$ 950,100 ÷ 10,000 jackets)	\$ 88.00 (\$ 880,000 ÷ 10,000 jackets)

The flexible-budget variance for revenues is called the **selling-price variance** because it arises solely from the difference between the actual selling price and the budgeted selling price:

$$\text{Selling-price variance} = \left(\text{Actual selling price} - \text{Budgeted selling price}\right) \times \text{Actual units sold}$$

$$= (\$125 \text{ per jacket} - \$120 \text{ per jacket}) \times 10{,}000 \text{ jackets}$$

$$= \$50{,}000 \text{ F}$$

Webb has a favorable selling-price variance because the $125 actual selling price exceeds the $120 budgeted amount, which increases operating income. Marketing managers are generally in the best position to understand and explain the reason for a selling price difference. For example, was the difference due to better quality? Or was it due to an overall increase in market prices? Webb's managers concluded it was due to a general increase in prices.

The flexible-budget variance for total variable costs is unfavorable ($70,100 U) for the actual output of 10,000 jackets. It's unfavorable because of one or both of the following:

- Webb used greater quantities of inputs (such as direct manufacturing labor-hours) compared to the budgeted quantities of inputs.
- Webb incurred higher prices per unit for the inputs (such as the wage rate per direct manufacturing labor-hour) compared to the budgeted prices per unit of the inputs.

Higher input quantities and/or higher input prices relative to the budgeted amounts could be the result of Webb deciding to produce a better product than what was planned or the result of inefficiencies related to Webb's manufacturing and purchasing operations or both. *You should always think of variance analysis as providing suggestions for further investigation rather than as establishing conclusive evidence of good or bad performance.*

The actual fixed costs of $285,000 are $9,000 more than the budgeted amount of $276,000. This unfavorable flexible-budget variance reflects unexpected increases in the cost of fixed indirect resources, such as the factory's rent or supervisors' salaries.

In the rest of this chapter, we will focus on variable direct-cost input variances.

DECISION POINT

How are flexible-budget and sales-volume variances calculated?

TRY IT! 3

Consider Zenefit Corporation again. With the same information for 2017 as provided in Try It 1, calculate Zenefit's flexible-budget and sales-volume variances for (a) revenues, (b) variable costs, (c) fixed costs, and (d) operating income.

Standard Costs for Variance Analysis

LEARNING OBJECTIVE 4

Explain why standard costs are often used in variance analysis

. . . standard costs exclude past inefficiencies and take into account expected future changes

To gain further insight, a company will subdivide the flexible-budget variance for its direct-cost inputs into two more-detailed variances:

1. A price variance that reflects the difference between an actual input price and a budgeted input price
2. An efficiency variance that reflects the difference between an actual input quantity and a budgeted input quantity

We will call these level 3 variances. Managers generally have more control over efficiency variances than price variances because the quantity of inputs used is primarily affected by factors inside the company (such as the efficiency with which operations are performed), whereas changes in the price of materials or in wage rates may be largely dictated by market forces outside the company.

Obtaining Budgeted Input Prices and Budgeted Input Quantities

To calculate price and efficiency variances, Webb needs to obtain budgeted input prices and budgeted input quantities. Webb's three main sources for this information are: (1) past data, (2) data from similar companies, and (3) standards. Each source has its advantages and disadvantages.

1. **Actual input data from past periods.** Most companies have past data on actual input prices and actual input quantities. These historical data could be analyzed for trends or patterns using some of the techniques to obtain estimates of budgeted prices and quantities.

   Advantages: Past data represent quantities and prices that are real rather than hypothetical, so they can be very useful benchmarks for measuring improvements in performance. Moreover, past data are typically easy to collect at a low cost.

   Disadvantages: A firm's inefficiencies, such as the wastage of direct materials, are incorporated in past data. Consequently, the data do not represent the performance the firm could have ideally attained, only the performance it achieved in the past. Past data also do not incorporate any changes expected for the budget period, such as improvements resulting from new investments in technology.

2. **Data from other companies that have similar processes.** Another source of information is data from peer companies or companies that have similar processes, which can serve as a benchmark. For example, Baptist Healthcare System in Louisville, Kentucky, benchmarks its labor performance data against those of similar top-ranked hospitals. (We will discuss benchmarking in more detail later in the chapter.)

   Advantages: Data from other companies can provide a firm useful information about how it's performing relative to its competitors.

   Disadvantages: Input-price and input-quantity data from other companies are often not available or may not be comparable to a particular company's situation. Consider Costco, which pays hourly workers an average of more than \$20 per hour, well above the national average of \$11.39 for a retail sales worker. Also unusually, Costco provides the vast majority of its workforce with company-sponsored health care. The reason is Costco's focus on employee satisfaction, with the idea that a more pleasant workplace will lead to lower employee turnover and higher productivity.

3. **Standards developed by the firm itself.** A **standard** is a carefully determined price, cost, or quantity that is used as a benchmark for judging performance. Standards are usually expressed on a per-unit basis. Consider how Webb determines its direct manufacturing labor standards. Webb conducts engineering studies to obtain a detailed breakdown of the steps required to make a jacket. Each step is assigned a standard time based on work performed by a *skilled* worker using equipment operating in an *efficient* manner. Similarly, Webb determines the standard quantity of square yards of cloth based on what is required by a skilled operator to make a jacket.

   Advantages: Standard times (1) aim to exclude past inefficiencies and (2) take into account changes expected to occur in the budget period. An example of the latter would be a decision by Webb's managers to lease new, faster, and more accurate sewing machines. Webb would incorporate the resulting higher level of efficiency into the new standards it sets.

   Disdvantages: Because they are not based on realized benchmarks, the standards might not be achievable, and workers could get discouraged trying to meet them.

The term *standard* refers to many different things:

- A **standard input** is a carefully determined quantity of input, such as square yards of cloth or direct manufacturing labor-hours, required for one unit of output, such as a jacket.
- A **standard price** is a carefully determined price a company expects to pay for a unit of input. In the Webb example, the standard wage rate the firm expects to pay its operators is an example of a standard price of a direct manufacturing labor-hour.

- A **standard cost** is a carefully determined cost of a unit of output, such as the standard direct manufacturing labor cost of a jacket at Webb.

$$\text{Standard cost per output unit for each variable direct-cost input} = \text{Standard input allowed for one output unit} \times \text{Standard price per input unit}$$

Standard direct material cost per jacket: 2 square yards of cloth input allowed per output unit (jacket) manufactured, at $30 standard price per square yard

$$\text{Standard direct material cost per jacket} = 2 \text{ square yards} \times \$30 \text{ per square yard} = \$60$$

Standard direct manufacturing labor cost per jacket: 0.8 manufacturing labor-hour of input allowed per output unit manufactured, at $20 standard price per hour

$$\text{Standard direct manufacturing labor cost per jacket} = 0.8 \text{ labor-hour} \times \$20 \text{ per labor-hour} = \$16$$

How are the words *budget* and *standard* related? Budget is the broader term. To clarify, budgeted input prices, input quantities, and costs need *not* be based on standards. As we saw previously, they could be based on past data or competitive benchmarks. However, when standards *are* used to obtain budgeted input quantities and prices, the terms *standard* and *budget* are used interchangeably. The standard cost of each input required for one unit of output is determined by the standard quantity of the input required for one unit of output and the standard price per input unit. Notice how the standard-cost computations shown previously for direct materials and direct manufacturing labor result in the budgeted direct material cost per jacket of $60 and the budgeted direct manufacturing labor cost of $16 referred to earlier.

In its standard costing system, Webb uses standards that are attainable by operating efficiently but that allow for normal disruptions. A normal disruption could include, for example, a short delay in the receipt of materials needed to produce the jackets or a production hold-up because a piece of equipment needed a minor repair. An alternative is to set more-challenging standards that are more difficult to attain. Setting challenging standards can increase the motivation of employees and a firm's performance. However, if workers believe the standards are unachievable, they can become frustrated and the firm's performance could suffer.

DECISION POINT

What is a standard cost and what are its purposes?

Price Variances and Efficiency Variances for Direct-Cost Inputs

LEARNING OBJECTIVE 5

Compute price variances

...each price variance is the difference between an actual input price and a budgeted input price

and efficiency variances

...each efficiency variance is the difference between an actual input quantity and a budgeted input quantity for actual output

for direct-cost categories

Consider Webb's two direct-cost categories. The actual cost for each of these categories for the 10,000 jackets manufactured and sold in April 2017 is as follows:

Direct Materials Purchased and Used[4]	
1. Square yards of cloth purchased and used	22,200
2. Actual price incurred per square yard	$ 28
3. Direct material costs (22,200 × $28) [shown in Exhibit 2, column 1]	$621,600

Direct Manufacturing Labor Used	
1. Direct manufacturing labor-hours used	9,000
2. Actual price incurred per direct manufacturing labor-hour	$ 22
3. Direct manufacturing labor costs (9,000 × $22) [shown in Exhibit 2, column 1]	$198,000

Let's use the Webb Company data to illustrate the price variance and the efficiency variance for direct-cost inputs.

A **price variance** is the difference between actual price and budgeted price, multiplied by the actual input quantity, such as direct materials purchased. A price variance is sometimes called a **rate variance**, especially when it's used to describe the price variance for direct

[4] The Problem for Self-Study (pages 269–270) relaxes the assumption that the quantity of direct materials used equals the quantity of direct materials purchased.

manufacturing labor. An **efficiency variance** is the difference between the actual input quantity used (such as square yards of cloth) and the budgeted input quantity allowed for actual output, multiplied by budgeted price. An efficiency variance is sometimes called a **usage variance.** Let's explore price and efficiency variances in greater detail so we can see how managers use them.

Price Variances

The formula for computing the price variance is as follows:

$$\text{Price variance} = \left(\text{Actual price of input} - \text{Budgeted price of input}\right) \times \text{Actual quantity of input}$$

The price variances for Webb's two direct-cost categories are as follows:

Direct-Cost Category	(Actual price of input	− Budgeted price of input)	× Actual quantity of input	= Price Variance
Direct materials	($28 per sq. yard)	− $30 per sq. yard)	× 22,200 square yards	= $44,400 F
Direct manufacturing labor	($22 per hour	− $20 per hour)	× 9,000 hours	= $18,000 U

The direct materials price variance is favorable because the actual price of cloth is less than the budgeted price, resulting in an increase in operating income. The direct manufacturing labor price variance is unfavorable because the actual wage rate paid to labor is more than the budgeted rate, resulting in a decrease in operating income.

Managers should always consider a broad range of possible causes for a price variance. For example, Webb's favorable direct materials price variance could be due to one or more of the following:

- Webb's purchasing manager negotiated the direct materials prices more skillfully than was planned for in the budget.
- The purchasing manager switched to a lower-price supplier.
- The purchasing manager ordered larger quantities than the quantities budgeted, thereby obtaining quantity discounts.
- Direct materials prices decreased unexpectedly due to an oversupply of materials in the industry.
- The budgeted purchase prices of direct materials were set too high because managers did not carefully analyze market conditions.
- The purchasing manager negotiated favorable prices because he was willing to accept unfavorable terms on factors other than prices (such as agree to lower-quality material).

How Webb's managers respond to the direct materials price variance depends on what they believe caused it. For example, if they believe the purchasing manager received quantity discounts by ordering a larger amount of materials than budgeted, Webb could investigate whether the larger quantities resulted in higher storage costs for the firm. If the increase in storage and inventory holding costs exceeds the quantity discounts, purchasing in larger quantities is not beneficial. Some companies have reduced their materials storage areas to prevent their purchasing managers from ordering in larger quantities.

Efficiency Variance

For any actual level of output, the efficiency variance is the difference between the actual quantity of input used and the budgeted quantity of input allowed for that output level, multiplied by the budgeted input price:

$$\text{Efficiency variance} = \left(\text{Actual quantity of input used} - \text{Budgeted quantity of input allowed for actual output}\right) \times \text{Budgeted price of input}$$

The idea here is that, given a certain output level, a company is inefficient if it uses a larger quantity of input than budgeted. Conversely, a company is efficient if it uses a smaller input quantity than was budgeted for that output level.

The efficiency variances for each of Webb's direct-cost categories are as follows:

Direct-Cost Category	(Actual quantity of input used − Budgeted quantity of input allowed for actual output)	× Budgeted price of input	= Efficiency variance
Direct materials	[22,200 sq. yds. − (10,000 units × 2 sq. yds./unit)]	× $30 per sq. yard	
	= (22,200 sq. yds. − 20,000 sq. yds.)	× $30 per sq. yard	= $66,000 U
Direct manufacturing labor	[9,000 hours − (10,000 units × 0.8 hour/unit)]	× $20 per hour	
	= (9,000 hours − 8,000 hours)	× $20 per hour	= $20,000 U

The two manufacturing efficiency variances—the direct materials efficiency variance and the direct manufacturing labor efficiency variance—are each unfavorable. Why? Because given the firm's actual output, more of these inputs were used than were budgeted for. This lowered Webb's operating income.

As with price variances, there is a broad range of possible causes for these efficiency variances. For example, Webb's unfavorable efficiency variance for direct manufacturing labor could be because of one or more of the following:

- Webb's workers took longer to make each jacket because they worked more slowly or made poor-quality jackets that required reworking.
- Webb's personnel manager hired underskilled workers.
- Webb's production scheduler inefficiently scheduled work, resulting in more manufacturing labor time than budgeted being used per jacket.
- Webb's maintenance department did not properly maintain machines resulting in more manufacturing labor time than budgeted being used per jacket.
- Webb's budgeted time standards were too tight because the skill levels of employees and the environment in which they operated weren't accurately evaluated.

Suppose Webb's managers determine that the unfavorable variance is due to poor machine maintenance. Webb could then establish a team consisting of plant engineers and machine operators to develop a maintenance schedule to reduce future breakdowns and prevent adverse effects on labor time and product quality.[5]

Exhibit 3 provides an alternative way to calculate price and efficiency variances. It shows how the price variance and the efficiency variance subdivide the flexible-budget variance. Consider direct materials. The direct materials flexible-budget variance of $21,600 U is the difference between the actual costs incurred (actual input quantity × actual price) of $621,600 shown in column 1 and the flexible budget (budgeted input quantity allowed for actual output × budgeted price) of $600,000 shown in column 3. Column 2 (actual input quantity × budgeted price) is inserted between column 1 and column 3. Then:

- The difference between columns 1 and 2 is the price variance of $44,400 F. This price variance occurs because the same actual input quantity (22,200 sq. yds.) is multiplied by the *actual price* ($28) in column 1 and the *budgeted price* ($30) in column 2.
- The difference between columns 2 and 3 is the efficiency variance of $66,000 U This efficieny variance occurs because the same budgeted price ($30) is multiplied by the *actual input quantity* (22,200 sq. yds.) in column 2 and the *budgeted input quantity allowed for actual output* (20,000 sq. yds.) in column 3.
- The sum of the direct materials price variance, $44,400 F, and the direct materials efficiency variance, $66,000 U, equals the direct materials flexible budget variance, $21,600 U.

[5] When there are multiple inputs, such as different types of materials, that can be substituted for one another, the efficiency variance can be further decomposed into mix and yield variances. The appendix to this chapter describes how these variances are calculated.

EXHIBIT 3 Columnar Presentation of Variance Analysis: Direct Costs for Webb Company for April 2017[a]

Level 3 Analysis

	Actual Costs Incurred (Actual Input Quantity × Actual Price) (1)	Actual Input Quantity × Budgeted Price (2)	Flexible Budget (Budgeted Input Quantity Allowed for Actual Output × Budgeted Price) (3)
Direct Materials	(22,200 sq. yds. × $28/sq. yd.) $621,600	(22,200 sq. yds. × $30/sq. yd.) $666,000	(10,000 units × 2 sq. yds./unit × $30/sq. yd.) $600,000
Level 3	$44,400 F Price variance		$66,000 U Efficiency variance
Level 2	$21,600 U Flexible-budget variance		
Direct Manufacturing Labor	(9,000 hours × $22/hr.) $198,000	(9,000 hours × $20/hr.) $180,000	(10,000 units × 0.8 hr./unit × $20/hr.) $160,000
Level 3	$18,000 U Price variance		$20,000 U Efficiency variance
Level 2	$38,000 U Flexible-budget variance		

[a]F = favorable effect on operating income; U = unfavorable effect on operating income.

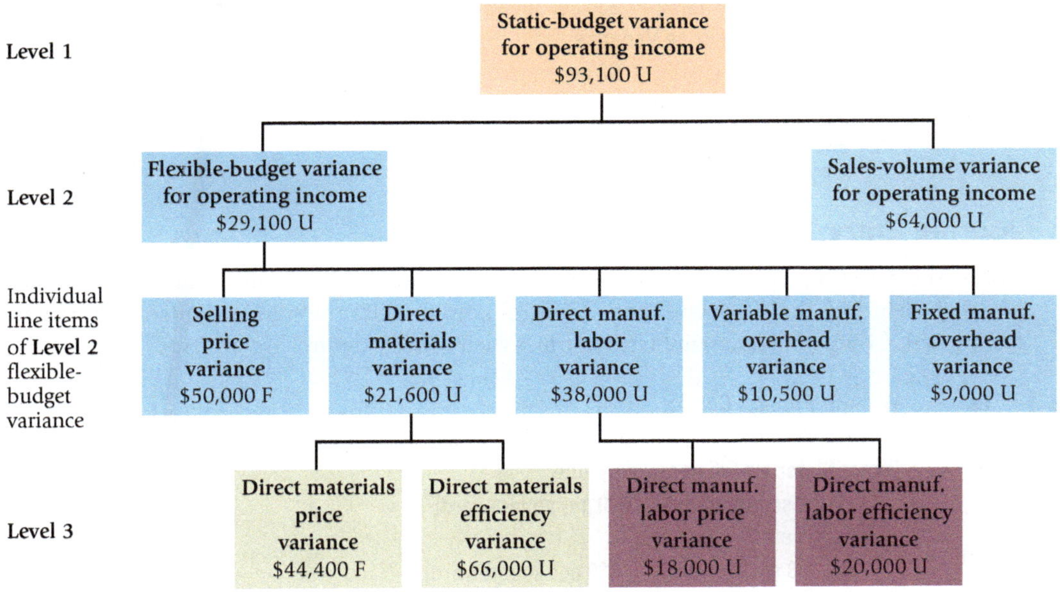

EXHIBIT 4

Summary of Level 1, 2, and 3 Variance Analyses

Exhibit 4 provides a summary of the different variances. Note how the variances at each higher level provide disaggregated and more detailed information for evaluating performance.

We now present Webb's journal entries under its standard costing system.

TRY IT! **4**

Jamie Draperies manufactures curtains. To complete a curtain, Jamie requires the following inputs:

Direct materials standard:	10 square yards at $5 per yard
Direct manufacturing labor standard:	5 hours at $10 per hour

During the second quarter, Jamie Draperies made 1,500 curtains and used 14,000 square yards of fabric costing $68,600. Direct manufacturing labor totaled 7,600 hours for $79,800.

a. Compute the direct materials price and efficiency variances for the quarter.
b. Compute the direct manufacturing labor price and efficiency variances for the quarter.

Journal Entries Using Standard Costs

We will now illustrate journal entries for Webb Company using standard costing. Our focus is on direct materials and direct manufacturing labor. All the numbers included in the following journal entries are found in Exhibit 3.

Note: In each of the following entries, unfavorable variances are always debits (they decrease operating income), and favorable variances are always credits (they increase operating income).

Journal Entry 1A

Isolate the direct materials price variance at the time the materials were purchased. This is done by increasing (debiting) the Direct Materials Control account by the standard price Webb established for purchasing the materials. This is the earliest time possible to isolate this variance.

1a.	Direct Materials Control		
	(22,200 square yards × $30 per square yard)	666,000	
	Direct Materials Price Variance		
	(22,200 square yards × $2 per square yard)		44,400
	Accounts Payable Control		
	(22,200 square yards × $28 per square yard)		621,600
	This records the direct materials purchased.		

Journal Entry 1B

Isolate the direct materials efficiency variance at the time the direct materials are used by increasing (debiting) the Work-in-Process Control account. Use the standard quantities allowed for the actual output units manufactured times their standard purchase prices.

1b.	Work-in-Process Control		
	(10,000 jackets × 2 yards per jacket × $30 per square yard)	600,000	
	Direct Materials Efficiency Variance		
	(2,200 square yards × $30 per square yard)	66,000	
	Direct Materials Control		
	(22,200 square yards × $30 per square yard)		666,000
	This records the direct materials used.		

Journal Entry 2

Isolate the direct manufacturing labor price variance and efficiency variance at the time the labor is used by increasing (debiting) the Work-in-Process Control by the standard hours and standard wage rates allowed for the actual units manufactured. Note that the Wages Payable Control account measures the actual amounts payable to workers based on the actual hours they worked and their actual wage rate.

2. Work-in-Process Control		
(10,000 jackets × 0.80 hour per jacket × $20 per hour)	160,000	
Direct Manufacturing Labor Price Variance		
(9,000 hours × $2 per hour)	18,000	
Direct Manufacturing Labor Efficiency Variance		
(1,000 hours × $20 per hour)	20,000	
Wages Payable Control		
(9,000 hours × $22 per hour)		198,000

This records the liability for Webb's direct manufacturing labor costs.

You have learned how standard costing and variance analysis help managers focus on areas not operating as expected. The journal entries here point to another advantage of standard costing systems: Standard costs simplify product costing. As each unit is manufactured, costs are assigned to it using the standard cost of direct materials, the standard cost of direct manufacturing labor, and the standard manufacturing overhead cost.

From the perspective of control, variances should be isolated at the earliest possible time. For example, the direct materials price variance should be calculated at the time materials are purchased. By doing so, managers can take corrective actions—such as trying to obtain cost reductions from the firm's current suppliers or obtaining price quotes from other potential suppliers—immediately when a large unfavorable variance is known rather than waiting until after the materials are used in production.

If the variance accounts are immaterial in amount at the end of the fiscal year, they are written off to the cost of goods sold. For simplicity, we assume that the balances in the different direct-cost variance accounts as of April 2017 are also the balances at the end of 2017 and are immaterial in total. Webb would record the following journal entry to write off the direct-cost variance accounts to the Cost of Goods Sold account.

Cost of Goods Sold	59,600	
Direct Materials Price Variance	44,400	
Direct Materials Efficiency Variance		66,000
Direct Manufacturing Labor Price Variance		18,000
Direct Manufacturing Labor Efficiency Variance		20,000

Alternatively, assuming Webb has inventories at the end of the fiscal year and the variances are material in their amounts, the variance accounts will be prorated among the cost of goods sold and various inventory accounts. For example, the Direct Materials Price Variance will be prorated among Materials Control, Work-in-Process Control, Finished Goods Control, and Cost of Goods Sold on the basis of the standard costs of direct materials in each account's ending balance. Direct Materials Efficiency Variance is prorated among Work-in-Process Control, Finished Goods Control, and Cost of Goods Sold on the basis of the direct material costs in each account's ending balance (after proration of the direct materials price variance).

Many accountants, industrial engineers, and managers argue that to the extent variances measure inefficiency during the year, they should be written off against income for that period instead of being prorated among inventories and the cost of goods sold. These people believe it's better to apply a combination of the write-off and proration methods for each individual variance. That way, unlike full proration, the firm doesn't end up carrying the costs of inefficiency as part of its inventoriable costs. Consider the efficiency variance: The portion of the variance due to avoidable inefficiencies should be written off to cost of goods sold. In contrast, the portion that is unavoidable should be prorated. Likewise, if a portion of the direct materials price variance is unavoidable because it is entirely caused by general market conditions, it too should be prorated.

Implementing Standard Costing

Standard costing provides valuable information that is used for the management and control of materials, labor, and other activities related to production.

Standard Costing and Information Technology

Both large and small firms are increasingly using computerized standard costing systems. For example, companies such as Sandoz, a maker of generic drugs, and Dell store standard prices and standard quantities in their computer systems. A bar code scanner records the receipt of materials, immediately costing each material using its stored standard price. The receipt of materials is then matched with the firm's purchase orders and recorded in accounts payable, and the direct material price variance is isolated.

The direct materials efficiency variance is calculated as output is completed by comparing the standard quantity of direct materials that should have been used with the computerized request for direct materials submitted by an operator on the production floor. Labor variances are calculated as employees log into production-floor terminals and punch in their employee numbers, start and end times, and the quantity of product they helped produce. Managers use this instantaneous feedback from variances to immediately detect and correct any cost-related problem.

Wide Applicability of Standard Costing

Manufacturing firms as well as firms in the service sector find standard costing to be a useful tool. Companies implementing total quality management programs use standard costing to control materials costs. Service-sector companies such as McDonald's are labor intensive and use standard costs to control labor costs. Companies that have implemented computer-integrated manufacturing (CIM), such as Toyota, use flexible budgeting and standard costing to manage activities such as materials handling and setups. The increased use of enterprise resource planning (ERP) systems has made it easy for firms to keep track of the standard, average, and actual costs of items in inventory and to make real-time assessments of variances. Managers use variance information to identify areas of the firm's manufacturing or purchasing process that most need attention.

DECISION POINT

Why should a company calculate price and efficiency variances?

Management's Use of Variances

LEARNING OBJECTIVE 6

Understand how managers use variances

. . . managers use variances to improve future performance

Managers and management accountants use variances to evaluate performance after decisions are implemented, to trigger organization learning, and to make continuous improvements. Variances serve as an early warning system to alert managers to existing problems or to prospective opportunities. When done well, variance analysis enables managers to evaluate the effectiveness of the actions and performance of personnel in the current period, as well as to fine-tune strategies for achieving improved performance in the future. Concepts in Action: Can Chipotle Wrap Up Its Materials-Cost Variance Increases? shows the importance to the fast casual dining giant of paying careful attention to variance analysis with respect to its direct costs.

Multiple Causes of Variances

To interpret variances correctly and make appropriate decisions based on them, managers need to recognize that variances can have multiple causes. Managers must not interpret variances in isolation of each other. The causes of variances in one part of the value chain can be

CONCEPTS IN ACTION

Can Chipotle Wrap Up Its Materials-Cost Variance Increases?

Patrick T. Fallon/Bloomberg/Getty Images

Along with burritos, Chipotle has cooked up profitable growth for many years. The company's build-your-own meal model and focus on organic and naturally raised ingredients successfully attracted millions of customers in the United States and beyond. As it continues to grow, Chipotle's success depends on the company's ability to wrap up keep its materials-cost variance increases.

For Chipotle, profitability depends on making each burrito at the lowest possible cost. In each Chipotle store, the two key direct costs are labor and materials costs. Labor costs include wages for restaurant managers and staff, along with benefits such as health insurance. Materials costs include the "critical seven" expensive food ingredients—steak, carnitas, barbacoa, chicken, cheese, guacamole, and sour cream—and items such as foil, paper bags, and plastic silverware.

To reduce labor costs, Chipotle often makes subtle recipe shifts to find the right balance between taste and cost. For example, it uses pre-chopped tomatoes shipped in plastic bags to make salsa because chopping tomatoes by hand takes too much labor. From 2010–2014, tweaks like that lowered Chipotle's labor costs from 24.7% of revenue to 22.0%. At the same time, however, materials costs rose from 30.5% of revenue to 34.6% due to the company's focus on naturally raised ingredients. Responsibly raised meat and fresh local produce cost Chipotle more than conventional ingredients, which reduces profitability. As a result, each Chipotle store aggressively manages portion control. While employees gladly oblige customers asking for extra rice, beans, or salsa, they are trained to be stingy with the "critical seven" food ingredients.

After E. coli and norovirus outbreaks in 2015, Chipotle made changes to its operations to improve food safety and reduce materials-cost variances. Cheese and some vegetables now arrive in stores pre-cut and shredded, while pork and barbacoa beef are now pre-cooked and delivered in sealed bags. With future profitability dependent on lowering its materials-cost variance, Chipotle's "food with integrity" will need to be managed very closely going forward.

Sources: Sarah Nassauer, "Inside Chipotle's Kitchen: What's Really Handmade," *The Wall Street Journal* (February 24, 2015); Candice Choi, "Chipotle Makes Food Prep Changes after E. Coli Scare," *Claims Journal* (December 28, 2015).

the result of decisions made in another part of the value chain. Consider an unfavorable direct materials efficiency variance on Webb's production line. Possible operational causes of this variance across the value chain of the company are:

1. Poor design of products or processes
2. Poor work on the production line because of underskilled workers or faulty machines
3. Inappropriate assignment of labor or machines to specific jobs
4. Congestion due to scheduling a large number of rush orders placed by Webb's sales representatives
5. Webb's cloth suppliers not manufacturing materials of uniformly high quality

Item 5 offers an even broader reason for the cause of the unfavorable direct materials efficiency variance by considering inefficiencies in the supply chain of companies—in this case, by the cloth suppliers for Webb's jackets. Whenever possible, managers must attempt to understand the root causes of the variances.

When to Investigate Variances

Because a standard is not a single measure but rather a range of acceptable input quantities, costs, output quantities, or prices, managers should expect small variances to arise. A variance within an acceptable range is considered to be an "in-control occurrence" and calls for no investigation or action by managers. So when do managers need to investigate variances?

Frequently, managers investigate variances based on subjective judgments or rules of thumb. For critical items, such as product defects, even a small variance can prompt an investigation. For other items, such as direct material costs, labor costs, and repair costs, companies generally have rules such as "investigate all variances exceeding $5,000 or 20% of the budgeted cost, whichever is lower." The idea is that a 4% variance in direct material costs of $1 million—a $40,000 variance—deserves more attention than a 15% variance in repair costs of $10,000—a $1,500 variance. In other words, variance analysis is subject to the same cost–benefit test as all other phases of a management control system.

Using Variances for Performance Measurement

Managers often use variance analysis when evaluating the performance of their employees or business units. Two attributes of performance are commonly evaluated:

1. **Effectiveness**: the degree to which a predetermined objective or target is met, such as the sales, market share, and customer satisfaction ratings of Starbucks' VIA® Ready Brew line of instant coffees.
2. **Efficiency**: the relative amount of inputs used to achieve a given output level. For example, the smaller the quantity of Arabica beans used to make a given number of VIA packets or the greater the number of VIA packets made from a given quantity of beans, the greater the efficiency.

As we discussed earlier, it is important to understand the causes of a variance before using it for performance evaluation. Suppose a purchasing manager for Starbucks has just negotiated a deal that results in a favorable price variance for direct materials. The deal could have achieved a favorable variance for any or all of the following reasons:

1. The purchasing manager bargained effectively with suppliers.
2. The purchasing manager secured a discount for buying in bulk with fewer purchase orders. (However, buying larger quantities than necessary for the short run resulted in excessive inventory.)
3. The purchasing manager accepted a bid from the lowest-priced supplier without fully checking the supplier's quality-monitoring procedures.

If the purchasing manager's performance is evaluated solely on price variances, then the evaluation will be positive. Reason 1 would support this conclusion: The purchasing manager bargained effectively. Reasons 2 and 3, buying in bulk or buying without checking the supplier's quality-monitoring procedures, will lead to short-run gains. But should these lead to a positive evaluation for the purchasing manager? Not necessarily. These short-run gains could be offset by higher inventory storage costs or higher inspection costs and defect rates. Starbucks may ultimately lose more money because of reasons 2 and 3 than it gains from the favorable price variance.

Bottom line: Managers should not automatically interpret a favorable variance as "good news" or assume it means their subordinates performed well.

Firms benefit from variance analysis because it highlights individual aspects of performance. However, if any single performance measure (for example, achieving a certain labor efficiency variance or a certain consumer rating) is overemphasized, managers will tend to make decisions that will cause the particular performance measure to look good. These actions may conflict with the company's overall goals, inhibiting the goals from being achieved. This faulty perspective on performance usually arises when top management designs a performance evaluation and reward system that does not emphasize total company objectives.

Organization Learning

The goal of variance analysis is for managers to understand why variances arise, to learn, and to improve their firm's future performance. For instance, to reduce the unfavorable direct materials efficiency variance, Webb's managers may attempt to improve the design of its jackets, the commitment of its workers to do the job right the first time, and the quality of the materials. Sometimes an unfavorable direct materials efficiency variance may signal a need to change the strategy related to a product, perhaps because it cannot be made at a low enough cost. Variance analysis should not be used to "play the blame game" (find someone to blame for every unfavorable variance) but to help managers learn about what happened and how to perform better in the future.

Companies need to strike a delicate balance between using variances to evaluate the performance of managers and employees and improve learning within the organization. If the performance evaluation aspect is overemphasized, managers will focus on setting and meeting targets that are easy to attain rather than targets that are challenging, require creativity and resourcefulness, and result in continuous improvement. For example, Webb's manufacturing manager will prefer an easy standard that allows workers ample time to manufacture a jacket. But that will provide the manufacturing department little incentive to improve processes and identify methods to reduce production times and costs. Alternatively, the manufacturing manager might urge workers to produce jackets within the time allowed, even if this leads to poorer quality jackets being produced, which would later hurt revenues. If variance analysis is seen as a way to promote learning within the organization, negative effects such as these can be minimized.

Continuous Improvement

Managers can also use variance analysis to create a virtuous cycle of continuous improvement. How? By repeatedly identifying the causes of variances, taking corrective actions, and evaluating the results. Improvement opportunities are often easier to identify when the company first produces a product. Once managers identify easy improvements, much more ingenuity may be required to identify successive ones. Some companies use Kaizen budgeting to specifically target reductions in budgeted costs over successive periods. The advantage of Kaizen budgeting is that it makes continuous improvement goals explicit.

It is important to make sure though that continuous improvement goals are implemented thoughtfully. In a research or design setting, injecting too much discipline and focusing on incremental improvement may well dissuade creativity and truly innovative approaches. An overt reliance on gaining efficiencies should not deter employees from a willingness to take risky approaches or from challenging the basic assumptions of how business is carried out.

Financial and Nonfinancial Performance Measures

Almost all companies use a combination of financial and nonfinancial performance measures for planning and control rather than relying exclusively on either type of measure. To control a production process, supervisors cannot wait for an accounting report with variances reported in dollars. Instead, timely nonfinancial performance measures are frequently used for control purposes. For example, Nissan and many other manufacturers display real-time defect rates and production levels on large screens throughout their plants for workers and managers to see.

In Webb's cutting room, cloth is laid out and cut into pieces, which are then matched and assembled. Managers exercise control in the cutting room by observing workers and by focusing on *nonfinancial measures*, such as number of square yards of cloth used to produce 1,000 jackets or the percentage of jackets started and completed without requiring any rework. Webb's production workers find these nonfinancial measures easy to understand. Webb's managers also use *financial measures* to evaluate the overall cost efficiency with which operations are being run and to help guide decisions about, say, changing the mix of inputs used in manufacturing jackets. Financial measures are critical in a company because they indicate the economic impact of diverse physical activities. This knowledge allows managers to make trade-offs, such as increasing the costs of one physical activity (say, cutting) to reduce the costs of another physical measure (say, defects).

DECISION POINT

How do managers use variances?

LEARNING OBJECTIVE 7

Describe benchmarking and explain its role in cost management

. . . benchmarking compares actual performance against the best levels of performance

Benchmarking and Variance Analysis

Webb Company based its budgeted amounts on analysis of its own operations. We now turn to the situation in which companies develop standards based on the operations of other companies. **Benchmarking** is the continuous process of comparing your firm's performance levels against the best levels of performance in competing companies or in companies having similar processes. When benchmarks are used as standards, managers and management accountants know that the company will be competitive in the marketplace if it can meet or beat those standards.

Companies develop benchmarks and calculate variances on items that are the most important to their businesses. A common unit of measurement used to compare the efficiency of airlines is cost per available seat mile. Available seat mile (ASM) is a measure of airline size and equals the total seats in a plane multiplied by the distance the plane traveled. Consider the cost per available seat mile for United. Assume United uses data from each of six competing U.S. airlines in its benchmark cost comparisons. Summary data are in Exhibit 5. The benchmark companies are in alphabetical order in column A. Also reported in Exhibit 5 are operating cost per ASM, operating revenue per ASM, operating income per ASM, fuel cost per ASM, labor cost per ASM, and total available seat miles for each airline. The recovery of the travel industry from the recession induced by the financial crisis as well as the benefits of lower fuel costs and greater industry consolidation are evident in the fact that all of the airlines have positive levels of operating income.

How well did United manage its costs? The answer depends on which specific benchmark is being used for comparison. United's actual operating cost of 13.65 cents per ASM is above the average operating cost of 12.78 cents per ASM of the six other airlines. Moreover, United's operating cost per ASM is 23.3% higher than Alaska Airways, the lowest-cost competitor at 11.07 cents per ASM [(13.65 − 11.07) ÷ 11.07 = 0.233]. So why is United's operating cost per ASM so high? Columns E and F suggest that both fuel cost and labor cost are possible reasons. These benchmarking data alert management at United that it needs to become more efficient in its use of both material and labor inputs to become cost competitive.

It can be difficult for firms to find appropriate benchmarks such as those in Exhibit 5. Many companies purchase benchmark data from consulting firms. Another problem is ensuring the benchmark numbers are comparable. In other words, there needs to be an "apples to apples" comparison. Differences can exist across companies in their strategies, inventory costing methods, depreciation methods, and so on. For example, JetBlue serves fewer cities and

EXHIBIT 5 Available Seat Mile (ASM) Benchmark Comparison of United Airlines with Six Other Airlines

	A	B	C	D	E	F	G
1–3	Airline	Operating Cost (cents per ASM) (1)	Operating Revenue (cents per ASM) (2)	Operating Income (cents per ASM) (3) = (2) – (1)	Fuel Cost (cents per ASM) (4)	Labor Cost (cents per ASM) (5)	Total ASMs (Millions) (6)
4							
5	United Airlines	13.65	13.66	0.01	4.30	4.27	214,061
6	Airlines used as benchmarks:						
7	Alaska Airlines	11.07	13.13	2.06	3.60	3.45	32,434
8	American Airlines	13.76	14.13	0.37	4.40	3.80	157,598
9	Delta Airlines	14.98	15.45	0.47	5.50	4.41	212,235
10	JetBlue Airways	11.69	12.47	0.78	4.10	3.04	45,200
11	Southwest Airlines	12.42	14.13	1.71	3.90	4.35	131,259
12	U.S. Airways	12.75	14.42	1.67	4.10	3.75	79,913
13	Average of airlines						
14	used as benchmarks	12.78	13.96	1.18	4.27	3.80	109,773
15							
16	*Source: 2014 data from the MIT Global Airline Industry Program*						

flies mostly long-haul routes compared with United, which serves almost all major U.S. cities and several international cities and flies both long-haul and short-haul routes. Southwest Airlines differs from United because it specializes in short-haul direct flights and offers fewer services on board its planes. Because United's strategy is different from the strategies of JetBlue and Southwest, one might expect its cost per ASM to be different, too. United's strategy is more comparable to the strategies of American and Delta. Note that its costs per ASM are relatively more competitive with these airlines. But United competes head to head with Alaska, JetBlue, and Southwest in several cities and markets, so it needs to benchmark against these carriers as well.

United's management accountants can use benchmarking data to address several questions. How do factors such as plane size and type or the duration of flights affect the cost per ASM? Do airlines differ in their fixed cost/variable cost structures? To what extent can United's performance be improved by rerouting flights, using different types of aircraft on different routes, or changing the frequency or timing of specific flights? What explains revenue differences per ASM across airlines? Is it differences in the service quality passengers perceive or differences in an airline's competitive power at specific airports? Management accountants are more valuable to managers when they use benchmarking data to provide insight into *why* costs or revenues differ across companies or within plants of the same company, as distinguished from simply reporting the magnitude of the differences.

DECISION POINT

What is benchmarking and why is it useful?

PROBLEM FOR SELF-STUDY

O'Shea Company manufactures ceramic vases. It uses its standard costing system when developing its flexible-budget amounts. In September 2017, O'Shea produced 2,000 finished units. The following information relates to its two direct manufacturing cost categories: direct materials and direct manufacturing labor.

Direct materials used were 4,400 kilograms (kg). The standard direct materials input allowed for one output unit is 2 kilograms at $15 per kilogram. O'Shea purchased 5,000 kilograms of materials at $16.50 per kilogram, a total of $82,500. (This Problem for Self-Study illustrates how to calculate direct materials variances when the quantity of materials purchased in a period differs from the quantity of materials used in that period.)

Actual direct manufacturing labor-hours were 3,250, at a total cost of $66,300. Standard manufacturing labor time allowed is 1.5 hours per output unit, and the standard direct manufacturing labor cost is $20 per hour.

Required

1. Calculate the direct materials price variance and efficiency variance and the direct manufacturing labor price variance and efficiency variance. Base the direct materials price variance on a flexible budget for *actual quantity purchased*, but base the direct materials efficiency variance on a flexible budget for *actual quantity used*.
2. Prepare journal entries for a standard costing system that isolates variances at the earliest possible time.

Solution

1. Exhibit 6 shows how the columnar presentation of variances introduced in Exhibit 3 can be adjusted for the difference in timing between purchase and use of materials. Note, in particular, the two sets of computations in column 2 for direct materials—the $75,000 for direct materials purchased and the $66,000 for direct materials used. The direct materials price variance is calculated on purchases so that managers responsible for the purchase can immediately identify and isolate reasons for the variance and initiate any desired corrective action. The efficiency variance is the responsibility of the production manager, so this variance is identified only at the time materials are used.

EXHIBIT 6 Columnar Presentation of Variance Analysis for O'Shea Company: Direct Materials and Direct Manufacturing Labor for September 2017[a]

Level 3 Analysis

	Actual Costs Incurred (Actual Input Quantity × Actual Price) (1)	Actual Input Quantity × Budgeted Price (2)	Flexible Budget (Budgeted Input Quantity Allowed for Actual Output × Budgeted Price) (3)
Direct Materials	(5,000 kg × \$16.50/kg) \$82,500	(5,000 kg × \$15.00/kg) \$75,000 / (4,400 kg × \$15.00/kg) \$66,000	(2,000 units × 2 kg/unit × \$15.00/kg) \$60,000
	\$7,500 U Price variance (1)–(2)		\$6,000 U Efficiency variance (2)–(3)
Direct Manufacturing Labor	(3,250 hrs. × \$20.40/hr.) \$66,300	(3,250 hrs. × \$20.00/hr.) \$65,000	(2,000 units × 1.50 hrs./unit × \$20.00/hr.) \$60,000
	\$1,300 U Price variance (1)–(2)		\$5,000 U Efficiency variance (2)–(3)

[a]F = favorable effect on operating income; U = unfavorable effect on operating income.

2.

Materials Control (5,000 kg × \$15 per kg)	75,000	
Direct Materials Price Variance (5,000 kg × \$1.50 per kg)	7,500	
Accounts Payable Control (5,000 kg × \$16.50 per kg)		82,500
Work-in-Process Control (2,000 units × 2 kg per unit × \$15 per kg)	60,000	
Direct Materials Efficiency Variance (400 kg × \$15 per kg)	6,000	
Materials Control (4,400 kg × \$15 per kg)		66,000
Work-in-Process Control (2,000 units × 1.5 hours per unit × \$20 per hour)	60,000	
Direct Manufacturing Labor Price Variance (3,250 hours × \$0.40 per hour)	1,300	
Direct Manufacturing Labor Efficiency Variance (250 hours × \$20 per hour)	5,000	
Wages Payable Control (3,250 hours × \$20.40 per hour)		66,300

Note: All the variances are debits because they are unfavorable and therefore reduce operating income.

DECISION POINTS

The following question-and-answer format summarizes the chapter's learning objectives. Each decision presents a key question related to a learning objective. The guidelines are the answer to that question.

Decision	Guidelines
1. What are static budgets and static-budget variances?	A static budget is based on the level of output planned at the start of the budget period. The static-budget variance is the difference between the actual result and the corresponding budgeted amount in the static budget.
2. How can managers develop a flexible budget, and why is it useful to do so?	A flexible budget is adjusted (flexed) to recognize the actual output level of the budget period. Managers use a three-step procedure to develop a flexible budget. When all costs are either variable or fixed with respect to output, these three steps require only information about the budgeted selling price, budgeted variable cost per output unit, budgeted fixed costs, and actual quantity of output units. Flexible budgets help managers gain more insight into the causes of variances than is available from static budgets.

Decision	Guidelines
3. How are flexible-budget and sales-volume variances calculated?	The static-budget variance can be subdivided into a flexible-budget variance (the difference between the actual result and the corresponding flexible-budget amount) and a sales-volume variance (the difference between the flexible-budget amount and the corresponding static-budget amount).
4. What is a standard cost and what are its purposes?	A standard cost is a carefully determined cost used as a benchmark for judging performance. The purposes of a standard cost are to exclude past inefficiencies and to take into account changes expected to occur in the budget period.
5. Why should a company calculate price and efficiency variables?	The computation of price and efficiency variances helps managers gain insight into two different—but not independent—aspects of performance. The price variance focuses on the difference between the actual input price and the budgeted input price. The efficiency variance focuses on the difference between the actual quantity of input and the budgeted quantity of input allowed for actual output.
6. How do managers use variances?	Managers use variances for control, decision making, performance evaluation, organization learning, and continuous improvement. When using variances for these purposes, managers should consider several variances together rather than focusing only on an individual variance.
7. What is benchmarking and why is it useful?	Benchmarking is the continuous process of comparing your firm's performance against the best levels of performance in competing companies or companies with similar processes. Benchmarking measures how well a company and its managers are doing in comparison to other organizations.

APPENDIX

Mix and Yield Variances for Substitutable Inputs

The Webb Company example illustrates how to calculate price and efficiency variances for production inputs when there is a single form of each input. Webb used a single material (cloth) and a single type of direct labor. But what if managers have leeway in combining and substituting inputs? For example, Del Monte Foods can combine material inputs (such as pineapples, cherries, and grapes) in varying proportions for its cans of fruit cocktail. Within limits, these individual fruits are *substitutable inputs* in making the fruit cocktail.

We illustrate how the efficiency variance discussed in this chapter can be subdivided into variances that highlight the financial impact of input mix and input yield when inputs are substitutable. We consider a variation of the Webb Company example. For simplicity, we focus on direct manufacturing labor inputs and substitution among three of these inputs. The same approach can also be used to examine substitutable direct materials inputs.

Mode Company also manufactures jackets but, unlike Webb, employs workers of different skill (or experience) levels. Workers are of Low, Medium, or High skill. Workers with greater skill levels focus on the more complicated aspects of the jacket, such as adding darts and fancy seam lines. They are compensated accordingly. Mode's production standards require 0.80 labor-hours to produce 1 jacket; 50% of the hours are budgeted to be Low skill,

30% Medium, and 20% High. The direct manufacturing labor inputs budgeted to produce 1 jacket are as follows:

0.40 (50% of 0.80) hours of Low at $12 per hour	$ 4.80
0.24 (30% of 0.80) hours of Medium at $20 per hour	4.80
0.16 (20% of 0.80) hours of High at $40 per hour	6.40
Total budgeted direct manufacturing labor cost of 1 jacket	$16.00

With an expected $16 in labor cost for a jacket that requires 0.80 labor hours, note that the production standards imply a weighted average labor rate of $20 per hour ($16 ÷ 0.80 hours).

In April 2017, Mode produced 10,000 jackets using a total of 9,000 labor-hours. The breakdown for this input usage is as follows:

4,500	hours of Low at actual cost of $12 per hour	$ 54,000
3,150	hours of Medium at actual cost of $26 per hour	81,900
1,350	hours of High at actual cost of $46 per hour	62,100
9,000	hours of direct manufacturing labor	198,000
Budgeted cost of 8,000 direct manufacturing labor-hours at $20 per hour		160,000
Flexible-budget variance for direct manufacturing labor		$ 38,000 U

Direct Manufacturing Labor Price and Efficiency Variances

Mode's flexible budget and actual costs for direct manufacturing labor are identical to those in the Webb Company example. As a result, Mode has the same flexible-budget variance for direct manufacturing labor ($38,000). The breakdown of this amount into price and efficiency variances is different, however, because Mode employs three categories of substitutable direct manufacturing labor inputs.

Exhibit 7 presents in columnar format the analysis of Mode's flexible-budget variance for direct manufacturing labor. The labor price and efficiency variances are calculated separately for each category of direct manufacturing labor and then added together. The variance analysis prompts Webb to investigate the unfavorable price and efficiency variances in each category. Why did it pay more for certain types of labor and use more hours than it had budgeted? Were actual wage rates higher, in general, or could the personnel department have negotiated lower rates? Did the additional labor costs result from inefficiencies in processing?

EXHIBIT 7 Direct Manufacturing Labor Price and Efficiency Variances for Mode Company for April 2017[a]

	Actual Costs Incurred: Actual Input Quantity × Actual Price (1)	Actual Input Quantity × Budgeted Price (2)	Flexible Budget: Budgeted Input Quantity Allowed for Actual Output × Budgeted Price (3)
Low:	4,500 × $12 = $ 54,000	4,500 × $12 = $ 54,000	4,000 × $12 = $ 48,000
Medium:	3,150 × $26 = 81,900	3,150 × $20 = 63,000	2,400 × $20 = 48,000
High:	1,350 × $46 = 62,100	1,350 × $40 = 54,000	1,600 × $40 = 64,000
	$198,000	$171,000	$160,000

Level 3: $27,000 U Price variance (between columns 1 and 2); $11,000 U Efficiency variance (between columns 2 and 3)

Level 2: $38,000 U Flexible-budget variance (between columns 1 and 3)

[a]F = favorable effect on operating income; U = unfavorable effect on operating income.

Direct Manufacturing Labor Mix and Yield Variances

Managers sometimes have discretion to substitute one input for another. The manager of Mode's operations has some leeway in combining Low, Medium, and High skill workers without affecting the quality of the jackets. We will assume that to maintain quality, mix percentages of each type of labor can only vary up to 5% from standard mix. For example, the percentage of Low skill labor in the mix can vary between 45% and 55% (50% ± 5%). When inputs are substitutable, direct manufacturing labor efficiency improvement relative to budgeted costs can come from two sources: (1) using a cheaper mix to produce a given quantity of output, measured by the mix variance, and (2) using less input to achieve a given quantity of output, measured by the yield variance.

Holding actual total quantity of all direct manufacturing labor inputs used constant, the total **direct manufacturing labor mix variance** is the difference between:

1. budgeted cost for actual mix of actual total quantity of direct manufacturing labor used and
2. budgeted cost of budgeted mix of actual total quantity of direct manufacturing labor used.

Holding budgeted input mix constant, the **direct manufacturing labor yield variance** is the difference between:

1. budgeted cost of direct manufacturing labor based on actual total quantity of direct manufacturing labor used and
2. flexible-budget cost of direct manufacturing labor based on budgeted total quantity of direct manufacturing labor allowed for actual output produced.

Exhibit 8 presents the direct manufacturing labor mix and yield variances for Mode Company. Note that column (1) in this exhibit is identical to column (2) in Exhibit 7, and column (3) is the same in both exhibits.

Direct Manufacturing Labor Mix Variance

The total direct manufacturing labor mix variance is the sum of the direct manufacturing labor mix variances for each input:

$$\begin{array}{c}\text{Direct}\\ \text{labor}\\ \text{mix variance}\\ \text{for each input}\end{array} = \begin{array}{c}\text{Actual total}\\ \text{quantity of all}\\ \text{direct labor}\\ \text{inputs used}\end{array} \times \left(\begin{array}{c}\text{Actual}\\ \text{direct labor}\\ \text{input mix}\\ \text{percentage}\end{array} - \begin{array}{c}\text{Budgeted}\\ \text{direct labor}\\ \text{input mix}\\ \text{percentage}\end{array}\right) \times \begin{array}{c}\text{Budegeted}\\ \text{price of}\\ \text{direct labor}\\ \text{input}\end{array}$$

EXHIBIT 8 Direct Manufacturing Labor Yield and Mix Variances for Mode Company for April 2017[a]

	Actual Total Quantity of All Inputs Used × Actual Input Mix × Budgeted Price (1)	Actual Total Quantity of All Inputs Used × Budgeted Input Mix × Budgeted Price (2)	Flexible Budget: Budgeted Total Quantity of All Inputs Allowed for Actual Output × Budgeted Input Mix × Budgeted Price (3)
Low:	9,000 × 0.50 × $12 = $ 54,000	9,000 × 0.50 × $12 = $ 54,000	8,000 × 0.50 × $12 = $ 48,000
Medium:	9,000 × 0.35 × $20 = 63,000	9,000 × 0.30 × $20 = 54,000	8,000 × 0.30 × $20 = 48,000
High:	9,000 × 0.15 × $40 = 54,000	9,000 × 0.20 × $40 = 72,000	8,000 × 0.20 × $40 = 64,000
	$171,000	$180,000	$160,000

Level 4: $9,000 F Mix variance (between (1) and (2)); $20,000 U Yield variance (between (2) and (3))

Level 3: $11,000 U Efficiency variance (between (1) and (3))

[a]F = favorable effect on operating income; U = unfavorable effect on operating income.

The direct manufacturing labor mix variances are as follows:

Low:	9,000 hours × (0.50 − 0.50) × $12 per hour = 9,000 × 0.00 × $12 =	$ 0
Medium:	9,000 hours × (0.35 − 0.30) × $20 per hour = 9,000 × 0.05 × $20 =	9,000 U
High:	9,000 hours × (0.15 − 0.20) × $40 per hour = 9,000 × −0.05 × $40 =	18,000 F
Total direct manufacturing labor mix variance		$ 9,000 F

The total direct manufacturing labor mix variance is favorable because, relative to the budgeted mix, Mode substitutes 5% of the cheaper Medium skill labor for 5% of the more-expensive High skill.

Direct Manufacturing Labor Yield Variance

The yield variance is the sum of the direct manufacturing labor yield variances for each input:

$$\begin{array}{c}\text{Direct}\\\text{labor}\\\text{yield variance}\\\text{for each input}\end{array} = \left(\begin{array}{c}\text{Actual total}\\\text{quantity of}\\\text{all direct}\\\text{labor}\\\text{inputs used}\end{array} - \begin{array}{c}\text{Budgeted total}\\\text{quantity of all}\\\text{direct labor}\\\text{input allowed}\\\text{for actual output}\end{array}\right) \times \begin{array}{c}\text{Budgeted}\\\text{direct labor}\\\text{input mix}\\\text{percentage}\end{array} \times \begin{array}{c}\text{Budegeted}\\\text{price of}\\\text{direct labor}\\\text{input}\end{array}$$

The direct manufacturing labor yield variances are as follows:

Low:	(9,000 − 8,000) hours × 0.50 × $12 per hour = 1,000 × 0.50 × $12 =	$ 6,000 U
Medium:	(9,000 − 8,000) hours × 0.30 × $20 per hour = 1,000 × 0.30 × $20 =	6,000 U
High:	(9,000 − 8,000) hours × 0.20 × $40 per hour = 1,000 × 0.20 × $40 =	8,000 U
Total direct manufacturing labor yield variance		$20,000 U

The total direct manufacturing labor yield variance is unfavorable because Mode used 9,000 hours of labor rather than the 8,000 hours that it should have used to produce 10,000 jackets. The budgeted cost per hour of labor in the budgeted mix is $20 per hour. The unfavorable yield variance represents the budgeted cost of using 1,000 more hours of direct manufacturing labor, (9,000 − 8,000) hours × $20 per hour = $20,000 U. Mode would want to investigate reasons for this unfavorable yield variance. For example, did the substitution of the cheaper Medium skill for High skill labor, which resulted in the favorable mix variance, also cause the unfavorable yield variance?

The direct manufacturing labor variances computed in Exhibits 7 and 8 can be summarized as follows:

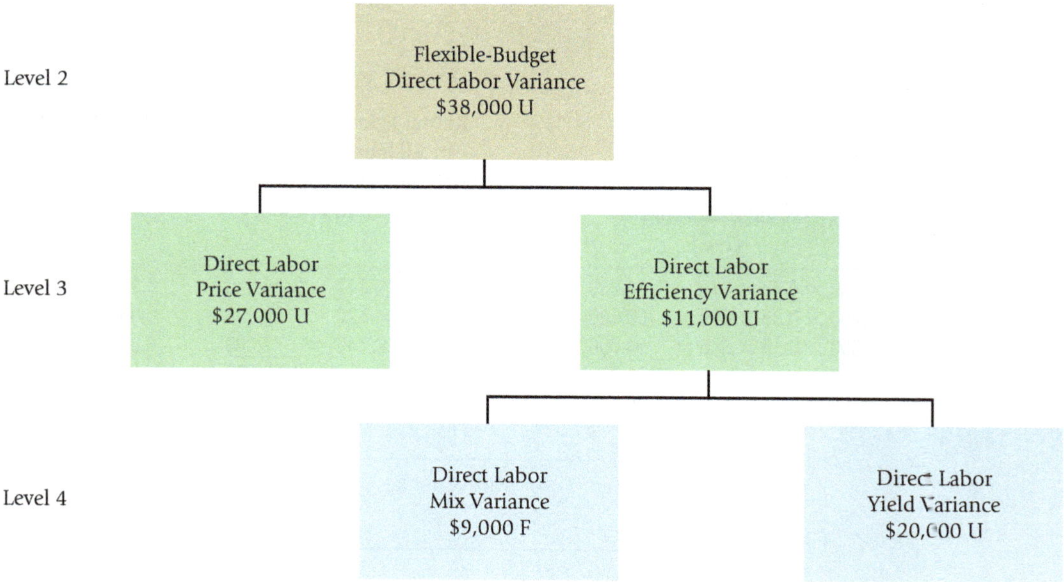

TERMS TO LEARN

This chapter and the Glossary at the end of the chapter contain definitions of the following important terms:

benchmarking
budgeted performance
direct manufacturing labor mix variance
direct manufacturing labor yield variance
effectiveness
efficiency
efficiency variance
favorable variance
flexible budget
flexible-budget variance
management by exception
price variance
rate variance
sales-volume variance
selling-price variance
standard
standard cost
standard input
standard price
static budget
static-budget variance
unfavorable variance
usage variance
variance

ASSIGNMENT MATERIAL

Questions

MyAccountingLab

1 What is the relationship between management by exception and variance analysis?

2 What are two possible sources of information a company might use to compute the budgeted amount in variance analysis?

3 Distinguish between a favorable variance and an unfavorable variance.

4 What is the key difference between a static budget and a flexible budget?

5 Why might managers find a flexible-budget analysis more informative than a static-budget analysis?

6 Describe the steps in developing a flexible budget.

7 List four reasons for using standard costs.

8 How might a manager gain insight into the causes of a flexible-budget variance for direct materials?

9 List three causes of a favorable direct materials price variance.

10 Describe three reasons for an unfavorable direct manufacturing labor efficiency variance.

11 How does variance analysis help in continuous improvement?

12 Why might an analyst examining variances in the production area look beyond that business function for explanations of those variances?

13 Comment on the following statement made by a plant manager: "Meetings with my plant accountant are frustrating. All he wants to do is pin the blame on someone for the many variances he reports."

14 When inputs are substitutable, how can the direct materials efficiency variance be decomposed further to obtain useful information?

15 "Benchmarking against other companies enables a company to identify the lowest-cost producer. This amount should become the performance measure for next year." Do you agree?

Multiple-Choice Questions

MyAccountingLab

In partnership with: BECKER PROFESSIONAL EDUCATION

16 Metal Shelf Company's standard cost for raw materials is $4.00 per pound and it is expected that each metal shelf uses two pounds of material. During October Year 2, 25,000 pounds of materials are purchased from a new supplier for $97,000 and 13,000 shelves are produced using 27,000 pounds of materials. Which statement is a possible explanation concerning the direct materials variances?

a. The production department had to use more materials since the quality of the materials was inferior.
b. The purchasing manager paid more than expected for materials.
c. Production workers were more efficient than anticipated.
d. The overall materials variance is positive; no further analysis is necessary.

17 All of the following statements regarding standards are accurate except:

a. Standards allow management to budget at a per-unit level.
b. Ideal standards account for a minimal amount of normal spoilage.
c. Participative standards usually take longer to implement than authoritative standards.
d. Currently attainable standards take into account the level of training available to employees.

18 Amalgamated Manipulation Manufacturing's (AMM) standards anticipate that there will be 3 pounds of raw material used for every unit of finished goods produced. AMM began the month of May with 5,000 pounds of raw material, purchased 15,000 pounds for $19,500 and ended the month with 4,000 pounds on hand. The company produced 5,000 units of finished goods. The company estimates standard costs at $1.50 per pound. The materials price and efficiency variances for the month of May were:

Price Variance	Efficiency Variance
1. $3,000 U	$1,500 F
2. $3,000 F	$ 0
3. $3,000 F	$1,500 U
4. $3,200 F	$1,500 U

19 Atlantic Company has a manufacturing facility in Brooklyn that manufactures robotic equipment for the auto industry. For Year 1, Atlantic collected the following information from its main production line:

Actual quantity purchased	200 units
Actual quantity used	110 units
Units standard quantity	100 units
Actual price paid	$ 8 per unit
Standard price	$ 10 per unit

Atlantic isolates price variances at the time of purchase. What is the materials price variance for Year 1?

1. $400 favorable.
2. $400 unfavorable.
3. $220 favorable.
4. $220 unfavorable.

20 Basix Inc. calculates direct manufacturing labor variances and has the following information:

Actual hours worked: 200
Standard hours: 250
Actual rate per hour: $12
Standard rate per hour: $10

Given the information above, which of the following is correct regarding direct manufacturing labor variances?

a. The price and efficiency variances are favorable.
b. The price and efficiency variances are unfavorable.
c. The price variance is favorable, while the efficiency variance is unfavorable.
d. The price variance is unfavorable, while the efficiency variance is favorable.

MyAccountingLab

Exercises

21 **Flexible budget.** Sweeney Enterprises manufactures tires for the Formula I motor racing circuit. For August 2017, it budgeted to manufacture and sell 3,600 tires at a variable cost of $71 per tire and total fixed costs of $55,000. The budgeted selling price was $114 per tire. Actual results in August 2017 were 3,500 tires manufactured and sold at a selling price of $116 per tire. The actual total variable costs were $280,000, and the actual total fixed costs were $51,000.

Required

1. Prepare a performance report (akin to Exhibit 2) that uses a flexible budget and a static budget.
2. Comment on the results in requirement 1.

22 **Flexible budget.** Bryant Company's budgeted prices for direct materials, direct manufacturing labor, and direct marketing (distribution) labor per attaché case are $43, $6, and $13, respectively. The president is pleased with the following performance report:

	Actual Costs	Static Budget	Variance
Direct materials	$438,000	$473,000	$35,000 F
Direct manufacturing labor	63,600	66,000	2,400 F
Direct marketing (distribution) labor	133,500	143,000	9,500 F

Actual output was 10,000 attaché cases. Assume all three direct-cost items shown are variable costs.

Required

Is the president's pleasure justified? Prepare a revised performance report that uses a flexible budget and a static budget.

23 **Flexible-budget preparation and analysis.** Bank Management Printers, Inc., produces luxury checkbooks with three checks and stubs per page. Each checkbook is designed for an individual customer and is ordered through the customer's bank. The company's operating budget for September 2017 included these data:

Number of checkbooks	15,000
Selling price per book	$ 20
Variable cost per book	$ 8
Fixed costs for the month	$145,000

The actual results for September 2017 were as follows:

Number of checkbooks produced and sold	12,000
Average selling price per book	$ 21
Variable cost per book	$ 7
Fixed costs for the month	$150,000

The executive vice president of the company observed that the operating income for September was much lower than anticipated, despite a higher-than-budgeted selling price and a lower-than-budgeted variable cost per unit. As the company's management accountant, you have been asked to provide explanations for the disappointing September results.

Bank Management develops its flexible budget on the basis of budgeted per-output-unit revenue and per-output-unit variable costs without detailed analysis of budgeted inputs.

Required

1. Prepare a static-budget-based variance analysis of the September performance.
2. Prepare a flexible-budget-based variance analysis of the September performance.
3. Why might Bank Management find the flexible-budget-based variance analysis more informative than the static-budget-based variance analysis? Explain your answer.

24 **Flexible budget, working backward.** The Clarkson Company produces engine parts for car manufacturers. A new accountant intern at Clarkson has accidentally deleted the company's variance analysis calculations for the year ended December 31, 2017. The following table is what remains of the data.

Home Insert Page Layout Formulas Data Review View

	A	B	C	D	E	F
1		**Performance Report, Year Ended December 31, 2017**				
2						
3		**Actual Results**	**Flexible-Budget Variances**	**Flexible Budget**	**Sales-Volume Variances**	**Static Budget**
4	Units sold	130,000				120,000
5	Revenues (sales)	$715,000				$420,000
6	Variable costs	515,000				240,000
7	Contribution margin	200,000				180,000
8	Fixed costs	140,000				120,000
9	Operating income	$ 60,000				$ 60,000

Required

1. Calculate all the required variances. (If your work is accurate, you will find that the total static-budget variance is $0.)
2. What are the actual and budgeted selling prices? What are the actual and budgeted variable costs per unit?
3. Review the variances you have calculated and discuss possible causes and potential problems. What is the important lesson learned here?

25 Flexible-budget and sales volume variances. Cascade, Inc., produces the basic fillings used in many popular frozen desserts and treats—vanilla and chocolate ice creams, puddings, meringues, and fudge. Cascade uses standard costing and carries over no inventory from one month to the next. The ice-cream product group's results for June 2017 were as follows:

	A	B	C
1	**Performance Report, June 2017**		
2		**Actual Results**	**Static Budget**
3	Units (pounds)	460,000	447,000
4	Revenues	$2,626,600	$2,592,600
5	Variable manufacturing costs	1,651,400	1,564,500
6	Contribution margin	$ 975,200	$1,028,100

Jeff Geller, the business manager for ice-cream products, is pleased that more pounds of ice cream were sold than budgeted and that revenues were up. Unfortunately, variable manufacturing costs went up, too. The bottom line is that contribution margin declined by $52,900, which is just over 2% of the budgeted revenues of $2,592,600. Overall, Geller feels that the business is running fine.

Required

1. Calculate the static-budget variance in units, revenues, variable manufacturing costs, and contribution margin. What percentage is each static-budget variance relative to its static-budget amount?
2. Break down each static-budget variance into a flexible-budget variance and a sales-volume variance.
3. Calculate the selling-price variance.
4. Assume the role of management accountant at Cascade. How would you present the results to Jeff Geller? Should he be more concerned? If so, why?

26 Price and efficiency variances. Sunshine Foods manufactures pumpkin scones. For January 2017, it budgeted to purchase and use 14,750 pounds of pumpkin at $0.92 a pound. Actual purchases and usage for January 2017 were 16,000 pounds at $0.85 a pound. Sunshine budgeted for 59,000 pumpkin scones. Actual output was 59,200 pumpkin scones.

Required

1. Compute the flexible-budget variance.
2. Compute the price and efficiency variances.
3. Comment on the results for requirements 1 and 2 and provide a possible explanation for them.

27 Materials and manufacturing labor variances. Consider the following data collected for Great Homes, Inc.:

	Direct Materials	Direct Manufacturing Labor
Cost incurred: Actual inputs × actual prices	$200,000	$90,000
Actual inputs × standard prices	214,000	86,000
Standard inputs allowed for actual output × standard prices	225,000	80,000

Required

Compute the price, efficiency, and flexible-budget variances for direct materials and direct manufacturing labor.

28 Direct materials and direct manufacturing labor variances. Rugged Life, Inc., designs and manufactures fleece quarter-zip jackets. It sells its jackets to brand-name outdoor outfitters in lots of one dozen. Rugged Life's May 2017 static budget and actual results for direct inputs are as follows:

Static Budget	
Number of jacket lots (1 lot = 1 dozen)	300
Per Lot of Jackets:	
Direct materials	18 yards at $4.65 per yard = $83.70
Direct manufacturing labor	2.4 hours at $12.50 per hour = $30.00
Actual Results	
Number of jacket lots sold	325
Total Direct Inputs:	
Direct materials	6,500 yards at $4.85 per yard = $31,525
Direct manufacturing labor	715 hours at $12.60 = $9,009

Rugged Life has a policy of analyzing all input variances when they add up to more than 8% of the total cost of materials and labor in the flexible budget, and this is true in May 2017. The production manager discusses the sources of the variances: "A new type of material was purchased in May. This led to faster cutting and sewing, but the workers used more material than usual as they learned to work with it. For now, the standards are fine."

Required

1. Calculate the direct materials and direct manufacturing labor price and efficiency variances in May 2017. What is the total flexible-budget variance for both inputs (direct materials and direct manufacturing labor) combined? What percentage is this variance of the total cost of direct materials and direct manufacturing labor in the flexible budget?
2. Comment on the May 2017 results. Would you continue the "experiment" of using the new material?

29 Price and efficiency variances, journal entries. The Schuyler Corporation manufactures lamps. It has set up the following standards per finished unit for direct materials and direct manufacturing labor:

Direct materials: 10 lb. at $4.50 per lb.	$45.00
Direct manufacturing labor: 0.5 hour at $30 per hour	15.00

The number of finished units budgeted for January 2017 was 10,000; 9,850 units were actually produced.

Actual results in January 2017 were as follows:

Direct materials: 98,055 lb. used	
Direct manufacturing labor: 4,900 hours	$154,350

Assume that there was no beginning inventory of either direct materials or finished units.

During the month, materials purchased amounted to 100,000 lb., at a total cost of $465,000. Input price variances are isolated upon purchase. Input-efficiency variances are isolated at the time of usage.

Required

1. Compute the January 2017 price and efficiency variances of direct materials and direct manufacturing labor.
2. Prepare journal entries to record the variances in requirement 1.
3. Comment on the January 2017 price and efficiency variances of Schuyler Corporation.
4. Why might Schuyler calculate direct materials price variances and direct materials efficiency variances with reference to different points in time?

30 Materials and manufacturing labor variances, standard costs. Dawson, Inc., is a privately held furniture manufacturer. For August 2017, Dawson had the following standards for one of its products, a wicker chair:

	Standards per Chair
Direct materials	3 square yards of input at $5.50 per square yard
Direct manufacturing labor	0.5 hour of input at $10.50 per hour

The following data were compiled regarding *actual performance*: actual output units (chairs) produced, 2,200; square yards of input purchased and used, 6,200; price per square yard, $5.70; direct manufacturing labor costs, $9,844; actual hours of input, 920; labor price per hour, $10.70.

1. Show computations of price and efficiency variances for direct materials and direct manufacturing labor. Give a plausible explanation of why each variance occurred.
2. Suppose 8,700 square yards of materials were purchased (at $5.70 per square yard), even though only 6,200 square yards were used. Suppose further that variances are identified at their most timely control point; accordingly, direct materials price variances are isolated and traced at the time of purchase to the purchasing department rather than to the production department. Compute the price and efficiency variances under this approach.

31 Journal entries and T-accounts (continuation of 30). Prepare journal entries and post them to T-accounts for all transactions in Exercise 30, including requirement 2. Summarize how these journal entries differ from the normal-costing entries.

32 Price and efficiency variances, benchmarking. Nantucket Enterprises manufactures insulated cold beverage cups printed with college and corporate logos, which it distributes nationally in lots of 12 dozen cups. In June 2017, Nantucket produced 5,000 lots of its most popular line of cups, the 24-ounce lidded tumbler, at each of its two plants, which are located in Providence and Amherst. The production manager, Shannon Bryant, asks her assistant, Joel Hudson, to find out the precise per-unit budgeted variable costs at the two plants and the variable costs of a competitor, Beverage Mate, who offers similar-quality tumblers at cheaper prices. Hudson pulls together the following information for each lot:

Per lot	Providence Plant	Amherst Plant	Beverage Mate
Direct materials	74 lbs. @ $3.20 per lb.	76.5 lbs. @ $3.10 per lb.	70 lbs. @ $2.90 per lb.
Direct manufacturing labor	2.5 hrs. @ $12.00 per hr.	2.4 hrs. @ $12.20 per hr.	2.4 hrs. @ $10.50 per hr.
Variable overhead	$20 per lot	$22 per lot	$20 per lot

Required

1. What is the budgeted variable cost per lot at the Providence Plant, the Amherst Plant, and at Beverage Mate?
2. Using the Beverage Mate data as the standard, calculate the direct materials and direct manufacturing labor price and efficiency variances for the Providence and Amherst plants.
3. What advantage does Nantucket get by using Beverage Mate's benchmark data as standards in calculating its variances? Identify two issues that Bryant should keep in mind in using the Beverage Mate data as the standards.

33 Static and flexible budgets, service sector. Student Finance (StuFi) is a start-up that aims to use the power of social communities to transform the student loan market. It connects participants through a dedicated lending pool, enabling current students to borrow from a school's alumni community. StuFi's revenue model is to take an upfront fee of 40 basis points (0.40%) *each* from the alumni investor and the student borrower for every loan originated on its platform.

StuFi hopes to go public in the near future and is keen to ensure that its financial results are in line with that ambition. StuFi's budgeted and actual results for the third quarter of 2017 are presented below.

Home | Insert | Page Layout | Formulas | Data | Review | View

	A	B	C	D	E
1		**Static Budget**		**Actual Results**	
2	New loans originated	8,200		10,250	
3	Average amount of loan	$145,000		$162,000	
4	Variable costs per loan:				
5	Professional labor	$360	(8 hrs at $45 per hour)	$475	(9.5 hrs at $50 per hour)
6	Credit verification	$100		$100	
7	Federal documentation fees	$120		$125	
8	Courier services	$50		$54	
9	Administrative costs (fixed)	$800,000		$945,000	
10	Technology costs (fixed)	$1,300,000		$1,415,000	

Required

1. Prepare StuFi's static budget of operating income for the third quarter of 2017.
2. Prepare an analysis of variances for the third quarter of 2017 along the lines of Exhibit 2; identify the sales volume and flexible budget variances for operating income.
3. Compute the professional labor price and efficiency variances for the third quarter of 2017.
4. What factors would you consider in evaluating the effectiveness of professional labor in the third quarter of 2017?

MyAccountingLab

Problems

34 Flexible budget, direct materials, and direct manufacturing labor variances. Emerald Statuary manufactures bust statues of famous historical figures. All statues are the same size. Each unit requires the same amount of resources. The following information is from the static budget for 2017:

Expected production and sales	7,000 units
Expected selling price per unit	$ 680
Total fixed costs	$1,400,000

Standard quantities, standard prices, and standard unit costs follow for direct materials and direct manufacturing labor:

	Standard Quantity	Standard Price	Standard Unit Cost
Direct materials	10 pounds	$ 8 per pound	$ 80
Direct manufacturing labor	3.7 hours	$50 per hour	$185

During 2017, actual number of units produced and sold was 4,800, at an average selling price of $720. Actual cost of direct materials used was $392,700, based on 66,000 pounds purchased at $5.95 per pound. Direct manufacturing labor-hours actually used were 18,300, at the rate of $48 per hour. As a result, actual direct manufacturing labor costs were $878,400. Actual fixed costs were $1,170,000. There were no beginning or ending inventories.

Required

1. Calculate the sales-volume variance and flexible-budget variance for operating income.
2. Compute price and efficiency variances for direct materials and direct manufacturing labor.

35 Variance analysis, nonmanufacturing setting. Joyce Brown has run Medical Maids, a specialty cleaning service for medical and dental offices, for the past 10 years. Her static budget and actual results for April 2017 are shown below. Joyce has one employee who has been with her for all 10 years that she has been in business. In addition, at any given time she also employs two other less-experienced workers. It usually takes each employee 2 hours to clean an office, regardless of his or her experience. Brown pays her experienced employee $30 per office and the other two employees $15 per office. There were no wage increases in April.

Medical Maids Actual and Budgeted Income Statements For the Month Ended April 30, 2017

	Budget	Actual
Offices cleaned	140	160
Revenue	$26,600	$36,000
Variable costs:		
Costs of supplies	630	680
Labor	3,360	4,200
Total variable costs	3,990	4,880
Contribution margin	22,610	31,120
Fixed costs	4,900	4,900
Operating income	$17,710	$26,220

Required

1. How many offices, on average, did Brown budget for each employee? How many offices did each employee actually clean?
2. Prepare a flexible budget for April 2017.
3. Compute the sales price variance and the labor efficiency variance for each labor type.
4. What information, in addition to that provided in the income statements, would you want Brown to gather, if you wanted to improve operational efficiency?

36 Comprehensive variance analysis review. Ellis Animal Health, Inc., produces a generic medication used to treat cats with feline diabetes. The liquid medication is sold in 100 ml vials. Ellis employs a team of sales representatives who are paid varying amounts of commission.

Given the narrow margins in the generic veterinary drugs industry, Ellis relies on tight standards and cost controls to manage its operations. Ellis has the following budgeted standards for the month of April 2017:

Average selling price per vial	$ 8.30
Total direct materials cost per vial	$ 3.60
Direct manufacturing labor cost per hour	$ 15.00
Average labor productivity rate (vials per hour)	100
Sales commission cost per vial	$ 0.72
Fixed administrative and manufacturing overhead	$990,000

Ellis budgeted sales of 700,000 vials for April. At the end of the month, the controller revealed that actual results for April had deviated from the budget in several ways:

- Unit sales and production were 90% of plan.
- Actual average selling price decreased to $8.20.
- Productivity dropped to 90 vials per hour.
- Actual direct manufacturing labor cost was $15.20 per hour.
- Actual total direct material cost per unit increased to $3.90.
- Actual sales commissions were $0.70 per vial.
- Fixed overhead costs were $110,000 above budget.

Calculate the following amounts for Ellis for April 2017:

Required

1. Static-budget and actual operating income
2. Static-budget variance for operating income
3. Flexible-budget operating income
4. Flexible-budget variance for operating income
5. Sales-volume variance for operating income
6. Price and efficiency variances for direct manufacturing labor
7. Flexible-budget variance for direct manufacturing labor

37 Possible causes for price and efficiency variances. You have been invited to interview for an internship with an international food manufacturing company. When you arrive for the interview, you are given the following information related to a fictitious Belgian chocolatier for the month of June. The chocolatier manufactures truffles in 12-piece boxes. The production is labor intensive, and the delicate nature of the chocolate requires a high degree of skill.

Actual	
Boxes produced	10,000
Direct materials used in production	2,150,000 g
Actual direct material cost	60,200 euro
Actual direct manufacturing labor-hours	1,100
Actual direct manufacturing labor cost	12,650 euro

Standards	
Purchase price of direct materials	0.03 euro/g
Materials per box	200 g
Wage rate	12 euro/hour
Boxes per hour	10

Please respond to the following questions as if you were in an interview situation:

Required

1. Calculate the materials efficiency and price variance and the wage and labor efficiency variances for the month of June.
2. Discuss some possible causes of the variances you have calculated. Can you make any possible connection between the material and labor variances? What recommendations do you have for future improvement?

38 Material-cost variances, use of variances for performance evaluation. Katharine Johnson is the owner of Best Bikes, a company that produces high-quality cross-country bicycles. Best Bikes participates in a supply chain that consists of suppliers, manufacturers, distributors, and elite bicycle shops. For several years Best Bikes has purchased titanium from suppliers in the supply chain. Best Bikes uses titanium for the bicycle frames because it is stronger and lighter than other metals and therefore increases the quality of the bicycle. Earlier this year, Best Bikes hired Michael Bentfield, a recent graduate from State University, as purchasing manager. Michael believed that he could reduce costs if he purchased titanium from an online marketplace at a lower price.

Best Bikes established the following standards based upon the company's experience with previous suppliers. The standards are as follows:

Cost of titanium	$18 per pound
Titanium used per bicycle	8 lbs.

Actual results for the first month using the online supplier of titanium are as follows:

Bicycles produced	400
Titanium purchased	5,200 lb. for $88,400
Titanium used in production	4,700 lb.

Required

1. Compute the direct materials price and efficiency variances.
2. What factors can explain the variances identified in requirement 1? Could any other variances be affected?
3. Was switching suppliers a good idea for Best Bikes? Explain why or why not.
4. Should Michael Bentfield's performance evaluation be based solely on price variances? Should the production manager's evaluation be based solely on efficiency variances? Why is it important for Katharine Johnson to understand the causes of a variance before she evaluates performance?
5. Other than performance evaluation, what reasons are there for calculating variances?
6. What future problems could result from Best Bikes' decision to buy a lower quality of titanium from the online marketplace?

39 Direct manufacturing labor and direct materials variances, missing data. (CMA, heavily adapted) Oyster Bay Surfboards manufactures fiberglass surfboards. The standard cost of direct materials and direct manufacturing labor is $248 per board. This includes 35 pounds of direct materials, at the budgeted price of $3 per pound, and 11 hours of direct manufacturing labor, at the budgeted rate of $13 per hour. Following are additional data for the month of July:

Units completed	5,600 units
Direct material purchases	230,000 pounds
Cost of direct material purchases	$759,000
Actual direct manufacturing labor-hours	43,000 hours
Actual direct manufacturing labor cost	$623,500
Direct materials efficiency variance	$ 1,200 F

There were no beginning inventories.

Required

1. Compute direct manufacturing labor variances for July.
2. Compute the actual pounds of direct materials used in production in July.
3. Calculate the actual price per pound of direct materials purchased.
4. Calculate the direct materials price variance.

40 Direct materials efficiency, mix, and yield variances. Sandy's Snacks produces snack mixes for the gourmet and natural foods market. Its most popular product is Tempting Trail Mix, a mixture of peanuts, dried cranberries, and chocolate pieces. For each batch, the budgeted quantities and budgeted prices are as follows:

	Quantity per Batch	Price per Cup
Peanuts	60 cups	$1
Dried cranberries	30 cups	$2
Chocolate pieces	10 cups	$3

Small changes to the standard mix of direct materials reflected in the above quantities do not significantly affect the overall end product. In addition, not all ingredients added to production end up in the finished product, as some are rejected during inspection.

In the current period, Sandy's Snacks made 100 batches of Tempting Trail Mix with the following actual quantity, cost, and mix of inputs:

	Actual Quantity	Actual Cost	Actual Mix
Peanuts	6,720 cups	$ 5,712	64%
Dried cranberries	2,625 cups	5,775	25%
Chocolate pieces	1,155 cups	3,350	11%
Total actual	10,500 cups	$14,837	100%

Required

1. What is the budgeted cost of direct materials for the 100 batches?
2. Calculate the total direct materials efficiency variance.
3. Calculate the total direct materials mix and yield variances.
4. How do the variances calculated in requirement 3 relate to those calculated in requirement 2? What do the variances calculated in requirement 3 tell you about the 100 batches produced this period? Are the variances large enough to investigate?

41 Direct materials and manufacturing labor variances, solving unknowns. (CPA, adapted) On May 1, 2017, Bovar Company began the manufacture of a new paging machine known as Dandy. The company installed a standard costing system to account for manufacturing costs. The standard costs for a unit of Dandy follow:

Direct materials (3 lb. at $4 per lb.)	$12.00
Direct manufacturing labor (1/2 hour at $20 per hour)	10.00
Manufacturing overhead (75% of direct manufacturing labor costs)	7.50
	$29.50

The following data were obtained from Bovar's records for the month of May:

	Debit	Credit
Revenues		$125,000
Accounts payable control (for May's purchases of direct materials)		55,000
Direct materials price variance	$3,500	
Direct materials efficiency variance	2,400	
Direct manufacturing labor price variance	1,890	
Direct manufacturing labor efficiency variance		2,200

Actual production in May was 4,000 units of Dandy, and actual sales in May were 2,500 units.

The amount shown for direct materials price variance applies to materials purchased during May. There was no beginning inventory of materials on May 1, 2017.

Compute each of the following items for Bovar for the month of May. Show your computations.

Required

1. Standard direct manufacturing labor-hours allowed for actual output produced
2. Actual direct manufacturing labor-hours worked

3. Actual direct manufacturing labor wage rate
4. Standard quantity of direct materials allowed (in pounds)
5. Actual quantity of direct materials used (in pounds)
6. Actual quantity of direct materials purchased (in pounds)
7. Actual direct materials price per pound

42 Direct materials and manufacturing labor variances, journal entries. Collegiate Corn Hole is a small business that Zach Morris developed while in college. He began building wooden corn hole game sets for friends, hand painted with college colors and logos. As demand grew, he hired some workers and began to manage the operation. Collegiate Corn Hole maintains two departments: construction and painting. In the construction department, the games require wood and labor. Collegiate Corn Hole has some employees who have been with the company for a very long time and others who are new and inexperienced.

Collegiate Corn Hole uses standard costing for the game sets. Zach expects that a typical set should take 4 hours of labor in the construction department, and the standard wage rate is $10.00 per hour. An average set uses 24 square feet of wood, allowing for a certain amount of scrap. Because of the nature of the wood, workers must work around flaws in the materials. Zach shops around for good deals and expects to pay $5.00 per square feet.

Zach does not store inventory, and buys the wood as he receives an order.

For the month of September, Zach's workers produced 60 corn hole sets using 250 hours and 1,500 square feet of wood. Zach bought wood for $7,350 (and used the entire quantity, and incurred labor costs of $2,375.

Required

1. For the construction department, calculate the price and efficiency variances for the wood and the price and efficiency variances for direct manufacturing labor.
2. Record the journal entries for the variances incurred.
3. Discuss logical explanations for the combination of variances that the construction department of Collegiate Corn Hole experienced.

43 Use of materials and manufacturing labor variances for benchmarking. You are a new junior accountant at In Focus Corporation, maker of lenses for eyeglasses. Your company sells generic-quality lenses for a moderate price. Your boss, the controller, has given you the latest month's report for the lens trade association. This report includes information related to operations for your firm and three of your competitors within the trade association. The report also includes information related to the industry benchmark for each line item in the report. You do not know which firm is which, except that you know you are Firm A.

Unit Variable Costs Member Firms
for the Month Ended September 30, 2017

	Firm A	Firm B	Firm C	Firm D	Industry Benchmark	
Materials input	2.15	2.00	2.20	2.60	2.15	oz. of glass
Materials price	$ 5.00	$ 5.25	$ 5.10	$ 4.50	$ 5.10	per oz.
Labor-hours used	0.75	1.00	0.65	0.70	0.70	hours
Wage rate	$14.50	$14.00	$14.25	$15.25	$12.50	per DLH
Variable overhead rate	$ 9.25	$14.00	$ 7.75	$11.75	$12.25	per DLH

Required

1. Calculate the total variable cost per unit for each firm in the trade association. Compute the percent of total for the material, labor, and variable overhead components.
2. Using the trade association's industry benchmark, calculate direct materials and direct manufacturing labor price and efficiency variances for the four firms. Calculate the percent over standard for each firm and each variance.
3. Write a brief memo to your boss outlining the advantages and disadvantages of belonging to this trade association for benchmarking purposes. Include a few ideas to improve productivity that you want your boss to take to the department heads' meeting.

44 Direct manufacturing labor variances: price, efficiency, mix, and yield. Elena Martinez employs two workers in her wedding cake bakery. The first worker, Gabrielle, has been making wedding cakes for 20 years and is paid $25 per hour. The second worker, Joseph, is less experienced and is paid $15 per hour. One wedding cake requires, on average, 6 hours of labor. The budgeted direct manufacturing labor quantities for one cake are as follows:

	Quantity
Gabrielle	3 hours
Joseph	3 hours
Total	6 hours

That is, each cake is budgeted to require 6 hours of direct manufacturing labor, composed of 50% of Gabrielle's labor and 50% of Joseph's, although sometimes Gabrielle works more hours on a particular cake and Joseph less, or vice versa, with no obvious change in the quality of the cake.

During the month of May, the bakery produces 50 cakes. Actual direct manufacturing labor costs are as follows:

Gabrielle (140 hours)	$ 3,500
Joseph (165 hours)	2,475
Total actual direct labor cost	$ 5,975

Required

1. What is the budgeted cost of direct manufacturing labor for 50 cakes?
2. Calculate the total direct manufacturing labor price and efficiency variances.
3. For the 50 cakes, what is the total actual amount of direct manufacturing labor used? What is the actual direct manufacturing labor input mix percentage? What is the budgeted amount of Gabrielle's and Joseph's labor that should have been used for the 50 cakes?
4. Calculate the total direct manufacturing labor mix and yield variances. How do these numbers relate to the total direct manufacturing labor efficiency variance? What do these variances tell you?

45 Direct-cost and selling price variances. MicroDisk is the market leader in the Secure Digital (SD) card industry and sells memory cards for use in portable devices such as mobile phones, tablets, and digital cameras. Its most popular card is the Mini SD, which it sells through outlets such as Target and Walmart for an average selling price of $8. MicroDisk has a standard monthly production level of 420,000 Mini SDs in its Taiwan facility. The standard input quantities and prices for direct-cost inputs are as follows:

	A	B	C	D	E
1		Quantity per		Standard	
2	Cost Item	Mini SD card		Unit Costs	
3	Direct materials:				
4	Specialty polymer	17	mm	$0.05	/mm
5	Connector pins	10	units	0.10	/unit
6	Wi-Fi transreceiver	1	unit	0.50	/unit
7					
8	Direct manufacturing labor:				
9	Setup	1	min.	24.00	/hr.
10	Fabrication	2	min.	30.00	/hr.

Phoebe King, the CEO, is disappointed with the results for June 2017, especially in comparison to her expectations based on the standard cost data.

13	Performance Report, June 2017						
14		Actual		Budget		Variance	
15	Output units	462,000		420,000		42,000	F
16	Revenues	$3,626,700		$3,360,000		$266,700	F
17	Direct materials	1,200,000		987,000		213,000	U
18	Direct manufacturing labor	628,400		588,000		40,400	U

King observes that despite the significant increase in the output of Mini SDs in June, the product's contribution to the company's profitability has been lower than expected. She gathers the following information to help analyze the situation:

	Home	Insert	Page Layout	Formulas	Data	Review	View

21	Input Usage Report, June 2017			
22	Cost Item	Quantity		Actual Cost
23	Direct materials:			
24	Specialty polymer	8,300,000	mm	$415,000
25	Connector pins	5,000,000	units	550,000
26	Wi-Fi transreceiver	470,000	units	235,000
27				
28	Direct manufacturing labor:			
29	Setup	455,000	min.	182,000
30	Fabrication	864,000	min.	446,400

Calculate the following variances. Comment on the variances and provide potential reasons why they might have arisen, with particular attention to the variances that may be related to one another:

Required

1. Selling-price variance
2. Direct materials price variance, for each category of materials
3. Direct materials efficiency variance, for each category of materials
4. Direct manufacturing labor price variance, for setup and fabrication
5. Direct manufacturing labor efficiency variance, for setup and fabrication

46 Variances in the service sector. Derek Wilson operates Clean Ride Enterprises, an auto detailing company with 20 employees. Jamal Jackson has recently been hired by Wilson as a controller. Clean Ride's previous accountant had done very little in the area of variance analysis, but Jackson believes that the company could benefit from a greater understanding of his business processes. Because of the labor-intensive nature of the business, he decides to focus on calculating labor variances.

Jackson examines past accounting records, and establishes some standards for the price and quantity of labor. While Clean Ride's employees earn a range of hourly wages, they fall into two general categories: skilled labor, with an average wage of $20 per hour, and unskilled labor, with an average wage of $10 per hour. One standard 5-hour detailing job typically requires a combination of 3 skilled hours and 2 unskilled hours.

Actual data from last month, when 600 detailing jobs were completed, are as follows:

Skilled (2,006 hours)	$ 39,117
Unskilled (944 hours)	9,292
Total actual direct labor cost	$ 48,409

Looking over last month's data, Jackson determines that Clean Ride's labor price variance was $1,151 favorable, but the labor efficiency variance was $1,560 unfavorable. When Jackson presents his findings to Wilson, the latter is furious. "Do you mean to tell me that my employees wasted $1,560 worth of time last month? I've had enough. They had better shape up, or else!" Jackson tries to calm him down, saying that in this case the efficiency variance doesn't necessarily mean that employees were wasting time. Jackson tells him that he is going to perform a more detailed analysis, and will get back to him with more information soon.

Required

1. What is the budgeted cost of direct labor for 600 detailing jobs?
2. How were the $1,151 favorable price variance and the $1,560 unfavorable labor efficiency variance calculated? What was the company's flexible-budget variance?
3. What do you think Jackson meant when said that "in this case the efficiency variance doesn't necessarily mean that employees were wasting time"?
4. For the 600 detailing jobs performed last month, what is the actual direct labor input mix percentage? What was the standard mix for labor?
5. Calculate the total direct labor mix and yield variances.
6. How could these variances be interpreted? Did the employees waste time? Upon further investigation, you discover that there were some unfilled vacancies last month in the unskilled labor positions that have recently been filled. How will this new information likely impact the variances going forward?

47 Price and efficiency variances, benchmarking and ethics. Sunto Scientific manufactures GPS devices for a chain of retail stores. Its most popular model, the Magellan XS, is assembled in a dedicated facility in Savannah, Georgia. Sunto is keenly aware of the competitive threat from smartphones that use Google Maps and has put in a standard cost system to manage production of the Magellan XS. It has also implemented a just-in-time system so the Savannah facility operates with no inventory of any kind.

Producing the Magellan XS involves combining a navigation system (imported from Sunto's plant in Dresden at a fixed price), an LCD screen made of polarized glass, and a casing developed from specialty plastic. The budgeted and actual amounts for Magellan XS for July 2017 were as follows:

	Budgeted Amounts	Actual Amounts
Magellan XS units produced	4,000	4,400
Navigation systems cost	$81,600	$89,000
Navigation systems	4,080	4,450
Polarized glass cost	$40,000	$40,300
Sheets of polarized glass used	800	816
Plastic casing cost	$12,000	$12,500
Ounces of specialty plastic used	4,000	4,250
Direct manufacturing labor costs	$36,000	$37,200
Direct manufacturing labor-hours	2,000	2,040

The controller of the Savannah plant, Jim Williams, is disappointed with the standard costing system in place. The standards were developed on the basis of a study done by an outside consultant at the start of the year. Williams points out that he has rarely seen a significant unfavorable variance under this system. He observes that even at the present level of output, workers seem to have a substantial amount of idle time. Moreover, he is concerned that the production supervisor, John Kelso, is aware of the issue but is unwilling to tighten the standards because the current lenient benchmarks make his performance look good.

Required

1. Compute the price and efficiency variances for the three categories of direct materials and for direct manufacturing labor in July 2017.
2. Describe the types of actions the employees at the Savannah plant may have taken to reduce the accuracy of the standards set by the outside consultant. Why would employees take those actions? Is this behavior ethical?
3. If Williams does nothing about the standard costs, will his behavior violate any of the standards of ethical conduct for practitioners described in the IMA Statement of Ethical Professional Practice (see Exhibit 7)?
4. What actions should Williams take?
5. Williams can obtain benchmarking information about the estimated costs of Sunto's competitors such as Garmin and TomTom from the Competitive Intelligence Institute (CII). Discuss the pros and cons of using the CII information to compute the variances in requirement 1.

GLOSSARY

Benchmarking. The continuous process of comparing the levels of performance in producing products and services and executing activities against the best levels of performance in competing companies or in companies having similar processes.

Budgeted performance. Expected performance or a point of reference to compare actual results.

Direct manufacturing labor mix variance. The difference between (1) budgeted cost for actual mix of the actual total quantity of direct manufacturing labor used and (2) budgeted cost of budgeted mix of the actual total quantity of direct manufacturing labor used.

Direct manufacturing labor yield variance. The difference between (1) budgeted cost of direct manufacturing labor based on the actual total quantity of direct manufacturing labor used and (2) flexible-budget cost of direct manufacturing labor based on the budgeted total quantity of direct manufacturing labor allowed for actual output produced.

Effectiveness. The degree to which a predetermined objective or target is met.

Efficiency. The relative amount of inputs used to achieve a given output level.

Efficiency variance. The difference between actual input quantity used and budgeted input quantity allowed for actual output, multiplied by budgeted price. Also called *usage variance*.

Favorable variance. Variance that has the effect of increasing operating income relative to the budgeted amount. Denoted F.

Flexible budget. Budget developed using budgeted revenues and budgeted costs based on the actual output in the budget period.

Flexible-budget variance. The difference between an actual result and the corresponding flexible-budget amount based on the actual output level in the budget period.

Management by exception. Practice of focusing management attention on areas not operating as expected and giving less attention to areas operating as expected.

Price variance. The difference between actual price and budgeted price multiplied by actual quantity of input. Also called *rate variance*.

Rate variance. See *price variance*.

Sales-volume variance. The difference between a flexible-budget amount and the corresponding static-budget amount.

Selling-price variance. The difference between the actual selling price and the budgeted selling price multiplied by the actual units sold.

Standard. A carefully determined price, cost, or quantity that is used as a benchmark for judging performance. It is usually expressed on a per unit basis.

Standard cost. A carefully determined cost of a unit of output.

Standard input. A carefully determined quantity of input required for one unit of output.

Standard price. A carefully determined price that a company expects to pay for a unit of input.

Static budget. Budget based on the level of output planned at the start of the budget period.

Static-budget variance. Difference between an actual result and the corresponding budgeted amount in the static budget.

Unfavorable variance. Variance that has the effect of decreasing operating income relative to the budgeted amount. Denoted U.

Usage variance. See *efficiency variance*.

Variance. The difference between actual result and expected performance.

Flexible Budgets, Overhead Cost Variances, and Management Control

Flexible Budgets, Overhead Cost Variances, and Management Control

LEARNING OBJECTIVES

1. Explain the similarities and differences in planning variable overhead costs and fixed overhead costs
2. Develop budgeted variable overhead cost rates and budgeted fixed overhead cost rates
3. Compute the variable overhead flexible-budget variance, the variable overhead efficiency variance, and the variable overhead spending variance
4. Compute the fixed overhead flexible-budget variance, the fixed overhead spending variance, and the fixed overhead production-volume variance
5. Show how the 4-variance analysis approach reconciles the actual overhead incurred with the overhead amounts allocated during the period
6. Explain the relationship between the sales-volume variance and the production-volume variance
7. Calculate variances in activity-based costing
8. Examine the use of overhead variances in nonmanufacturing settings

What do this week's weather forecast and an organization's performance have in common?

Much of the time, reality doesn't match what people expect. Rain that results in a little league game being canceled may suddenly give way to sunshine. Business owners expecting to "whistle their way to the bank" may change their tune after tallying their monthly bills and discovering that skyrocketing operational costs have significantly reduced their profits. Differences, or variances, are all around us.

Analyzing variances is a valuable activity for firms because the process highlights the areas where performance most lags expectations. By using this information to make corrective adjustments, companies can achieve significant savings. Furthermore, the process of setting up standards requires firms to have a thorough understanding of their fixed and variable overhead costs, which brings its own benefits, as the following article shows.

TESLA MOTORS GIGAFACTORY[1]

Tesla Motors is a Silicon Valley-based electric car manufacturer. To meet its planned production of 500,000 cars per year by 2018, Tesla is building the Gigafactory, a 5.8 million square foot state-of-the-art facility in Nevada that will produce the lithium ion batteries the company needs to power its electric vehicles. In building the $5 billion Gigafactory, Tesla Motors required an in-depth understanding of its fixed and variable overhead costs for planning and control purposes.

The Gigafactory has significant fixed overhead costs. Roughly the size of 100 football fields, the Gigafactory required Tesla to make up-front fixed-cost investments designed to benefit the company for many years. These include depreciation and taxes, construction costs, insurance, and environmentally friendly investments such as covering the Gigafactory in solar panels to ensure no fossil fuels are used in production. Variable costs at the Gigafactory will ultimately include production employee salaries, utilities, and office supplies, among others.

MShieldsPhotos/Alamy Stock Photo

Understanding its fixed and variable overhead costs will allow Tesla's management accountants to develop the company's budgeted fixed and variable overhead cost rates for each battery produced. Once the Gigafactory is complete, battery production for Tesla cars—all the way down to the cell level—will happen in one facility. As a result, the cost to produce batteries should decrease by at least 30% compared to 2016 costs.

Managers use flexible budgets and variance analysis to help plan and control the direct-cost categories of direct materials and direct manufacturing labor. In this chapter, you will learn how managers plan for and control the indirect-cost categories of variable manufacturing overhead and fixed manufacturing overhead.

---

[1] *Sources:* Dana Hull, "Inside the Gigafactory That Will Decide Tesla's Fate," *Bloomberg.com*, May 6, 2016; Max Chafkin, "Elon Musk Powers Up: Inside Tesla's $5 billion Gigafactory," *Fast Company*, November 17, 2015; Colin Lecher, "Inside Nevada's $1.3 Billion Gamble on Tesla," *The Verge*, February 8, 2016.

Planning of Variable and Fixed Overhead Costs

We'll use the Webb Company example again to illustrate the planning and control of variable and fixed overhead costs. Recall that Webb manufactures jackets it sells to distributors, who in turn sell them to independent clothing stores and retail chains. Because we assume Webb's only costs are manufacturing costs, for simplicity we use the term "overhead costs" instead of "manufacturing overhead costs" in this chapter. Webb's variable overhead costs include energy, machine maintenance, engineering support, and indirect materials. Webb's fixed overhead costs include plant leasing costs, depreciation on plant equipment, and the salaries of the plant managers.

LEARNING OBJECTIVE 1

Explain the similarities and differences in planning variable overhead costs and fixed overhead costs

...for both, plan only essential activities and be efficient; fixed overhead costs are usually determined well before the budget period begins

Planning Variable Overhead Costs

To effectively plan variable overhead costs for a product or service, managers must focus on the activities that create a superior product or service for their customers and eliminate activities that do not add value. For example, customers expect Webb's jackets to last, so Webb's managers consider sewing to be an essential activity. Therefore, maintenance activities for sewing machines, which are included in Webb's variable overhead costs, are also essential activities for which management must plan. Such maintenance should be done in a cost-effective way, such as by scheduling periodic equipment maintenance rather than waiting for sewing machines to break down. For many companies today, it is critical to plan for ways to reduce the consumption of energy, a rapidly growing component of variable overhead costs. Webb installs smart meters in order to monitor energy use in real time and steer production operations away from peak consumption periods.

Planning Fixed Overhead Costs

Planning fixed overhead costs is similar to planning variable overhead costs—undertake only essential activities and then plan to be efficient in that undertaking. But there is an additional strategic issue when it comes to planning fixed overhead costs: choosing the appropriate level of capacity or investment that will benefit the company in the long run. Consider Webb's leasing of sewing machines, each of which has a fixed cost per year. Leasing too many machines will result in overcapacity and unnecessary fixed leasing costs. Leasing too few machines will result in an inability to meet demand, lost sales of jackets, and unhappy customers. Consider AT&T, which did not initially foresee the iPhone's appeal or the proliferation of "apps" and consequently did not upgrade its network sufficiently to handle the resulting data traffic. AT&T subsequently had to impose limits on how customers could use the iPhone (such as by curtailing tethering and the streaming of Webcasts). This explains why, at one point following the iPhone's release, AT&T had the lowest customer satisfaction ratings among all major carriers.

The planning of fixed overhead costs differs from the planning of variable overhead costs in another regard as well: timing. At the start of a budget period, management will have made most of the decisions determining the level of fixed overhead costs to be incurred. But it's the day-to-day, ongoing operating decisions that mainly determine the level of variable overhead costs incurred in that period. For example, the variable overhead costs of hospitals, which include the costs of disposable supplies, doses of medication, suture packets, and medical waste disposal, are a function of the number and nature of procedures carried out, as well as the practice patterns of the physicians. However, most of the costs of providing hospital service are fixed overhead costs—those related to buildings, equipment, and salaried labor. These costs are unrelated to a hospital's volume of activity.[2]

DECISION POINT

How do managers plan variable overhead costs and fixed overhead costs?

[2] Free-standing surgery centers have thrived because they have lower fixed overhead costs compared to traditional hospitals. For an enlightening summary of costing issues in health care, see A. Macario, "What Does One Minute of Operating Room Time Cost?" *Journal of Clinical Anesthesia*, June 2010.

Standard Costing at Webb Company

LEARNING OBJECTIVE 2

Develop budgeted variable overhead cost rates

...budgeted variable costs divided by quantity of costallocation base

and budgeted fixed overhead cost rates

...budgeted fixed costs divided by quantity of costallocation base

Webb uses standard costing. This chapter explains how the standards for Webb's manufacturing overhead costs are developed. **Standard costing** is a costing system that (1) traces direct costs to output produced by multiplying the standard prices or rates by the standard quantities of inputs allowed for actual outputs produced, and (2) allocates overhead costs on the basis of the standard overhead cost rates times the standard quantities of the allocation bases allowed for the actual outputs produced.

The standard cost of Webb's jackets can be computed at the start of the budget period. This feature of standard costing simplifies recordkeeping because no record is needed of the actual overhead costs or of the actual quantities of the cost-allocation bases used for making the jackets. What managers *do* need are the standard overhead cost rates for Webb's variable and fixed overhead. Management accountants calculate these cost rates based on the planned amounts of variable and fixed overhead and the standard quantities of the allocation bases. We describe these computations next. Note that once managers set these standards, the costs of using standard costing are low relative to the costs of using actual costing or normal costing.

Developing Budgeted Variable Overhead Rates

Budgeted variable overhead cost-allocation rates can be developed in four steps. Throughout the chapter, we use the broader term *budgeted rate* rather than *standard rate*. When standard costing is used, as is the case with Webb, the budgeted rates are standard rates.

Step 1: Choose the Period to Be Used for the Budget. Webb uses a 12-month budget period. Two reasons are provided for using annual overhead rates rather than, say, monthly rates. The first relates to the numerator, such as reducing the influence of seasonality on the firm's cost structure. The second relates to the denominator, such as reducing the effect of varying output and number of days in a month. In addition, setting overhead rates once a year rather than 12 times a year saves managers time.

Step 2: Select the Cost-Allocation Bases to Use in Allocating the Variable Overhead Costs to the Output Produced. Webb's operating managers select machine-hours as the cost-allocation base because they believe that the number of machine-hours is the sole cost driver of variable overhead. Based on an engineering study, Webb estimates it will take 0.40 of a machine-hour per actual output unit. For its budgeted output of 144,000 jackets in 2017, Webb budgets 57,600 (0.40 × 144,000) machine-hours.

Step 3: Identify the Variable Overhead Costs Associated with Each Cost-Allocation Base. Webb groups all of its variable overhead costs, including the costs of energy, machine maintenance, engineering support, indirect materials, and indirect manufacturing labor, in a single cost pool. Webb's total budgeted variable overhead costs for 2017 are $1,728,000.

Step 4: Compute the Rate per Unit of Each Cost-Allocation Base Used to Allocate the Variable Overhead Costs to the Output Produced. Dividing the amount in Step 3 ($1,728,000) by the amount in Step 2 (57,600 machine-hours), Webb estimates a rate of $30 per standard machine-hour for allocating its variable overhead costs.

When standard costing is used, the variable overhead rate per unit of the cost-allocation base ($30 per machine-hour for Webb) is generally expressed as a standard rate per output unit. Webb calculates the budgeted variable overhead cost rate per output unit as follows:

$$\begin{aligned}\begin{matrix}\text{Budgeted variable}\\\text{overhead cost rate}\\\text{per output unit}\end{matrix} &= \begin{matrix}\text{Budgeted input}\\\text{allowed per}\\\text{output unit}\end{matrix} \times \begin{matrix}\text{Budgeted variable}\\\text{overhead cost rate}\\\text{per input unit}\end{matrix}\\ &= 0.40 \text{ hour per jacket} \times \$30 \text{ per hour}\\ &= \$12 \text{ per jacket}\end{aligned}$$

The $12-per-jacket rate is the budgeted variable overhead cost rate in Webb's static budget for 2017 as well as in the monthly performance reports the firm prepares during 2017.

The $12-per-jacket rate represents the amount by which managers expect Webb's variable overhead costs to change when the amount of output changes. As the number of jackets manufactured increases, the variable overhead costs allocated to output (for inventory costing) increase at the rate of $12 per jacket. The $12 per jacket constitutes the firm's total variable overhead costs per unit of output, including the costs of energy, repairs, indirect labor, and so on. Managers control variable overhead costs by setting a budget for each of these line items and then investigating the possible causes of any significant variances.

Developing Budgeted Fixed Overhead Rates

Fixed overhead costs are, by definition, a lump sum of costs that remains unchanged for a given period, despite wide changes in a firm's level of activity or output. Fixed costs are included in flexible budgets, but they remain the same within the relevant range of activity regardless of the output level chosen to "flex" the variable costs and revenues. Recall from Exhibit 2 and the steps in developing a flexible budget that Webb's monthly fixed overhead costs of $276,000 are the same in the static budget as they are in the flexible budget. Do not assume, however, that these costs can never be changed. Managers can reduce them by selling equipment or laying off employees, for example. But the costs are fixed in the sense that, unlike variable costs such as direct material costs, fixed costs do not *automatically* increase or decrease with the level of activity within the relevant range.

The process of developing the budgeted fixed overhead rate is the same as the one for calculating the budgeted variable overhead rate. The steps are as follows:

Step 1: Choose the Period to Use for the Budget. As with variable overhead costs, the budget period for fixed overhead costs is typically one year, to help smooth out seasonal effects.

Step 2: Select the Cost-Allocation Bases to Use in Allocating the Fixed Overhead Costs to the Output Produced. Webb uses machine-hours as the only cost-allocation base for the firm's fixed overhead costs. Why? Because Webb's managers believe that, in the long run, the company's fixed overhead costs will increase or decrease to the levels needed to support the amount of machine-hours. Therefore, in the long run, the amount of machine-hours used is the only cost driver of fixed overhead costs. The number of machine-hours is the denominator in the budgeted fixed overhead rate computation and is called the **denominator level.** For simplicity, we assume Webb expects to operate at capacity in fiscal year 2017, with a budgeted usage of 57,600 machine-hours for a budgeted output of 144,000 jackets.[3]

Step 3: Identify the Fixed Overhead Costs Associated with Each Cost-Allocation Base. Because Webb identifies a single cost-allocation base—machine-hours—to allocate fixed overhead costs, it groups all such costs into a single cost pool. Costs in this pool include depreciation on plant and equipment, plant and equipment leasing costs, and the plant manager's salary. Webb's fixed overhead budget for 2017 is $3,312,000.

Step 4: Compute the Rate per Unit of Each Cost-Allocation Base Used to Allocate Fixed Overhead Costs to the Output Produced. By dividing the $3,312,000 from Step 3 by the 57,600 machine-hours from Step 2, Webb estimates a fixed overhead cost rate of $57.50 per machine-hour:

$$\text{Budgeted fixed overhead cost per unit of cost-allocation base} = \frac{\text{Budgeted total costs in fixed overhead cost pool}}{\text{Budgeted total quantity of cost-allocation base}} = \frac{\$3{,}312{,}000}{57{,}600} = \$57.50 \text{ per machine-hour}$$

[3] Because Webb plans its capacity over multiple periods, anticipated demand in 2017 could be such that budgeted output for 2017 is less than Webb's capacity. Companies vary in the denominator levels they choose. Some choose budgeted output and others choose capacity. In either case, the approach and analysis presented in this chapter is unchanged.

Under standard costing, the $57.50 fixed overhead cost per machine-hour is usually expressed as a standard cost per output unit. Recall that Webb's engineering study estimates that it will take 0.40 machine-hour per output unit. Webb can now calculate the budgeted fixed overhead cost per output unit as follows:

$$\text{Budgeted fixed overhead cost per output unit} = \text{Budgeted quantity of cost-allocation base allowed per output unit} \times \text{Budgeted fixed overhead cost per unit of cost-allocation base}$$
$$= 0.40 \text{ of a machine-hour per jacket} \times \$57.50 \text{ per machine-hour}$$
$$= \$23.00 \text{ per jacket}$$

DECISION POINT

How are budgeted variable overhead and fixed overhead cost rates calculated?

When preparing monthly budgets for 2017, Webb divides the $3,312,000 annual total fixed costs into 12 equal monthly amounts of $276,000.

Variable Overhead Cost Variances

LEARNING OBJECTIVE 3

Compute the variable overhead flexible-budget variance,

...difference between actual variable overhead costs and flexible-budget variable overhead amounts

the variable overhead efficiency variance,

...difference between actual quantity of cost-allocation base and budgeted quantity of cost-allocation base

and the variable overhead spending variance

...difference between actual variable overhead cost rate and budgeted variable overhead cost rate

We now illustrate how the budgeted variable overhead rate is used to compute Webb's variable overhead cost variances. The following data are for April 2017, when Webb produced and sold 10,000 jackets:

	Actual Result	Flexible-Budget Amount
1. Output units (jackets)	10,000	10,000
2. Machine-hours per output unit	0.45	0.40
3. Machine-hours (1 × 2)	4,500	4,000
4. Variable overhead costs	$130,500	$120,000
5. Variable overhead costs per machine-hour (4 ÷ 3)	$ 29.00	$ 30.00
6. Variable overhead costs per output unit (4 ÷ 1)	$ 13.05	$ 12.00

The flexible budget enables Webb to highlight the differences between actual costs and actual quantities versus budgeted costs and budgeted quantities for the actual output level of 10,000 jackets.

Flexible-Budget Analysis

The **variable overhead flexible-budget variance** measures the difference between actual variable overhead costs incurred and flexible-budget variable overhead amounts.

$$\text{Variable overhead flexible-budget variance} = \text{Actual costs incurred} - \text{Flexible-budget amount}$$
$$= \$130{,}500 - \$120{,}000$$
$$= \$10{,}500 \text{ U}$$

This $10,500 unfavorable flexible-budget variance means Webb's actual variable overhead exceeded the flexible-budget amount by $10,500 for the 10,000 jackets actually produced and sold. Webb's managers would want to know why. Did Webb use more machine-hours than planned to produce the 10,000 jackets? If so, was it because workers were less skilled than expected in using machines? Or did Webb spend more on variable overhead costs, such as maintenance?

As with the flexible-budget variance for direct-cost items, Webb's managers can get further insight into the reason for the $10,500 unfavorable variance by subdividing it into the efficiency variance and spending variance.

Variable Overhead Efficiency Variance

The **variable overhead efficiency variance** is the difference between the actual quantity of the cost-allocation base used and budgeted quantity of the cost-allocation base that should have been used to produce the actual output, multiplied by the budgeted variable overhead cost per unit of the cost-allocation base.

$$\text{Variable overhead efficiency variance} = \left(\begin{array}{c}\text{Actual quantity of}\\ \text{variable overhead}\\ \text{cost-allocation base}\\ \text{used for actual}\\ \text{output}\end{array} - \begin{array}{c}\text{Budgeted quantity of}\\ \text{variable overhead}\\ \text{cost-allocation base}\\ \text{allowed for}\\ \text{actual output}\end{array}\right) \times \begin{array}{c}\text{Budgeted variable}\\ \text{overhead cost per unit}\\ \text{of cost-allocation base}\end{array}$$

$$= (4{,}500\text{ hours} - 0.40\text{ hr./unit} \times 10{,}000\text{ units}) \times \$30\text{ per hour}$$

$$= (4{,}500\text{ hours} - 4{,}000\text{ hours}) \times \$30\text{ per hour}$$

$$= \$15{,}000\text{ U}$$

Columns 2 and 3 of Exhibit 1 depict the variable overhead efficiency variance. The variance arises solely because of the difference between the actual quantity (4,500 hours) and budgeted quantity (4,000 hours) of the cost-allocation base. The variable overhead efficiency variance is computed the same way the efficiency variance for direct-cost items is. However, the interpretation of the variance is different. The efficiency variances for direct-cost items are based on the differences between the actual inputs used and the budgeted inputs allowed for the actual output produced. For example, a forensic laboratory (the kind popularized by television shows such as *CSI* and *Dexter*) would calculate a direct labor efficiency variance based on whether the lab used more or fewer hours than the standard hours allowed for the actual number of DNA tests. In contrast, the efficiency variance for variable overhead is based on the efficiency with which *the cost-allocation base* is used. Webb's unfavorable variable overhead efficiency variance of $15,000 means that the actual machine-hours (the cost-allocation base) of 4,500 hours was higher than the budgeted machine-hours of 4,000 hours allowed to manufacture 10,000 jackets and this, to the extent machine-hours are a cost driver for variable overhead, pushed up the potential spending on variable overhead.

EXHIBIT 1 Columnar Presentation of Variable Overhead Variance Analysis: Webb Company for April 2017[a]

	Actual Costs Incurred: Actual Input Quantity × Actual Rate (1)		**Actual Input Quantity × Budgeted Rate (2)**		**Flexible Budget: Budgeted Input Quantity Allowed for Actual Output × Budgeted Rate (3)**
	(4,500 hrs. × $29/hr.) = $130,500		(4,500 hrs. × $30/hr.) = $135,000		(0.40 hr./unit × 10,000 units × $30/hr.) 4,000 hrs. × $30/hr. $120,000
Level 3		$4,500 F Spending variance		$15,000 U Efficiency variance	
Level 2			$10,500 U Flexible-budget variance		

[a]F = favorable effect on operating income; U = unfavorable effect on operating income.

The following table shows possible causes for Webb's actual machine-hours exceeding the budgeted machine-hours and Webb's potential responses to each of these causes.

Possible Causes for Exceeding Budget	Potential Management Responses
1. Workers were less efficient than expected in using machines.	1. Encourage the human resources department to implement better employee-hiring practices and training procedures.
2. The production scheduler inefficiently scheduled jobs, resulting in more machine-hours used than budgeted.	2. Improve plant operations by installing production-scheduling software.
3. Machines were not maintained in good operating condition.	3. Ensure preventive maintenance is done on all machines.
4. Webb's sales staff promised a distributor a rush delivery, which resulted in more machine-hours used than budgeted.	4. Coordinate production schedules with sales staff and distributors and share information with them.
5. Budgeted machine time standards were set too tight.	5. Commit more resources to develop appropriate standards.

Note how, depending on the cause(s) of the $15,000 U variance, corrective actions may need to be taken not just in manufacturing but also in other business functions of the value chain, such as sales and distribution.

Webb's managers discovered that one reason for the unfavorable variance was that workers were underskilled. As a result, Webb is improving its hiring and training practices. Insufficient maintenance performed in the two months prior to April 2017 was another reason. A former plant manager had delayed the maintenance in an attempt to meet Webb's monthly cost targets. Managers should not focus on meeting short-run cost targets if they are likely to result in harmful long-run consequences. For example, if Webb's employees were to hurt themselves while operating poorly maintained machinery, the consequences would not only be harmful, they could be deadly. Webb is now strengthening its internal maintenance procedures so that failure to do monthly maintenance as needed will raise a "red flag" that must be immediately explained to management. Webb is also taking a hard look at its evaluation practices to determine if they inadvertently pressure managers to fixate on short-term targets to the long-run detriment of the firm.

Variable Overhead Spending Variance

The **variable overhead spending variance** is the difference between the actual variable overhead cost per unit of the cost-allocation base and the budgeted variable overhead cost per unit of the cost-allocation base, multiplied by the actual quantity of variable overhead cost-allocation base used.

$$\text{Variable overhead spending variance} = \left(\begin{array}{c}\text{Actual variable}\\\text{overhead cost per unit}\\\text{of cost-allocation base}\end{array} - \begin{array}{c}\text{Budgeted variable}\\\text{overhead cost per unit}\\\text{of cost-allocation base}\end{array}\right) \times \begin{array}{c}\text{Actual quantity of}\\\text{variable overhead}\\\text{cost-allocation base}\\\text{used}\end{array}$$

$$= (\$29 \text{ per machine-hour} - \$30 \text{ per machine-hour}) \times 4{,}500 \text{ machine-hours}$$

$$= (-\$1 \text{ per machine-hour}) \times 4{,}500 \text{ machine-hours}$$

$$= \$4{,}500 \text{ F}$$

Webb operated in April 2017 with a lower-than-budgeted variable overhead cost per machine-hour, so there is a favorable variable overhead spending variance. Columns 1 and 2 in Exhibit 1 depict this variance.

To understand why the favorable variable overhead spending variance occurred, Webb's managers need to recognize why *actual* variable overhead cost per unit of the cost-allocation base ($29 per machine-hour) is *lower* than the *budgeted* variable overhead cost per unit of the cost-allocation base ($30 per machine-hour).

Overall, Webb used 4,500 machine-hours, which is 12.5% greater than the flexible-budget amount of 4,000 machine-hours. However, actual variable overhead costs of $130,500 are only 8.75% greater than the flexible-budget amount of $120,000. Thus, relative to the flexible budget, the percentage increase in actual variable overhead costs is *less* than the percentage increase in machine-hours. Consequently, the actual variable overhead cost per machine-hour is lower than the budgeted amount, resulting in a favorable variable overhead spending variance.

Why might the percentage increase in actual variable overhead costs come in lower than the percentage increase in machine-hours? Here are two possible reasons:

1. The actual prices of the individual inputs included in variable overhead costs, such as the price of energy, indirect materials, or indirect labor, are lower than budgeted prices of these inputs. For example, the actual price of electricity may only be $0.09 per kilowatt-hour, compared with a price of $0.10 per kilowatt-hour in the flexible budget.
2. Relative to the flexible budget, the percentage increase in the actual use of individual items in the variable overhead-cost pool is less than the percentage increase in machine-hours. Compared with the flexible-budget amount of 30,000 kilowatt-hours, suppose the actual energy use was 32,400 kilowatt-hours, or 8% higher. The fact that this is a smaller percentage increase than the 12.5% increase in machine-hours (4,500 actual machine-hours versus a flexible budget of 4,000 machine-hours) will lead to a favorable variable overhead spending variance, which can be partially or completely traced to the efficient use of energy and other variable overhead items.

As part of the last stage of the five-step decision-making process, Webb's managers will need to examine the signals provided by the variable overhead variances to *evaluate the firm's performance and learn.* By understanding the reasons for these variances, Webb can take appropriate actions and make more precise predictions in order to achieve improved results in future periods.

For example, Webb's managers must examine why the actual prices of variable overhead cost items are different from the budgeted prices. The differences could be the result of skillful negotiation on the part of the purchasing manager, oversupply in the market, or lower quality of inputs such as indirect materials. Webb's response depends on what is believed to be the cause of the variance. If the concerns are about quality, for instance, Webb may want to put in place new quality management systems.

Similarly, Webb's managers should understand the possible causes for the efficiency with which variable overhead resources are used. These causes include the skill levels of workers, maintenance of machines, and the efficiency of the manufacturing process. Webb's managers discovered that Webb used fewer indirect labor resources per machine-hour because of manufacturing process improvements. As a result, the firm began organizing cross-functional teams to see if more process improvements could be achieved.

We emphasize that a manager should not always view a favorable variable overhead spending variance as desirable. For example, the variable overhead spending variance would be favorable if Webb's managers purchased lower-priced, poor-quality indirect materials, hired less-talented supervisors, or performed less machine maintenance. These decisions, however, are likely to hurt product quality and harm the long-run prospects of the business.

To clarify the concepts of variable overhead efficiency variance and variable overhead spending variance, consider the following example. Suppose that (a) energy is the only item of variable overhead cost and machine-hours is the cost-allocation base; (b) actual machine-hours used equals the number of machine-hours under the flexible budget; and (c) the actual price of energy equals the budgeted price. From (a) and (b), it follows that there is no efficiency variance—the company has been efficient with respect to the number of machine-hours (the cost-allocation base) used to produce the actual output. However, and despite (c), there could still be a spending variance. Why? Because even though the company used the correct number of machine-hours, the energy consumed *per machine-hour* could be higher than budgeted (for example, because the machines have not been maintained correctly). The cost of this higher energy usage would be reflected in an unfavorable spending variance.

TRY IT! 1

Duvet Company manufactures pillows. The 2017 operating budget was based on production of 25,000 pillows, with 0.75 machine-hours allowed per pillow. Budgeted variable overhead per hour was $25.

Actual production for 2017 was 27,000 pillows using 19,050 machine-hours. Actual variable costs were $23 per machine-hour.

Calculate the following:

a. the budgeted variable overhead for 2017;

b. the variable overhead spending variance; and

c. the variable overhead efficiency variance.

Journal Entries for Variable Overhead Costs and Variances

We now prepare journal entries for the Variable Overhead Control account and the contra account Variable Overhead Allocated.

Entries for variable overhead for April 2017 (data from Exhibit 1) are as follows:

1. Variable Overhead Control	130,500	
Accounts Payable and various other accounts		130,500
To record actual variable overhead costs incurred.		
2. Work-in-Process Control	120,000	
Variable Overhead Allocated		120,000
To record variable overhead cost allocated (0.40 machine-hour/unit × 10,000 units × $30/machine-hour). (The costs accumulated in Work-in-Process Control are transferred to Finished-Goods Control when production is completed and to Cost of Goods Sold when the products are sold.)		
3. Variable Overhead Allocated	120,000	
Variable Overhead Efficiency Variance	15,000	
Variable Overhead Control		130,500
Variable Overhead Spending Variance		4,500
This records the variances for the accounting period.		

These variances are the underallocated or overallocated variable overhead costs. At the end of the fiscal year, the variance accounts are written off to cost of goods sold if immaterial in amount. If the variances are material in amount, they are prorated among the Work-in-Process Control, Finished-Goods Control, and Cost of Goods Sold accounts on the basis of the variable overhead allocated to these accounts. Only unavoidable costs are prorated. Any part of the variances attributable to avoidable inefficiency is written off in the period. Assume that the balances in the variable overhead variance accounts as of April 2017 are also the balances at the end of the 2017 fiscal year and are immaterial in amount. The following journal entry records the write-off of the variance accounts to the Cost of Goods Sold:

DECISION POINT

What variances can be calculated for variable overhead costs?

Cost of Goods Sold	10,500	
Variable Overhead Spending Variance	4,500	
Variable Overhead Efficiency Variance		15,000

Next we demonstrate how to calculate fixed overhead cost variances.

Fixed Overhead Cost Variances

LEARNING OBJECTIVE 4

Compute the fixed overhead flexible-budget variance,

...difference between actual fixed overhead costs and flexible-budget fixed overhead amounts

the fixed overhead spending variance,

...same as the preceding explanation

and the fixed overhead production-volume variance

...difference between budgeted fixed overhead and fixed overhead allocated on the basis of actual output produced

The flexible-budget amount for a fixed-cost item is also the amount included in the static budget prepared at the start of the period. No adjustment is required for differences between actual output and budgeted output for fixed costs because fixed costs are unaffected by changes in the output level within the relevant range. At the start of 2017, Webb budgeted its fixed overhead costs to be \$276,000 per month. The actual amount for April 2017 turned out to be \$285,000. The **fixed overhead flexible-budget variance** is the difference between actual fixed overhead costs and fixed overhead costs in the flexible budget:

$$\begin{aligned}\text{Fixed overhead flexible-budget variance} &= \text{Actual costs incurred} - \text{Flexible-budget amount}\\ &= \$285{,}000 - \$276{,}000\\ &= \$9{,}000\text{ U}\end{aligned}$$

The variance is unfavorable because the \$285,000 actual fixed overhead costs exceed the \$276,000 budgeted for April 2017, which decreases that month's operating income by \$9,000.

The variable overhead flexible-budget variance described earlier in this chapter was subdivided into a spending variance and an efficiency variance. There is no efficiency variance for fixed overhead costs. That's because a given lump sum of fixed overhead costs will be unaffected by how efficiently machine-hours are used to produce output in a given budget period. As Exhibit 2 shows, because there is no efficiency variance, the **fixed overhead spending variance** is the same amount as the fixed overhead flexible-budget variance:

$$\begin{aligned}\text{Fixed overhead spending variance} &= \text{Actual costs incurred} - \text{Flexible-budget amount}\\ &= \$285{,}000 - \$276{,}000\\ &= \$9{,}000\text{ U}\end{aligned}$$

Reasons for the unfavorable spending variance could be higher plant-leasing costs, higher depreciation on plant and equipment, or higher administrative costs, such as a higher-than-budgeted salary paid to the plant manager. Webb investigated this variance and found that there was a \$9,000 per month unexpected increase in its equipment-leasing costs. However,

EXHIBIT 2 Columnar Presentation of Fixed Overhead Variance Analysis: Webb Company for April 2017[a]

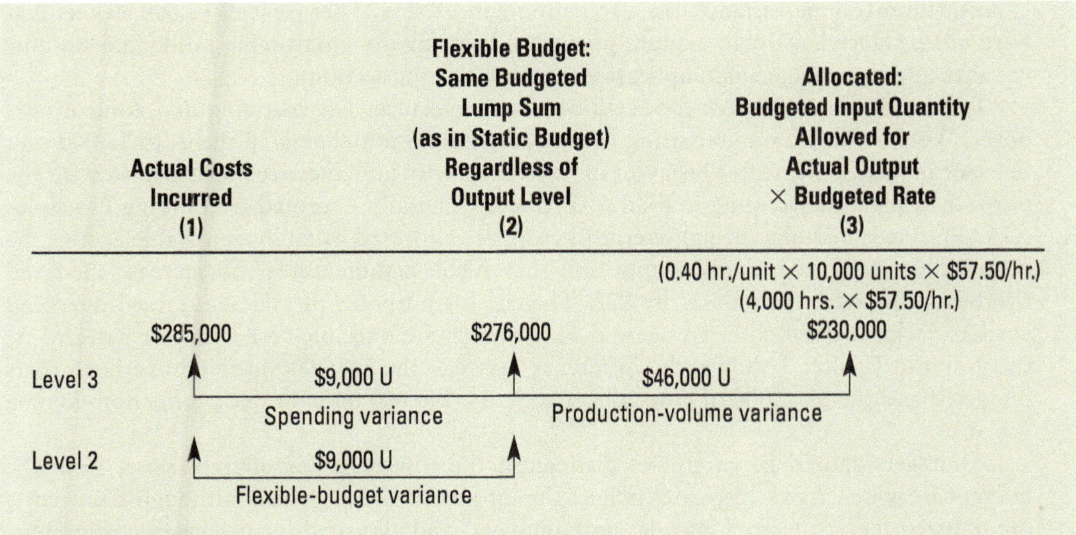

[a]F = favorable effect on operating income; U = unfavorable effect on operating income.

managers concluded that the new lease rates were competitive with lease rates available elsewhere. If this were not the case, Webb would look to lease equipment from other suppliers.

Production-Volume Variance

The **production-volume variance** arises only for fixed costs. It is the difference between the budgeted fixed overhead and the fixed overhead allocated on the basis of actual output produced. Recall that at the start of the year, Webb calculated a budgeted fixed overhead rate of $57.50 per machine-hour based on monthly budgeted fixed overhead costs of $276,000. Under standard costing, Webb's fixed overhead costs are allocated to the actual output produced during each period at the rate of $57.50 per standard machine-hour, which is equivalent to a rate of $23 per jacket (0.40 machine-hour per jacket × $57.50 per machine-hour). If Webb produces 1,000 jackets, $23,000 ($23 per jacket × 1,000 jackets) out of April's budgeted fixed overhead costs of $276,000 will be allocated to the jackets. If Webb produces 10,000 jackets, $230,000 ($23 per jacket × 10,000 jackets) will be allocated. Only if Webb produces 12,000 jackets (that is, operates, as budgeted, at capacity) will all $276,000 ($23 per jacket × 12,000 jackets) of the budgeted fixed overhead costs be allocated to the jacket output. The key point here is that even though Webb budgeted its fixed overhead costs to be $276,000, it does not necessarily allocate all these costs to output. The reason is that Webb budgets $276,000 of fixed costs to support its planned production of 12,000 jackets. If Webb produces fewer than 12,000 jackets, it only allocates the budgeted cost of capacity actually needed and used to produce the jackets.

The production-volume variance, also referred to as the **denominator-level variance**, is the difference between the budgeted and allocated fixed overhead amounts. Note that the allocated overhead can be expressed in terms of allocation-base units (machine-hours for Webb) or in terms of the budgeted fixed cost per unit:

$$\begin{aligned}\text{Production volume variance} &= \text{Budgeted fixed overhead} - \text{Fixed overhead allocated for actual output units producted}\\ &= \$276{,}000 - (0.40 \text{ hour per jacket} \times \$57.50 \text{ per hour} \times 10{,}000 \text{ jackets})\\ &= \$276{,}000 - (\$23 \text{ per jacket} \times 10{,}000 \text{ jackets})\\ &= \$276{,}000 - \$230{,}000\\ &= \$46{,}000\text{ U}\end{aligned}$$

As shown in Exhibit 2, the budgeted fixed overhead ($276,000) will be the lump sum shown in the static budget and also in any flexible budget within the relevant range. The fixed overhead allocated ($230,000) is calculated by multiplying the number of output units produced during the budget period (10,000 units) by the budgeted cost per output unit ($23). The $46,000 U production-volume variance can also be thought of as $23 per jacket × 2,000 jackets that were *not* produced. We will explore possible causes for the unfavorable production-volume variance and its management implications in the following section.

Exhibit 3 shows Webb's production-volume variance. For planning and control purposes, Webb's fixed (manufacturing) overhead costs do not change in the 0- to 12,000-unit relevant range. Contrast this behavior of fixed costs with how these costs are depicted for the purpose of inventory costing in Exhibit 3. Under Generally Accepted Accounting Principles (GAAP), fixed (manufacturing) overhead costs are allocated as an inventoriable cost to the output units produced. Every output unit that Webb manufactures will increase the fixed overhead allocated to products by $23. That is, for purposes of allocating fixed overhead costs to jackets, these costs are viewed *as if* they had a variable-cost behavior pattern. As the graph in Exhibit 3 shows, the difference between the $276,000 in fixed overhead costs budgeted and the $230,000 of costs allocated is the $46,000 unfavorable production-volume variance.

Managers should be careful to distinguish the true behavior of fixed costs from the manner in which fixed costs are assigned to products. In particular, although fixed costs are unitized (i.e., converted into per-unit amounts) and allocated for inventory-costing purposes, managers should be wary of using the same per-unit fixed overhead costs for planning and control purposes. When forecasting fixed costs, managers should concentrate on total

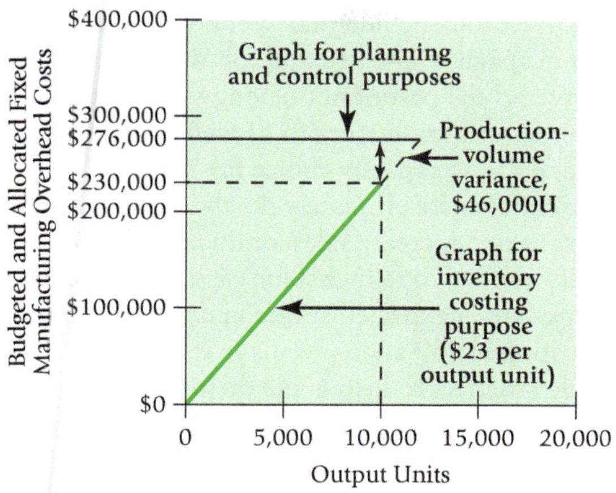

EXHIBIT 3

Behavior of Fixed Manufacturing Overhead Costs: Budgeted for Planning and Control Purposes and Allocated for Inventory Costing Purposes for Webb Company for April 2017

lump-sum costs instead of unitized costs. Similarly, when managers are looking to assign costs for control purposes or identify the best way to use capacity resources fixed in the short run, the use of unitized fixed costs often leads to incorrect decisions.

Interpreting the Production-Volume Variance

Lump-sum fixed costs represent the costs of acquiring capacity. These costs do not decrease automatically if the capacity needed turns out to be less than the capacity acquired. Sometimes costs are fixed for a specific time period for contractual reasons, such as an annual lease contract for a plant. At other times, costs are fixed because capacity has to be acquired or disposed of in fixed increments, or lumps. For example, suppose that acquiring a sewing machine gives Webb the ability to produce 1,000 jackets. If it is not possible to buy or lease a fraction of a machine, Webb can add capacity only in increments of 1,000 jackets. That is, Webb may choose capacity levels of 10,000, 11,000, or 12,000 jackets, but nothing in between.

Webb's management would want to analyze the $46,000 unfavorable production-volume variance. Why did this overcapacity occur? Why were 10,000 jackets produced instead of 12,000? Is demand weak? Should Webb reevaluate its product and marketing strategies? Is there a quality problem? Or did Webb make a strategic mistake by acquiring too much capacity? The causes of the $46,000 unfavorable production-volume variance will determine the actions Webb's managers take in response to the variance.

In contrast, a favorable production-volume variance indicates an overallocation of fixed overhead costs. That is, the overhead costs allocated to the actual output produced exceed the budgeted fixed overhead costs of $276,000. The favorable production-volume variance is composed of the fixed costs recorded in excess of $276,000.

Be careful when drawing conclusions about a company's capacity planning on the basis of the production-volume variance. To correctly interpret Webb's $46,000 unfavorable production-volume variance, its managers should consider why it sold only 10,000 jackets in April. Suppose a new competitor gained market share by pricing its jackets lower than Webb's. To sell the budgeted 12,000 jackets, Webb might have had to reduce its own selling price on all 12,000 jackets. Suppose it decided that selling 10,000 jackets at a higher price yielded higher operating income than selling 12,000 jackets at a lower price. The production-volume variance does not take into account such information. The failure of the production-volume variance to consider such information is why Webb should not interpret the $46,000 U amount as the total economic cost of selling 2,000 jackets fewer than the 12,000 jackets budgeted. If, however, Webb's managers anticipate they will not need capacity beyond 10,000 jackets, they may reduce the excess capacity, for example, by canceling the lease on some of the machines.

Companies plan their plant capacity strategically on the basis of market information about how much capacity will be needed over some future time horizon. For 2017, Webb's budgeted quantity of output is equal to the maximum capacity of the plant for that budget period. Actual demand (and quantity produced) turned out to be below the budgeted quantity of output, so Webb reports an unfavorable production-volume variance for April 2017.

However, it would be incorrect to conclude that Webb's management made a poor planning decision regarding its plant capacity. The demand for Webb's jackets might be highly uncertain. Given this uncertainty and the cost of not having sufficient capacity to meet sudden demand surges (including lost contribution margins as well as reduced repeat business), Webb's management may have made a wise capacity choice for 2017.

So what should Webb's managers ultimately do about the unfavorable variance in April? Should they try to reduce capacity, increase sales, or do nothing? Based on their analysis of the situation, Webb's managers decided to reduce some capacity, but continued to maintain some excess capacity to accommodate unexpected surges in demand. Concepts in Action: Variance Analysis and Standard Costing Help Sandoz Manage Its Overhead Costs highlights another example of managers using variances to help guide their decisions.

Next we describe the journal entries Webb would make to record fixed overhead costs using standard costing.

TRY IT! **2**

Sanjana Company makes watches. For 2017, the company expected fixed overhead costs of $648,000. Sanjana uses direct labor-hours to allocate fixed overhead and anticipates 21,600 hours during the year for an expected output of 540,000 units. An equal number of units are budgeted for each month.

During October, 48,000 watches were produced and $52,000 was spent on fixed overhead.

Calculate the following:

a. the fixed overhead rate for 2017;

b. the fixed overhead spending variance for October; and

c. the production-volume variance for October.

Journal Entries for Fixed Overhead Costs and Variances

We illustrate journal entries for fixed overhead costs for April 2017 using the Fixed Overhead Control account and the contra account Fixed Overhead Allocated (data from Exhibit 2).

1. Fixed Overhead Control	285,000	
Salaries Payable, Accumulated Depreciation, and various other accounts		285,000
To record actual fixed overhead costs incurred.		
2. Work-in-Process Control	230,000	
Fixed Overhead Allocated		230,000
To record fixed overhead costs allocated. (0.40 machine-hour/unit × 10,000 units × $57.50/machine-hour). (The costs accumulated in Work-in-Process Control are transferred to Finished-Goods Control when production is completed and to the Cost of Goods Sold when the products are sold.)		
3. Fixed Overhead Allocated	230,000	
Fixed Overhead Spending Variance	9,000	
Fixed Overhead Production-Volume Variance	46,000	
Fixed Overhead Control		285,000
To record variances for the accounting period.		

Overall, $285,000 of fixed overhead costs were incurred during April, but only $230,000 were allocated to jackets. The difference of $55,000 is precisely the underallocated fixed overhead costs. The third entry illustrates how the fixed overhead spending variance of $9,000 and the fixed overhead production-volume variance of $46,000 together record this amount in a standard costing system.

CONCEPTS IN ACTION

Variance Analysis and Standard Costing Help Sandoz Manage Its Overhead Costs

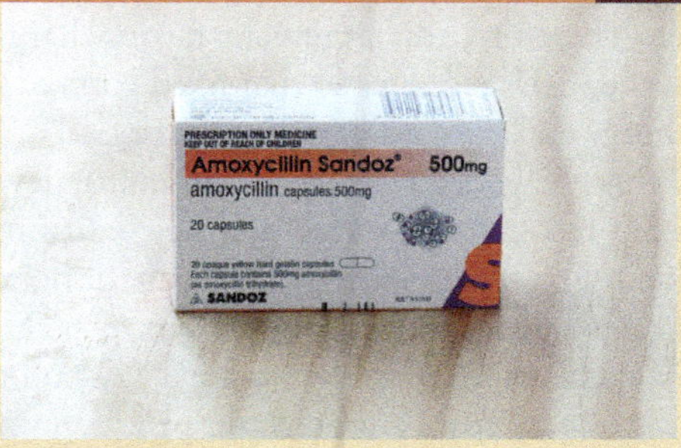

Fir Mamat/Alamy Stock Photo

Sandoz, the $10.1 billion generics division of Swiss-based Novartis AG, is the world's second largest generic drug manufacturer. Generic pharmaceuticals help reduce the cost of health care around the world. In the United States, for example, 88% of all prescription drugs dispensed were generics, but they accounted for only 28% of total drug costs. Market pricing pressure means that Sandoz operates on razor-thin margins. As a result, the company must ensure that managers have a full and accurate understanding of its costs, including of accounting for overhead costs. Sandoz uses standard costing and variance analysis to manage its overhead costs.

Each year, Sandoz prepares an overhead budget based on a detailed production plan, planned overhead spending, and other factors. Sandoz then uses activity-based costing to assign budgeted overhead costs to different work centers (for example, mixing, blending, tableting, testing, and packaging). Finally, overhead costs are assigned to products based on the activity levels required by each product at each work center. The resulting standard product cost is used in product profitability analysis and as a basis for making pricing decisions. The two main focal points in Sandoz's performance analyses are overhead absorption analysis and manufacturing overhead variance analysis.

Each month, Sandoz uses absorption analysis to compare actual production and actual costs to the standard costs of processed inventory. The monthly analysis evaluates two key trends:

1. Are costs in line with the budget? If not, the reasons are examined and the accountable managers are notified.
2. Are production volume and product mix conforming to plan? If not, Sandoz reviews and adjusts machine capacities and the absorption trend is deemed to be permanent.

Manufacturing overhead variances are examined at the work center level. These variances help determine when equipment is not running as expected so it can be repaired or replaced. Variances also help in identifying inefficiencies in processing and setup and cleaning times, which leads to more efficient ways to use equipment. Sometimes, the manufacturing overhead variance analysis leads to the review and improvement of the standards themselves—a critical element in planning the level of plant capacity. Management also reviews current and future capacity on a monthly basis to identify constraints and future capital needs.

Sources: Novartis AG, 2015 Form 20-F (Basel, Switzerland: Novartis AG, 2016); IMS Institute for Healthcare Informatics/Generic *Pharmaceutical Association, Generic Drug Savings in the United States*, November 2015; Conversations with, and documents prepared by, Eric Evans and Erich Erchr of Sandoz, 2004; Conversations with, and documents prepared by, Tobias Hestler and Chris Lewis of Sandoz, 2016.

At the end of the fiscal year, the fixed overhead spending variance is written off to the Cost of Goods Sold if it is immaterial in amount or prorated among Work-in-Process Control, Finished-Goods Control, and Cost of Goods Sold on the basis of the fixed overhead allocated to these accounts. Some companies combine the write-off and proration methods—that is, they write off the portion of the variance that is due to inefficiency and could have been avoided and prorate the portion of the variance that is unavoidable. Assume that the balance in the Fixed Overhead Spending Variance account as of April 2017 is also the balance at the end of 2017 and is immaterial in amount. The following journal entry records the write-off to Cost of Goods Sold.

Cost of Goods Sold	9,000	
Fixed Overhead Spending Variance		9,000

We now consider the production-volume variance. Assume that the balance in the Fixed Overhead Production-Volume Variance account as of April 2017 is also the balance at the end of 2017. Also assume that some of the jackets manufactured during 2017 are in work-in-process and finished-goods inventory at the end of the year. Many management accountants make a strong argument for writing off to Cost of Goods Sold and not prorating an unfavorable production-volume variance. Proponents of this argument contend that the unfavorable production-volume variance of $46,000 measures the cost of resources expended for 2,000 jackets that were not produced ($23 per jacket × 2,000 jackets = $46,000). Prorating these costs would inappropriately allocate the fixed overhead costs incurred for the 2,000 jackets not produced to the jackets that were produced. The jackets produced already bear their representative share of fixed overhead costs of $23 per jacket. Therefore, this argument favors charging the unfavorable production-volume variance against the year's revenues so that fixed costs of unused capacity are not carried in work-in-process inventory and finished-goods inventory.

There is, however, an alternative view. This view regards the denominator level as a "soft" rather than a "hard" measure of the fixed resources required and needed to produce each jacket. Suppose that, either because of the design of the jacket or the functioning of the machines, it took more machine-hours than previously thought to manufacture each jacket. Consequently, Webb could make only 10,000 jackets rather than the planned 12,000 in April. In this case, the $276,000 of budgeted fixed overhead costs support the production of the 10,000 jackets manufactured. Under this reasoning, prorating the fixed overhead production-volume variance would appropriately spread the fixed overhead costs among the Work-in-Process Control, Finished-Goods Control, and Cost of Goods Sold accounts.

What about a favorable production-volume variance? Suppose Webb manufactured 13,800 jackets in April 2017.

$$\text{Production-volume variance} = \begin{matrix}\text{Budgeted}\\\text{fixed}\\\text{overhead}\end{matrix} - \begin{matrix}\text{Fixed overhead allocated using}\\\text{budgeted cost per output unit overhead}\\\text{allowed for actual output produced}\end{matrix}$$

$$= \$276{,}000 - (\$23 \text{ per jacket} \times 13{,}800 \text{ jackets})$$

$$= \$276{,}000 - \$317{,}400 = \$41{,}400 \text{ F}$$

Because actual production exceeded the planned capacity level, clearly the fixed overhead costs of $276,000 supported the production of all 13,800 jackets and should therefore be allocated to them. Prorating the favorable production-volume variance achieves this outcome and reduces the amounts in the Work-in-Process Control, Finished-Goods Control, and Cost of Goods Sold accounts. Proration is also the more conservative approach in the sense that it results in a lower operating income than if the entire favorable production-volume variance were credited to Cost of Goods Sold.

Another point relevant to this discussion is that if variances are always written off to Cost of Goods Sold, a company could set its standards to either increase (for financial reporting purposes) or decrease (for tax purposes) its operating income. In other words, always writing off variances invites gaming behavior. For example, Webb could generate a favorable production-volume variance by setting the denominator level used to allocate the firm's fixed overhead costs low and thereby increase its operating income. Or the firm could do just the opposite if it wanted to decrease its operating income to lower its taxes. The proration method has the effect of approximating the allocation of fixed costs based on actual costs and actual output, so it is not susceptible to this type of manipulation.

There is no clear-cut or preferred approach for closing out the production-volume variance. The appropriate accounting procedure is a matter of judgment and depends on the circumstances of each case. Variations of the proration method may be desirable. For example, a company may choose to write off a portion of the production-volume variance and prorate the rest. The goal is to write off that part of the production-volume variance that represents the cost of capacity not used to support the production of output during the period. The rest of the production-volume variance is prorated to Work-in-Process Control, Finished-Goods Control, and Cost of Goods Sold.

DECISION POINT

What variances can be calculated for fixed overhead costs?

If Webb were to write off the production-volume variance to Cost of Goods Sold, it would make the following journal entry.

Cost of Goods Sold	46,000	
Fixed Overhead Production-Volume Variance		46,000

Integrated Analysis of Overhead Cost Variances

LEARNING OBJECTIVE 5

Show how the 4-variance analysis approach reconciles the actual overhead incurred with the overhead amounts allocated during the period

...the 4-variance analysis approach identifies spending and efficiency variances for variable overhead costs and spending and production-volume variances for fixed overhead costs

As our discussion indicates, the variance calculations for variable overhead and fixed overhead differ:

- Variable overhead has no production-volume variance.
- Fixed overhead has no efficiency variance.

Exhibit 4 presents an integrated summary of the variable overhead variances and the fixed overhead variances computed using standard costs for April 2017. Panel A shows the variances for variable overhead, whereas Panel B contains the fixed overhead variances. As you study Exhibit 4, note how the columns in Panels A and B are aligned to measure the different variances. In both Panels A and B,

- the difference between columns 1 and 2 measures the spending variance.
- the difference between columns 2 and 3 measures the efficiency variance (if applicable).
- the difference between columns 3 and 4 measures the production-volume variance (if applicable).

Panel A contains an efficiency variance; Panel B has no efficiency variance for fixed overhead. As we discussed, a lump-sum amount of fixed costs will be unaffected by the degree of operating efficiency in a given budget period.

Panel A does not have a production-volume variance because the amount of variable overhead allocated is always the same as the flexible-budget amount. Variable costs never have any unused capacity. When production and sales decline from 12,000 jackets to 10,000 jackets, budgeted variable overhead costs proportionately decline. Fixed costs are different. Panel B has a production-volume variance (see Exhibit 3) because Webb did not use some of the fixed overhead capacity it had acquired when it planned to produce 12,000 jackets.

4-Variance Analysis

When all of the overhead variances are presented together as in Exhibit 4, we refer to it as a 4-variance analysis:

	4-Variance Analysis		
	Spending Variance	**Efficiency Variance**	**Production-Volume Variance**
Variable overhead	\$4,500 F	\$15,000 U	Never a variance
Fixed overhead	\$9,000 U	Never a variance	\$46,000 U

The 4-variance analysis provides the same level of information as the variance analysis carried out earlier for variable overhead and fixed overhead separately (in Exhibits 1 and 2, respectively), but does so in a unified presentation that also indicates those variances that are never present.

As with other variances, the variances in Webb's 4-variance analysis are not necessarily independent of each other. For example, Webb may purchase lower-quality machine fluids (leading to a favorable variable overhead spending variance), which results in the machines taking longer to operate than budgeted (causing an unfavorable variable overhead efficiency variance), and producing less than budgeted output (causing an unfavorable production-volume variance).

Combined Variance Analysis

To keep track of all that is happening within their areas of responsibility, managers in large, complex businesses, such as General Electric and Disney, use detailed 4-variance analysis. Doing so helps them identify and focus attention on the areas not operating as expected. Managers of small businesses understand their operations better based on personal

EXHIBIT 4 Columnar Presentation of Integrated 4-Variance Analysis: Webb Company for April 2017[a]

PANEL A: Variable (Manufacturing) Overhead

Actual Costs Incurred: Actual Input Quantity × Actual Rate (1)		Actual Input Quantity × Budgeted Rate (2)		Flexible Budget: Budgeted Input Quantity Allowed for Actual Output × Budgeted Rate (3)		Allocated: Budgeted Input Quantity Allowed for Actual Output × Budgeted Rate (4)
				(0.40 hrs./unit × 10,000 units × $30/hr.)		(0.40 hrs./unit × 10,000 units × $30/hr.)
(4,500 hrs. × $29/hr.)		(4,500 hrs. × $30/hr.)		(4,000 hrs. × $30/hr.)		(4,000 hrs. × $30/hr.)
$130,500		$135,000		$120,000		$120,000
	$4,500 F Spending variance		$15,000 U Efficiency variance		Never a variance	
		$10,500 U Flexible-budget variance			Never a variance	
			$10,500 U Underallocated variable overhead (Total variable overhead variance)			

PANEL B: Fixed (Manufacturing) Overhead

Actual Costs Incurred (1)		Same Budgeted Lump Sum (as in Static Budget) Regardless of Output Level (2)		Flexible Budget: Same Budgeted Lump Sum (as in Static Budget) Regardless of Output Level (3)		Allocated: Budgeted Input Quantity Allowed for Actual Output × Budgeted Rate (4)
						(0.40 hrs./unit × 10,000 units × $57.50/hr.)
						(4,000 hrs. × $57.50/hr.)
$285,000		$276,000		$276,000		$230,000
	$9,000 U Spending variance		Never a variance		$46,000 U Production-volume variance	
		$9,000 U Flexible-budget variance			$46,000 U Production-volume variance	
			$55,000 U Underallocated fixed overhead (Total fixed overhead variance)			

[a]F = favorable effect on operating income; U = unfavorable effect on operating income.

observations and nonfinancial measures. They find less value in doing the additional measurements required for 4-variance analyses. For example, to simplify their costing systems, small companies may not distinguish variable overhead incurred from fixed overhead incurred because making this distinction is often not clear-cut. Many costs such as supervision, quality control, and materials handling have both variable- and fixed-cost components that may not be easy to separate. Managers may therefore use a less detailed analysis that *combines* the variable overhead and fixed overhead into a single total overhead cost.

When a single total overhead cost category is used, it can still be analyzed in depth. The variances are now the sums of the variable overhead and fixed overhead variances for that level, as computed in Exhibit 4. The combined variance analysis looks as follows:

	Combined 3-Variance Analysis		
	Spending Variance	Efficiency Variance	Production-Volume Variance
Total overhead	$4,500 U	$15,000 U	$46,000 U

The accounting for 3-variance analysis is simpler than for 4-variance analysis, but some information is lost because the variable and fixed overhead spending variances are combined into a single total overhead spending variance.

Finally, the overall **total-overhead variance** is given by the sum of the preceding variances. In the Webb example, this equals $65,500 U. Note that this amount, which aggregates the flexible-budget and production-volume variances, equals the total amount of underallocated (or underapplied) overhead costs. Using figures from Exhibit 4, the $65,500 U total-overhead variance is the difference between (a) the total actual overhead incurred ($130,500 + $285,000 = $415,500) and (b) the overhead allocated ($120,000 + $230,000 = $350,000) to the actual output produced. If the total-overhead variance were favorable, it would have corresponded instead to the amount of overapplied overhead costs.

DECISION POINT

What is the most detailed way for a company to reconcile actual overhead incurred with the amount allocated during a period?

3

TRY IT!

You are given the following information about Proton Equipment, Inc.

Variances	Spending	Efficiency	Production-Volume
Variable manufacturing overhead	$ 7,500 F	$30,000 U	(B)
Fixed manufacturing overhead	$28,000 U	(A)	$80,000 U

a. What are the amounts (A) and (B) in the above table?
b. In a combined 3-variance analysis, what is the total spending variance?
c. What is the total overhead variance?

Production-Volume Variance and Sales-Volume Variance

LEARNING OBJECTIVE 6

Explain the relationship between the sales-volume variance and the production-volume variance

...the production-volume and operating-income volume variances together comprise the sales-volume variance

As we complete our study of variance analysis for Webb Company, it is helpful to step back to see the "big picture" and to link the accounting and performance evaluation functions of standard costing. This chapter presents more detailed variances that subdivided, whenever possible, individual flexible-budget variances for the selling price, direct materials, direct manufacturing labor, and variable overhead. For the fixed overhead, the flexible-budget variance is the same as the spending variance. Where does the production-volume variance belong then? As you shall see, the production-volume variance is a component of the sales-volume variance. Under our assumption of actual production and sales of 10,000 jackets, Webb's costing system debits to Work-in-Process Control the standard costs of the 10,000 jackets produced. These amounts are then transferred to Finished Goods and finally to Cost of Goods Sold:

Direct materials	
($60 per jacket × 10,000 jackets)	$ 600,000
Direct manufacturing labor	
($16 per jacket × 10,000 jackets)	160,000
Variable overhead	
($12 per jacket × 10,000 jackets)	120,000
Fixed overhead	
($23 per jacket × 10,000 jackets)	230,000
Cost of goods sold at standard cost	
($111 per jacket × 10,000 jackets)	$1,110,000

Webb's costing system also records the revenues from the 10,000 jackets sold at the budgeted selling price of $120 per jacket. The net effect of these entries on Webb's budgeted operating income is as follows:

Revenues at budgeted selling price	
($120 per jacket × 10,000 jackets)	$1,200,000
Cost of goods sold at standard cost	
($111 per jacket × 10,000 jackets)	1,110,000
Operating income based on budgeted profit per jacket	
($9 per jacket × 10,000 jackets)	$ 90,000

A crucial point to keep in mind is that under standard costing, fixed overhead costs are treated as if they are a variable cost. That is, in determining the budgeted operating income of $90,000, only $230,000 ($23 per jacket × 10,000 jackets) of the fixed overhead costs are considered, whereas the budgeted fixed overhead costs are $276,000. Webb's accountants then record the $46,000 unfavorable production-volume variance (the difference between the budgeted fixed overhead costs, $276,000, and allocated fixed overhead costs, $230,000), as well as the various flexible-budget variances (including the fixed overhead spending variance) that total $29,100 unfavorable. This results in actual operating income of $14,900 as follows:

Operating income based on budgeted profit per jacket	
($9 per jacket × 10,000 jackets)	$ 90,000
Unfavorable production-volume variance	(46,000)
Flexible-budget operating income	44,000
Unfavorable flexible-budget variance for operating income	(29,100)
Actual operating income	$ 14,900

In contrast, the static-budget operating income of $108,000 is not entered in Webb's costing system because standard costing records budgeted revenues, standard costs, and variances only for the 10,000 jackets actually produced and sold, not for the 12,000 jackets that were *planned* to be produced and sold. As a result, the sales-volume variance of $64,000 U, which is the difference between the static-budget operating income of $108,000 and the flexible-budget operating income of $44,000, is never actually recorded under standard costing. Nevertheless, the sales-volume variance is useful because it helps managers understand the lost contribution margin from selling 2,000 fewer jackets (the sales-volume variance assumes fixed costs remain at the budgeted level of $276,000).

The sales-volume variance has two components. They are as follows

1. A difference between the static-budget operating income of $108,000 for 12,000 jackets and the budgeted operating income of $90,000 for 10,000 jackets. This is the **operating-income volume variance** of $18,000 U ($108,000 − $90,000). It reflects the fact that Webb produced and sold 2,000 fewer units than budgeted.

EXHIBIT 5 Summary of Levels 1, 2, and 3 Variance Analysis: Webb Company for April 2017

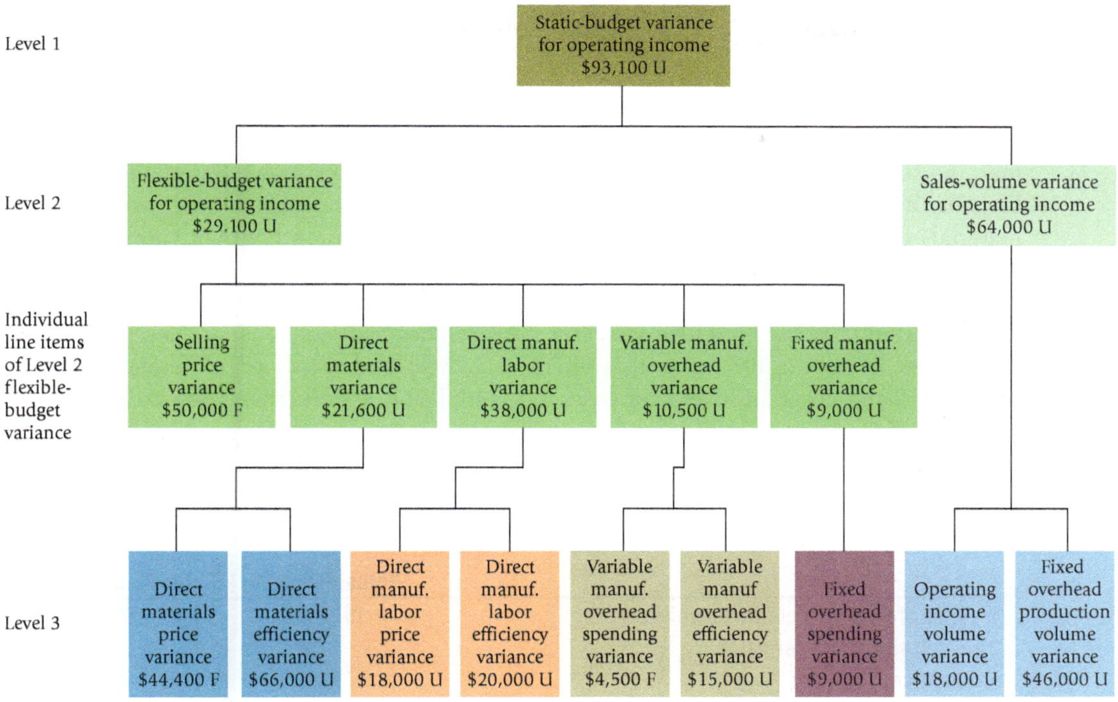

2. A difference between the budgeted operating income of $90,000 and the flexible-budget operating income of $44,000 for the 10,000 actual units. This difference arises because Webb's costing system treats fixed costs as if they behave in a variable manner and assumes fixed costs equal the allocated amount of $230,000, rather than the budgeted fixed costs of $276,000. Of course, this difference is precisely the production-volume variance of $46,000 U.

In summary, we have the following:

	Operating-income volume variance	$18,000 U
(+)	Production-volume variance	46,000 U
Equals	Sales-volume variance	$64,000 U

We can now provide a summary (see Exhibit 5) that formally disaggregates the static-budget variance of $93,100 U into its components. Note how the comprehensive chart incorporates all of the variances.

We next describe the use of variance analysis in activity-based costing systems.

DECISION POINT

What is the relationship between the sales-volume variance and the production-volume variance?

Variance Analysis and Activity-Based Costing

LEARNING OBJECTIVE 7

Calculate variances in activity-based costing

...compare budgeted and actual overhead costs of activities

Activity-based costing (ABC) systems focus on individual activities as the fundamental cost objects. ABC systems classify the costs of various activities into a cost hierarchy—output unit-level costs, batch-level costs, product-sustaining costs, and facility-sustaining costs. In this section, we show how a company that has an ABC system and batch-level costs can benefit from variance analysis. Batch-level costs are the costs of activities related to a group of units of products or services rather than to each individual unit of product or service. We illustrate variance analysis for variable batch-level direct costs and fixed batch-level overhead costs.[4]

[4] The techniques we demonstrate can be applied to analyze variable batch-level overhead costs as well.

Consider Lyco Brass Works, which manufactures many different types of faucets and brass fittings. Because of the wide range of products it produces, Lyco uses an activity-based costing system. In contrast, Webb uses a simple costing system because it makes only one type of jacket. One of Lyco's products is Elegance, a decorative brass faucet for home spas. Lyco produces Elegance in batches.

For each product Lyco makes, it uses dedicated materials-handling labor to bring materials to the production floor, transport items in process from one work center to the next, and take the finished goods to the shipping area. Therefore, materials-handling labor costs for Elegance are direct costs of Elegance. Because the materials for a batch are moved together, materials-handling labor costs vary with the number of batches rather than with the number of units in a batch. Materials-handling labor costs are variable direct batch-level costs.

To manufacture a batch of Elegance, Lyco must set up the machines and molds. Employees must be highly skilled to set up the machines and molds. Hence, a separate setup department is responsible for setting up the machines and molds for different batches of products. Setup costs are overhead costs. For simplicity, assume that setup costs are fixed with respect to the number of setup-hours. The costs consist of salaries paid to engineers and supervisors and the costs of leasing setup equipment.

Information regarding Elegance for 2017 follows:

	Actual Result	Static-Budget Amount
1. Units of Elegance produced and sold	151,200	180,000
2. Batch size (units per batch)	140	150
3. Number of batches (Line 1 ÷ Line 2)	1,080	1,200
4. Materials-handling labor-hours per batch	5.25	5
5. Total materials-handling labor-hours (Line 3 × Line 4)	5,670	6,000
6. Cost per materials-handling labor-hour	$ 14.50	$ 14
7. Total materials-handling labor costs (Line 5 × Line 6)	$ 82,215	$ 84,000
8. Setup-hours per batch	6.25	6
9. Total setup-hours (Line 3 × Line 8)	6,750	7,200
10. Total fixed setup overhead costs	$220,000	$216,000

Flexible Budget and Variance Analysis for Direct Materials-Handling Labor Costs

To prepare the flexible budget for the materials-handling labor costs, Lyco starts with the actual units of output produced, 151,200 units, and proceeds with the following steps.

Step 1: Using the Budgeted Batch Size, Calculate the Number of Batches that Should Have Been Used to Produce the Actual Output. At the budgeted batch size of 150 units per batch, Lyco should have produced the 151,200 units of output in 1,008 batches (151,200 units ÷ 150 units per batch).

Step 2: Using the Budgeted Materials-Handling Labor-Hours per Batch, Calculate the Number of Materials-Handling Labor-Hours that Should Have Been Used. At the budgeted quantity of 5 hours per batch, 1,008 batches should have required 5,040 materials-handling labor-hours (1,008 batches × 5 hours per batch).

Step 3: Using the Budgeted Cost per Materials-Handling Labor-Hour, Calculate the Flexible-Budget Amount for the Materials-Handling Labor-Hours. The flexible-budget amount is 5,040 materials-handling labor-hours × the $14 budgeted cost per materials-handling labor-hour = $70,560.

Note how the flexible-budget calculations for the materials-handling labor costs focus on batch-level quantities (materials-handling labor-hours per batch rather than per unit). The flexible-budget quantity computations focus at the appropriate level of the cost hierarchy. For example, because materials handling is a batch-level cost, the flexible-budget quantity calculations are made at the batch level—the quantity of materials-handling labor-hours that Lyco should have used based on the number of batches it should have used to produce the actual quantity of 151,200 units. If a cost had been a product-sustaining cost—such as product design cost—the flexible-budget quantity computations would focus at the product-sustaining level by, for example, evaluating the actual complexity of the product's design relative to the budget.

The flexible-budget variance for the materials-handling labor costs can now be calculated as follows:

$$
\begin{aligned}
\text{Flexible-budget variance} &= \text{Actual costs} - \text{Flexible-budget costs}\\
&= (5{,}670 \text{ hours} \times \$14.50 \text{ per hour}) - (5{,}040 \text{ hours} \times \$14 \text{ per hour})\\
&= \$82{,}215 - \$70{,}560\\
&= \$11{,}655 \text{ U}
\end{aligned}
$$

The unfavorable variance indicates that materials-handling labor costs were $11,655 higher than the flexible-budget target. We can get some insight into the possible reasons for this unfavorable outcome by examining the price and efficiency components of the flexible-budget variance. Exhibit 6 presents the variances in columnar form.

$$
\begin{aligned}
\text{Price variance} &= \left(\text{Actual price of input} - \text{Budgeted price of input}\right) \times \text{Actual quantity of input}\\
&= (\$14.50 \text{ per hour} - \$14 \text{ per hour}) \times 5{,}670 \text{ hours}\\
&= \$0.50 \text{ per hour} \times 5{,}670 \text{ hours}\\
&= \$2{,}835 \text{ U}
\end{aligned}
$$

The unfavorable price variance for materials-handling labor indicates that the $14.50 actual cost per materials-handling labor-hour exceeds the $14.00 budgeted cost per materials-handling labor-hour. This variance could be the result of Lyco's human resources manager negotiating wage rates less skillfully or of wage rates increasing unexpectedly due to a scarcity of labor.

$$
\begin{aligned}
\text{Efficiency variance} &= \left(\text{Actual quantity of input used} - \text{Budgeted quantity of input allowed for actual output}\right) \times \text{Budgeted price of input}\\
&= (5{,}670 \text{ hours} - 5{,}040 \text{ hours}) \times \$14 \text{ per hour}\\
&= 630 \text{ hours} \times \$14 \text{ per hour}\\
&= \$8{,}820 \text{ U}
\end{aligned}
$$

EXHIBIT 6 Columnar Presentation of Variance Analysis for Direct Materials-Handling Labor Costs: Lyco Brass Works for 2017[a]

	Actual Costs Incurred: Actual Input Quantity × Actual Rate (1)		Actual Input Quantity × Budgeted Rate (2)		Flexible Budget: Budgeted Input Quantity Allowed for Actual Output × Budgeted Rate (3)
	(5,670 hours × $14.50 per hour) $82,215		(5,670 hours × $14 per hour) $79,380		(5,040 hours × $14 per hour) $70,560
Level 3		$2,835 U Price variance		$8,820 U Efficiency variance	
Level 2			$11,655 U Flexible-budget variance		

[a]F = favorable effect on operating income; U = unfavorable effect on operating income.

The unfavorable efficiency variance indicates that the 5,670 actual materials-handling labor-hours exceeded the 5,040 budgeted materials-handling labor-hours for the actual output. Possible reasons for the unfavorable efficiency variance are as follows:

- Smaller actual batch sizes of 140 units, instead of the budgeted batch sizes of 150 units, resulted in Lyco producing the 151,200 units in 1,080 batches instead of 1,008 (151,200 ÷ 150) batches
- The actual materials-handling labor-hours per batch (5.25 hours) were higher than the budgeted materials-handling labor-hours per batch (5 hours)

Reasons for smaller-than-budgeted batch sizes could include quality problems when batch sizes exceed 140 faucets and high costs of carrying inventory.

Possible reasons for the larger actual materials-handling labor-hours per batch are as follows:

- Inefficient layout of the Elegance production line
- Materials-handling labor having to wait at work centers before picking up or delivering materials
- Unmotivated, inexperienced, and underskilled employees
- Very tight standards for materials-handling time

Identifying the reasons for the efficiency variance helps Lyco's managers develop a plan for improving its materials-handling labor efficiency and take corrective action that will be incorporated into future budgets.

We now consider fixed setup overhead costs.

Flexible Budget and Variance Analysis for Fixed Setup Overhead Costs

Exhibit 7 presents the variances for fixed setup overhead costs in columnar form.

Lyco's fixed setup overhead flexible-budget variance is calculated as follows:

$$\text{Fixed-setup overhead flexible-budget variance} = \text{Actual costs incurred} - \text{Flexible-budget costs}$$

$$= \$220{,}000 - \$216{,}000$$

$$= \$4{,}000\ \text{U}$$

Note that the flexible-budget amount for the fixed setup overhead costs equals the static-budget amount of $216,000. That's because there is no "flexing" of fixed costs. Moreover, because the fixed overhead costs have no efficiency variance, the fixed setup overhead spending variance is the same as the fixed overhead flexible-budget variance. The spending variance could be unfavorable because of higher leasing costs of new setup equipment or higher salaries paid to engineers and supervisors. Lyco may have incurred these costs to alleviate some of the difficulties it was having in setting up machines.

To calculate the production-volume variance, Lyco first computes the budgeted cost-allocation rate for the fixed setup overhead costs using the same four-step approach.

Step 1: Choose the Period to Use for the Budget. Lyco uses a period of 12 months (the year 2017).

Step 2: Select the Cost-Allocation Base to Use in Allocating the Fixed Overhead Costs to the Output Produced. Lyco uses budgeted setup-hours as the cost-allocation base for fixed setup overhead costs. Budgeted setup-hours in the static budget for 2017 are 7,200 hours.

Step 3: Identify the Fixed Overhead Costs Associated with the Cost-Allocation Base. Lyco's fixed setup overhead cost budget for 2017 is $216,000.

EXHIBIT 7 Columnar Presentation of Fixed Setup Overhead Variance Analysis: Lyco Brass Works for 2017[a]

	Actual Costs Incurred (1)		Flexible Budget: Same Budgeted Lump Sum (as in Static Budget) Regardless of Output Level (2)		Allocated: Budgeted Input Quantity Allowed for Actual Output × Budgeted Rate (3)
					(1,008[b] batches × 6 hours/batch × \$30/hour)
					(6,048 hours × \$30/hour)
	\$220,000		\$216,000		\$181,440
Level 3		\$4,000 U Spending variance		\$34,560 U Production-volume variance	
Level 2		\$4,000 U Flexible-budget variance			

[a]F = favorable effect on operating income; U = unfavorable effect on operating income.
[b]1,008 batches = 151,200 units ÷ 150 units per batch.

Step 4: Compute the Rate per Unit of the Cost-Allocation Base Used to Allocate the Fixed Overhead Costs to the Output Produced. Dividing the \$216,000 from Step 3 by the 7,200 setup-hours from Step 2, Lyco estimates a fixed setup overhead cost rate of \$30 per setup-hour:

$$\begin{array}{c}\text{Budgeted fixed}\\\text{setup overhead}\\\text{cost per unit of}\\\text{cost-allocation base}\end{array} = \frac{\text{Budgeted total costs in fixed overhead cost pool}}{\text{Budgeted total quantity of cost-allocation base}} = \frac{\$216{,}000}{7{,}200 \text{ setup hours}}$$

$$= \$30 \text{ per setup-hour}$$

$$\begin{array}{c}\text{Production-volume}\\\text{variance for}\\\text{fixed setup}\\\text{overhead costs}\end{array} = \begin{array}{c}\text{Budgeted}\\\text{fixed setup}\\\text{overhead}\\\text{costs}\end{array} - \begin{array}{c}\text{Fixed setup overhead}\\\text{allocated using budgeted}\\\text{input allowed for actual}\\\text{output units produced}\end{array}$$

$$= \$216{,}000 - (1{,}008 \text{ batches} \times 6 \text{ hours/batch} \times \$30/\text{hour})$$

$$= \$216{,}000 - (6{,}048 \text{ hours} \times \$30/\text{hour})$$

$$= \$216{,}000 - \$181{,}440$$

$$= \$34{,}560 \text{ U}$$

During 2017, Lyco planned to produce 180,000 units of Elegance but actually produced 151,200 units. The unfavorable production-volume variance measures the amount of extra fixed setup costs Lyco incurred for setup capacity it did not use. One interpretation is that the unfavorable \$34,560 production-volume variance represents an inefficient use of the company's setup capacity. However, Lyco may have earned higher operating income by selling 151,200 units at a higher price than 180,000 units at a lower price. As a result, Lyco's managers should interpret the production-volume variance cautiously because it does not consider the effect of output on selling prices and operating income.

DECISION POINT

How can variance analysis be used in an activity-based costing system?

TRY IT! 4

Matterhorn, Inc., produces a special line of toy racing cars. Matterhorn produces the cars in batches. To manufacture each batch of the cars, Matterhorn must set up the machines and molds. Setup costs are batch-level costs and are fixed with respect to the number of setup-hours. A separate Setup Department is responsible for setting up machines and molds for each style of car. The following information pertains to July 2017:

	Actual Amounts	Static-budget Amounts
Units produced and sold	15,000	11,250
Batch size (number of units per batch)	250	225
Setup-hours per batch	5	5.25
Total fixed setup overhead costs	$12,000	$9,975

Calculate the following:

a. the spending variance for fixed setup overhead costs;

b. the budgeted fixed setup overhead rate; and

c. the production-volume variance for fixed overhead setup costs.

Overhead Variances in Nonmanufacturing Settings

LEARNING OBJECTIVE 8

Examine the use of overhead variances in nonmanufacturing settings

...analyze nonmanufacturing variable overhead costs for decision making and cost management; fixed overhead variances are especially important in service settings

Our Webb Company example examined variable and fixed manufacturing overhead costs. Managers can also use variance analysis to examine the overhead costs of the nonmanufacturing areas of the company and to make decisions about (1) pricing, (2) managing costs, and (3) the mix of products to make. For example, when product distribution costs are high, as they are in the automobile, consumer durables, cement, and steel industries, standard costing can provide managers with reliable and timely information on variable distribution overhead spending variances and efficiency variances.

What about service-sector companies such as airlines, hospitals, hotels, and railroads? How can they benefit from variance analyses? The output measures these companies commonly use are passenger-miles flown, patient-days provided, room-days occupied, and ton-miles of freight hauled, respectively. Few costs can be traced to these outputs in a cost-effective way. Most of the costs are fixed overhead costs, such as the costs of equipment, buildings, and staff. Using capacity effectively is the key to profitability, and fixed overhead variances can help managers in this task. Retail businesses, such as Kmart, also have high-capacity–related fixed costs (lease and occupancy costs). In the case of Kmart, sales declines resulted in unused capacity and unfavorable fixed-cost variances. Kmart reduced its fixed costs by closing some of its stores.

Consider the following data for United Airlines for selected years from the past 15 years. Available seat miles (ASMs) are the actual seats in an airplane multiplied by the distance the plane traveled.

Year	Total ASMs (Millions) (1)	Operating Revenue per ASM (2)	Operating Cost per ASM (3)	Operating Income per ASM (4) = (2) − (3)
2000	175,493	10.2 cents	10.0 cents	0.2 cents
2003	136,566	8.6 cents	9.8 cents	−1.2 cents
2006	143,085	10.6 cents	10.8 cents	−0.2 cents
2008	135,859	11.9 cents	13.6 cents	−1.7 cents
2011	118,973	13.1 cents	13.5 cents	−0.4 cents
2015	219,956	13.1 cents	12.2 cents	0.9 cents

When air travel declined after the events of September 11, 2001, United's revenues fell. However, most of the company's fixed costs—for its airport facilities, equipment, personnel, and so on—did not. United had a large unfavorable production-volume variance because its capacity was underutilized. As column 1 of the table indicates, United responded by reducing its capacity substantially. Available seat miles (ASMs) declined from 175,493 million in 2000 to 136,566 million in 2003. Yet United was unable to fill even the planes it had retained, so its revenue per ASM declined (column 2) and its cost per ASM stayed roughly the same (column 3). United filed bankruptcy in December 2002 and began seeking government guarantees to obtain the loans it needed. Subsequently, strong demand for airline travel, as well as productivity improvements resulting from the more efficient use of resources and networks, led to increased traffic and higher average ticket prices. By maintaining a disciplined approach to capacity and tight control over growth, United saw over a 20% increase in its revenue per ASM between 2003 and 2006. The improvement in performance allowed United to come out of bankruptcy on February 1, 2006. Subsequently, however, the global recession and soaring jet fuel prices had a significant negative impact on United's performance, as reflected in the continued negative operating incomes and the further decline in capacity. In May 2010, a merger agreement was reached between United and Continental Airlines. Continental was formally dissolved in 2012. The merger is reflected in the 85% growth in United's ASM between 2011 and 2015. The revenue benefits from this greater scale and the recent plunge in fuel prices have led United to new heights of profitability.

Financial and Nonfinancial Performance Measures

The overhead variances discussed in this chapter are examples of financial performance measures. As the preceding examples illustrate, nonfinancial measures such as those related to capacity utilization and physical measures of input usage also provide useful information. The nonfinancial measures that managers of Webb would likely find helpful in planning and controlling its overhead costs include the following:

1. Quantity of actual indirect materials used per machine-hour, relative to the quantity of budgeted indirect materials used per machine-hour
2. Actual energy used per machine-hour, relative to the budgeted energy used per machine-hour
3. Actual machine-hours per jacket, relative to the budgeted machine-hours per jacket

These performance measures, like the financial variances discussed in this chapter, alert managers to problems and probably would be reported daily or hourly on the production floor. The overhead variances we discussed in this chapter capture the financial effects of items such as the three factors listed, which in many cases first appear as nonfinancial performance measures. An especially interesting example along these lines comes from Japan: Some Japanese companies have begun reining in their CO_2 emissions in part by doing a budgeted-to-actual variance analysis of the emissions. The goal is to make employees aware of the emissions and reduce them in advance of greenhouse-gas reduction plans being drawn up by the Japanese government.

Finally, both financial and nonfinancial performance measures are used to evaluate the performance of managers. Exclusive reliance on either is always too simplistic because each gives a different perspective on performance. Nonfinancial measures (such as those described previously) provide feedback on individual aspects of a manager's performance, whereas financial measures evaluate the overall effect of and the tradeoffs among different nonfinancial performance measures.

DECISION POINT

How are overhead variances useful in nonmanufacturing settings?

PROBLEM FOR SELF-STUDY

Nina Garcia is the newly appointed president of Laser Products. She is examining the May 2017 results for the Aerospace Products Division. This division manufactures solar arrays for satellites. Garcia's current concern is with manufacturing overhead costs at the Aerospace Products Division. Both variable and fixed overhead costs are allocated to the solar arrays on the basis of laser-cutting-hours. The following budget information is available:

Budgeted variable overhead rate	$200 per hour
Budgeted fixed overhead rate	$240 per hour
Budgeted laser-cutting time per solar array	1.5 hours
Budgeted production and sales for May 2017	5,000 solar arrays
Budgeted fixed overhead costs for May 2017	$1,800,000

Actual results for May 2017 are as follows:

Solar arrays produced and sold	4,800 units
Laser-cutting-hours used	8,400 hours
Variable overhead costs	$1,478,400
Fixed overhead costs	$1,832,200

Required

1. Compute the spending variance and the efficiency variance for variable overhead.
2. Compute the spending variance and the production-volume variance for fixed overhead.
3. Give two explanations for each of the variances calculated in requirements 1 and 2.

Solution

1 and 2. See Exhibit 8.

3. a. Variable overhead spending variance, $201,600 F. One possible reason for this variance is that the actual prices of individual items included in variable overhead (such as cutting fluids) are lower than budgeted prices. A second possible reason is that the percentage increase in the actual quantity usage of individual items in the variable overhead cost pool is less than the percentage increase in laser-cutting-hours compared to the flexible budget.

   b. Variable overhead efficiency variance, $240,000 U. One possible reason for this variance is inadequate maintenance of laser machines, causing them to take more laser-cutting time per solar array. A second possible reason is use of undermotivated, inexperienced, or underskilled workers operating the laser-cutting machines, resulting in more laser-cutting time per solar array.

   c. Fixed overhead spending variance, $32,200 U. One possible reason for this variance is that the actual prices of individual items in the fixed-cost pool unexpectedly increased from the prices budgeted (such as an unexpected increase in the cost of leasing each machine). A second possible reason is that the Aerospace Products Division had to lease more machines or hire more supervisors than had been budgeted.

   d. Production-volume variance, $72,000 U. Actual production of solar arrays is 4,800 units, compared with 5,000 units budgeted. One possible reason for this variance is demand factors, such as a decline in an aerospace program that led to a decline in demand for satellites. A second possible reason is supply factors, such as a production stoppage due to labor problems or machine breakdowns.

EXHIBIT 8 Columnar Presentation of Integrated Variance Analysis: Laser Products for May 2017[a]

PANEL A: Variable (Manufacturing) Overhead

Actual Costs Incurred: Actual Input Quantity × Actual Rate (1)	Actual Input Quantity × Budgeted Rate (2)	Flexible Budget: Budgeted Input Quantity Allowed for Actual Output × Budgeted Rate (3)	Allocated: Budgeted Input Quantity Allowed for Actual Output × Budgeted Rate (4)
		(1.5 hrs./unit × 4,800 units × $200/hr.)	(1.5 hrs./unit × 4,800 units × $200/hr.)
(8,400 hrs. × $176/hr.)	(8,400 hrs. × $200/hr.)	(7,200 hrs. × $200/hr.)	(7,200 hrs. × $200/hr.)
$1,478,400	$1,680,000	$1,440,000	$1,440,000

(1)–(2): $201,600 F, Spending variance; (2)–(3): $240,000 U, Efficiency variance; (3)–(4): Never a variance

(1)–(3): $38,400 U, Flexible-budget variance; (3)–(4): Never a variance

(1)–(4): $38,400 U, Underallocated variable overhead (Total variable overhead variance)

PANEL B: Fixed (Manufacturing) Overhead

Actual Costs Incurred (1)	Same Budgeted Lump Sum (as in Static Budget) Regardless of Output Level (2)	Flexible Budget: Same Budgeted Lump Sum (as in Static Budget) Regardless of Output Level (3)	Allocated: Budgeted Input Quantity Allowed for Actual Output × Budgeted Rate (4)
			(1.5 hrs./unit × 4,800 units × $240/hr.)
			(7,200 hrs. × $240/hr.)
$1,832,200	$1,800,000	$1,800,000	$1,728,000

(1)–(2): $32,200 U, Spending variance; (2)–(3): Never a variance; (3)–(4): $72,000 U, Production-volume variance

(1)–(3): $32,200 U, Flexible-budget variance; (3)–(4): $72,000 U, Production-volume variance

(1)–(4): $104,200 U, Underallocated fixed overhead (Total fixed overhead variance)

[a]F = favorable effect on operating income; U = unfavorable effect on operating income.

Source: Republished with permission of Strategic Finance by Paul Sherman. Copyright 2003 by Institute of Management Accountants. Permission conveyed through Copyright Clearance Center, Inc.

DECISION POINTS

The following question-and-answer format summarizes the chapter's learning objectives. Each decision presents a key question related to a learning objective. The guidelines are the answer to that question.

Decision	Guidelines
1. How do managers plan variable overhead costs and fixed overhead costs?	Planning of both variable and fixed overhead costs involves undertaking only activities that add value and then being efficient in that undertaking. The key difference is that for variable-cost planning, ongoing decisions during the budget period play a much larger role; for fixed-cost planning, most key decisions are made before the start of the period.
2. How are budgeted variable overhead and fixed overhead cost rates calculated?	The budgeted variable (fixed) overhead cost rate is calculated by dividing the budgeted variable (fixed) overhead costs by the denominator level of the cost-allocation base.
3. What variances can be calculated for variable overhead costs?	When the flexible budget for variable overhead is developed, an overhead efficiency variance and an overhead spending variance can be computed. The variable overhead efficiency variance focuses on the difference between the actual quantity of the cost-allocation base used relative to the budgeted quantity of the cost-allocation base. The variable overhead spending variance focuses on the difference between the actual variable overhead cost per unit of the cost-allocation base relative to the budgeted variable overhead cost per unit of the cost-allocation base.
4. What variances can be calculated for fixed overhead costs?	For fixed overhead, the static and flexible budgets coincide. The difference between the budgeted and actual amount of fixed overhead is the flexible-budget variance, also referred to as the spending variance. The production-volume variance measures the difference between the budgeted fixed overhead and the fixed overhead allocated on the basis of actual output produced.
5. What is the most detailed way for a company to reconcile actual overhead incurred with the amount allocated during a period?	A 4-variance analysis presents spending and efficiency variances for variable overhead costs and spending and production-volume variances for fixed overhead costs. By analyzing these four variances together, managers can reconcile the actual overhead costs with the amount of overhead allocated to the output produced during a period.
6. What is the relationship between the sales-volume variance and the production-volume variance?	The production-volume variance is a component of the sales-volume variance. The production-volume and operating-income volume variances together comprise the sales-volume variance.
7. How can variance analysis be used in an activity-based costing system?	Flexible budgets in ABC systems give insight into why actual activity costs differ from budgeted activity costs. Using output and input measures for an activity, a comprehensive variance analysis can be conducted.
8. How are overhead variances useful in nonmanufacturing settings?	Managers can analyze variances for all variable overhead costs, including those outside the manufacturing function. The analysis can be used to make pricing and product-mix decisions and to manage costs. Fixed overhead variances are especially important in service settings, where using capacity effectively is the key to profitability. In all cases, the information provided by variances can be supplemented by the use of suitable nonfinancial metrics.

TERMS TO LEARN

The chapter and the Glossary at the end of the chapter contain definitions of the following important terms:

denominator level
denominator-level variance
fixed overhead flexible-budget variance
fixed overhead spending variance
operating-income volume variance
production-volume variance
standard costing
total-overhead variance
variable overhead efficiency variance
variable overhead flexible-budget variance
variable overhead spending variance

ASSIGNMENT MATERIAL

Questions

MyAccountingLab

1 How do managers plan for variable overhead costs?
2 How does the planning of fixed overhead costs differ from the planning of variable overhead costs?
3 How does standard costing differ from actual costing?
4 What are the steps in developing a budgeted variable overhead cost-allocation rate?
5 What are the factors that affect the spending variance for variable manufacturing overhead?
6 Assume variable manufacturing overhead is allocated using machine-hours. Give three possible reasons for a favorable variable overhead efficiency variance.
7 Describe the difference between a direct materials efficiency variance and a variable manufacturing overhead efficiency variance.
8 What are the steps in developing a budgeted fixed overhead rate?
9 Why is the flexible-budget variance the same amount as the spending variance for fixed manufacturing overhead?
10 Explain how the analysis of fixed manufacturing overhead costs differs for (a) planning and control and (b) inventory costing for financial reporting.
11 Provide one caveat that will affect whether a production-volume variance is a good measure of the economic cost of unused capacity.
12 "The production-volume variance should always be written off to Cost of Goods Sold." Do you agree? Explain.
13 What are the variances in a 4-variance analysis?
14 "Overhead variances should be viewed as interdependent rather than independent." Give an example.
15 Describe how flexible-budget variance analysis can be used in the control of costs of activity areas.

Multiple-Choice Questions

MyAccountingLab

In partnership with: BECKER PROFESSIONAL EDUCATION

16 Each of the following statements is correct regarding overhead variances except:

a. Actual overhead greater than applied overhead is unfavorable.
b. The efficiency overhead variance ignores the standard variable overhead rate.
c. Variable overhead rates are not a factor in the production-volume variance calculation.
d. Favorable spending and efficiency variances imply that the flexible budget variance must be favorable.

17 Steed Co. budgets production of 150,000 units in the next year. Steed's CFO expects that each unit will take 8 hours to produce at an hourly wage rate of $10 per hour. If factory overhead is applied on the basis of direct labor hours at $6 per hour, the budget for factory overhead will total:

a. $7,200,000. **c.** $12,000,000.
b. $9,000,000. **d.** $19,200,000.

18 As part of her annual review of her company's budgets versus actuals, Mary Gerard isolates unfavorable variances with the hope of getting a better understanding of what caused them and how to avoid them next year. The variable overhead efficiency variance was the most unfavorable over the previous year, which Gerard will specifically be able to trace to:

a. Actual overhead costs below applied overhead costs.
b. Actual production units below budgeted production units.
c. Standard direct labor hours below actual direct labor hours.
d. The standard variable overhead rate below the actual variable overhead rate.

19 Culpepper Corporation had the following inventories at the beginning and end of the month of January:

	January 1	January 31
Finished goods	$125,000	$117,000
Work-in-process	235,000	251,000
Direct materials	134,000	124,000

The following additional manufacturing data was available for the month of January.

Direct materials purchased	$189,000
Transportation in	3,000
Direct labor	400,000
Actual factory overhead	175,000

Culpepper Corporation applies factory overhead at a rate of 40% of direct labor cost, and any overapplied or underapplied factory overhead is deferred until the end of the year.
Culpepper's balance in its factory overhead control account at the end of January was:

1. $15,000 overapplied. **3.** $5,000 underapplied.
2. $15,000 underapplied. **4.** $5,000 overapplied.

20 Fordham Corporation produces a single product. The standard costs for one unit of its Concourse product are as follows:

Direct materials (6 pounds at $0.50 per pound)	$ 3
Direct labor (2 hours at $10 per hour)	20
Variable manufacturing overhead (2 hours at $5 per hour)	10
Total	33

During November Year 2, 4,000 units of Concourse were produced. The costs associated with November operations were as follows:

Material purchased (36,000 pounds at $0.60 per pound)	$21,600
Material used in production (28,000 pounds)	
Direct labor (8,200 hours at $9.75 per hour)	79,950
Variable manufacturing overhead incurred	41,820

What is the variable overhead efficiency variance for Concourse for November Year 2?

1. $2,000 favorable. **3.** $1,000 favorable.
2. $2,000 unfavorable. **4.** $1,000 unfavorable.

Exercises

MyAccountingLab

21 Variable manufacturing overhead, variance analysis. Esquire Clothing is a manufacturer of designer suits. The cost of each suit is the sum of three variable costs (direct material costs, direct manufacturing labor costs, and manufacturing overhead costs) and one fixed-cost category (manufacturing overhead costs). Variable manufacturing overhead cost is allocated to each suit on the basis of budgeted direct manufacturing labor-hours per suit. For June 2017, each suit is budgeted to take 4 labor-hours. Budgeted variable manufacturing overhead cost per labor-hour is $12. The budgeted number of suits to be manufactured in June 2017 is 1,040.

Actual variable manufacturing costs in June 2017 were $52,164 for 1,080 suits started and completed. There were no beginning or ending inventories of suits. Actual direct manufacturing labor-hours for June were 4,536.

Required

1. Compute the flexible-budget variance, the spending variance, and the efficiency variance for variable manufacturing overhead.
2. Comment on the results.

22 Fixed manufacturing overhead, variance analysis (continuation of 21). Esquire Clothing allocates fixed manufacturing overhead to each suit using budgeted direct manufacturing labor-hours per suit. Data pertaining to fixed manufacturing overhead costs for June 2017 are budgeted, $62,400, and actual, $63,916.

Required

1. Compute the spending variance for fixed manufacturing overhead. Comment on the results.
2. Compute the production-volume variance for June 2017. What inferences can Esquire Clothing draw from this variance?

23 Variable manufacturing overhead variance analysis. The Sourdough Bread Company bakes baguettes for distribution to upscale grocery stores. The company has two direct-cost categories: direct materials and direct manufacturing labor. Variable manufacturing overhead is allocated to products on the basis of standard direct manufacturing labor-hours. Following is some budget data for the Sourdough Bread Company:

Direct manufacturing labor use	0.02 hours per baguette
Variable manufacturing overhead	$10.00 per direct manufacturing labor-hour

The Sourdough Bread Company provides the following additional data for the year ended December 31, 2017:

Planned (budgeted) output	3,100,000 baguettes
Actual production	2,600,000 baguettes
Direct manufacturing labor	46,800 hours
Actual variable manufacturing overhead	$617,760

Required

1. What is the denominator level used for allocating variable manufacturing overhead? (That is, for how many direct manufacturing labor-hours is Sourdough Bread budgeting?)
2. Prepare a variance analysis of variable manufacturing overhead. Use Exhibit 4 for reference.
3. Discuss the variances you have calculated and give possible explanations for them.

24 Fixed manufacturing overhead variance analysis (continuation of 23). The Sourdough Bread Company also allocates fixed manufacturing overhead to products on the basis of standard direct manufacturing labor-hours. For 2017, fixed manufacturing overhead was budgeted at $3.00 per direct manufacturing labor-hour. Actual fixed manufacturing overhead incurred during the year was $294,000.

Required

1. Prepare a variance analysis of fixed manufacturing overhead cost. Use Exhibit 4 as a guide.
2. Is fixed overhead underallocated or overallocated? By what amount?
3. Comment on your results. Discuss the variances and explain what may be driving them.

25 Manufacturing overhead, variance analysis. The Rotations Corporation is a manufacturer of centrifuges. Fixed and variable manufacturing overheads are allocated to each centrifuge using budgeted assembly-hours. Budgeted assembly time is 2 hours per unit. The following table shows the budgeted amounts and actual results related to overhead for June 2017.

	A B C D E	F	G
1	**The Rotations Corporation (June 2017)**	**Actual Results**	**Static Budget**
2	Number of centrifuges assembled and sold	220	150
3	Hours of assembly time	396	
4	Variable manufacturing overhead cost per hour of assembly time		$31.00
5	Variable manufacturing overhead costs	$12,693	
6	Fixed manufacturing overhead costs	$15,510	$14,100

Required

1. Prepare an analysis of all variable manufacturing overhead and fixed manufacturing overhead variances using the columnar approach in Exhibit 4.
2. Prepare journal entries for Rotations' June 2017 variable and fixed manufacturing overhead costs and variances; write off these variances to Cost of Goods Sold for the quarter ending June 30, 2017.
3. How does the planning and control of variable manufacturing overhead costs differ from the planning and control of fixed manufacturing overhead costs?

26 4-variance analysis, fill in the blanks. ProChem, Inc., produces chemicals for large biotech companies. It has the following data for manufacturing overhead costs during August 2017:

	Variable	**Fixed**
Actual costs incurred	$35,000	$16,500
Costs allocated to products	36,000	15,200
Flexible budget	———	16,000
Actual input × budgeted rate	31,500	———

Fill in the blanks. Use F for favorable and U for unfavorable:

	Variable	**Fixed**
(1) Spending variance	$____	$____
(2) Efficiency variance	____	____
(3) Production-volume variance	____	____
(4) Flexible-budget variance	____	____
(5) Underallocated (overallocated) manufacturing overhead	____	____

27 Straightforward 4-variance overhead analysis. The Lopez Company uses standard costing in its manufacturing plant for auto parts. The standard cost of a particular auto part, based on a denominator level of 4,000 output units per year, included 6 machine-hours of variable manufacturing overhead at $8 per hour and 6 machine-hours of fixed manufacturing overhead at $15 per hour. Actual output produced was 4,400 units. Variable manufacturing overhead incurred was $245,000. Fixed manufacturing overhead incurred was $373,000. Actual machine-hours were 28,400.

Required

1. Prepare an analysis of all variable manufacturing overhead and fixed manufacturing overhead variances, using the 4-variance analysis in Exhibit 4.
2. Prepare journal entries using the 4-variance analysis.
3. Describe how individual fixed manufacturing overhead items are controlled from day to day.
4. Discuss possible causes of the fixed manufacturing overhead variances.

28 Straightforward coverage of manufacturing overhead, standard-costing system. The Brazil division of an American telecommunications company uses standard costing for its machine-paced production of telephone equipment. Data regarding production during June are as follows:

Variable manufacturing overhead costs incurred	$537,470
Variable manufacturing overhead cost rate	$7 per standard machine-hour
Fixed manufacturing overhead costs incurred	$146,101
Fixed manufacturing overhead costs budgeted	$136,000
Denominator level in machine-hours	68,000
Standard machine-hour allowed per unit of output	1.2
Units of output	66,500
Actual machine-hours used	75,700
Ending work-in-process inventory	0

Required

1. Prepare an analysis of all manufacturing overhead variances. Use the 4-variance analysis framework illustrated in Exhibit 4.
2. Prepare journal entries for manufacturing overhead costs and their variances.
3. Describe how individual variable manufacturing overhead items are controlled from day to day.
4. Discuss possible causes of the variable manufacturing overhead variances.

29 Overhead variances, service sector. Meals Made Easy (MME) operates a meal home-delivery service. It has agreements with 20 restaurants to pick up and deliver meals to customers who place orders on MME's website. MME allocates variable and fixed overhead costs on the basis of delivery time. MME's owner, Thomas Stewart, obtains the following information for May 2017 overhead costs:

	A	B	C
1	**Meals Made Easy (May 2017)**	**Actual Results**	**Static Budget**
2	Output units (number of deliveries)	8,750	13,000
3	Hours per delivery		0.70
4	Hours of delivery time	5,600	
5	Variable overhead cost per hour of delivery time		$1.60
6	Variable overhead costs	$10,640	
7	Fixed overhead costs	$39,200	$36,400

Required

1. Compute spending and efficiency variances for MME's variable overhead in May 2017.
2. Compute the spending variance and production-volume variance for MME's fixed overhead in May 2017.
3. Comment on MME's overhead variances and suggest how Thomas Stewart might manage MME's variable overhead differently from its fixed overhead costs.

30 Total overhead, 3-variance analysis. Pampered Pets, Inc., makes embellished accessories primarily for dogs. For 2017, budgeted variable overhead is $70,000 for 10,000 direct labor-hours. Budgeted total overhead is $100,000 at 8,000 direct labor-hours. The standard costs allocated to the production of these accessories included a total overhead rate of 80% of standard direct labor costs.

In May 2017, Pampered Pets incurred total overhead of $133,000 and direct labor costs of $178,125. The direct labor efficiency variance was $7,500 unfavorable. The direct labor flexible-budget variance was $1,875 favorable. The standard labor price was $15 per hour. The production-volume variance was $16,000 favorable.

Required

1. Compute the direct labor price variance.
2. Compute the denominator level and the spending and efficiency variances for total overhead.
3. Describe how individual variable overhead items are controlled from day to day. Also, describe how individual fixed overhead items are controlled.

31 Production-volume variance analysis and sales-volume variance. Chart Hills Company makes customized golf shirts for sale to golf courses. Each shirt requires 3 hours to produce because of the customized logo for each golf course. Chart Hills uses direct labor-hours to allocate the overhead cost to production. Fixed overhead costs, including rent, depreciation, supervisory salaries, and other production expenses, are budgeted at $28,500 per month. The facility currently used is large enough to produce 5,000 shirts per month.

During March, Chart Hills produced 4,200 shirts and actual fixed costs were $28,000.

Required

1. Calculate the fixed overhead spending variance and indicate whether it is favorable (F) or unfavorable (U).
2. If Chart Hills uses direct labor-hours available at capacity to calculate the budgeted fixed overhead rate, what is the production-volume variance? Indicate whether it is favorable (F) or unfavorable (U).
3. An unfavorable production-volume variance could be interpreted as the economic cost of unused capacity. Why would Chart Hills be willing to incur this cost?
4. Chart Hills' budgeted variable cost per unit is $18, and it expects to sell its shirts for $35 apiece. Compute the sales-volume variance and reconcile it with the production-volume variance calculated in requirement 2. What does each concept measure?

32 Overhead variances, service setting. Carlyle Capital Company offers financial services to its clients. Recently, Carlyle has experienced rapid growth and has increased both its client base and the variety of services it offers. The company is becoming concerned about its rising costs, however, particularly related to technology overhead.

After some study, Carlyle determines that its variable and fixed technology overhead costs are both driven by the processing time involved in meeting client requests. This is typically measured in CPU units of their computer usage. Carlyle's measure of output is the number of client interactions in a given period.

The technology budget for Carlyle for the first quarter of 2017 was as follows:

Client interactions	12,000
Fixed Overhead	$14,400
Variable Overhead	4,800 CPU units @ $2 per CPU unit

The actual results for the first quarter of 2017 are given below:

Client interactions	13,600
Fixed Overhead	$14,100
Variable Overhead	$11,200
CPU Units used	5,500

Required

1. Calculate the variable overhead spending and efficiency variances, and indicate whether each is favorable (F) or unfavorable (U).
2. Calculate the fixed overhead spending and production-volume variances, and indicate whether each is favorable (F) or unfavorable (U).
3. Comment on Carlyle Capital's overhead variances. In your view, is the firm right to be worried about its control over technology spending?

33 Identifying favorable and unfavorable variances. Tred-America, Inc., manufactures tires for large auto companies. It uses standard costing and allocates variable and fixed manufacturing overhead based on machine-hours. For each independent scenario given, indicate whether each of the manufacturing variances will be favorable or unfavorable or, in case of insufficient information, indicate "CBD" (cannot be determined).

Scenario	Variable Overhead Spending Variance	Variable Overhead Efficiency Variance	Fixed Overhead Spending Variance	Fixed Overhead Production-Volume Variance
Production output is 8% more than budgeted, and actual fixed manufacturing overhead costs are 7% less than budgeted				
Production output is 11% more than budgeted; actual machine-hours are 5% less than budgeted				
Production output is 15% less than budgeted				
Actual machine-hours are 18% greater than flexible-budget machine-hours				
Relative to the flexible budget, actual machine-hours are 10% greater, and actual variable manufacturing overhead costs are 15% less				

34 Flexible-budget variances. Eric Williams is a cost accountant and business analyst for Diamond Design Company (DDC), which manufactures expensive brass doorknobs. DDC uses two direct-cost categories: direct materials and direct manufacturing labor. Williams feels that manufacturing overhead is most closely related to material usage. Therefore, DDC allocates manufacturing overhead to production based upon pounds of materials used.

At the beginning of 2017, DDC budgeted annual production of 420,000 doorknobs and adopted the following standards for each doorknob:

	Input	Cost/Doorknob
Direct materials (brass)	0.3 lb. @ $10/lb.	$ 3.00
Direct manufacturing labor	1.2 hours @ $17/hour	20.40
Manufacturing overhead:		
Variable	$5/lb. × 0.3 lb.	1.50
Fixed	$15/lb. × 0.3 lb.	4.50
Standard cost per doorknob		$29.40

Actual results for April 2017 were as follows:

Production	29,000 doorknobs
Direct materials purchased	12,400 lb. at $11/lb.
Direct materials used	8,500 lbs.
Direct manufacturing labor	29,200 hours for $671,600
Variable manufacturing overhead	$ 65,100
Fixed manufacturing overhead	$158,000

Required

1. For the month of April, compute the following variances, indicating whether each is favorable (F) or unfavorable (U):
   a. Direct materials price variance (based on purchases)
   b. Direct materials efficiency variance
   c. Direct manufacturing labor price variance
   d. Direct manufacturing labor efficiency variance
   e. Variable manufacturing overhead spending variance
   f. Variable manufacturing overhead efficiency variance
   g. Production-volume variance
   h. Fixed manufacturing overhead spending variance
2. Can Williams use any of the variances to help explain any of the other variances? Give examples.

Problems

MyAccountingLab

35 Comprehensive variance analysis. Cooking Whiz manufactures premium food processors. The following are some manufacturing overhead data for Cooking Whiz for the year ended December 31, 2017:

Manufacturing Overhead	Actual Results	Flexible Budget	Allocated Amount
Variable	$ 71,808	$ 80,640	$ 80,640
Fixed	360,672	351,360	368,640

Budgeted number of output units: 915

Planned allocation rate: 2 machine-hours per unit

Actual number of machine-hours used: 1,632

Static-budget variable manufacturing overhead costs: $76,860

Required

Compute the following quantities (you should be able to do so in the prescribed order):

1. Budgeted number of machine-hours planned
2. Budgeted fixed manufacturing overhead costs per machine-hour
3. Budgeted variable manufacturing overhead costs per machine-hour
4. Budgeted number of machine-hours allowed for actual output produced
5. Actual number of output units
6. Actual number of machine-hours used per output unit

36 Journal entries (continuation of 35).

Required

1. Prepare journal entries for variable and fixed manufacturing overhead (you will need to calculate the various variances to accomplish this).
2. Overhead variances are written off to the Cost of Goods Sold (COGS) account at the end of the fiscal year. Show how COGS is adjusted through journal entries.

37 Graphs and overhead variances. Best Around, Inc., is a manufacturer of vacuums and uses standard costing. Manufacturing overhead (both variable and fixed) is allocated to products on the basis of budgeted machine-hours. In 2017, budgeted fixed manufacturing overhead cost was $17,000,000. Budgeted variable manufacturing overhead was $10 per machine-hour. The denominator level was 1,000,000 machine-hours.

Required

1. Prepare a graph for fixed manufacturing overhead. The graph should display how Best Around, Inc.'s fixed manufacturing overhead costs will be depicted for the purposes of (a) planning and control and (b) inventory costing.
2. Suppose that 1,125,000 machine-hours were allowed for actual output produced in 2017, but 1,200,000 actual machine-hours were used. Actual manufacturing overhead was $12,075,000, variable, and $17,100,000, fixed. Compute (a) the variable manufacturing overhead spending and efficiency variances and (b) the fixed manufacturing overhead spending and production-volume variances. Use the columnar presentation illustrated in Exhibit 4.

3. What is the amount of the under- or overallocated variable manufacturing overhead and the under- or overallocated fixed manufacturing overhead? Why are the flexible-budget variance and the under- or overallocated overhead amount always the same for variable manufacturing overhead but rarely the same for fixed manufacturing overhead?
4. Suppose the denominator level was 1,700,000 rather than 1,000,000 machine-hours. What variances in requirement 2 would be affected? Recompute them.

38 Overhead variance, missing information. Consider the following two situations—cases A and B—independently. Data refer to operations for April 2017. For each situation, assume standard costing. Also assume the use of a flexible budget for control of variable and fixed manufacturing overhead based on machine-hours.

		Cases	
		A	B
(1)	Fixed manufacturing overhead incurred	$27,000	$132,900
(2)	Variable manufacturing overhead incurred	$10,511	—
(3)	Denominator level in machine-hours	—	45,000
(4)	Standard machine-hours allowed for actual output achieved	4,700	—
(5)	Fixed manufacturing overhead (per standard machine-hour)	—	—
Flexible-Budget Data:			
(6)	Variable manufacturing overhead (per standard machine-hour)	—	$ 2.10
(7)	Budgeted fixed manufacturing overhead	$23,375	$130,500
(8)	Budgeted variable manufacturing overhead[a]	—	—
(9)	Total budgeted manufacturing overhead[a]	—	—
Additional Data:			
(10)	Standard variable manufacturing overhead allocated	$10,340	—
(11)	Standard fixed manufacturing overhead allocated	$19,975	—
(12)	Production-volume variance	—	$ 580 F
(13)	Variable manufacturing overhead spending variance	$ 457 U	$ 1,490 F
(14)	Variable manufacturing overhead efficiency variance	—	$ 1,680 F
(15)	Fixed manufacturing overhead spending variance	—	—
(16)	Actual machine-hours used	—	—

[a]For standard machine-hours allowed for actual output produced.

Required

Fill in the blanks under each case. [*Hint*: Prepare a worksheet similar to that in Exhibit 4. Fill in the knowns and then solve for the unknowns.]

39 Flexible budgets, 4-variance analysis. (CMA, adapted) Wilson Products uses standard costing. It allocates manufacturing overhead (both variable and fixed) to products on the basis of standard direct manufacturing labor-hours (DLH). Wilson Products develops its manufacturing overhead rate from the current annual budget. The manufacturing overhead budget for 2017 is based on budgeted output of 672,000 units, requiring 3,360,000 DLH. The company is able to schedule production uniformly throughout the year.

A total of 72,000 output units requiring 321,000 DLH was produced during May 2017. Manufacturing overhead (MOH) costs incurred for May amounted to $355,800. The actual costs, compared with the annual budget and 1/12 of the annual budget, are as follows:

Annual Manufacturing Overhead Budget 2017

	Total Amount	Per Output Unit	Per DLH Input Unit	Monthly MOH Budget May 2017	Actual MOH Costs for May 2017
Variable MOH					
Indirect manufacturing labor	$1,008,000	$1.50	$0.30	$ 84,000	$ 84,000
Supplies	672,000	1.00	0.20	56,000	117,000
Fixed MOH					
Supervision	571,200	0.85	0.17	47,600	41,000
Utilities	369,600	0.55	0.11	30,800	55,000
Depreciation	705,600	1.05	0.21	58,800	88,800
Total	$3,326,400	$4.95	$0.99	$277,200	$355,800

Calculate the following amounts for Wilson Products for May 2017:

Required

1. Total manufacturing overhead costs allocated
2. Variable manufacturing overhead spending variance
3. Fixed manufacturing overhead spending variance
4. Variable manufacturing overhead efficiency variance
5. Production-volume variance

Be sure to identify each variance as favorable (F) or unfavorable (U).

40 Activity-based costing, batch-level variance analysis. Audrina's Fleet Feet, Inc., produces dance shoes for stores all over the world. While the pairs of shoes are boxed individually, they are crated and shipped in batches. The shipping department records both variable direct batch-level costs and fixed batch-level overhead costs. The following information pertains to shipping department costs for 2017.

	Static-Budget Amounts	Actual Results
Pairs of shoes shipped	225,000	180,000
Average number of pairs of shoes per crate	15	10
Packing hours per crate	0.9 hours	1.1 hour
Variable direct cost per hour	$18	$16
Fixed overhead cost	$54,000	$56,500

Required

1. What is the static budget number of crates for 2017?
2. What is the flexible budget number of crates for 2017?
3. What is the actual number of crates shipped in 2017?
4. Assuming fixed overhead is allocated using crate-packing hours, what is the predetermined fixed overhead allocation rate?
5. For variable direct batch-level costs, compute the price and efficiency variances.
6. For fixed overhead costs, compute the spending and the production-volume variances.

41 Overhead variances and sales-volume variance. The Roller Bag Company manufactures extremely light and rolling suitcases. It was one of the first companies to produce rolling suitcases and sales have increased for the past several years. In 2017, Roller Bag budgeted to sell 150,000 suitcases for $80 each.

The budgeted standard machine hours for production in 2017 were 375,000 machine hours. Budgeted fixed overhead costs are $525,000, and variable overhead cost was budgeted at $1.75 per machine-hour.

In 2017, Roller Bag experienced a drop in sales due to increased competition for rolling suitcases. Roller Bag used 310,000 machine-hours to produce the 120,000 suitcases it sold in 2017. Actual variable overhead costs were $488,000 and actual fixed overhead costs were $532,400. The average selling price of the suitcases sold in 2017 was $72.

Actual direct materials and direct labor costs were the same as standard costs, which were $20 per unit and $18 per unit, respectively.

Required

1. Calculate the variable overhead and fixed overhead variances (spending, efficiency, spending, and volume).
2. Create a chart like that in Exhibit 2 showing Flexible Budget Variances and Sales-Volume Variances for revenues, costs, contribution margin, and operating income.
3. Calculate the operating income based on budgeted profit per suitcase.
4. Reconcile the budgeted operating income from requirement 3 to the actual operating income from your chart in requirement 2.
5. Calculate the operating income volume variance and show how the sales-volume variance is composed of the production-volume variance and the operating income volume variance.

42 Activity-based costing, batch-level variance analysis. The Saluki Company specializes in making fraternity and sorority T-shirts for the college market. Due to the high setup costs for each batch printed, Saluki holds the T-shirt requests until demand is approximately 100 shirts. At that point Saluki will schedule the setup and production of the shirts. For rush orders, Saluki will produce smaller batches for an additional charge of $175 per setup.

Budgeted and actual costs for the production process for 2017 were as follows:

	Static-Budget Amounts	Actual Results
Number of shirts produced	125,000	114,000
Average number of shirts per setup	100	95
Hours to set up machines	5	5.20
Direct variable cost per setup-hour	$ 30	$ 32
Total fixed setup overhead costs	$56,250	$56,000

Required

1. What is the static budget number of setups for 2017?
2. What is the flexible-budget number of setups for 2017?
3. What is the actual number of setups in 2017?
4. Assuming fixed setup overhead costs are allocated using setup-hours, what is the predetermined fixed setup overhead allocation rate?
5. Does Saluki's charge of $175 cover the budgeted direct variable cost of an order? The budgeted total cost?
6. For direct variable setup costs, compute the price and efficiency variances.
7. For fixed setup overhead costs, compute the spending and the production-volume variances.
8. What qualitative factors should Saluki consider before accepting or rejecting a special order?

43 Comprehensive review of working backward from given variances. The Gallo Company uses a flexible budget and standard costs to aid planning and control of its machining manufacturing operations. Its costing system for manufacturing has two direct-cost categories (direct materials and direct manufacturing labor—both variable) and two overhead-cost categories (variable manufacturing overhead and fixed manufacturing overhead, both allocated using direct manufacturing labor-hours).

At the 50,000 budgeted direct manufacturing labor-hour level for August, budgeted direct manufacturing labor is $1,250,000, budgeted variable manufacturing overhead is $500,000, and budgeted fixed manufacturing overhead is $1,000,000.

The following actual results are for August:

Direct materials price variance (based on purchases)	$179,300 F
Direct materials efficiency variance	75,900 U
Direct manufacturing labor costs incurred	535,500
Variable manufacturing overhead flexible-budget variance	10,400 U
Variable manufacturing overhead efficiency variance	18,100 U
Fixed manufacturing overhead incurred	957,550

The standard cost per pound of direct materials is $11.50. The standard allowance is 6 pounds of direct materials for each unit of product. During August, 20,000 units of product were produced. There was no beginning inventory of direct materials. There was no beginning or ending work in process. In August, the direct materials price variance was $1.10 per pound.

In July, labor unrest caused a major slowdown in the pace of production, resulting in an unfavorable direct manufacturing labor efficiency variance of $40,000. There was no direct manufacturing labor price variance. Labor unrest persisted into August. Some workers quit. Their replacements had to be hired at higher wage rates, which had to be extended to all workers. The actual average wage rate in August exceeded the standard average wage rate by $0.50 per hour.

Required

1. Compute the following for August:
   a. Total pounds of direct materials purchased
   b. Total number of pounds of excess direct materials used
   c. Variable manufacturing overhead spending variance
   d. Total number of actual direct manufacturing labor-hours used
   e. Total number of standard direct manufacturing labor-hours allowed for the units produced
   f. Production-volume variance
2. Describe how Gallo's control of variable manufacturing overhead items differs from its control of fixed manufacturing overhead items.

44 Review of 3-variance analysis. (CPA, adapted) The Beal Manufacturing Company's costing system has two direct-cost categories: direct materials and direct manufacturing labor. Manufacturing overhead (both variable and fixed) is allocated to products on the basis of standard direct manufacturing labor-hours (DLH). At the beginning of 2017, Beal adopted the following standards for its manufacturing costs:

	Input	Cost per Output Unit
Direct materials	5 lb. at $4 per lb.	$ 20.00
Direct manufacturing labor	4 hrs. at $16 per hr.	64.00
Manufacturing overhead:		
Variable	$8 per DLH	32.00
Fixed	$9 per DLH	36.00
Standard manufacturing cost per output unit		$152.00

The denominator level for total manufacturing overhead per month in 2017 is 37,000 direct manufacturing labor-hours. Beal's budget for January 2017 was based on this denominator level. The records for January indicated the following:

Direct materials purchased	40,300 lb. at $3.80 per lb.
Direct materials used	37,300 lb.
Direct manufacturing labor	31,400 hrs. at $16.25 per hr.
Total actual manufacturing overhead (variable and fixed)	$650,000
Actual production	7,600 output units

Required

1. Prepare a schedule of total standard manufacturing costs for the 7,600 output units in January 2017.
2. For the month of January 2017, compute the following variances, indicating whether each is favorable (F) or unfavorable (U):
   a. Direct materials price variance, based on purchases
   b. Direct materials efficiency variance
   c. Direct manufacturing labor price variance
   d. Direct manufacturing labor efficiency variance
   e. Total manufacturing overhead spending variance
   f. Variable manufacturing overhead efficiency variance
   g. Production-volume variance

45 Nonfinancial variances. Kathy's Kettle Potato Chips produces gourmet chips distributed to chain sub shops throughout California. To ensure that their chips are of the highest quality and have taste appeal, Kathy has a rigorous inspection process. For quality control purposes, Kathy has a standard based on the number of pounds of chips inspected per hour and the number of pounds that pass or fail the inspection.

Kathy expects that for every 1,000 pounds of chips produced, 200 pounds of chips will be inspected. Inspection of 200 pounds of chips should take 1 hour. Kathy also expects that 1% of the chips inspected will fail the inspection. During the month of May, Kathy produced 113,000 pounds of chips and inspected 22,300 pounds of chips in 120 hours. Of the 22,300 pounds of chips inspected, 215 pounds of chips failed to pass the inspection.

Required

1. Compute two variances that help determine whether the time spent on inspections was more or less than expected. (Follow a format similar to the one used for the variable overhead spending and efficiency variances, but without prices.)
2. Compute two variances that can be used to evaluate the percentage of the chips that fails the inspection.

46 Overhead variances, service sector. Cavio is a cloud service provider that offers computing resources to handle enterprise-wide applications. For March 2017, Cavio estimates that it will provide 18,000 RAM hours of services to clients. The budgeted variable overhead rate is $6 per RAM hour.

At the end of March, there is a $500 favorable spending variance for variable overhead and a $1,575 unfavorable spending variance for fixed overhead. For the services actually provided during the month, 14,850 RAM hours are budgeted and 15,000 RAM hours are actually used. Total actual overhead costs are $119,875.

Required

1. Compute efficiency and flexible-budget variances for Cavio's variable overhead in March 2017. Will variable overhead be over- or underallocated? By how much?
2. Compute production-volume and flexible-budget variances for Cavio's fixed overhead in March 2017. Will fixed overhead be over- or underallocated? By how much?

47 Direct-cost and overhead variances, income statement. The Greenspace Company started business on January 1, 2017. The company adopted a standard costing system for the production of ergonomic backpacks. Greenspace chose direct labor as the application base for overhead and decided to use the proration method to account for variances at year-end.

In 2017, Greenspace expected to make and sell 160,000 backpacks; each was budgeted to use 2 yards of fabric and require 0.5 hours of direct labor work. The company expected to pay $2 per yard for fabric and compensate workers at an hourly wage of $12. Greenspace has no variable overhead costs, but budgeted $800,000 for fixed manufacturing overhead in 2017.

In 2017, Greenspace actually made 180,000 backpacks and sold 144,000 of them for a total revenue of $2,592,000.

The costs incurred were as follows:

Fixed manufacturing costs	$ 875,000
Fabric costs (370,000 yards bought and used)	$ 758,500
Direct manufacturing labor costs (100,000 hours)	$1,260,000

Required

1. Compute the following variances for 2017, and indicate whether each is favorable (F) or unfavorable (U):
   a. Direct materials efficiency variance
   b. Direct materials price variance
   c. Direct manufacturing labor efficiency variance
   d. Direct manufacturing labor price variance
   e. Fixed overhead flexible-budget variance
   f. Fixed overhead production-volume variance
2. Compute Greenspace Company's gross margin for its first year of operation.

48 Overhead variances, ethics. Carpenter Company uses standard costing. The company has a manufacturing plant in Georgia. Standard labor-hours per unit are 0.50, and the variable overhead rate for the Georgia plant is $3.50 per direct labor-hour. Fixed overhead for the Georgia plant is budgeted at $1,800,000 for the year. Firm management has always used variance analysis as a performance measure for the plant.

Tom Saban has just been hired as a new controller for Carpenter Company. Tom is good friends with the Georgia plant manager and wants him to get a favorable review. Tom decides to underestimate production, and budgets annual output of 1,200,000 units. His explanation for this is that the economy is slowing and sales are likely to decrease.

At the end of the year, the plant reported the following actual results: output of 1,500,000 using 760,000 labor-hours in total, at a cost of $2,700,000 in variable overhead and $1,850,000 in fixed overhead.

Required

1. Compute the budgeted fixed cost per labor-hour for the fixed overhead.
2. Compute the variable overhead spending variance and the variable overhead efficiency variance.
3. Compute the fixed overhead spending and volume variances.
4. Compute the budgeted fixed cost per labor-hour for the fixed overhead if Tom Saban had estimated production more realistically at the expected sales level of 1,500,000 units.
5. Summarize the fixed overhead variance based on both the projected level of production of 1,200,000 units and 1,500,000 units.
6. Did Tom Saban's attempt to make his friend, the plant manager, look better work? Why or why not?
7. What do you think of Tom Saban's behavior overall?

GLOSSARY

Denominator level. The denominator in the budgeted fixed overhead rate computation.

Denominator-level variance. See *production-volume variance*.

Fixed overhead flexible-budget variance. The difference between actual fixed overhead costs and fixed overhead costs in the flexible budget.

Fixed overhead spending variance. Same as the fixed overhead flexible-budget variance. The difference between actual fixed overhead costs and fixed overhead costs in the flexible budget.

Operating-income volume variance. The difference between static-budget operating income and the operating income based on budgeted profit per unit and actual units of output.

Production-volume variance. The difference between budgeted fixed overhead and fixed overhead allocated on the basis of actual output produced. Also called *denominator-level variance*.

Standard costing. Costing system that traces direct costs to output produced by multiplying the standard prices or rates by the standard quantities of inputs allowed for actual outputs produced and allocates overhead costs on the basis of the standard overhead-cost rates times the standard quantities of the allocation bases allowed for the actual outputs produced.

Total-overhead variance. The sum of the flexible-budget variance and the production-volume variance.

Variable overhead efficiency variance. The difference between the actual quantity of variable overhead cost-allocation base used and budgeted quantity of variable overhead cost-allocation base that should have been used to produce actual output, multiplied by budgeted variable overhead cost per unit of cost-allocation base.

Variable overhead flexible-budget variance. The difference between actual variable overhead costs incurred and flexible-budget variable overhead amounts.

Variable overhead spending variance. The difference between actual variable overhead cost per unit and budgeted variable overhead cost per unit of the cost-allocation base, multiplied by actual quantity of variable overhead cost-allocation base used for actual output.

Incentive Pay

Learning Objectives

When you finish studying this chapter, you should be able to:

1. Explore the incentive pay approach.
2. Describe the differences between incentive pay methods and traditional pay methods.
3. Summarize five types of individual incentive pay plans.
4. Explain two types of group incentive plans.
5. Discuss two types of company-wide incentive plans.
6. Summarize considerations when designing incentive pay programs.

CHAPTER WARM-UP!

If your professor has assigned this, go to the Assignments section of **mymanagementlab.com** to complete the Chapter Warm-Up! and see what you already know. After reading the chapter, you'll have a chance to take the Chapter Quiz! and see what you've learned.

As we will discuss momentarily, incentive pay places some portion of employee compensation at risk. When employees, groups of employees, or entire companies fail to meet preestablished performance standards (e.g., annual sales), they forfeit some or all of their compensation. Expert incentive pay consultants argue that a critical element of successful incentive pay plans is the provision of regular, honest communication to employees. We will explore this issue and several others related to effective incentive pay design.

EXPLORING INCENTIVE PAY

1 Explore the incentive pay approach.

Incentive pay or **variable pay** rewards employees for partially or completely attaining a predetermined work objective. Incentive or variable pay is defined as compensation, other than base wages or salaries that fluctuate according to employees' attainment of some standard, such as a preestablished formula, individual or group goals, or company earnings.[1]

Effective incentive pay systems are based on three assumptions:[2]

- Individual employees and work teams differ in how much they contribute to the company, both in what they do as well as in how well they do it.
- The company's overall performance depends to a large degree on the performance of individuals and groups within the company.
- To attract, retain, and motivate high performers and to be fair to all employees, a company needs to reward employees on the basis of their relative performance.

Much like seniority and merit pay approaches, incentive pay augments employees' base pay, but incentive pay appears as a one-time payment. Employees usually receive a combination of recurring base pay and incentive pay, with base pay representing the greater portion of core compensation. More employees are presently eligible for incentive pay than ever before, as companies seek to control costs and motivate personnel continually to strive for exemplary performance. Companies increasingly recognize the importance of applying incentive pay programs to various kinds of employees as well, including production workers, technical employees, and service workers.

Some companies use incentive pay extensively. Lincoln Electric Company, a manufacturer of welding machines and motors, is renowned for its use of incentive pay plans. At Lincoln Electric, production employees receive recurring base pay as well as incentive pay. The company determines incentive pay awards according to five performance criteria: quality, output, dependability, cooperation, and ideas. The company has awarded incentive payments every year since 1934, through prosperous and poor economic times. In 2014, the average profit sharing payment per employee was $33,984.[3] Coupled with average base pay, total core compensation for Lincoln employees was $82,903. Over the past 10 years, Lincoln's profit-sharing payments averaged approximately 40 percent of annual salary.[4] Similarly, Southwest Airlines has distributed profit-sharing payments to employees every year for the past 40 years.[5] In 2014, Southwest announced that it would share $228 million in profits.[6]

Companies generally institute incentive pay programs to control payroll costs or to motivate employee productivity. Companies can control costs by replacing annual merit or seniority increases or fixed salaries with incentive plans that award pay raises only when the company enjoys an offsetting rise in productivity, profits, or some other measure of business success. Well-developed incentive programs base pay on performance, so employees control their own compensation levels. Companies can choose incentives to further business objectives. For example, the management of H. Lee Moffitt Cancer Center and Research Institute at the University of South Florida continually strives to improve patient care as well as control costs. Moffitt's incentives are usually tied to net income or operating surplus, quality of care measures, patient satisfaction scores, and operating efficiencies.

CONTRASTING INCENTIVE PAY WITH TRADITIONAL PAY

2 Describe the differences between incentive pay methods and traditional pay methods.

In traditional pay plans, employees receive compensation based on a fixed hourly pay rate or annual salary. Some companies use incentive pay programs that replace all or a portion of base pay in order to control payroll expenditures and to link pay to performance. Since 1998, there has been a 47 percent increase in the use of incentive pay programs. Companies use incentive pay programs in varying degrees for different kinds of positions.[7] Nowadays, most companies use a mix of traditional and incentive pay methods. The mix has steadily changed. In 1998, traditional pay increases totaled 4.2 percent of payroll while incentive pay increases amounted to 8.0 percent. In 2014, the amounts were 2.9 percent and 12.7 percent, respectively.[8]

Employees under traditional pay structures earn raises according to their length of service in the organization or to supervisors' subjective appraisals of employees' job performance. Again, both merit pay raises and seniority pay raises are permanent increases to base pay. Annual merit pay increase amounts usually total no more than a small percentage of base pay (approximately 3 percent), but the dollar impact represents a significant cost to employers over time. Table 1 shows the contrast in rate of compensation increase between a traditional merit compensation plan and an incentive plan.

Companies use incentive pay to reward individual employees, teams of employees, or whole companies based on their performance. Incentive pay plans are not limited solely to production or nonsupervisory workers. Many incentive plans apply to such categories of employees as sales

TABLE 1 Permanent Annual Merit Increases versus Incentive Awards: A Comparison

(At the end of 2015, John Smith earned an annual salary of $35,000.)

		Cost of Increase (Total Current Salary—2015 Annual Salary equals $35,000)		Total Salary under	
Year	Increase Amount (%)	Permanent Merit Increase ($)	Incentive Award ($)	Permanent Merit Increase (Percent Increase × Previous Year Annual Salary) + Previous Annual Salary ($)	Incentive Award (Percent Increase × 2015 Salary) + Fixed Base Pay ($35,000) ($)
2016	3	1,050	1,050	36,050	36,050
2017	5	2,853	1,750	37,853	36,750
2018	4	4,367	1,400	39,367	36,400
2019	7	7,122	2,450	42,122	37,450
2020	6	9,649	2,100	44,649	37,100

professionals, managers, and executives. Management typically relies on business objectives to determine incentive pay levels such as company profits and sales growth. Management then communicates these planned incentive levels and performance goals to managers. Although merit pay performance standards aim to be measurable and objective, incentive levels tend to be based on even more objective criteria, such as quantity of items an employee produces per production period or market indicators of a company's performance (e.g., an increase in market share for the fiscal year). Moreover, supervisors communicate the incentive award amounts in advance that correspond to objective performance levels. On the other hand, supervisors generally do not communicate the merit award amounts until after they offer subjective assessments of employees' performance.

Incentive pay plans can be broadly classified into three categories:

- ***Individual incentive plans.*** These plans reward employees whose work is performed independently. Some companies have piecework plans, typically for their production employees. Under piecework plans, an employee's compensation depends on the number of units she or he produces over a given period.
- ***Group incentive plans.*** These plans promote supportive, collaborative behavior among employees. Group incentives work well in manufacturing and service delivery environments that rely on interdependent teams. In gain sharing programs, group improvements in productivity, cost savings, or product quality are shared by employees within the group.
- ***Company-wide incentive plans.*** These plans tie employee compensation to a company's performance over a short time frame, usually from a one-month period to a five-year period.

Table 2 lists common performance measures used in individual, group, and company-wide incentive plans[9].

INDIVIDUAL INCENTIVES

3 Summarize five types of individual incentive pay plans.

Individual incentive pay plans are most appropriate under three conditions. First, employees' performance can be measured objectively. Examples of objective performance measures include:

- Number of units produced—an automobile parts production worker's completion of a turn signal lighting assembly
- Sales amount—a Mary Kay Cosmetics sales professional's monthly sales revenue
- Reduction in error rate—a word processor's reduction in typing errors

Second, individual incentive plans are appropriate when employees have sufficient control over work outcomes. Factors such as frequent equipment breakdowns and delays in receipt

TABLE 2 Typical Performance Measures for Individual, Group, and Company-wide Incentive Plans

Individual Incentive Plans
Quantity of work output
Quality of work output
Monthly sales
Work safety record
Work attendance
Group Incentive Plans
Customer satisfaction
Labor cost savings (through gain sharing plans)
Materials cost savings
Services cost savings (e.g., utilities)
Company-wide Incentive Plans
Operational Measures:
Customer satisfaction
Operational efficiency
Service/quality
Safety/occupational injury
Financial Measures:
Revenue
Earnings per company stock share
Operating income
Revenue growth

Note: Measures such as safety records and customer satisfaction can be measured on an individual, group, or company-wide basis according to a company's objectives.

of raw materials limit employees' ability to control their performance levels. Employees are not likely to be diligent when they encounter interference: Chances are good that employees who previously experienced interference will expect to encounter interference in the future. Employees' resistance threatens profits because companies will find it difficult to motivate people to work hard when problem factors are not present.

Third, individual incentive plans are appropriate when they do not create a level of unhealthy competition among workers that ultimately leads to poor quality. For example, a company may create unhealthy competition when it limits the number of incentive awards to only 10 percent of the employees who have demonstrated the highest levels of performance. If the company judges performance according to volume, then employees may sacrifice quality as they compete against each other to outmatch quantity. In addition, under an incentive plan that rewards quantity of output, those employees who meet or exceed the highest standard established by their employer may be subject to intimidation by workers whose work falls below the standard.[10] Unions may use these intimidation tactics to prevent plan standards from being raised.

Defining Individual Incentives

Individual incentive plans reward employees for meeting such work-related performance standards as quality, productivity, customer satisfaction, safety, or attendance. Any one of these standards by itself or in combination may be used. A company ultimately should employ the standards that represent work that an employee actually performs. For instance, take the case of telemarketers. Customer satisfaction and sales volume measures indicate telemarketers' performance. Tardiness would not be as relevant unless absenteeism was a general management problem.

Managers should also choose factors that are within the individual employee's control when they create individual performance standards. Furthermore, employees must know about standards and potential awards before the performance period starts. When designed and implemented well, individual incentive plans reward employees based on results for which they are directly responsible. The end result should be that excellent performers receive higher incentive awards than poor performers.

Types of Individual Incentive Plans

There are five common types of individual incentive plans:

- Piecework plans
- Management incentive plans
- Behavioral encouragement plans
- Referral plans
- Spot bonuses

PIECEWORK PLANS Companies generally use one of two **piecework plans.**[11] The first, which is typically found in manufacturing settings, rewards employees based on their individual hourly production against an objective output standard and are determined by the pace at which manufacturing equipment operates. For each hour, workers receive piecework incentives for every item produced over the designated production standard. Workers also receive a guaranteed hourly pay rate regardless of whether they meet the designated production standard. Table 3 illustrates the calculation of a piecework incentive.

Companies use piecework plans when the time to produce a unit is relatively short, usually less than 15 minutes, and the cycle repeats continuously. Piecework plans are usually found in such manufacturing industries as textiles and apparel.

Quality is also an important consideration. Companies do not reward employees for producing defective products. In the apparel industry, manufacturers attempt to minimize defect rates because they cannot sell defective clothing for the same price as nondefective clothing. Selling defective clothing at a lower price reduces company profits.

The second type of piecework incentive plan establishes individual performance standards that include both objective and subjective criteria. Units produced represent an objective standard. Overall work quality is a subjective criterion that is based on supervisors' interpretations and judgments. For example, supervisors may judge customer service representatives' performance to be higher when

TABLE 3 Calculation of a Piecework Award for a Garment Worker

Piecework standard: 15 stitched garments per hour

Hourly base pay rate awarded to employees when the standard is not met: $4.50 per hour

That is, workers receive $4.50 per hour worked regardless of whether they meet the piecework standard of 15 stitched garments per hour.

Piecework incentive award: $0.75 per garment stitched per hour above the piecework standard

	Guaranteed Hourly Base Pay ($)	Piecework Award (No. of Garments Stitched above the Piecework Standard × Piecework Incentive Award)	Total Hourly Earnings ($)
First hour	4.50	10 garments × $0.75/garment = $7.50	12.00
Second hour	4.50	Fewer than 15 stitched garments, thus piecework award equals $0	4.50

sales professionals emphasize the benefits of purchasing extended product warranties than when sales professionals merely mention the availability and price of extended product warranties.

Economists argue that there are two advantages to companies of using piecework plans in manufacturing settings known as the **incentive effect** and **sorting effect**.[12] The incentive effect refers to a worker's willingness to work diligently to produce more quality output than simply attending work without putting in the effort. To put this simply, employees earn much less under the piecework system than they would under a standard hourly pay system. Whereas employees are certainly expected to perform without an incentive (piece rate), research shows that incentives often are associated with higher employee performance.

The sorting effect addresses an employee's choice to stay versus leave his or her employer for another job, presumably one without an incentive pay contingency. Specifically, a hardworking, highly skilled employee is likely to choose to remain employed under an incentive system because both diligence and skill presumably contribute to higher quantity and quality of output—thus, higher pay.

MANAGEMENT INCENTIVE PLANS **Management incentive plans** award bonuses to managers when they meet or exceed objectives based on sales, profit, production, or other measures for their division, department, or unit. Management incentive plans differ from piecework plans in that piecework plans base rewards on the attainment of one specific objective, and management incentive plans often require multiple complex objectives. For example, management incentive plans reward managers for increasing market share or reducing their budgets without compromising the quality and quantity of output. The best-known management incentive plan is management by objectives (MBO).[13] MBO was presented as an outcome-oriented performance appraisal technique for merit pay systems. When MBO is used as part of merit pay systems, superiors make subjective assessments of managers' performance, and they use these assessments to determine permanent merit pay increases. When used as part of incentive programs, superiors communicate the amount of incentive pay managers will receive based on the attainment of specific goals.

BEHAVIORAL ENCOURAGEMENT PLANS Under **behavioral encouragement plans**, employees receive payments for specific behavioral accomplishments (e.g., good attendance or safety records). For example, companies usually award monetary bonuses to employees who have exemplary attendance records for a specified period. When behavioral encouragement plans are applied to safety records, workers earn awards for lower personal injury or accident rates associated with the improper use of heavy equipment or hazardous chemicals. Table 4 contains an illustration of a sample behavioral encouragement plan that rewards employees for

TABLE 4 A Sample Behavioral Encouragement Plan that Rewards Employee Attendance

At the end of each 3-month period, employees with exemplary attendance records will receive monetary incentive awards according to the following schedule. Note that the number of days absent does not refer to such company-approved absences as vacation, personal illness, jury duty, bereavement leave, military duty, scheduled holidays, and educational leave.

Number of Days Absent	Monetary Incentive Award ($)
0 (perfect attendance)	250
1	200
2	100
3	50
4	25

excellent attendance. Employees can earn $250 for perfect attendance during a three-month period. With perfect attendance for an entire year, employees can earn $1,000. Behavioral encouragement plans have the potential to save companies substantially more money than the cost of these awards. For example, frequent absenteeism in a company's workforce could disrupt production goals and quality. Customers may respond by choosing to make purchases for better quality products from other companies. Loss of customer bases will have a negative impact on profitability and reputation that prompts prospective customers to choose alternate sources to purchase products.

REFERRAL PLANS Employees may receive monetary bonuses under **referral plans** for referring new customers or recruiting successful job applicants. Companies commonly rely on referral bonuses to enhance recruitment of highly qualified employees, particularly when the supply of highly qualified individuals is low, or the company is experiencing explosive growth. HubSpot, the developer of inbound marketing software, recently experienced growth in excess of 80 percent.[14] The company relies heavily on the work of talented software engineers and designers. In response to this substantial growth, HubSpot offered a $30,000 bonus to employees whose referral was hired as a software engineer or designer. This program expands eligibility to any individual regardless of employment status.

A successful referral usually means that companies award bonuses only if hired referrals remain employed with the company in good standing beyond a designated period, often at least 30 days. Referral plans rely on the idea that current employees' familiarity with company culture should enable them to identify viable candidates for job openings more efficiently than employment agencies could because agents are probably less familiar with client companies' cultures. Employees are likely to make only those referrals they truly believe are worthwhile because their personal reputations are at stake.

SPOT BONUSES Many organizations today are providing *spot bonuses* for critical areas and talents. **Spot bonuses** are relatively small monetary gifts provided to employees for outstanding work or effort during a reasonably short period of time. If an employee's performance has been exceptional, the employer may reward the worker with a one-time bonus with an amount as low as $50. For certain professional jobs it is not unheard of for a highly productive worker to receive $5,000 shortly after a noteworthy achievement.

Advantages of Individual Incentive Pay Programs

There are three key advantages of individual incentive pay plans. First, individual incentive plans can promote the relationship between pay and performance. Employees in the United States are highly motivated by earning money. Employees strive for excellence when they expect to earn incentive awards commensurate with their job performance.

Second, individual incentive plans promote an equitable distribution of compensation within companies (i.e., the amount employees earn depends on their job performance). The better they perform, the more they earn. Equitable pay ultimately enables companies to retain the best performers. Paying better performers more money sends a signal that the company appropriately values positive job performance.

A third advantage of individual incentive plans is their compatibility with such individualistic cultures as the United States. Because U.S. employees are socialized to make individual contributions and be recognized for them, the national culture of the United States probably enhances the motivational value of individual incentive programs.

Disadvantages of Individual Incentive Pay Programs

Although individual incentive plans can prove effective in certain settings, these programs also have serious limitations. Supervisors, human resource (HR) managers, and compensation professionals should know about three potential problems with individual incentive plans.

First, individual incentive plans possess the potential to promote inflexibility. Because supervisors determine employee performance levels, workers under individual incentive plans become dependent on supervisors for setting work goals. If employees become highly proficient performers, they are not likely to increase their performance beyond their reward compensation. For example, let's assume that management defines the maximum incentive award as $500 per month, which is awarded to employees whose productivity rates 15 percent above the performance standard. Employees who produce more than 15 percent above the production standard will not receive additional incentive pay beyond the $500. With this design, employees would not be motivated to further improve their performance.

Second, with merit pay systems, supervisors must develop and maintain comprehensive performance measures to properly grant incentive awards. Individual incentive programs pose measurement problems when management implements improved work methods or equipment. When such changes occur, it will take some time for employees to become proficient performers. Thus, it will be difficult for companies to determine equitable incentive awards, which may lead to employees' resistance to the new methods.

A third limitation of individual incentive plans is that they may encourage undesirable workplace behavior when these plans reward only one or a subset of dimensions that constitute employees' total job performance. Let's assume that an incentive plan rewards employees for quantity of output. If employees' jobs address such various dimensions as quantity of output, quality, and customer satisfaction, employees may focus on the one dimension—in this case, quantity of output—that leads to incentive pay and thereby neglect the other dimensions.

Our focus has been on financial incentive awards. Companies may provide nonfinancial incentives to employees, including companies such as hotels that operate in a low-paying industry. Hotel chain Joie de Vivre Hospitality does just that. Several times a year, employees are given the opportunity to stay in any of the company's hotels at no charge and to take full advantage of the amenities. By assuming the customer role, Joie de Vivre Hospitality employees can improve job performance because they gain a better understanding of their guests' needs.

WATCH IT!

If your professor has assigned this, go to the Assignments section of **mymangementlab.com** to complete the video exercise titled Joie de Vivre Hospitality: Pay for Performance and Financial Incentives.

GROUP INCENTIVES

4 Explain two types of group incentive plans.

U.S. employers are increasingly using teams to get work done. Two main changes in the business environment have led to an increased use of teams in the workplace.[15] First, in the 1980s, many more Japanese companies were conducting business in the United States, particularly in the automobile industry. A common feature of Japanese companies was the use of teams, which contributed to superior product quality. Second, team-based job design promotes innovation in the workplace.[16] At Newell Rubbermaid, a manufacturer of such plastic household products as snap-together furniture and storage boxes, product innovation has become the rule since the implementation of project teams. Team members represent various cross-functional areas, including research and development (R&D), marketing, finance, and manufacturing. Rubbermaid attributes the rush on innovation to the cross-fertilization of ideas that has resulted from the work of these diverse teams.[17]

Companies that use work teams need to change individualistic compensation practices so that groups are rewarded for their behavior together.[18] Team-based pay plans should accordingly emphasize cooperation between and within teams, compensate employees for additional responsibilities they often must assume in their roles as members of a team, and encourage team members to attain predetermined objectives for the team.[19] Merit, seniority, or individual incentives do not encourage team behaviors and may potentially limit team effectiveness. Experts suggest that traditional pay programs will undermine the ability of teams to function effectively.[20] Both merit- and seniority-based pay emphasize hierarchy among employees, which is incompatible with the very concept of a team.

Team-based organizational structures encourage team members to learn new skills and assume broader responsibility than is expected of them under traditional pay structures that are geared toward individuals. Rather than following specific orders from a supervisor, employees who work in teams must initiate plans for achieving their team's production. A pay plan for teams usually emphasizes cooperation and rewards its members for the additional responsibilities they must take on, as well as the skills and knowledge they must acquire.

Defining Group Incentives

Group incentive programs reward employees for their collective performance, rather than for each employee's individual performance. Group incentive programs are most effective when all group members have some impact on achieving the goal, even though individual contributions might not be equal. Boeing utilizes a team-based approach to manufacture its model 777 jumbo jet. More than 200 cross-functional teams contribute to the construction of each jet, and the contribution of each individual is clearly not equal. Installing such interior trim features as upholstery is not nearly as essential to the airworthiness of each jet as are the jobs of ensuring the aerodynamic integrity of each aircraft.

Well-designed group incentive plans ultimately reinforce teamwork, cultivate loyalty to the company, and increase productivity. For instance, the Morning Star Company, which processes tomato production, is based almost entirely on self-management principles: "We envision an organization of self-managing professionals who initiate communication and coordination of their activities with fellow colleagues, customers, suppliers, and fellow industry participants, absent directives from others."[21] Annually, each employee negotiates a Colleague Letter of Understanding with other employees who are most affected by his or her work.[22] Morning Star leadership believes that voluntary agreements among individuals can produce effective coordination.

Types of Group Incentive Plans

Companies use two major types of group incentive plans:

- *Team-based or small-group incentive plans.* A small group of employees shares a financial reward when a specific objective is met.
- *Gain sharing plans.* A group of employees, generally a department or work unit, is rewarded for productivity gains.

TEAM-BASED OR SMALL-GROUP INCENTIVE PLANS **Team-based incentives** are similar to individual incentives with one exception. Each group member receives a financial reward for the attainment of a group goal. There are many kinds of team incentive programs. Most companies define these programs based on the type of team:[23]

Work (process) teams refer to organizational units that perform the work of the organization on an ongoing basis. Membership is relatively permanent, and members work full time in the team. Customer service teams and assembly teams on production lines represent excellent examples of work teams. Work teams are effective when individuals are cross-trained to perform team members' work when they are absent. The goal is to maintain consistency in performance quality (e.g., addressing customer concerns promptly even when one or more team members are absent) and output (e.g., in the case of assembly teams). Team members ultimately engage in performance sharing rather than focusing exclusively on one set of tasks. The knowledge and skill sets required to contribute effectively to the work of a process team can be acquired with the assistance of person-focused pay.

Project teams consist of a group of people assigned to complete a one-time project. Members usually have well-defined roles and may work on specific phases of the project, either full time or in addition to other work responsibilities of the team. Project teams usually work across such functions as engineering, product development, and marketing to ensure that the final product meets company specifications in terms of cost, quality, and responsiveness to market demands (e.g., Toyota's hybrid vehicles). Many individuals collaborated to ensure the production of cars that rely less on fossil fuels, demonstrate excellent gas mileage, and offer the same driving experience that people have come to expect of gasoline-powered automobiles.

Parallel teams, or task forces, include employees assigned to work on a specific task in addition to normal work duties. The modifier *parallel* indicates that an employee works on the team task while continuing to work on normal duties. Also, parallel teams or task forces operate on a temporary basis until their work culminates in a recommendation to top management. Task forces are used to evaluate existing systems and processes, to select new technology, and to improve existing products. There is some evidence that team interactions on complex tasks are likely to influence creativity more than individual efforts, and group incentive plans may foster creativity. This especially seems to be the case when incentive compensation is truly an add-on, and independent of employees' regular base pay.[24]

Teams or groups may ultimately receive incentive pay based on such criteria as customer satisfaction (i.e., customer service quality), safety records, quality, and production records. Although these criteria apply to other categories of incentive programs as well (individual, company-wide, and group plans), companies allocate awards to each worker based on the group's attainment of predetermined performance standards.

Human resource managers must devise methods for allocating incentives to team members. Although the team-based reward is generated by the performance of the team, the incentive payments are typically distributed to members of the team individually. Human resource experts allocate rewards in one of three ways:

- Equal incentive payments to all team members.
- Differential incentive payments to team members based on their contribution to the team's performance.
- Differential payments determined by a ratio of each team member's base pay to the total base pay of the group.

The first method—the equal incentives payment approach—reinforces cooperation among team members except when team members perceive differences in members' contributions or performance. The second method—the differential incentive payments approach—distributes rewards based to some extent on individual performance. Differential approaches obviously can hinder cooperative behavior. Some employees may focus on their own performance rather than on the group's performance because they wish to maximize their income. As a compromise, companies may base part of the incentive on individual performance, with the remainder based on the team's performance. The third disbursement method—differential payments by ratio of base pay—rewards each group member in proportion to her or his base pay. This approach assumes that employees with higher base pay contribute more to the company and so should be rewarded in accord with that worth.

GAIN SHARING PLANS **Gain sharing** describes group incentive systems that provide participating employees with an incentive payment based on improved company performance for increased productivity, increased customer satisfaction, lower costs, or better safety records.[25] Gain sharing was developed so that all employees could benefit financially from productivity improvements resulting from the suggestion system. In addition to serving as a compensation tool, most gain sharing reflects a management philosophy that emphasizes employee involvement. The use of gain sharing is most appropriate where workplace technology does not constrain productivity improvements. For example, assembly line workers' abilities to improve productivity may be limited. Increasing the speed of the conveyor belts may compromise workers' safety.

Most gain sharing programs have three components:[26]

- Leadership philosophy
- Employee involvement systems
- Bonus

The first component—leadership philosophy—refers to a cooperative organizational climate that promotes high levels of trust, open communication, and participation. The second component—employee involvement systems—drives organizational productivity improvements. Employee involvement systems use broadly based suggestion systems. Anyone can make suggestions to a committee made up of both hourly and management employees who oversee the suggestion implementation. This involvement system also may include other innovative employee involvement practices (e.g., problem-solving task forces).

The bonus is the third component of a gain sharing plan. A company awards gain sharing bonuses when its actual productivity exceeds its targeted productivity level. The gain sharing bonuses are usually based on a formula that measures productivity that employees perceive as fair and the employer believes will result in improvements in company performance. Employees typically receive gain sharing bonuses on a monthly basis. Most bonuses range between 5 and 10 percent of an employee's base annual pay. A noteworthy exception to this norm is AmeriSteel. On average, AmeriSteel's gain sharing plan pays out between 35 and 45 percent of base pay.

Although many accounts of gain sharing use can be found in the practitioner and scholarly literature, no one has completed a comprehensive, soundly designed investigation of the effectiveness of gain sharing programs.[27] Meanwhile, gain sharing programs' success has been attributed to company cultures that support cooperation among employees.[28] Some gain sharing attempts have failed. Such organizational, external environmental and financial information factors, including poor communications within and across departments, highly competitive product markets, and variable corporate profits over time can inhibit effective gain sharing programs.[29] Poor communications will stifle the creativity needed to improve the efficiency of work processes when employees focus exclusively on their own work. Highly competitive product markets often require companies to make frequent changes to their production methods, as in the automobile industry, where such changes occur each year with the introduction of new models. When companies make frequent or sudden changes, employees must have time to learn the new processes well before they can offer productive suggestions. Companies that experience variable profits from year to year most likely do not use gain sharing because management sets aside as much excess cash as possible in reserve for periods when profits are down and excess cash is scarce.

The Scanlon, Rucker, and Improshare gain sharing plans are the most common forms used in companies, and they were also the first types of gain sharing plans developed and used by employers. These plans were adopted wholesale in the early days of gain sharing. Employers today generally modify one of these traditional plans to meet their needs or adopt hybrid plans.

THE SCANLON PLAN Joseph Scanlon first developed the gain sharing concept in 1935 as an employee involvement system without a pay element.[30] The hallmark of the **Scanlon plan** is its emphasis on employee involvement. Scanlon believed that employees will exercise self-direction and self-control if they are committed to company objectives and that employees will accept and seek out responsibility if given the opportunity.[31] Current Scanlon plans include monetary rewards to employees for productivity improvements. Scanlon plans assume that companies will be able to offer higher pay to workers, generate increased profits for stockholders, and lower prices for consumers. The *Scanlon plan* is a generic term referring to any gain sharing plan that has characteristics common to the original gain sharing plan devised by Scanlon. Scanlon plans have the following three components:[32]

- An emphasis on teamwork to reduce costs, assisted by management-supplied information on production concerns.
- Suggestion systems that route cost-saving ideas from the workforce through a labor–management committee that evaluates and acts on accepted suggestions.
- A monetary reward based on productivity improvements to encourage employee involvement.

Scanlon plan employee involvement systems include a formal suggestion program structured at two levels. Production-level committees, usually including a department foreman or supervisor and at least one elected worker, communicate the suggestion program and its reward features to workers. Production committee members encourage and assist workers in making suggestions and formally record suggestions for consideration. Production committees may also reject suggestions that are not feasible, but they must provide a written explanation of the reasons for the rejection to the worker who made the suggestion. Providing the written rationale under this circumstance is key to helping employees understand why the suggestions are not feasible and, thus, workers are not discouraged from making suggestions in the future. After employees' suggestions have been fully implemented, they typically receive bonuses on a monthly basis.

The production committee forwards appropriate suggestions to a company-wide screening committee, which also includes worker representatives. This committee reviews suggestions referred by the production committees, serves as a communications link between management and employees, and reviews the company's performance each month.

Actual gain sharing formulas are designed to suit the individual needs of the company.[33] Formulas are usually based on the ratio between labor costs and **sales value of production (SVOP).**[34] The SVOP is the sum of sales revenue plus the value of goods in inventory.

Smaller Scanlon ratios indicate that labor costs are lower relative to SVOP. Companies definitely strive for lower ratios, as Table 5 illustrates. In addition, Table 5 shows the calculation for a bonus distribution under a Scanlon plan.

THE RUCKER PLAN Similar to Scanlon's plan, the **Rucker plan** was developed by Allan W. Rucker in 1933. Both the Scanlon and Rucker plans emphasize employee involvement and provide monetary incentives to encourage employee participation. The main difference lies in the formula used to measure productivity. Rucker plans use a **value-added formula** to measure productivity. Value added is the difference between the value of the sales price of a product and the value of materials purchased to make the product. The following example illustrates the concept of value added based on the sequence of events that eventually lead to selling bread to consumers. These events include growing the wheat, milling the wheat, adding the wheat to other ingredients to make bread, and selling the bread to consumers.

A farmer grows the wheat and sells it to a miller; the added value is the difference in the income the farmer receives for the wheat and the costs incurred for purchasing seed, fertilizer, fuel, and other supplies. The miller, in turn, buys the wheat from the farmer, mills it, and then sells it to a bakery. The difference in the cost of buying the wheat and the price it is sold for to the baker is the amount of "value" the miller "adds" in the milling processes. The same process is repeated by the baker, as the flour that was milled by the miller is mixed with other ingredients, baked, and sold as bread either to the consumer or to a retailer who in turn sells it to the consumer. The baker "adds value" by blending in the other ingredients to the flour and baking the bread. If the bread is sold to the consumer through a retailer, then the retailer also "adds value" by buying the bread from the bakery, transporting it to a store convenient for the consumer, displaying the bread, and selling it. The total of all the added values from each step along the way equals the total contribution to the overall economy from the chain of events.[35]

TABLE 5 Illustration of a Scanlon Plan

For the period 2012–2014, the labor costs of XYZ Manufacturing Company have averaged $44,000,000 per year. During the same 3-year period, the sales value of XYZ's production (SVOP) averaged $83,000,000 per year. (As an aside, of the $83,000,000, $65,000,000 represents sales revenue and $18,000,000 represents the value of goods held in inventory.) The Scanlon ratio for XYZ Manufacturing Company is:

$$\$44{,}000{,}000/\$83{,}000{,}000 = 0.53$$

The ratio of 0.53 is the base line or standard. Any benefits that result from an improvement in production methods produce results. Labor cost savings are shared with workers. In other words, when improvements lead to a Scanlon ratio that is lower than the standard of 0.53, employees will receive gain sharing bonuses.

The operating information for XYZ Manufacturing Company for March 2015 was as follows:

Total labor costs	$3,100,000
SVOP	$7,200,000

The Scanlon ratio, based on March 2015 information was

$$\frac{\$3{,}100{,}000}{\$7{,}200{,}000} = 0.43$$

The Scanlon ratio for March 2015 was less than the standard of 0.53. In order for there to be a payout, labor costs for March 2015 must be less than $3,816,000 (i.e., 0.53 × $7,200,000); $3,816,000 represents allowable labor costs for March 2015 based on the Scanlon standard established for XYZ Manufacturing.

In summary, the allowable labor costs for March 2015 were $3,816,000. The actual labor costs were $3,100,000. Thus, the savings $716,000 ($3,816,000–$3,100,000) is available for distribution as a bonus.

The following ratio is used to determine whether bonuses will be awarded under a Rucker plan:

$$\frac{\text{Value added}}{\text{Total employment costs}}$$

In contrast to the Scanlon ratio, companies prefer a larger Rucker ratio. A larger Rucker ratio indicates that the value added is greater than total employment costs. Table 6 illustrates the calculation for bonus distribution under the Rucker plan.

Invented by Mitchell Fein in 1973, **Improshare**—Improved Productivity through Sharing—measures productivity physically rather than in terms of dollar savings like those used in the Scanlon and Rucker plans. These programs aim to produce more products with fewer labor hours. Under Improshare, the emphasis is on providing employees with an incentive to finish products. The Improshare bonus is based on a **labor hour ratio formula**. A standard is determined by analyzing historical accounting data to find the number of labor hours needed to complete a product. Productivity is then measured as a ratio of standard labor hours and actual labor hours. Unlike the Rucker and Scanlon plans, employee participation is not a feature, and workers receive bonuses on a weekly basis.

In summary, the Scanlon, Rucker, and Improshare plans are among the best-known kinds of gain sharing programs that are used by companies. Although the principle underlying these different plans is the same (i.e., a group incentive system that provides all or most employees a bonus payment based on improved performance), they each rest on slightly different assumptions.

Advantages of Group Incentives

The use of group incentive plans has two advantages for companies. First, companies can more easily develop performance measures for group incentive plans than they can for individual

TABLE 6 Illustration of a Rucker Plan

Calculating the Standard:

For the 2012 – 2015 period, ABC Manufacturing Company generated average net sales of $7,500,000. The company paid $3,200,000 for materials, $250,000 for sundry supplies, and $225,000 for such services as liability insurance, basic maintenance, and utilities. On the basis of these data, average value added was $3,825,000 (i.e., net sales – costs of materials, supplies, and services rendered), for this example, $7,500,000 - ($3,200,000 + $250,000 + $225,000).

For the same period, average total employment costs were $2,400,000, which includes hourly wages for nonexempt workers, annual salaries for exempt employees, payroll taxes, and all benefit costs. Based on the Rucker formula, the ratio of value added to total employment costs was 1.59 ($3,825,000/$2,400,000).

If there are to be bonuses at the end of 2016, each dollar attributed to employment costs must be accompanied by creating at least $1.59 of value added.

Value added	$3,825,000
Total employment costs	$2,400,000

The Rucker ratio, based on this information, was:

$$\frac{\$3{,}825{,}000}{\$2{,}400{,}000} = 1.59$$

Applying the Standard to a 2016 Performance:

The operating information for ABC Manufacturing Company for 2016 was as follows:

Value added	$670,000
Total employment costs	$625,000

The Rucker ratio, based on 2016 data, was:

$$\frac{\$670{,}000}{\$625{,}000} = 1.07$$

This Rucker ratio for 2016 was less than the standard of 1.59. In order for there to be a payout, value added for 2016 must be more than the standard, which would be $1,065,300 (1.59 × $670,000). However, based on the Rucker ratio obtained for this month (1.07), value added was only $716,900 (1.07 × $670,000). Therefore, employees of ABC Manufacturing will not receive any gain sharing bonuses based on 2016 performance.

incentive plans. There are obviously fewer groups in a company than individuals. Thus, companies generally use fewer resources (e.g., staff time) to develop performance measures. In addition, judging the quality of the final product makes the most sense because companies must deliver high-quality products to maintain competitiveness. During the late 1970s and early 1980s, U.S. automobile manufacturers lost substantial market share to foreign automobile manufacturers because foreign automakers marketed automobiles of substantially higher quality than U.S. automakers. The trend did not change until U.S. automakers manufactured high-quality vehicles on a consistent basis.

Greater group cohesion is the second advantage associated with group incentive plans.[36] Cohesive groups usually work more effectively toward achieving common goals than do individual group members focusing on the specific tasks for which they are responsible. Working collaboratively is undoubtedly in group members' best interests in order to maximize their incentive awards.

Disadvantages of Group Incentives

The main disadvantage of group incentive compensation is employee turnover. Companies' implementation of group incentive programs may lead to turnover because of the **free-rider**

effect. Some employees may make fewer contributions to the group goals because they possess lower ability, skills, or experience than other group members. In some groups, members may deliberately choose to put forth less effort, particularly when each group member receives the same incentive compensation regardless of individual contributions to the group goals. In any case, the free-rider effect initially leads to feelings of inequity among those who make the greatest contributions to the attainment of the group goal. Over time, members who make the greatest contributions are likely to leave.

Group members may feel uncomfortable with the fact that other members' performance influences their compensation level. Exemplary performers are more likely to feel this way when other group members are not contributing equally to the attainment of group goals. The lower performance of a few group members may lead to lower earnings for all members of the group. Discomfort with group incentive plans is likely to be heightened where incentive compensation represents the lion's share of core compensation.

COMPANY-WIDE INCENTIVES

The use of company-wide incentive plans can be traced to the nineteenth century. Companies instituted profit sharing programs to ease workers' dissatisfaction with low pay and to change their beliefs that company management paid workers substandard wages while earning substantial profits. Quite simply, management believed that workers would be less likely to challenge managerial practices if they received a share of company profits.

5 Discuss two types of company-wide incentive plans.

Defining Company-wide Incentives

Company-wide incentive plans reward employees when the company exceeds minimum acceptable performance standards (e.g., profits or the overall value of the company based on its stock price). As competitive pressures on companies increased, management sought methods to improve employee productivity. Companies presently use company-wide incentive programs to motivate employees to work harder for increased profits or increased company value to owners. Advocates of company-wide incentive plans believe that well-designed programs make workers' and owners' goals more compatible as workers strive toward increasing company profits or value.

Types of Company-wide Incentive Plans

Companies use two major types of company-wide incentive plans:

- ***Profit sharing plans.*** Employees earn a financial reward when their company's profit objective is met.
- ***Employee stock option plans.*** Companies grant employees the right to purchase shares of company stock.

PROFIT SHARING PLANS **Profit sharing plans** pay a portion of company profits to employees, separate from base pay, cost-of-living adjustments, or permanent merit pay increases. Two basic kinds of profit sharing plans are used widely today. First, **current profit sharing** plans award cash to employees, typically on a quarterly or annual basis. Current profit sharing represents a form of short-term incentive because of the frequency of payout potential. Second, **deferred profit sharing** plans place cash awards in trust accounts for employees. These trusts are set aside on employees' behalf as a source of retirement income, and can also be considered a long-term incentive. Aircraft manufacturer Boeing offers current profit sharing plans to all employee groups, except for ones that are represented by labor unions. Under the plan, nonmanagement employees can earn from 1 to 20 days of regular pay.[37] In 2015, nonmanagement employees were granted 12.5 days' extra pay.[38] Management employees received awards that ranged from 12.5 to 22.5 of their salaries.

Calculating Profit Sharing Awards HR professionals determine the pool of profit sharing money with any of three possible formulas. A fixed *first-dollar-of-profits* formula uses a specific percentage of annual profits, contingent upon the successful attainment of a company goal. For instance, a company might establish that the profit sharing fund will equal 7 percent of corporate profits; however, payment is contingent on a specified reduction in scrap rates.

Second, companies may use a *graduated first-dollar-of-profits* formula instead of a fixed percentage. For example, a company may choose to share 3 percent of the first $8 million of profits and 6 percent of the profits in excess of that level. Graduated formulas motivate employees to strive for extraordinary profit targets by sharing even more of the incremental gain.

Third, *profitability threshold* formulas fund profit sharing pools only if profits exceed a predetermined minimum level but fall below some established maximum level. Companies establish minimums to guarantee a return to shareholders before they distribute profits to employees. They establish maximums because they attribute any profits beyond this level to factors other than employee productivity or creativity (e.g., technological innovation).

After management selects a funding formula for the profit sharing pool, they must consider how to distribute pool money among employees. Companies usually make distributions in one of three ways: equal payments to all employees, proportional payments to employees based on annual salary, and proportional payments to employees based on their contribution to profits. Equal payments to all employees reflect a belief that all employees should share equally in the company's gain in order to promote cooperation among employees; however, employee contributions to profits probably vary. Most employers accordingly divide the profit sharing pool among employees based on a differential basis.

Companies may disburse profits based on *proportional payments to employees based on their annual salaries.* Higher-paying jobs presumably indicate more potential to influence a company's competitive position. For any given job, pay will differ according to performance or seniority.

Still another approach is to disburse profits as *proportional payments to employees based on their contribution to profits.* Some companies measure employee contributions to profit based on job performance; however, this approach is not very feasible because it is difficult to isolate each employee's contributions to profits. For example, how does a secretary's performance (based on answering telephones, greeting visitors, and typing memos) directly contribute to company performance?

Advantages of Profit Sharing Plans The use of a profit sharing plan has two main advantages, one for employees and the other for companies. When properly designed, profit sharing plans enable employees to share in companies' fortunes. As employees benefit from profit sharing plans, they will be more likely to work productively to promote profits. The upshot of enhanced employee productivity obviously is greater profits for companies that use profit sharing plans.

Companies that use profit sharing programs gain greater financial flexibility. As we discussed, monetary payouts to employees vary with profit levels. During economic downturns, payout levels are significantly lower than they are during economic boom periods. This feature of profit sharing plans enables companies to use limited cash reserves where needed (e.g., for R&D activities).

Disadvantages of Profit Sharing Plans There are two main disadvantages associated with profit sharing plans. The first one directly affects employees; the second affects companies. Profit sharing plans may undermine the economic security of employees, particularly if profit sharing represents a sizable portion of direct compensation. Because company profits vary from year to year, so do employees' earnings. Thus, employees will find it difficult to predict their earnings, which will affect their saving and buying behavior. If there is significant variability in earnings, a company's excellent performers are likely to leave for employment with competitors. The turnover of excellent performers certainly represents a significant disadvantage to companies.

Employers also find profit sharing programs to be problematic under certain conditions. Profit sharing plans may fail to motivate employees because they do not see a direct link between their efforts and corporate profits. Hourly employees in particular may have trouble seeing this connection because their efforts appear to be several steps removed from the company's performance. For instance, an assembly line worker who installs interior trim (e.g., carpeting and seats) in automobiles may not find any connection between his or her efforts and the level of company profits because interior trim represents just one of many steps in the production of automobiles.

EMPLOYEE STOCK OPTION PLANS **Employee stock option plans** represent a long-term company-wide incentive plan that provide employees with stock options. Under these plans, companies grant employees the right to purchase shares of company stock. **Company stock** represents total equity of a company. **Company stock shares** represent equity segments of equal value. Equity interest increases positively with the number of stock shares. **Stock options** describe an employee's right to purchase company stock. Employees do not actually own stock until they exercise the stock option rights. This is done by purchasing stock at a designated price after a company-chosen time period lapses, usually no more than 10 years. Employee stock options provide an incentive to work productively, with the expectation that collective employee productivity will increase the value of company stock over time. Employees earn monetary compensation when they sell the stock at a higher price than they originally paid for it.

DESIGNING INCENTIVE PAY PROGRAMS

6 Summarize considerations when designing incentive pay programs.

When designing an incentive pay plan, HR professionals and line managers should consider five key factors:

- Whether the plan should be based on group or individual employee performance.
- The level of risk employees will be willing to accept in their overall compensation package.
- Whether incentive pay should replace or complement traditional pay.
- The criteria by which performance should be judged.
- The time horizon for goals—long term, short term, or a combination of both.

Group versus Individual Incentives

Companies considering various design alternatives should choose a design that fits the structure of the company. Group incentive programs are most suitable where the nature of the work is interdependent and the contributions of individual employees are difficult to measure. In such situations, companies require cooperative behavior among their employees. Companies may be able to encourage team behavior by linking compensation to the achievement of department or division goals and eliminating from the pay determination process such factors that are outside the group's control as the late delivery of raw materials by an independent vendor.

On the other hand, individual incentive plans reward employees for meeting or surpassing such predetermined individual goals as production or sales quotas. The attainment of individual goals should be well within employees' grasp as is the case for group incentives. Moreover, goals for individual incentive programs should be based on independent work rather than interdependent work. For example, it would be appropriate to base an employee's incentive on typing accuracy because the work can be performed independently and there are few external constraints on an employee's ability to complete such work. At the group level, it would be reasonable to provide incentives to the individual members of a sales team. In the case of computer hardware and networks, the sale and implementation of these products involve a team of marketing professionals and technical experts who depend on the others' expertise to identify the appropriate configuration of hardware and networking equipment (i.e., meeting the client's needs) and to install the equipment in the client's company successfully.

Level of Risk

Careful consideration should be given to the level of risk employees are willing to accept. Incentive pay may complement base salary or may be used in place of all or a portion of base salary. The level of risk clearly increases as incentive pay represents a greater proportion of total core compensation. The level of risk tends to be greater among higher-level employees than among those who are at the lower levels of a company's job structure. It is reasonable to infer that the attainment of a first-line supervisor's goal of maintaining a packing department's level of productivity above a predetermined level is less risky than the achievement of a sales manager's goal of increasing market share by 10 percent in a market where the competition is already quite stiff. Apart from an employee's rank, the level of risk chosen should depend on the extent to which employees control the attainment of the desired goal. The adoption of incentive pay programs makes the most sense when participants have a reasonable degree of control over the attainment of the plan's goals. Incentive programs logically are bound to fail when the goals are simply out of reach because they are too difficult or because extraneous factors are hampering employees' efforts to meet goals.

Complementing or Replacing Base Pay

When complementing base pay, a company awards incentive pay in addition to an employee's base pay and benefits. On the other hand, companies may reduce base pay by placing the reduced portion at risk in an incentive plan. For instance, if a company grants its employees 10 percent raises each year, the company could, instead, grant its employees a 4 percent cost-of-living increase and use the remaining 6 percent as incentive by awarding none of it to below-average performers, only half of it to employees whose performance is average, and the entire 6 percent to employees whose performance is above average. In this scenario, the 6 percent that was expected by the employees to become part of their base pay is no longer a guarantee because that potential salary has been placed at risk. By introducing risk into the pay program, employees have the potential to earn more than the 6 percent because poor performers will receive less, leaving more to be distributed to exemplary performers.

Companies in such cyclical industries as retail sales could benefit by including an incentive component in the core compensation programs they offer to employees. During slow business periods, the use of regular merit pay programs that add permanent increments to base pay can create budget problems. If incentive pay were used instead of permanent merit raises, then the level of expenditure on compensation would vary with levels of business activity. In effect, the use of incentive pay can lower payroll costs during lean periods and enhance the level of rewards when business activity picks up.

Performance Criteria

The measures used to appraise employee performance obviously should be quantifiable and accessible. For incentive pay programs, common measures of employee performance are company profits, sales revenue, and number of units produced by a business unit. The measures chosen preferably should relate to the company's competitive strategy. For instance, if a company is attempting to enhance quality, its incentive plan would probably reward employees on the basis of customer satisfaction with quality.

In reality, more than one performance measure may be relevant. In such instances, a company is likely to employ all of the measures as a basis for awarding incentives. The weighting scheme would reflect the relative importance of each performance criterion to the company's competitive strategy [e.g., company performance (10 percent), unit performance (40 percent), and individual performance (50 percent), incorporating all of the organizational levels]. An employee clearly would receive an incentive even if company or departmental performance was poor. In effect, the relative weights are indicative of the degree of risk to an employee that is inherent in these plans. Compared with the previous example, the following plan would be quite risky: 50 percent company performance, 35 percent departmental performance, and 15 percent individual performance. Employees' earnings would depend mainly on company and departmental performance over which they possess less control than they do over their own performance.

Time Horizon: Short Term versus Long Term

A key feature of incentive pay plans is the time orientation. There are no definitive standards to distinguish between short term and long term. A general rule of thumb is that short-term goals generally can be achieved in five years or less and that long-term goals may require even longer. Most companies offer one or more short-term plans.[39] Among the most popular plans are spot awards, profit sharing, and team-based incentives.

On the other hand, incentive programs for professionals and executives also have a long-term orientation. Stock option plans are among the most commonly used.[40] For instance, rewarding an engineer's innovation in product design requires a long-term orientation because it takes an extended amount of time to move through the series of steps required to bring the innovation to the marketplace (e.g., patent approval, manufacturing, and market distribution). The incentives that executives receive are based on a long-term horizon because their success is matched against the endurance of a company over time.

COMPENSATION IN ACTION

The use of incentive pay by an employer can be an effective way to tie individual or team performance to compensation. Many of the items in the *Action Checklist* are critical to the proper formation and administration of an incentive pay program (i.e., accurate criteria and measurement along with ongoing and honest performance discussions). Once this critical foundation is established, line managers and HR and compensation specialists must ensure that the plan is understood by employees and they can see the link between their performance and the portion of pay at risk.

Action checklist for line managers and HR—establishing an incentive pay program

HR takes the lead

- Work with compensation specialists on your team to benchmark industry competitors to identify whether individual, group, or company-wide programs are being used (to stay current with trends and ensure that the best people are retained).
- Work with line managers, based on the chosen program (individual, group, or company-wide), to choose which types of plan are utilized.
- Hold roundtable discussions with employees to gather feedback on the proposed program and to identify potential areas where additional buy-in may be necessary.

Line managers take the lead

- Work with HR to identify the desired behavior(s) you want to tie to incentives—ensuring that the focus on these behaviors does not come at the expense of other desired outcomes.
- Seek the education of HR to understand limitations of the chosen plan and how to overcome some of the potential pitfalls; plan should be monitored and/or tailored if these obstacles lead to the wrong behaviors being rewarded.
- Provide proper information to HR so that a communication plan is created for rollout and implementation of the program—HR will form frequently asked questions (FAQs) and talking points that detail rationale for the change.

END OF CHAPTER REVIEW

MyManagementLab

Go to **mymanagementlab.com** to complete the problems marked with this icon ✪.

Summary

Learning Objective 1: Incentive pay or variable pay is defined as compensation, other than base wages or salaries, which fluctuates according to employees' attainment of some standard, such as a preestablished formula, individual or group goals, or company earnings.

Learning Objective 2: In traditional pay plans, employees receive compensation based on a fixed hourly pay rate or annual salary. Annual raises are added to base pay according to seniority or a supervisor's evaluation of past performance. In incentive plans, employees receive one-time payments that correspond to the level of performance attainment based on objective goals.

Learning Objective 3: Individual incentive plans reward employees whose work is performed independently and can be quantified objectively such as by sales volume or number of units produced.

Learning Objective 4: Group incentive plans promote supportive, collaborative behavior among employees. In general, members of a group or team receive the same incentive award for the group's performance.

Learning Objective 5: Company-wide incentive plans tie employee compensation to a company's performance over a relatively short time frame, not uncommonly, from three months to five years.

Learning Objective 6: Compensation professionals give consideration to at least five important factors when designing effective incentive pay plans. These include: (a) group versus individual incentives, (b) level of risk, (c) compensating or replacing base pay, (d) performance criteria, and (e) short- or long-term time horizon.

Key Terms

incentive pay
variable pay
piecework plans
incentive effect
sorting effect
management incentive plans
behavioral encouragement plans
referral plans
spot bonuses
group incentive programs
team-based incentives
gain sharing
Scanlon plan
sales value of production (SVOP)
Rucker plan
value-added formula
Improshare
labor hour ratio formula
free-rider effect
profit sharing plans
current profit sharing
deferred profit sharing
employee stock option plans
company stock
company stock shares
stock options

MyManagementLab

CHAPTER QUIZ!

If your professor has assigned this, go to the Assignments section of **mymanagementlab.com** to complete the Chapter Quiz! and see what you've learned.

Discussion Questions

1. Indicate whether you agree or disagree with the following statement: "Individual incentive plans are less preferable than group incentives and company-wide incentives." Explain your answer.
2. There is currently a tendency among business professionals to endorse the use of incentive pay plans. Identify two jobs for which individual incentive pay is appropriate and two jobs for which individual incentive pay is inappropriate. Be sure to include your justification.
3. Critics of profit sharing plans maintain that these plans do not motivate employees to perform at

higher levels. Under what conditions are profit sharing plans not likely to motivate employees?

4. Unlike individual incentive programs, group and company-wide incentive programs reward individuals based on group (e.g., cost savings in a department) and company-wide (e.g., profits) performance standards, respectively. Under group and company-wide incentive programs, it is possible for poor performers to benefit without making substantial contributions to group or company goals. What can companies do to ensure that poor performers do not benefit?
5. Opponents of incentive pay programs argue that these programs manipulate employees more than seniority and merit pay programs. Discuss your views of this statement.

CASE
Individual or Team Reward?

An additional Supplemental Case can be found on MyManagementLab.

Jack Hopson has been making wood furniture for more than 10 years. He recently joined Metropolitan Furniture and has some ideas for Sally Boston, the company's CEO. Jack likes working for Sally because she is very open to employee suggestions and is serious about making the company a success. Metropolitan is currently paying Jack a competitive hourly pay rate for him to build various designs of tables and chairs. However, Jack thinks that an incentive pay plan might convince him and his coworkers to put forth more effort.

At Jack's previous employer, a competing furniture maker, Jack was paid on a piece-rate pay plan. The company paid Jack a designated payment for every chair or table that he completed. Jack felt this plan provided him an incentive to work harder to build the furniture pieces. Sally likes Jack's idea; however, Sally is concerned about how such a plan would affect the employees' need to work together as a team.

While the workers at Metropolitan build most furniture pieces individually, they often need to pitch in and work as a team. Each worker receives individual assignments, but as a delivery date approaches for a preordered furniture set due to a customer, the workers must help each other complete certain pieces of the set to ensure on-time delivery. A reputation for on-time delivery differentiates Metropolitan from its competitors. Several companies that compete against Metropolitan have a reputation of late deliveries, which gives Metropolitan a competitive edge. Because their promise of on-time delivery is such a high priority, Sally is concerned that a piece-rate pay plan may prevent employees from working together to complete furniture sets.

Sally agrees with Jack that an incentive pay plan would help boost productivity, but she thinks that a team-based incentive pay plan may be a better approach. She has considered offering a team-based plan that provides a bonus payment when each set of furniture is completed in time for scheduled delivery. However, after hearing from Jack about the success of the piece-rate pay plan at his previous employer, she is unsure of which path to take.

Questions:

6. What are some advantages of offering a piece-rate pay plan to the furniture builders at Metropolitan Furniture?
7. What are some advantages of offering a team-based incentive pay plan?
8. What do you think Sally should do?

Crunch the Numbers!
Calculating Piecework Pay Awards

An additional Crunch the Numbers! exercise can be found on **mymanagementlab.com**.

Table 3 illustrates the calculation of a piecework award for a garment worker who has completed two hours of service. Over the course of a six-hour shift, his productivity varies:

First hour: 10 garments above the hourly standard
Second hour: no garments above the hourly standard
Third hour: 15 garments above the hourly standard

Fourth hour: 13 garments above the hourly standard
Fifth hour: 9 garments above the hourly standard
Sixth hour: 3 garments above the hourly standard

Questions:

9. Calculate the worker's total earnings for his shift.
10. How many dollars did the garment worker earn in incentive payments?
11. On the following day, the garment worker completed a six-hour shift, but did not exceed the standard at any time during this shift. How much did he earn for the day?

MyManagementLab

Go to **mymanagementlab.com** for Auto-graded writing questions as well as the following Assisted-graded writing questions:

12. How can incentive pay systems, when properly applied, contribute to companies meeting the goals of lowest cost and differentiation strategies?
13. Considering our discussion of employee roles in strategic compensation, how can companies explain employees' contributions to company profits? How would the conversation go with administrative staff members compared to sales professionals?
14. MyManagementLab Only – comprehensive writing assignment for this chapter.

Endnotes

1. Peck, C. (1993). *Variable Pay: Nontraditional Programs for Motivation and Reward*. New York: The Conference Board.
2. Gómez-Mejía, L. R., & Balkin, D. R. (1992). *Compensation, Organizational Strategy and Firm Performance*. Cincinnati, OH: South-Western.
3. Kinchen, D. M. (2014). *Lincoln Electric Celebrates 81 Uninterrupted Years of Paying Employee Profit-Sharing Bonus* (December 13). Available: https://davidkinchen.files.wordpress.com, accessed February 5, 2015.
4. Lincoln Electric. (2015). *I Choose Lincoln....* Available: *www.lincolnelectric.com*, accessed February 5, 2015.
5. Southwest Airlines. (2015). *WorkPerks*. Available: *http://www.southest.com*, accessed February 23, 2015.
6. Blasi, J., & Freeman, R. (2014). Southwest Airlines' profit-sharing payout: What capitalism should be. *Fortune* (April 14). Available: *http://www.fortune.com*, accessed February 23, 2015.
7. WorldatWork and Deloitte Consulting LLP (2014). *Incentive Pay Practices Survey: Publicly Traded Companies* (February). Available: *http://www.worldatwork.org*, accessed February 12, 2015.
8. Abosch, K. (2014). Making the most of your variable pay program. *Workspan* (November): 30–34.
9. WorldatWork and Deloitte Consulting LLP (2014). *Incentive Pay Practices Survey: Publicly Traded Companies* (February). Available: *http://www.worldatwork.org*, accessed February 12, 2015.
10. Dulles, F. R., & Dubofsky, M. (1984). *Labor in America: A History* (4th ed.). Arlington Heights, IL: Harlan Davidson.
11. Peck, *Variable Pay*.
12. Lazear, E. P. (1998). *Personnel Economics for Managers*. New York: John Wiley & Sons.
13. Drucker, P. (1954). *The Practice of Management*. New York: Harper.
14. Fleishman, H. (2013). HubSpot launches $30,000 referral program for developers and designers. (HubSpot Company News). Available: *http://www.hubspot.com/company-news/*, accessed December 3, 2014.
15. Jackson, S. E. (1992). Team composition in organizational settings: Issues in managing an increasingly diverse workforce. In S. Worchel, W. Wood & J. A. Simpson (Eds.), *Group Process and Productivity* (pp. 138–173). Newbury Park, CA: Sage.

16. Kanter, R. M. (1988). When a thousand flowers bloom: Structural, collective, and social conditions for innovation in organizations. In B. M. Staw & L. L. Cummings (Eds.), *Research in Organizational Behavior* (Vol. 10, pp. 169–211). Greenwich, CT: JAI.
17. Newell Rubbermaid (2015). Design Center. Available: http:// http://design.newellrubbermaid.com/index.html, accessed January 31, 2015.
18. Worchel, S., Wood, W., & Simpson, J. A. (Eds.). (1992). *Group Process and Productivity*. Newbury Park, CA: Sage.
19. Kanin-Lovers, J., & Cameron, M. (1993). Team-based reward systems. *Journal of Compensation and Benefits*, January–February, pp. 55–60.
20. Schuster, J. R., & Zingheim, P. K. (1993). Building pay environments to facilitate high-performance teams. *ACA Journal, 2*, pp. 40–51.
21. "Our Vision" in the "Morning Star College Guidelines" Used by permission from The Morning Star Company.
22. Hamel, G. (2011). First, let's fire all the managers. *Harvard Business Review* (December). Available: *http://www.hbr.org*, accessed January 31, 2015.
23. Greene, R. J. (2007). Team incentives. In D. Scott (Ed.), *Incentive Pay: Creating a Competitive Advantage*. Phoenix, AZ: WorldatWork Press.
24. Silverman, R. E. (2014). How to pay employees for great ideas. *The Wall Street Journal* (December 4). Available: *http://www.wsj.com*, accessed December 10, 2014.
25. Belcher, J. G., Jr. (1994). Gain sharing and variable pay: The state of the art. *Compensation & Benefits Review*, May–June, pp. 50–60.
26. Doyle, R. J. (1983). *Gain Sharing and Productivity*. New York: American Management Association.
27. Peck, *Variable Pay*.
28. Milkovich, G. T., & Newman, J. M. (1993). *Compensation* (4th ed.). Homewood, IL: Irwin.
29. Ross, T. (1990). Why gain sharing sometimes fails. In B. Graham-Moore & T. Ross (Eds.), *Gain Sharing: Plans for Improving Performance* (pp. 100–115). Washington, DC: Bureau of National Affairs.
30. Schuster, M. H. (2013). Gainsharing: Research and practice. *WorldatWork Journal* (Second Quarter): 30–39.
31. Lesiur, F. G. (Ed.). (1958). *The Scanlon Plan: A Frontier in Labor–Management Cooperation*. Cambridge, MA: MIT Press.
32. Bullock, R. J., & Lawler, E. E., III. (1984). Gain sharing: A few questions and fewer answers. *Human Resource Management, 23*, pp. 18–20.
33. Smith, B. T. (1986). The Scanlon Plan revisited: A way to a competitive tomorrow. *Production Engineering, 33*, pp. 28–31.
34. Geare, A. J. (1976). Productivity from Scanlon type plans. *Academy of Management Review, 1*, pp. 99–108.
35. Myers, D. W. (1989). *Compensation Management*. Chicago, IL: Commerce Clearing House.
36. Lawler, E. E., III, & Cohen, S. G. (1992). Designing a pay system for teams. *American Compensation Association Journal, 1*, pp. 6–19.
37. Boeing (2015). *Employee Performance Incentive Plans Summary*. Available: *http://www.boeing.com*, accessed February 23, 2015.
38. Gates, D. (2015). Boeing managers to get annual bonuses of 12.5% to 22.5%. *Seattle Times* (February 23). Available: *http://www.seattletimes.com*, accessed February 23, 2015.
39. WorldatWork and Deloitte Consulting LLP (2014). *Incentive Pay Practices Survey: Publicly Traded Companies* (February). Available: *http://www.worldatwork.org*, accessed February 12, 2015.
40. WorldatWork and Deloitte Consulting LLP (2014). *Incentive Pay Practices Survey: Publicly Traded Companies* (February). Available: *http://www.worldatwork.org*, accessed February 12, 2015.

Glossary

Behavioral encouragement plans are individual incentive pay plans that reward employees for specific such behavioral accomplishments as good attendance or safety records.

Company stock represents the total equity or worth of the company.

Company stock shares represent equity segments of equal value. Equity interest increases with the number of stock shares held.

Current profit sharing plans award cash to employees, typically on a quarterly or annual basis.

Deferred profit sharing plans place cash awards in trust accounts for employees. These trusts are set aside on employees' behalf as a source of retirement income.

Employee stock option plans represent one type of companywide incentives. Companies grant employees the right to purchase shares of company stock.

Free-rider effect occurs when employees of lower ability, skill, and effort benefit equally as employees of higher ability, skill, and effort in group incentive plans. The free-rider effect can lead to resentment and turnover of stronger contributors because weaker contributors are getting a "free ride."

Gain sharing describes group incentive systems that provide participating employees an incentive payment based on improved company performance, whether for increased productivity, increased customer satisfaction, lower costs, or better safety records.

Group incentive programs reward employees for their collective performance, rather than for each employee's individual performance.

Improshare is a specific kind of gain sharing program that rewards employees based on a labor hour ratio formula. A standard is determined by analyzing historical accounting data to find the number of labor hours needed to complete a product. Productivity is then measured as a ratio of standard labor hours and actual labor hours.

Incentive effect refers to a worker's willingness to work diligently to produce more quality output than simply attending work without putting in the effort.

Incentive pay or variable pay is defined as compensation, other than base wages or salaries, that fluctuates according to employees' attainment of some standard (e.g., a preestablished formula, individual or group goals, or company earnings).

Labor hour ratio formula used in determining the payouts in Improshare plans, refers to a standard determined by analyzing historical accounting data to find the number of labor hours needed to complete a product. Productivity is then measured as a ratio of standard labor hours and actual labor hours.

Management incentive plans award bonuses to managers who meet or exceed objectives based on sales, profit, production, or other measures for their division, department, or unit.

Piecework plan an individual incentive pay program, rewards employees based on their individual hourly production against an objective output standard, determined by the pace at which manufacturing equipment operates. For each hour, workers receive piecework incentives for every item produced over the designated production standard. Workers also receive a guaranteed hourly pay rate regardless of whether they meet the designated production standard.

Profit sharing plans pay a portion of company profits to employees, separate from base pay, cost-of-living adjustments, or permanent merit pay increases. Two kinds of profit sharing plans are used widely today: current profit sharing and deferred profit sharing.

Referral plans are individual incentive pay plans that reward employees for referring new customers or recruiting successful job applicants.

Rucker plan is a particular type of gain sharing program that emphasizes employee involvement. Gain sharing awards are based on the ratio between value added (less the costs of materials, supplies, and services rendered) and the total cost of employment.

Sales value of production (SVOP) is the sum of sales revenue plus the value of goods in inventory. This is part of the equation to determine payout amounts in Scanlon gain sharing plans.

Scanlon plan is a specific type of gain sharing program that emphasizes employee involvement. Gain sharing awards are based on the ratio between labor costs and sales value of production.

Sorting effect addresses an employee's choice to stay versus leave his or her employer for another job, presumably one without an incentive pay contingency

Spot bonuses are relatively small monetary gifts provided to employees for outstanding work or effort during a reasonably short period of time.

Stock options describe an employee's right to purchase company stock.

Team-based (or small-group) incentive plans a small group of employees shares a financial reward when a specific objective is met.

Value-added formula is the difference between the value of the sales price of a product and the value of materials purchased to make the product. This is part of the equation to determine payout amounts in Rucker gain sharing plans.

Building Internally Consistent Compensation Systems

Building Internally Consistent Compensation Systems

Learning Objectives

When you finish studying this chapter, you should be able to:

1. Explain the concept of internal consistency.
2. Summarize the practice of job analysis.
3. Describe the practice of job evaluation.
4. Summarize various job evaluation techniques.
5. Explain how internally consistent compensation systems and competitive strategy relate to each other.

CHAPTER WARM-UP!

If your professor has assigned this, go to the Assignments section of **mymanagementlab.com** to complete the Chapter Warm-Up! and see what you already know. After reading the chapter, you'll have a chance to take the Chapter Quiz! and see what you've learned.

Job descriptions serve as a cornerstone in the development of internally consistent compensation systems as well as in describing selection standards and performance criteria in performance evaluation systems. Well-written job descriptions provide compensation professionals with sufficiently well-specified information about job duties and worker requirements upon where to begin making judgments about the relative worth of jobs based on differences in job content. With these judgments in hand, compensation professionals will be well positioned to survey market pay rates to establish competitive pay levels to attract and retain talented employees.

INTERNAL CONSISTENCY

1 Explain the concept of internal consistency.

Internally consistent compensation systems clearly define the relative value of each job among all jobs within a company. This ordered set of jobs represents the job structure or hierarchy. Companies rely on a simple, yet fundamental principle for building internally consistent compensation systems: Jobs that require higher qualifications, more responsibilities, and more complex job duties should be paid more than jobs that require lower qualifications, fewer responsibilities, and less-complex job duties. Internally consistent job structures formally recognize differences in job characteristics that enable compensation managers to set pay accordingly. Figure 1 illustrates an internally consistent job structure for employee benefits professionals. As Figure 1 indicates, a benefits manager should earn substantially more than a benefits counselor I. Benefits

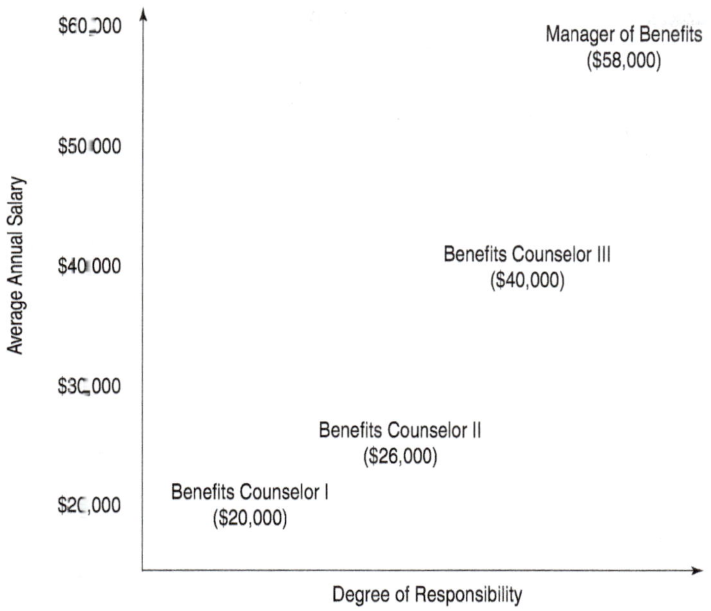

Benefits Counselor I

Provides basic counseling services to employees and assistance to higher-level personnel in more complex benefits activities. Works under general supervision of higher-level counselors or other personnel.

Benefits Counselor II

Provides skilled counseling services to employees concerning specialized benefits programs or complex areas of other programs. Also completes special projects or carries out assigned phases of the benefits counseling service operations. Works under general supervision from Benefits Counselor III or other personnel.

Benefits Counselor III

Coordinates the daily activities of an employee benefits counseling service and supervises its staff. Works under direction from higher-level personnel.

Manager of Benefits

Responsible for managing the entire benefits function from evaluating benefits programs to ensuring that Benefits Counselors are adequately trained. Reports to the Director of Compensation and Benefits.

FIGURE 1 Internally Consistent Compensation Structure

managers have far greater responsibility for ensuring effective benefits practices than does the entry-level counselor. The difference in average pay rates between benefits counselor II and benefits counselor I jobs should be far less than that between benefits manager and benefits counselor I jobs because the differences in responsibility between benefits counselor II and benefits counselor I are far less than the differences between benefits manager and benefits counselor I.

Compensation experts and HR professionals create internally consistent job structures through two processes—job analysis followed by job evaluation. **Job analysis** is almost purely a descriptive procedure; job evaluation reflects value judgments. Effective job analysis identifies and defines **job content**. Job content describes job duties and tasks as well as such pertinent factors as the skill and effort (i.e., compensable factors) needed to perform the job adequately.

Human resource specialists lead the job analysis process. As we will discuss shortly, they solicit the involvement of employees and supervisors, who offer their perspectives on the nature of the jobs being analyzed. Based on this information, HR specialists write job descriptions that describe the job duties and minimum qualifications required of individuals to perform their jobs effectively.

Job evaluation is key for casting internally consistent compensation systems as strategic tools. Compensation professionals use job evaluation to establish pay differentials among employees within a company. The descriptive job analysis results directly aid compensation professionals in their pay-setting decisions by quantifying the key similarities and differences between jobs based on job content identified in the job analysis process.

JOB ANALYSIS

2 Summarize the practice of job analysis.

Competent compensation professionals are familiar with job analysis concepts, the process of conducting job analysis, and fundamental job analysis techniques. Job analysis is a systematic process for gathering, documenting, and analyzing information in order to describe jobs. Job analyses describe content or job duties, worker requirements or job specifications, and, sometimes, the job context or working conditions.

Job content refers to the actual activities that employees must perform on the job. Job-content descriptions may be broad, general statements of job activities or detailed descriptions of duties and tasks performed on the job. Greeting clients is common to receptionist jobs. The job activity of greeting clients represents a broad statement. Describing the particular activities associated with greeting clients (e.g., saying "hello," asking the clients' names, using the telephone to notify the employees of their clients' arrivals, and offering beverages) represents a detailed statement.

Worker requirements represent the minimum qualifications and the knowledge, skills, and abilities (KSAs) that people must have to perform a particular job. Such requirements usually include education; experience; licenses; permits; and specific abilities and skills such as typing, drafting, or editing. For example, HR managers must have knowledge of principles and procedures for recruitment, selection, training, compensation and benefits, labor relations and negotiations, and HR information systems. Active listening and critical thinking are two examples of many necessary skills for effective HR managers. Human resource managers must possess abilities such as oral comprehension and written comprehension.

Working conditions are the social context or physical environment where work will be performed. For instance, social context is a key factor for jobs in the hospitality industry. Hospitality industry managers emphasize the importance of employees' interactions with guests. Hotel registration desk clerks should convey an air of enthusiasm toward guests and be willing to accommodate each guest's specific requests for a nonsmoking room or an early check-in time.

Physical environments vary along several dimensions, based on the level of noise and possible exposure to hazardous factors, including hazardous chemicals. Work equipment also defines the character of the physical environment. Nuclear power plant employees work in rather hazardous physical environments because of possible exposure to dangerous radiation levels. Accountants perform their jobs in relatively safe working environments because office buildings must meet local building safety standards.

Steps in the Job Analysis Process

The job analysis process has five main activities:

- Determine a job analysis program.
- Select and train analysts.
- Direct job analyst orientation.
- Conduct the study: data collection methods and sources of data.
- Summarize the results: writing job descriptions.

DETERMINE A JOB ANALYSIS PROGRAM A company must decide between using an established system or developing its own system tailored to specific requirements. Both established and custom job analysis programs vary in the method of gathering data. The most typical methods for collecting job analysis information are questionnaires, interviews, observation, and participation. Administrative costs often represent a major consideration in selecting a job analysis method.

SELECT AND TRAIN ANALYSTS Job analysts generally must be able to collect job-related information through various methods, relate to a wide variety of employees, analyze the information, and write clearly and succinctly. A task force of representatives from throughout the company ideally conducts the analysis, and HR staff members coordinate it. Although some companies rely on HR professionals to coordinate and conduct job analysis, many use teams to represent varying perspectives on work because virtually all employees interact with coworkers and supervisors.

Before the task force embarks on a job analysis, members need to be taught about the basic assumptions of the model and the procedures they must follow. The training should include discussions of the study's objectives, how the information will be used, methodology overviews, and discussions and demonstrations of the information-gathering techniques. Analysts also should be trained to minimize the chance that they will conduct ineffective job analyses. For example, analysts should involve as many job incumbents as possible within the constraints of staff time to have representative samples of job incumbents' perceptions.

Finally, job analysts must be familiar with the structure of pertinent job data. Job analysis data are configured in levels, hierarchically from specific bits of information to progressively broader categories that include the prior specific pieces. Table 1 defines representative analysis

TABLE 1 Units of Analysis in the Job Analysis Process

1. An element is the smallest step into which it is practical to subdivide any work activity without analyzing separate motions, movements, and mental processes involved. Connecting a flash drive into a USB port is an example of a job element.
2. A task is one or more elements and is one of the distinct activities that constitute logical and necessary steps in the performance of work by the worker. A task is created whenever human effort, physical or mental, is exerted to accomplish a specific purpose. Keyboarding text into memo format represents a job task.
3. A position is a collection of tasks constituting the total work assignment of a single worker. There are as many positions as there are workers. John Smith's position in the company is clerk typist. His tasks, which include keyboarding text into memo format, running a spell check on the text, and printing the text on company letterhead, combine to represent John Smith's position.
4. A job is a group of positions within a company that are identical, with respect to their major or significant tasks, and sufficiently alike to justify their being covered by a single analysis. There may be one or many persons employed in the same job. For example, Bob Arnold, John Smith, and Jason Colbert are clerk typists. With minor variations, they essentially perform the same tasks.
5. A job family is a group of two or more jobs that call for either similar worker characteristics or similar work tasks. File clerk, clerk typist, and administrative clerk represent a clerical job family because each job mainly requires employees to perform clerical tasks.
6. An occupation is a group of jobs, found at more than one establishment, in which a common set of tasks are performed or are related in terms of similar objectives, methodologies, materials, products, worker actions, or worker characteristics. File clerk, clerk typist, administrative clerk, staff secretary, and administrative secretary represent an office support occupation. Compensation analyst, training and development specialist, recruiter, and benefits counselor represent jobs from the human resources management occupation.

Source: U.S. Department of Labor (1991). *The Revised Handbook for Analyzing Jobs*. Washington, DC: U.S. Government Printing Office.

levels and lists examples of each one. The most specific information is a job element, and the broadest element is an occupation.

The U.S. Office of Management and Budget published *The Standard Occupational Classification System* (*SOC*), which identifies 840 detailed occupations. These detailed occupations are subdivided into 461 broad occupational groups. The broad occupational groups are subdivided into 97 minor groups. These minor groups are subdivided into the broadest category of 23 major occupational groups. Table 2 lists the 23 major occupational groups based. The following is an example:

- *Major occupational group*: Architecture and Engineering Occupations
- *Minor group*: Engineers
- *Broad occupational group*: Industrial Engineers
- *Detailed occupation*: Health and Safety Engineers[1]

These occupational group concepts are relevant for making compensation decisions. As we will see shortly, this classification system links to the Occupational Information Network (O*NET), which contains detailed information to facilitate compensation professionals making precise comparisons for pay-setting purposes.

DIRECT JOB ANALYST ORIENTATION Before analysts start specific job analysis techniques, they must analyze the context in which employees perform their work to better understand influencing

TABLE 2 Major Occupational Groups of the Standard Occupational Classification

- Management occupations
- Business and financial operations occupations
- Computer and mathematical occupations
- Architecture and engineering occupations
- Life, physical, and social science occupations
- Community and social service occupations
- Legal occupations
- Education, training, and library occupations
- Arts, design, entertainment, sports, and media occupations
- Health care practitioners and technical occupations
- Health care support occupations
- Protective service occupations
- Food preparation and serving-related occupations
- Building and grounds cleaning and maintenance occupations
- Personal care and service occupations
- Sales and related occupations
- Office and administrative support occupations
- Farming, fishing, and forestry occupations
- Construction and extraction occupations
- Installation, maintenance, and repair occupations
- Production occupations
- Transportation and material-moving occupations
- Military-specific occupations

Source: U.S. Bureau of Labor Statistics (2010). *2010 SOC User Guide*. Available: *www.bls.gov/soc/*, accessed August 25, 2013.

factors. In addition, analysts should obtain and review such internal information as organizational charts, listings of job titles, classifications of each position to be analyzed, job incumbent names and pay rates, and any instructional booklets or handbooks for operating equipment. Job analysts may also find pertinent job information in such external sources as *The Standard Occupational Classification System* trade associations, professional societies, and trade unions.

CONDUCT THE STUDY: DATA COLLECTION METHODS AND SOURCES OF DATA Once analysts have gathered and made sense of these preliminary data, they can begin gathering and recording information for each job in the company. Analysts should carefully choose the method of data collection and the sources of data. The most common methods are questionnaires and observation. Questionnaires direct job incumbents' and supervisors' descriptions of the incumbents' work through a series of questions and statements, for example:

- Describe the task you perform most frequently.
- How often do you perform this task?
- List any licenses, permits, or certifications required to perform duties assigned to your position.
- List any equipment, machines, or tools you normally operate as part of your position's duties.
- Does your job require any contacts with other department personnel, other departments, outside companies, or agencies? If yes, please describe.
- Does your job require supervisory responsibilities? If yes, for which jobs and for how many employees?

Observation requires job analysts to record perceptions they form while watching employees perform their jobs.

The most common sources of job analysis data are job incumbents, supervisors, and the job analysts. Job incumbents should provide the most extensive and detailed information about how they perform job duties. Experienced job incumbents will probably offer the most details and insights. Supervisors also should provide extensive and detailed information, but with a different focus. Supervisors specifically are most familiar with the interrelationships among jobs within their departments. They are probably in the best position to describe how employees performing different jobs interact. Job analysts also should involve as many job incumbents and supervisors as possible because employees with the same job titles may have different experiences.

For example, parts assembler John Smith reports that a higher level of manual dexterity is required than parts assembler Barbara Bleen reports. Parts assembler supervisor Jan Johnson indicates that assemblers interact several times a day to help each other solve unexpected problems, and supervisor Bill Black reports no interaction among parts assemblers. Including as many job incumbents and supervisors as possible will provide a truer assessment of the parts assembler job duties.

Of course, job analysts represent a source of information. In the case of observation, job analysts write descriptions. Job analysts, when using questionnaires, often ask follow-up questions to clarify job incumbents' and supervisors' answers. In either case, job analysts' HR expertise should guide the selection of pertinent follow-up questions.

Companies ultimately strive to conduct job analyses that meet reliability and validity criteria. A **reliable job analysis method** yields consistent results under similar conditions. For example, let's assume that two job analysts independently observe John Smith perform his job as a retail store manager. The method is reliable if the two analysts reach similar conclusions about the duties that constitute the retail store manager job. Although important, reliable job analysis methods are not enough. Job analyses also must be valid.

A **valid job analysis method** accurately assesses each job's duties or content. In this regard, we are referring to a particular type of validity – content validity. Unfortunately, neither researchers nor practitioners can demonstrate whether job analysis results are definitively accurate or content valid. At present, the *best* approach to producing valid job descriptions requires that results among multiple sources of job data (e.g., job incumbents, analysts, supervisors, and customers) and multiple methods (e.g., interview, questionnaire, and observation) converge.[2]

Reliable and valid job analysis methods are essential to building internally consistent compensation systems. The factors that describe a particular job should indeed reflect the actual work. Failure to match accurately compensable factors with the work employees perform may result in either inadequate or excessive pay rates. Both cases are detrimental to the company. Inadequate pay may lead to dysfunctional turnover (i.e., the departure of high-quality employees). Excessive pay represents a cost burden to the company that can ultimately undermine its competitive position. Moreover, basing pay on factors that do not relate to job duties leaves a company vulnerable to allegations of illegal discrimination.

What can compensation professionals do to increase the likelihood that they will use reliable and valid job analysis methods? Whenever time and budgetary constraints permit, job analysts should use more than one data collection method, and they should collect data from more than one source. Including multiple data collection methods and sources minimizes the inherent biases associated with any particular one. For example, job incumbents may view their work as having greater impact on the effectiveness of the company than does the incumbents' supervisor. Observation techniques do not readily indicate why an employee performs a task in a specific way, but the interview method provides analysts with an opportunity to make probing inquiries.

SUMMARIZE THE RESULTS: WRITING JOB DESCRIPTIONS **Job descriptions** summarize a job's purpose and list its tasks, duties, and responsibilities, as well as the KSAs necessary to perform the job at a minimum level. Effective job descriptions generally explain:

- What the employee must do to perform the job
- How the employee performs the job
- Why the employee performs the job in terms of its contribution to the functioning of the company
- Supervisory responsibilities, if any
- Contacts (and purpose of these contacts) with other employees inside or outside the company
- The skills, knowledge, and abilities the employee should have or must have to perform the job duties
- The physical and social conditions under which the employee must perform the job

Job descriptions usually contain four sections:

- Job title
- Job summary
- Job duties
- Worker specifications

Table 3 contains a job description for a training and development specialist.

Job titles indicate the name of each job within a company's job structure. In Table 3, the job title is training and development specialist. The **job summary** statement concisely summarizes the job with two to four descriptive statements. This section usually indicates whether the job incumbent receives supervision and by whom. The training and development specialist works under general supervision from higher-level training and development professionals or other designated administrators.

The **job duties** section describes the major work activities and, if pertinent, supervisory responsibilities. For instance, the training and development specialist evaluates training needs of employees and departments by conducting personal interviews, questionnaires, and statistical studies.

The **worker specifications** section lists the education, KSAs, and other qualifications individuals must possess to perform the job adequately. **Education** refers to formal training.

TABLE 3 Job Description: Training and Development Specialist

Job Title

Training and Development Specialist

Job Summary

Training and development specialists perform training and development activities for supervisors, managers, and staff to improve efficiency, effectiveness, and productivity. They work under general supervision from higher-level training and development professionals.

Job Duties

A training and development specialist typically:

1. Recommends, plans, and implements training seminars and workshops for administrators and supervisors, and evaluates program effectiveness.
2. Evaluates training needs of employees and departments by conducting personal interviews, questionnaires, and statistical studies.
3. Researches, writes, and develops instructional materials for career, staff, and supervisor workshops and seminars.
4. Counsels supervisors and employees on policies and rules.
5. Performs related duties as assigned.

Worker Specifications

1. Any one or any combination of the following types of preparation:
   a. credit for college training leading to a major or concentration in education or other fields closely related to training and development (such as human resource management or vocational education).

   —or—

   b. Two years of work experience as a professional staff member in a human resource management department.
2. Two years of professional work experience in the training and development area in addition to the training and experience required in item 1, above.

Minimum educational levels can be a high school diploma or a general equivalency diploma (GED) through such advanced levels as masters' or doctoral degrees.

The **Equal Employment Opportunity Commission (EEOC)** guidelines distinguish among the terms *skill, ability*, and *knowledge*. **Skill** refers to an observable competence to perform a learned psychomotor act. Typing 50 words per minute is an example of a psychomotor act. Typing requires knowledge of the keyboard layout and manual dexterity. According to the EEOC, **ability** refers to a present competence to perform an observable behavior or a behavior that results in an observable product. For example, possessing the competence to mediate a dispute between labor and management successfully reflects ability. **Knowledge** refers to a body of information applied directly to the performance of a function. Companies measure knowledge with tests, or they infer that employees have knowledge based on formal education completed. For instance, compensation professionals should know about the Fair Labor Standards Act's overtime pay requirements. Since these definitions were issued, the United States slightly modified the definitions of KSAs. These definitions are largely consistent with each other. We will work with the revised definitions when we review O*NET later in this chapter.

Legal Considerations for Job Analysis

The government does not require companies to conduct job analysis; however, conducting job analyses increases the chance that employment decisions are based solely on pertinent job requirements. Under the Equal Pay Act companies must justify pay differences between men and women who perform equal work. Different job titles do not suffice as justification. Instead, companies must demonstrate substantive differences in job functions. Job analysis helps HR professionals discern whether substantive differences between job functions exist. Job analysis is also useful for determining whether a job is exempt or nonexempt under the Fair Labor Standards Act (FLSA).

Companies may perform job analysis to see if they comply with the Americans with Disabilities Act (ADA) and the American with Disabilities Act Amendments Act of 2008. The amendments emphasize that the definition of disability should be construed in favor of broad coverage of individuals to the maximum extent permitted by the terms of the ADA. As long as disabled applicants can perform the essential functions of a job with reasonable accommodation, companies must not discriminate against these applicants by paying them less than other employees performing the same job. Human resource professionals use job analysis to define essential job functions systematically.

Job Analysis Techniques

Human resource professionals can either choose from a variety of established job analysis techniques or custom-design them. Most companies generally choose to use established job analysis techniques because the costs of custom-made job analysis techniques often outweigh the benefits. Besides, many of the established job analysis techniques apply to a wide variety of jobs and both researchers and practitioners have already tested and refined them.

Choosing one established plan over another depends on two considerations: applicability and cost. Some job analysis techniques apply only to particular job families (e.g., managerial jobs), but others can be applied more broadly. In addition, some methods are proprietary, yet others are available to the public at no charge. Private consultants or consulting firms charge substantial fees to companies that use their methods, but the U.S. Department of Labor does not charge fees to use its job analysis resources. Next, we will review the U.S. Department of Labor's **Occupational Information Network (O*NET)**.

U.S. Department of Labor's Occupational Information Network (O*NET)

O*NET is a database. The U.S. Department of Labor's employment and training administration spearheaded its creation for two reasons: First, it is designed to describe jobs in the relatively new service sector of the economy (e.g., wireless telecommunications). Second, O*NET more accurately describes jobs that evolved as the result of technological advances (e.g., software and hardware engineering).

O*NET is comprehensive because it incorporates information about both jobs and workers. The O*NET **Content Model** lists six categories of job and worker information. Job information contains the components that relate to the actual work activities of a job (i.e., information that HR professionals should include in the summary and duties sections of job descriptions). Worker information represents characteristics of employees that contribute to successful job performance. Figure 2 shows the six categories of the O*NET Content Model. According to the creators of O*NET, the Content Model was developed using research on job and organizational analysis. It embodies a view that reflects the character of occupations (via job-oriented descriptors) and people (via worker-oriented descriptors). The Content Model also allows occupational information to be applied across jobs, sectors, or industries (cross-occupational descriptors) and within occupations (occupational-specific descriptors). A description of each content area follows.

EXPERIENCE REQUIREMENTS Experience requirements include:

- Experience and training
- Licensing

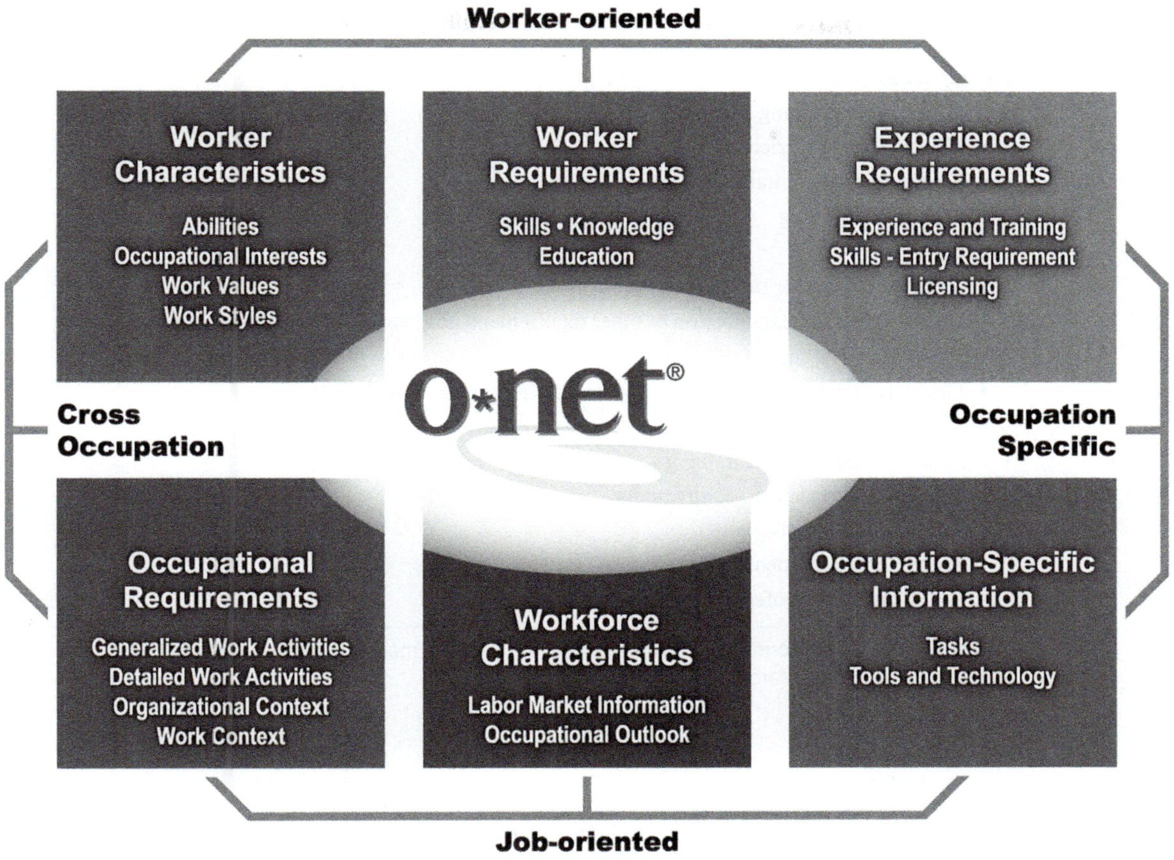

FIGURE 2 O*Net Content Model

Experience and training information describes specific preparation required for entry into a job plus past work experience contributing to qualifications for an occupation. **Licensing** information describes licenses, certificates, or registrations that are used to identify levels of skill that are required for entry and advancement in an occupation. Preferred education or training, and required apprenticeships will be documented by this part of the model. Table 4 lists the specific experience requirements.

OCCUPATIONAL REQUIREMENTS **Occupational requirements** include:

- Generalized work activities
- Organizational context
- Work context

The occupational requirements domain includes information about typical activities required across occupations. Identifying generalized work activities and detailed work activities summarizes the broad and more specific types of job behaviors and tasks that may be performed within multiple occupations. Using this framework makes it possible to use a single set of descriptors to describe many occupations. Contextual variables such as the physical, social, or structural context of work that may impose specific demands on the worker or activities are also included in this section.

Generalized work activities information describes general types of job behaviors occurring on multiple jobs. **Organizational context** information indicates the characteristics of the organization that influence how people do their work. **Work context** information describes

TABLE 4 O*NET Content Model: Experience Requirements (sample of full list)

Experience Requirements
- Experience and training
  - Related work experience
  - On-site or in-plant training
  - On-the-job training
- Licensing
- License, certificate, or registration required
- Education, training, examination or other requirements for license, certificate, or registration
  - Post-secondary degree
  - Graduate degree
  - On-the-job training
- Additional education and training
- Organization and agency requirements
  - Legal requirement
  - Employer requirement
  - Union, guild, or professional association requirement

Source: Occupational Information Network Consortium. Content model. Available: *www.onetcenter.org/content.html*, accessed March 1, 2015.

TABLE 5 O*NET Content Model: Occupational Requirements (sample of full list)

- Human resources systems and practices
  - Recruitment and selection
    - Recruitment operations
    - Reward system
  - Basis of compensation
  - Which of the following is part of your compensation package?
    - Profit sharing
    - Gain sharing
    - Knowledge/skill-based pay
    - Pay based on your individual performance
    - Pay based on the performance of your team
    - Pay based on customer satisfaction
    - Pay based on job tenure/seniority

Pay based on job attributes

Source: Occupational Information Network Consortium. Content model. Available: *www.onetcenter.org/content.html*, accessed March 1, 2015.

physical and social factors that influence the nature of work. Table 5 lists examples of particular occupational requirements.

OCCUPATION-SPECIFIC INFORMATION REQUIREMENTS **Occupation-specific information requirements** detail a comprehensive set of elements that apply to a single occupation or a narrowly defined job family. These particular requirements are occupational skills, knowledge, tasks, duties, machines, tools, and equipment. This domain parallels other Content Model domains because it includes requirements such as work-related knowledge, skills, and tasks in addition to the machines, equipment, tools, software, and information technology workers may use in their workplace.

WORKFORCE CHARACTERISTICS **Workforce characteristics** refer to variables that define and describe the general characteristics of occupations that may influence occupational requirements. Organizations do not exist in isolation. They must operate within a broader social and economic structure. To be useful, an occupational classification system must incorporate global contextual characteristics. O*NET provides this information by linking descriptive occupational information to statistical labor market information. This includes compensation and wage data, employment outlook, and industry size information. Much of this information is collected outside of the O*NET program's immediate scope. Collaborative efforts with such organizations as the Bureau of Labor Statistics, the Department of Commerce, the Department of Defense, Career One Stop, the U.S. Bureau of the Census, and the Employment and Training Administration facilitate these labor market information linkages. These characteristics include:

- Labor market information
- Occupational outlook

Labor market information describes current labor force characteristics of occupations. Occupational outlook describes future labor force characteristics of occupations.

WORKER CHARACTERISTICS **Worker characteristics** information includes:

- Abilities
- Interests
- Work styles

Abilities are enduring attributes of the individual that influence performance. **Interests** describe preferences for work environments and outcomes. **Work styles** are personal characteristics that describe important interpersonal and work style requirements in jobs and occupations. Table 6 lists a sample of worker characteristics.

Worker characteristics, such as interests and work styles, often rank highly in the employee selection process. Patagonia is a designer of outdoor clothing and gear for a variety of sports. The company strives to hire new employees whose interests and work styles are consistent with the company's mission and work culture. For example, Patagonia requires that new employees have a passion for and participate in outdoor activities as well as are fanatical about protecting the environment. The following video describes Patagonia's requirements.

WATCH IT!

If your professor has assigned this, go to the Assignments section of **mymanagementlab.com** to complete the video exercise titled Patagonia: Employee Testing and Selection.

WORKER REQUIREMENTS Worker requirements include:

- Basic skills
- Cross-functional skills
- Knowledge
- Education

Worker requirements represent developed or acquired attributes of an individual that may be related to work performance such as work-related knowledge and skill. Knowledge represents the acquisition of facts and principles about a domain of information. Experience lays

TABLE 6 O*NET Content Model: Worker Characteristics (sample of full list)

- Abilities
- Cognitive abilities
  - Verbal abilities
    - Oral comprehension
    - Written comprehension
    - Oral expression
    - Written expression
  - Idea generation and reasoning abilities
    - Fluency of ideas
    - Originality
    - Problem sensitivity
  - Quantitative abilities
    - Mathematical reasoning
    - Number facility
  - Memory
    - Memorization
  - Perceptual abilities
    - Speed of closure
    - Flexibility of closure
    - Perceptual speed

Source: Occupational Information Network Consortium. Content model. Available: *www.onetcenter.org/content.html*, accessed March 1, 2015.

the foundation for establishing procedures to work with given knowledge. These procedures are more commonly known as skills. Skills may be divided further into basic skills and cross-functional skills. Basic skills (e.g., reading) facilitate the acquisition of new knowledge. Cross-functional skills (e.g., problem solving) extend across several domains of activities.

Basic skills information describes developed capacities that facilitate learning or the more rapid acquisition of knowledge. **Cross-functional skills** information indicates developed capacities that facilitate performance of activities that occur across jobs. Knowledge information describes organized sets of principles and facts applying in general domains. Education information details prior educational experience required to perform in a job. **Knowledge** refers to organized sets of principles and facts applying in general domains. **Education** refers to prior educational experience required to perform in a job. Table 7 lists a sample of worker requirements.

USING O*NET Human resource professionals use O*NET by consulting the **O*NET User's Guide** as well as the most current **O*NET database.**[3] They may find the latest O*NET information on the U.S. Department of Labor Employment and Training Administration's Web site (*http://online.onetcenter.org*).

JOB EVALUATION

3 Describe the practice of job evaluation.

Compensation professionals use job evaluation to systematically recognize differences in the relative worth among a set of jobs and to establish pay differentials accordingly. Whereas job analysis is almost purely descriptive, job evaluation partly reflects the values and priorities that

TABLE 7 O*NET Content Model: Worker Requirements (sample of full list)

- Basic Skills
  - Content
    - Reading comprehension
    - Active listening
    - Writing
  - Process
    - Critical thinking
    - Active learning
    - Learning strategies
  - Cross-functional skills
    - Social skills
    - Social perceptiveness
    - Coordination
    - Persuasion
  - Complex problem-solving skills
    - Problem identification
    - Information gathering
    - Information organization

Source: Occupational Information Network Consortium. Content model. Available: *www.onetcenter.org/content.html*, accessed March 1, 2015.

management places on various positions. Based on job content and the firm's priorities, managers establish pay differentials for virtually all positions within the company.

Compensable Factors

Compensation professionals generally base job evaluations on **compensable factors**, which are the salient job characteristics by which companies establish relative pay rates. Most companies consider skill, effort responsibility, and working conditions, which were derived from the Equal Pay Act. These four dimensions help managers determine whether dissimilar jobs are "equal."

Skill, effort, responsibility, and working conditions are **universal compensable factors** because virtually every job contains these four factors. How, then, can meaningful distinctions regarding the value of jobs be made with such broad factors? Many companies break these general factors into more specific factors. For example, responsibility required could be further classified as responsibility for financial matters and responsibility for personnel matters.

Most jobs today can be described broadly in terms of KSAs given the evolution of jobs that require greater cognitive skills and mental (versus physical) effort. A working conditions compensable factor is most helpful when a company expects a substantial difference in working conditions for similar jobs. For example, a company may employ geologists, but while some of them are required to work in the field where possible dangers are greater, other geologists are required to work within the safe confines of a laboratory.

In any event, compensation professionals should choose compensable factors based on two considerations. First, factors must be job related. The factors that describe a particular job should indeed reflect the actual work that is performed.

Second, compensation professionals should select compensable factors that further a company's strategies. For example, companies that value product differentiation probably consider innovation to be an important compensable factor for research scientist and marketing manager jobs. Companies that distinguish themselves through high-quality customer relations are likely to place great value on such compensable factors as product knowledge and interpersonal skills. Lowest-cost strategies may emphasize different kinds of compensable factors (e.g., efficiency and timeliness).

The Job Evaluation Process

The job evaluation process entails six steps:

- Determining single versus multiple job evaluation techniques
- Choosing the job evaluation committee
- Training employees to conduct job evaluations
- Documenting the job evaluation plan
- Communicating with employees
- Setting up the appeals process

DETERMINING SINGLE VERSUS MULTIPLE JOB EVALUATION TECHNIQUES Compensation professionals must determine whether a single job evaluation technique is sufficiently broad to assess a diverse set of jobs. In particular, the decision is prompted by such questions as, "Can we use the same compensable factors to evaluate a forklift operator's job and the plant manager's job?" If the answer is *yes*, then a single job evaluation technique is appropriate. If not, then more than one job evaluation approach should be employed. Job evaluation plans are differentiated based on sets of compensable factors that are common to one set of jobs, but different from others. It is not reasonable to expect that a single job evaluation technique, based on one set of compensable factors, can adequately assess diverse sets of jobs (i.e., operative, clerical, administrative, managerial, professional, technical, and executive). A carpenter's job is clearly distinct from a certified public accountant's position because manual dexterity is an important compensable factor that describes carpentry work and is not nearly as central to an accounting position. Ultimately, compensation professionals will create as many job structures as there are job evaluation techniques that are appropriate for groups of like jobs. As described earlier, Figure 1 illustrates an internally consistent job structure for employee benefits professionals.

CHOOSING THE JOB EVALUATION COMMITTEE Human resource professionals help put together a committee of rank-and-file employees, supervisors, managers, and, if relevant, union representatives to design, oversee, and evaluate job evaluation results. The functions, duties, responsibilities, and authority of job evaluation committees vary considerably from company to company. In general, committees simply review job descriptions and analyses and then evaluate jobs. Larger companies with a multitude of jobs often establish separate committees to evaluate particular job classifications such as nonexempt, exempt, managerial, and executive jobs. The immense number of jobs in large companies would otherwise preclude committee members from performing their regular duties.

Job evaluation is an important determinant of a job's worth within many companies. All employees, regardless of their functions, wish to be compensated and valued for their efforts. All employees strive for a reasonable pay-effort bargain (i.e., a compensation level consistent with their contributions). Managers strive to balance employee motivation with cost control because they have limited resources for operating their departments. Union representatives strive to ensure that members enjoy a good standard of living. Therefore, unions try to prevent the undervaluation of jobs.

Job evaluation committees help ensure commitment from employees throughout companies. They also provide a checks-and-balances system. Job evaluation procedures are not scientifically accurate because these evaluation decisions are based on ordinary human judgment. Therefore, a consensus of several employees helps to minimize the biases of individual job evaluators.

TRAINING EMPLOYEES TO CONDUCT JOB EVALUATIONS Individuals should understand the process objectives. In addition to knowing company objectives, evaluators also should practice using the chosen job evaluation criteria before applying them to actual jobs. Similar to job analysis procedures, evaluators should base their decisions on sound job- and business-related rationales to ensure legal compliance.

DOCUMENTING THE JOB EVALUATION PLAN Documenting the job evaluation plan is useful for legal and training purposes. From an employer's perspective, a well-documented evaluation plan clearly specifies job- and business-related criteria against which jobs are evaluated. Well-documented plans can allow employees to understand clearly how their jobs were evaluated and the outcome of the process. In addition, well-documented plans provide guidelines for clarifying ambiguities in the event of employee appeals or legal challenges.

COMMUNICATING WITH EMPLOYEES Job evaluation results matter personally to all employees. Companies must formally communicate with employees throughout the job analysis and evaluation processes to ensure employees' understanding and acceptance of the job evaluation process and results. Information sessions and memoranda are useful media. Employers should share basic information, and employees should be given the opportunity to respond to what they believe are either unsatisfactory procedures or inaccurate outcomes of the job evaluation process.

SETTING UP THE APPEALS PROCESS Companies should set up appeals procedures that permit reviews on a case-by-case basis to provide a check on the process through reexamination. Such appeals reduce charges of illegal discrimination that would be more likely to occur if employees were not given a voice. Compensation professionals usually review employees' appeals. Companies increasingly process appeals through committees made up of compensation professionals and a representative sample of employees and supervisors. Grievants are more likely to judge appeal decisions as fair if committees are involved: Committee decisions should reflect the varied perspectives of participants rather than the judgment of one individual.

JOB EVALUATION TECHNIQUES

4 Summarize various job evaluation techniques.

Compensation professionals categorize job evaluation methods as either market-based evaluation or job-content evaluation techniques. **Market-based evaluation** plans use market data to determine differences in job worth. Many companies choose market-based evaluation methods because they wish to assign job pay rates that are neither too low nor too high relative to the market. Setting pay rates too low will make it difficult to recruit talented candidates, whereas setting pay rates too high will result in an excessive cost burden for the employer. Compensation professionals rely on compensation surveys to determine prevailing pay rates of jobs in the relevant labor market.

Job-content evaluation plans emphasize the company's internal value system by establishing a hierarchy of internal job worth based on each job's function in company strategy. Compensation professionals review preliminary structures for consistency with market pay rates on a representative sample of jobs known as benchmark jobs. Compensation professionals ultimately must balance external market considerations with internal consistency objectives. In practice, compensation professionals judge the adequacy of pay differentials by comparing both market rates and pay differences among jobs within their companies. They consult with the top HR official and chief financial officer when discrepancies arise, particularly if company pay rates are generally lower than the market rates. Upon careful consideration of the company's financial resources and the strategic value of the jobs in question, these executives decide whether to adjust internal pay rates for jobs with below-market pay rates.

Neither market-based nor job-content evaluation approaches alone enable compensation professionals to balance internal and external considerations. Most companies therefore rely on both approaches. The point method is the most popular job-content method because it gives compensation professionals better control over balancing internal and market considerations.

The Point Method

The **point method** is a job-content valuation technique that uses quantitative methodology. Quantitative methods assign numerical values to compensable factors that describe jobs, and these values are summed as an indicator of the overall value for the job. The relative worth of jobs is established by the magnitude of the overall numerical value for the jobs.

The point method evaluates jobs by comparing compensable factors. Each factor is defined and assigned a range of points based on the factor's relative value to the company. Compensable factors are weighted to represent the relative importance of each factor to the job. Job evaluation committees follow seven steps to complete the point method.

STEP 1: SELECT BENCHMARK JOBS Point method job evaluations use **benchmark jobs** to develop factors and their definitions to select jobs to represent the entire range of jobs in the company. Benchmark jobs, found outside the company, provide reference points against which jobs within the company are judged.

STEP 2: CHOOSE COMPENSABLE FACTORS BASED ON BENCHMARK JOBS Managers must define compensable factors that adequately represent the scope of jobs slated for evaluation. Each benchmark job should be described by those factors that help distinguish it from the value of all other jobs. In addition to the "universal" factors (e.g., skill, effort, responsibility, and working conditions), additional factors may be developed to the extent that they are job- and business-related.

Compensable factor categories may be broken down further into specific related factors or subfactors. For example, skill may include job knowledge, education, mental ability, physical ability, accuracy, and dexterity. Effort may include factors relating to both physical and mental exertion. Responsibility may include considerations related to fiscal, material, or personnel responsibilities. Working conditions may be unpleasant because of extreme temperatures or possible exposure to hazardous chemicals.

The number of compensable factors companies should use varies. Compensation professionals should select as many compensable factors as are needed to describe the range of benchmark jobs adequately.

STEP 3: DEFINE FACTOR DEGREES Although compensable factors describe the range of benchmark jobs, individual jobs vary in scope and content. Evaluators must therefore divide each factor into a sufficient number of degrees to identify the level of a factor present in each job. To clarify this idea of factor degrees, it is helpful to think about a paint sample that can be found in any home improvement store. Specifying a color such as gray is not straightforward because there are various shades of gray. Likewise, a compensable factor is similar to a color. For example, the compensable factor *writing ability* can be described in degrees (shades of color) ranging from the ability to write simple sentences to the ability to write paragraphs of complex information.

Table 8 illustrates a factor definition for writing ability and its degree statements. Degree definitions should set forth and limit the meaning of each degree so evaluators can uniformly interpret job descriptions. It is generally helpful to include a few actual work examples as anchors.

The number of degrees will vary based on the comprehensiveness of the plan. For example, if the plan covers only a limited segment of jobs (e.g., clerical employees), fewer degrees will be required than if the plan covered every group of employees. Take education as an example.

TABLE 8 Writing Ability: Factor Definition and Degree Statements

Definition	Capacity to communicate with others in written form.
First Degree	Print simple phrases and sentences, using normal work order and present and past tenses.
Sample Anchor	Prints shipping labels for packages, indicating the destination and the contents of the packages.
Second Degree	Write compound and complex sentences, using proper end punctuation and adjectives and adverbs.
Sample Anchor	Fills requisitions, work orders, or requests for materials, tools, or other stock items.
Third Degree	Write reports and essays with proper format, punctuation, spelling, and grammar, using all parts of speech.
Sample Anchor	Types letters, reports, or straight-copy materials from rough draft or corrected copy.
Fourth Degree	Prepare business letters, expositions, summaries, and reports using prescribed format and conforming to all rules of punctuation, grammar, diction, and style.
Sample Anchor	Composes letters in reply to correspondence concerning such items as request for merchandise, damage claims, credit information, or delinquent accounts or to request information.
Fifth Degree	Write manuals or speeches.
Sample Anchor	Writes service manuals and related technical publications concerned with installation, operation, and maintenance of electronic, electrical, mechanical, and other equipment.

Only two degrees may be necessary to describe the educational requirements for clerical jobs (i.e., high school diploma or equivalent and an associate's degree). More than two degrees would be required to describe adequately the educational requirements for administrative, production, managerial, and professional jobs (i.e., high school diploma or equivalent, associate's degree, bachelor's degree, master's degree, and doctorate). Most analyses anchor minimum and maximum degrees, with specific jobs representing these points.

STEP 4: DETERMINE THE WEIGHT OF EACH FACTOR Weighting compensable factors represents the importance of the factor to the overall value of the job. The weights of compensable factors are usually expressed as percentages. Weighting is often done by management or by a job evaluation committee's decision. All of the factors are ranked according to their relative importance, and final weights are assigned after discussion and consensus. For example, let's assume the relative importance of skill, effort, responsibility, and working conditions to ABC Manufacturing Corporation:

- Skill is the most highly valued compensable factor, weighted at 60 percent.
- Responsibility is the next most important factor, weighted at 25 percent.
- Effort is weighted at 10 percent.
- The working conditions factor is least important, weighted at 5 percent.

STEP 5: DETERMINE POINT VALUES FOR EACH COMPENSABLE FACTOR Compensation professionals set point values for each compensable factor in three stages. First, they must establish the maximum possible point values for the complete set of compensable factors. This total number is arbitrary, but it represents the possible maximum value jobs can possess. As a rule of thumb, the total point value for a set of compensable factors should be determined by a simple formula (e g., the number of compensable factors times 250). ABC Manufacturing sets 1,000 (4 compensable factors x 250) as the possible maximum number of points.

Second, the maximum possible point value for each compensable factor is based on total weight as described in Step 4. Again, for ABC Manufacturing, skill equals 60 percent, responsibility 25 percent, effort 10 percent, and working conditions 5 percent:

- The maximum possible total points for skills equal 600 points (60 percent × 1,000 points).
- The maximum possible total points for responsibility equal 250 points (25 percent × 1,000 points).
- The maximum possible total points for effort equal 100 points (10 percent × 1,000 points).
- The maximum possible total points for working conditions equal 50 points (5 percent × 1,000 points).

Third, compensation professionals distribute these points across degree statements within each compensable factor. The point progression by degrees from the lowest to the highest point value advances arithmetically (i.e., a scale of even incremental values). This characteristic is essential for conducting regression analysis in the discussion of integrating internal job structures—based on job evaluation points—with external pay rates for benchmark jobs).

How do compensation professionals assign point values to each degree? Let's illustrate this procedure by example, using the skill compensable factor. Let's also assume that the skill factor has five degree statements. Degree 1 represents the most basic skill level, and degree 5 represents the most advanced skill level. The increment from one degree to the next highest is 120 points (600 point maximum divided by 5 degree statements).

- Degree 1 = 120 points (120 points × 1)
- Degree 2 = 240 points (120 points × 2)
- Degree 3 = 360 points (120 points × 3)
- Degree 4 = 480 points (120 points × 4)
- Degree 5 = 600 points (120 points × 5)

STEP 6: VERIFY FACTOR DEGREES AND POINT VALUES Committee members should independently calculate the point values for a random sample of jobs. Table 9 shows a sample job evaluation worksheet. After calculating the point values for this sample, committee members should review the point totals for each job. Committee members give careful consideration to whether the hierarchy of jobs makes sense in the context of the company's strategic plan, as well as to the inherent content of the jobs. For instance, sales jobs should rank relatively high on the job hierarchy within a sales-oriented company, such as the pharmaceuticals industry. Research scientist jobs ought to rank relatively high for a company that pursues a differentiation strategy. Messenger jobs should not rank more highly than claims analyst jobs in an insurance company. In short, where peculiarities are apparent, committee members reconsider compensable factor definitions, weights, and actual ratings of the benchmark jobs.

STEP 7: EVALUATE ALL JOBS Committee members evaluate all jobs in the company once the evaluation system has been tested and refined. Each job then is evaluated by determining which degree definition best fits the job and by assigning the corresponding point factors. All points are totaled for each job, and all jobs are ranked according to their point values.

BALANCING INTERNAL AND MARKET CONSIDERATIONS USING THE POINT METHOD How do compensation professionals balance internal and market considerations with point method results? They convert point values into the market value of jobs through regression analysis, a statistical technique. Regression analysis enables compensation professionals to set base pay rates in line with market rates for benchmark or representative jobs. Companies identify market pay rates through compensation surveys. Of course, a company's value structure for jobs based on the point method will probably differ somewhat from the market pay rates for similar jobs. Regression analysis indicates base pay rates that minimize the differences between the company's point method results and the market pay rates.

TABLE 9 Sample Job Evaluation Worksheet

Job Title: _______________
Evaluation Date: _______________
Name of Evaluator: _______________

	Degree					
Compensable Factor	*1*	*2*	*3*	*4*	*5*	*Total*
Skill						
Mental skill	60	120	180	240	(300)	300
Manual skill	60	(120)	180	240	300	120
Effort						
Mental effort	10	20	30	40	(50)	50
Physical effort	10	20	(30)	40	50	30
Responsibility						
Supervisory	25	50	(75)	100	125	75
Department budgeting	(25)	50	75	100	125	25
Working conditions						
Hazards	10	20	30	(40)	50	40
Total job value						640

Alternative Job-Content Evaluation Approaches

Most other job-content approaches use qualitative methods. Qualitative methods evaluate entire jobs and typically compare jobs with each other or some general criteria. These criteria are usually vague (e.g., importance of jobs to departmental effectiveness). Four prevalent kinds of qualitative job evaluation techniques include:

- Simple ranking plans
- Paired comparisons
- Alternation ranking
- Classification plans

SIMPLE RANKING PLANS **Simple ranking plans** order all jobs from lowest to highest according to a single criterion (e.g., job complexity or the centrality of the job to the company's competitive strategy). This approach considers each job in its entirety, usually used in small companies that have relatively few employees. In large companies that classify many jobs, members of job evaluation committees independently rank jobs on a departmental basis. Different rankings will likely result. When this occurs, job evaluation committees discuss the differences in rankings and choose one set of rankings by consensus.

PAIRED COMPARISON AND ALTERNATION RANKING Two common variations of the ranking plan are paired comparison and alternation ranking. The **paired comparison** technique is useful if there are many jobs to rate, usually more than 20. Job evaluation committees generate every possible pair of jobs. For each pair, committee members assign a point to the job with the highest value, whereas the lowest-value job does not receive a point. After evaluating each pair, the evaluator sums the points for each job. Jobs with higher points are more valuable than are jobs with fewer points. The job with the most points is ranked the highest; the job with the fewest points is ranked the lowest.

The **alternation ranking** method orders jobs by extremes. Yet again, committee members judge the relative value of jobs according to a single criterion (e.g., job complexity or the centrality of the job to the company's competitive strategy). This ranking process begins by determining which job is the most valuable, followed by determining which job is the least valuable. Committee members then judge the next most valuable job and the next least valuable job. This process continues until all jobs have been evaluated.

Despite the simplicity of ranking plans, they exhibit three limitations. First, ranking results rely on purely subjective data; the process lacks objective standards, guidelines, and principles that would aid in resolving differences of opinion among committee members. Companies usually do not fully define their ranking criteria. For example, the criterion job complexity can be defined as level of education or as number of distinct tasks that the workers must perform daily.

Second, ranking methods use neither job analyses nor job descriptions, which makes this method difficult to defend legally. Committee members rely on their own impressions of the jobs.

Third, ranking approaches do not incorporate objective scales that indicate how different in value one job is from another. For instance, let's assume that a committee decides on the following ranking for training and development professionals (listed from most valuable to least valuable):

- Director of training and development
- Manager of training and development
- Senior training and development specialist
- Training and development specialist
- Training and development assistant

Rankings do not offer standards for compensation professionals to facilitate answering such questions as, "Is the director of training and development job worth four times as much as the training and development assistant job?" Compensation professionals' inability to answer such questions makes it difficult to establish pay levels according to job-content differences.

CLASSIFICATION PLANS Companies use **classification plans** to place jobs into categories based on compensable factors. Public sector organizations (e.g., civil service systems) use classification systems most prevalently. The federal government's classification system is a well-known example. The General Schedule classifies federal government jobs into 15 classifications (GS-1 through GS-15) based on such factors as skill, education, and experience levels. In addition, jobs that require high levels of specialized education (e.g., a physicist), significantly influence public policy (e.g., law judges), or require executive decision making are classified in separate categories: Senior Level (SL) positions, Scientific and Professional (SP) positions, and the Senior Executive Service (SES).

Alternatives to Job Evaluation

Compensation professionals assign pay rates to jobs in numerous ways other than through the job evaluation process. These alternate methods include reliance on market pay rates, pay incentives, individual rates, and collective bargaining. Many companies determine the value of jobs by paying the average rate in the external labor market.

In addition to the market pay rate, pay incentives may also be the basis for establishing the core compensation for jobs. Incentives tie part or all of an employee's core compensation to the attainment of a predetermined performance objective. Next, both core and fringe compensation may be determined through negotiations between an individual and an employer. The employer typically uses the market rate as a basis for negotiations, agreeing to higher pay if the supply of talented individuals is scarce and the individual in question has an established track record of performance. Finally, when unions are present, pay rates are established through the collective bargaining process.

INTERNALLY CONSISTENT COMPENSATION SYSTEMS AND COMPETITIVE STRATEGY

5 Explain how internally consistent compensation systems and competitive strategy relate to each other.

We established the importance of instituting internally consistent compensation systems. Tightly specified job descriptions that focus on work efficiency may be appropriate for companies that pursue a lowest cost strategy. There may be limitations; however, that hamper agility for companies that strive to differentiate themselves from their competition. For example, internally consistent pay systems may reduce a company's flexibility to respond to changes in competitors' pay practices because job analysis leads to structured job descriptions and job structures. In addition, job evaluation establishes the relative worth of jobs within the company. Responding to the competition may require employees to engage in duties that extend beyond what's written in their job descriptions whenever competitive pressures demand. In the process, the definitions of jobs become more fluid, which makes equity assessments more difficult.

Another potential limitation of internally consistent compensation structures is the resultant bureaucracy. Companies that establish job hierarchies tend to create narrowly defined jobs that lead to greater numbers of jobs and staffing levels.[4] Such structures promote heavy compensation burdens. Employees' core compensation depends on the jobs they perform, how well they perform their jobs, or the skills they possess. Employee benefits, however, represent fixed costs that typically do not vary with employees' job performance or their skills. Employing a larger number of workers to staff a multitude of narrowly defined jobs contributes substantially to exorbitant fixed costs for employee benefits.

COMPENSATION IN ACTION

Creating a clear expectation of performance and organizing employee roles in a way that aligns strategy, pay, and performance will benefit you as a line manager or HR professional. Line managers and HR should employ the help of those who know roles the best—the employees who fill those roles—in order to arrive at conclusions that are fair, informed, and consistent. Line managers will have insight in many cases to choose the right people to help out in this process. HR will ensure that these individuals receive proper training and are equipped to assess roles and provide appropriate and objective recommendations. As a line manager or HR professional, your main responsibility in creating a system is to ensure that employee compensation is equitable internally and competitive externally.

Action checklist for line managers and HR—building an equitable and competitive system

HR takes the lead

- Capture the analysis provided by incumbents and create job descriptions for each role.
- Compare the newly created job descriptions with those found on O*NET to validate the decisions made based on the incumbent information.
- Compensation specialists work with HR professionals to identify the compensable factors within each job description; these factors will serve as the basis for pay differentials (the more critical these factors are to company strategy, the more they will be compensated).
- Work with compensation specialists to evaluate differentials across departments in the organization and compare them with similar jobs in other organizations (ideally competitors); consult with line managers and senior finance executives as discrepancies arise and adjustments appear to be necessary.
- Monitor the match of performance expectations and job descriptions to guard against role stagnation in the face of competition that could require jobs to flex and people to take on unexpected responsibilities—monitor equity carefully.

Line managers take the lead

- Partner with job incumbents to understand job content of their roles.
- Select workers to sit on committees that will be given the task of assessing the accuracy of the assigned pay differentials.

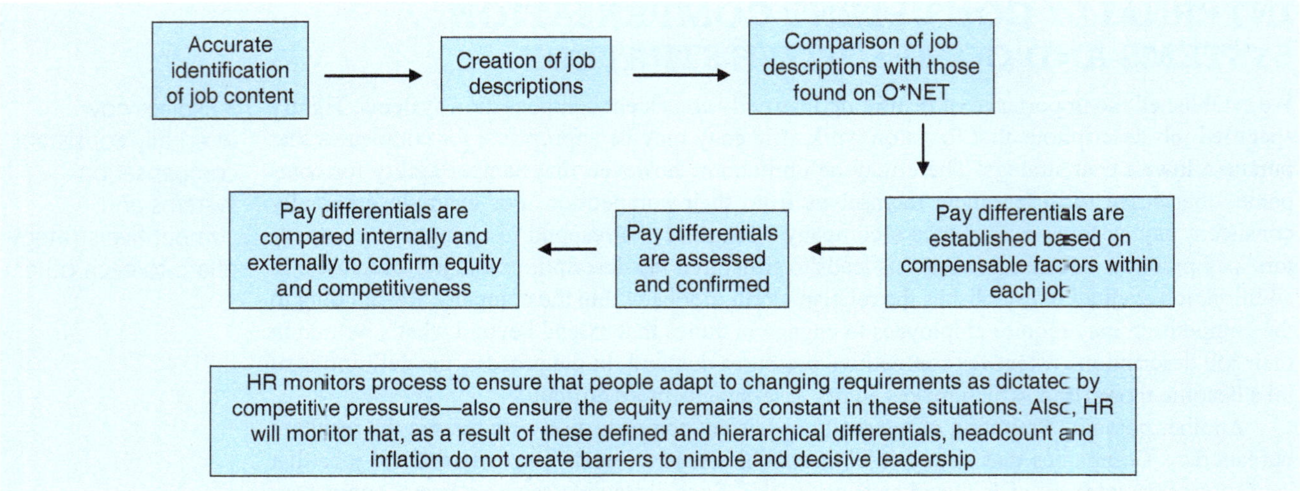

END OF CHAPTER REVIEW

MyManagementLab

Go to **mymanagementlab.com** to complete the problems marked with this icon ✪.

Summary

Learning Objective 1: Internal consistency is a characteristic of job structures that clearly define the relative value of each job among all jobs within a company.

Learning Objective 2: Job analysis is a systematic process that describes job content.

Learning Objective 3: Job evaluation is a systematic process that recognizes differences in the relative worth among a set of jobs and helps to establish pay differentials accordingly.

Learning Objective 4: There are a variety of job evaluation techniques. A clear distinction is made between two approaches: job-content evaluation and market-based evaluation. There are a variety of job-content job evaluation practices. The point method is among the most prominent.

Learning Objective 5: Internally consistent compensation systems can facilitate lowest cost strategies by clearly defining job duties and responsibilities that focus on efficiency. On the other hand, internal consistency could create rigid job structures that limit flexibility.

Key Terms

internally consistent compensation systems
job analysis
job content
job evaluation
worker requirements
working conditions
reliable job analysis method
valid job analysis method
job descriptions
job titles
job summary
job duties
worker specifications
education
Equal Employment Opportunity Commission (EEOC)
skill
ability
knowledge
Occupational Information Network (O*NET)
Content Model
experience and training
licensing
occupational requirements
generalized work activities

organizational context
work context
occupation-specific information requirements
workforce characteristics
worker characteristics
abilities
interests
work styles
basic skills
cross-functional skills
knowledge
education
O*NET User's Guide
O*NET database
compensable factors
universal compensable factors
market-based evaluation
job-content evaluation
point method
benchmark jobs
simple ranking plans
paired comparison
alternation ranking
classification plans

MyManagementLab

CHAPTER QUIZ!

If your professor has assigned this, go to the Assignments section of **mymanagementlab.com** to complete the Chapter Quiz! and see what you've learned.

Discussion Questions

1. Discuss the differences between job analysis and job evaluation. How do these practices help establish internally consistent job structures?
2. Write a draft job description (no longer than one page) for a job that you have had according to the principles described in this chapter.
3. This chapter provides rationale for conducting job analysis, and indicates some of the limitations. Take a stand for or against the use of job analysis, and provide convincing arguments for your position.
4. Respond to the statement "Building an internally consistent job structure is burdensome to companies. Instead, it is best to simply define and evaluate the worth of jobs by surveying the market."
5. Do you consider job evaluation to be an art or a science? Please explain.

CASE

Internal Consistency at Customers First

An additional Supplemental Case can be found on MyManagementLab.

After 3 months in her new role as Director of Human Resources (HR) at Customers First, Deborah Ketson feels confident she has identified the significant HR issues at the company. She has prioritized the issues and is meeting with company president Joan Bates to make her recommendations. Deborah is prepared to discuss her top priority, which is to conduct an organization-wide job analysis and job evaluation project in order to start building a more internally consistent pay structure.

Customers First is a company that provides customer service for other companies. Small-to-medium-sized companies outsource their customer service function to Customers First, which manages all customer service for their clients through a call center and also via an online customer service center. The company works with a diverse group of clients ranging from small retail stores to larger online retailers. Customers First has grown quickly in the 5 years since Joan started the company, and now employs more than 150 customer service representatives (CSRs) and other support staff.

The company's quick growth has led to several problems with its compensation structure. Much of the company's hiring has occurred in response to a new contract, and pay was set based on the current market rate for CSRs in order to attract the right talent. For example, an early client was a small retail store that needed fairly simple customer support. Four CSRs were hired and their pay was set at just slightly above minimum wage. In comparison, a more recent client required hiring 18 CSRs. The labor market was competitive at the time, and the company hired these 18 new employees at a pay rate well above what others at the company were paid. Such variance has occurred often in the hiring process, resulting in groups of CSRs at much different levels of pay for doing substantially similar work.

Deborah has heard many complaints from the supervisors about inequities in the pay of the CSRs. The supervisors are concerned that the inequities may lead to turnover among some of the staff. Deborah has examined the pay rates of the CSRs across the organization and agrees with the supervisors that there are some concerns. One particular concern is that the lowest paid group of CSRs is primarily female, while the highest paid group includes all male employees. By talking with the supervisors, Deborah has learned that there are some CSRs with different levels of responsibilities and skills, but they all hold the same job title. Deborah believes that an organization-wide job analysis and job evaluation is necessary to build an internally consistent compensation structure.

However, when she shared her recommendation with Joan, she did not receive the response she expected. Joan is resistant of the job analysis and job evaluation process as she thinks that having such a structured compensation system will limit the company's ability to be flexible in the marketplace. Often hiring happens quickly in response to a new client contract, and they must hire the right skill set, which might vary based on the current market rates. Further, Joan suggested the entire project would be too time-consuming for Deborah and the other staff that would need to be involved. She felt their time would be better spent on other concerns such as recruiting new staff.

Questions:

6. Do you think that job analysis and job evaluation will benefit Customers First?
7. What is your opinion on Joan's view on job analysis and job evaluation?
8. What do you recommend Customers First do? Why?

Crunch the Numbers!
Modifying a Job Evaluation Worksheet

An additional Crunch the Numbers! exercise can be found on **mymanagementlab.com**.

This chapter discusses the concept and practice of the point method system. The discussion also specifies the six steps necessary to develop and implement a plan. Table 9 shows the job evaluation sheet template, which compensation professionals will use to rate the relative worth of jobs based on content.

9. Refer to Step 5 in the discussion of the point method (in this chapter), and let's assume that the total possible number of job evaluation points is 875 rather than 1,000. Based on the following weighting scheme, what is the possible maximum value of each compensable factor?
   - Skill: 20%
   - Effort: 15%
   - Responsibility: 60%
   - Working Conditions: 5%
10. The sample worksheet (Table 9) shows point values for each compensable factor degree. Based on the information provided in and your answers to question **6-9,** calculate the revised amounts.
11. Based on the revised sample worksheet (question **6-10**), calculate the job point total with the following degree selection per compensable factor:
    - Skill: 3
    - Effort: 3
    - Responsibility: 5
    - Working Conditions: 1

MyManagementLab

Go to **mymanagementlab.com** for Auto-graded writing questions as well as the following Assisted-graded writing questions:

12. Why must a job analysis be reliable and valid? What can a compensation professional do to ensure that a job analysis is reliable and valid?

13. After completing the job analysis, your boss has asked you to conduct a job evaluation of the various positions in the company. Detail the steps you would take in accomplishing this task.
14. MyManagementLab Only – comprehensive writing assignment for this chapter.

Endnotes

1. U.S. Bureau of Labor Statistics (2010). *Standard Occupational Classification*. Available: http://www.bls.gov/soc/, accessed February 20, 2015.
2. Cascio, W. F., & Aguinis, H. (2011). *Applied Psychology in Personnel Management* (7th ed.). Upper Saddle River, NJ: Prentice Hall.
3. U.S. Department of Labor, Employment and Training Administration. (2011). *O*NET*. Washington, DC: Government Printing Office. Available: *www.onetcenter.gov*, accessed January 11, 2011.
4. Lawler, E. E., III. (1986). What's wrong with point-factor job evaluation? *Compensation and Benefits Review, 18*, pp. 20–28.

Glossary

Abilities are enduring attributes of the individual that influence performance.

Ability based on Equal Employment Opportunity Commission guidelines, refers to a present competence to perform an observable behavior or a behavior that results in an observable product.

Alternation ranking a variation of simple ranking job evaluation plans, orders all jobs from lowest to highest, based on alternately identifying the jobs of lowest and highest worth.

Basic skills information describes developed capacities that facilitate learning or the more rapid acquisition of knowledge.

Benchmark jobs found outside the company, provide reference points against which the values of jobs within the company are judged.

Classification plans particular methods of job evaluation, place jobs into categories based on compensable factors.

Compensable factors are job attributes (e.g., skill, effort, responsibility, and working conditions) that compensation professionals use to determine the value of jobs.

Content Model of O*NET lists six categories of job and worker information. Job information contains the components that relate to the actual work activities of a job (i.e., information that HR professionals should include in the summary and duties sections of job descriptions). Worker information represents characteristics of employees that contribute to successful job performance.

Cross-functional skills information indicates developed capacities that facilitate performance of activities that occur across jobs.

Education based on Equal Employment Opportunity Commission guidelines, refers to formal training.

Equal Employment Opportunity Commission a federal government agency, oversees and enforces various employment laws that guard against illegal discrimination including Title VII of the Civil Rights Act of 1964.

Experience and training information describes specific preparation required for entry into a job plus past work experience contributing to qualifications for an occupation.

Generalized work activities information describes general types of job behaviors occurring on multiple jobs.

Interests represent individuals' liking or preference for performing specific jobs.

Internally consistent compensation systems clearly define the relative value of each job among all jobs within a company. This ordered set of jobs represents the job structure or hierarchy. Companies rely on a simple, yet fundamental, principle for building internally consistent compensation systems: Jobs that require greater qualifications, more responsibilities, and more complex duties should be paid more highly than jobs that require lesser qualifications, fewer responsibilities, and less complex job duties.

Job analysis is a systematic process for gathering, documenting, and analyzing information in order to describe jobs.

Job content refers to the actual activities that employees must perform in the job. Job content descriptions may be broad, general statements of job activities or detailed descriptions of duties and tasks performed in the job.

Job-content evaluation an approach to evaluating job worth, takes skill, effort, responsibility, and working conditions into account.

Job descriptions summarize a job's purpose and list its tasks, duties, and responsibilities, as well as the skills, knowledge, and abilities necessary to perform the job at a minimum level.

Job duties a section in job descriptions, describe the major work activities and, if pertinent, supervisory responsibilities.

Job evaluation systematically recognizes differences in the relative worth among a set of jobs and establishes pay differentials accordingly.

Job summary a statement contained in job descriptions, summarizes the job based on two to four descriptive statements.

Job titles listed in job descriptions, indicate job designations.

Knowledge based on Equal Employment Opportunity Commission guidelines, refers to a body of information applied directly to the performance of a function. Similarly, according to O*NET, knowledge refers to organized sets of principles and facts applying in general domains.

Licensing information describes licenses, certificates, or registrations that are used to identify levels of skill or performance relevant to occupations.

Market-based evaluation an approach to job evaluation, uses market data to determine differences in job worth.

Occupation requirements in O*NET include information about typical activities required across occupations. Identifying generalized work activities and detailed work activities summarizes the broad and more specific types of job behaviors and tasks that may be performed within multiple occupations.

Occupation-specific requirements information describes the characteristics of a particular occupation. These particular requirements are occupational skills, knowledge, tasks, duties, machines, tools, and equipment.

Occupational Information Network (O*NET) is a database designed to describe jobs in the relatively new service sector of the economy and to more accurately describe jobs that evolved as the result of technological advances. O*NET replaces the **Revised Handbook for Analyzing Jobs.**

O*NET database See also *Occupational Information Network (O*NET).*

O*NET User's Guide provides detailed information about the O*NET job content model, its applications, and how to use the system.

Organizational context information indicates the characteristics of the organization that influence how people do their work.

Paired comparison a variation of simple ranking job evaluation plans, orders all jobs from lowest to highest based on comparing the worth of each job in all possible job pairs. Paired comparison also refers to a specific kind of comparison method for appraising job performance. Supervisors compare each employee to every other employee, identifying the better performer in each pair.

Point method represents a job-content evaluation technique that uses quantitative methodology. Quantitative methods assign numerical values to compensable factors that describe jobs, and these values are summed as an indicator of the overall value for the job.

Reliable job analysis method yields consistent results under similar conditions.

Simple ranking plan a specific method of job evaluation, orders all jobs from lowest to highest according to a single criterion (e.g., job complexity or the centrality of the job to the company's competitive strategy).

Skill based on Equal Employment Opportunity Commission guidelines, refers to an observable competence to perform a learned psychomotor act.

Universal compensable factors based on the Equal Pay Act of 1963, include skill, effort, responsibility, and working conditions.

Valid job analysis method accurately assesses each job's duties or content. In this regard, we are referring to a particular type of validity—content validity.

Work context information describes physical and social factors that influence the nature of work.

Work styles are personal characteristics that describe important interpersonal and work style requirements in jobs and occupations.

Worker characteristics refer to ability, interests, and work styles.

Worker requirements represent the minimum qualifications and skills that people must have to perform a particular job. Such requirements usually include education, experience, licenses, permits, and specific abilities such as typing, drafting, or editing.

Worker specifications a section in job descriptions, lists the education, skills, abilities, knowledge, and other qualifications individuals must possess to perform the job adequately.

Workforce characteristics refer to variables that define and describe the general characteristics of occupations that may influence occupational requirements.

Working conditions are the social context or physical environment where work will be performed.

Building Pay Structures That Recognize Employee Contributions

Learning Objectives

When you finish studying this chapter, you should be able to:

1. Explain the concept of pay structures and the five steps necessary to construct pay structures.
2. Discuss the components of merit pay systems.
3. Summarize the features of sales compensation plan design.
4. Describe the essentials of person-focused pay program design.
5. Summarize pay structure variations.

CHAPTER WARM-UP!

If your professor has assigned this, go to the Assignments section of **mymanagementlab.com** to complete the Chapter Warm-Up! and see what you already know. After reading the chapter, you'll have a chance to take the Chapter Quiz! and see what you've learned.

Pay structures assign different pay rates for jobs of unequal worth and provide the framework for recognizing differences in individual employee contributions. No two employees possess identical credentials, nor do they perform the same jobs equally well. Companies recognize these differences by paying individuals according to their credentials, knowledge, or job performance. When completed, pay structures should define the boundaries for recognizing employee contributions. Employee contributions in this context correspond to the pay bases (i.e., seniority, merit, incentive pay, and person-based pay). Pay structures also have strategic value. Well-designed structures should promote the retention of valued employees.

In this chapter, we will address how companies structure these pay bases, with the exception of seniority. We will start out by considering the fundamental process of constructing pay structures. Then we will move on to specific pay structures, including merit pay, sales incentive pay, person-focused pay, broadbanding, and two-tier structures.

CONSTRUCTING A PAY STRUCTURE

1. Explain the concept of pay structures and the five steps necessary to construct pay structures.

Compensation specialists develop pay structures based on five steps:

- Deciding on the number of pay structures
- Determining a market pay line

From Chapter 8 of *Strategic Compensation: A Human Resource Management Approach*, Ninth Edition. Joseph J. Martocchio.

- Defining pay grades
- Calculating pay ranges for each pay grade
- Evaluating the results

Step 1: Deciding on the Number of Pay Structures

Most companies often establish more than one pay structure, depending on market rates and the company's job structure.[1] Common pay structures include exempt and nonexempt structures, pay structures based on job families, and pay structures based on geography. A large-scale survey estimates that approximately 37 percent of companies establish pay structures on the basis of job exemption criteria, 17 percent based on job families, and 30 percent based on geographic scope.[2]

EXEMPT AND NONEXEMPT PAY STRUCTURES These categories reflect a distinction in the Fair Labor Standards Act (FLSA). Exempt jobs are not subject to the overtime pay provisions of the act. Core compensation terms for these jobs are usually expressed as an annual salary. Nonexempt jobs are subject to the overtime pay provision of the act. The core compensation for these jobs is therefore expressed as an hourly pay rate. Companies establish these pay structures for administrative ease. Some broadly consistent features distinguish exempt from nonexempt jobs: Exempt jobs, by the definition of the Fair Labor Standards Act, are generally supervisory, professional, managerial, or executive jobs that contain a wide variety of duties. Nonexempt jobs are generally nonsupervisory in nature, and the duties tend to be narrowly defined.

PAY STRUCTURES BASED ON JOB FAMILY Executive, managerial, professional, technical, clerical, and craft jobs represent distinct job families. Pay structures are also defined on the basis of job family, each of which shows a distinct salary pattern in the market. For example, the Davis–Bacon Act requires contractors and subcontractors to pay wages at least equal to those prevailing in the area where work is performed. This act applies only to employers with federal or federally financed contracts worth more than $2,000 for the construction, alteration, or repair of public works or buildings. Moreover, the Davis–Bacon Act also applies only to laborers and mechanics, excluding clerical, professional, and managerial employees. Thus, companies holding federal contracts meeting these criteria have limited latitude for setting pay for certain jobs; however, the latitude for setting pay rates for other jobs is greater.

PAY STRUCTURES BASED ON GEOGRAPHY Companies with multiple, geographically dispersed locations such as sales offices, manufacturing plants, service centers, and corporate offices may establish pay structures based on going rates in different geographic regions because local conditions may influence pay levels. The cost of living is an important consideration. Cost of living varies considerably between broad regions (e.g., the northeast versus the southeast) and more narrowly focused areas (e.g., Boston, Massachusetts versus Fargo, North Dakota). Cost-of-living comparison calculators (for example, one furnished by CNN, *http://money.cnn.com/calculator/pf/cost-of-living/*) may be useful. Based on this calculator, a $50,000 salary in Fargo was equivalent to a $73,000 salary in Boston as of mid-2015. Among companies that deploy geographic-based pay structures, approximately half do so according to U.S. city or metropolitan area.[3]

Step 2: Determining a Market Pay Line

We discussed that companies rely on surveys to help establish pay policy levels and mixes. Our focus here will be on pay level policy considerations. Again, the market pay line is representative of typical market pay rates relative to a company's job structure. Pay levels that correspond with the market pay line are market-competitive pay rates. It is important to remember that surveys can provide a plethora of information pertaining to competitors' full range of compensation practices, including base pay levels, types and value of incentives, and employee benefits. Approximately

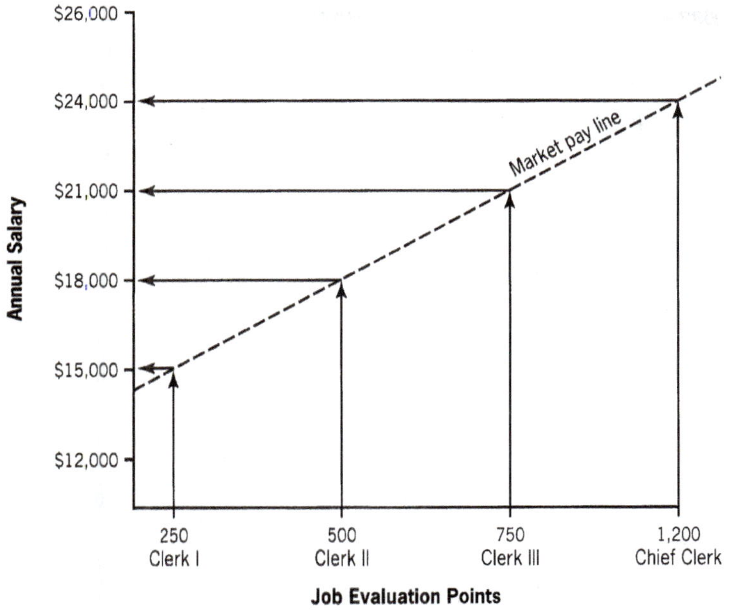

Clerk I
Employees receive training in basic office support procedures, the operation of office equipment, and the specific activities of the unit. Tasks assigned are simple and repetitive in nature and are performed in accordance with explicit instructions and clearly established guidelines. Sample duties include: files materials in established alphabetical order and prepares new file folders and affixes labels. Clerk Is must possess a high school diploma or equivalent.
Clerk II
Employees work under general supervision in support of an office. They perform routine office support tasks that require a knowledge of standard office procedures and the ability to operate a variety of office equipment. Sample duties include: prepares simple factual statements or reports involving computations such as totals or subtotals and composes memos requesting or transmitting factual information. Clerk IIs must possess a high school diploma or equivalent and 1 year work experience performing simple clerical tasks.
Clerk III
Employees work under general supervision in support of an office. They perform office support tasks requiring knowledge of general office and departmental procedures and methods and ability to operate a variety of office equipment. Sample duties include: reconciles discrepancies between unit records and those of other departments and assigns and reviews work performed by Clerks I and II. Clerk IIIs must possess a high school diploma or equivalent, 2 years work experience performing moderately complex clerical tasks, and completed coursework (five in all) in such related topics as word processing and basic accounting principles.
Chief Clerk
Employees work under direction in support of an office. They perform a wide variety of office support tasks that require the use of judgment and initiative. A knowledge of the organization, programs, practices, and procedures of the unit is central to the performance of the duties. Chief clerks must possess a high school diploma or equivalent, 4 years work experience performing moderately difficult clerical tasks, and an associate's degree in office management.

FIGURE 1 Pay Structure for Clerk Jobs

more than 80 percent of companies establish their competitive pay-level position (matching, leading, or lagging the market) on base pay.[4]

Figure 1 illustrates a market pay line for a series of clerical jobs. Pay rates that fall along the market pay line represent competitive pay rates based on the company's selection of a relevant labor market, and these rates promote internal consistency because pay rates increase with the value of jobs based on a company's systematic job evaluation. The clerk I job has the least complex and demanding duties, and it has fewer worker requirements than do the remaining clerk jobs (clerk II, clerk III, and chief clerk).

Step 3: Defining Pay Grades

Pay grades group jobs for pay policy application. Human resource (HR) professionals typically group jobs into pay grades based on similar compensable factors and value. These criteria are not precise. In fact, no one formula determines what is sufficiently similar in terms of content and value to warrant grouping jobs into a pay grade.

Job groupings are ultimately influenced by such other factors as management's philosophy. Wider pay grades (i.e., grades that include a relatively larger number of jobs) minimize hierarchy and social distance between employees. Narrower pay grades tend to promote hierarchy and social distance. Figure 2 illustrates pay grade definitions, based on the jobs used in Figure 1.

Human resource professionals can develop pay grade widths as either "absolute" job evaluation point spreads or as percentage-based job evaluation point spreads. When absolute point spreads are used, grades are based on a set number of job evaluation points for each grade. For example, a compensation professional establishes pay grades equal to 200 points each. Grade 1 includes jobs that range from 1 to 200 job evaluation points, Grade 2 contains jobs that range from 201 to 400 points, and so on.

Companies may choose to vary the "absolute" point spread by increasing the point spread as they move up the pay structure, in recognition of the broader range of skills that higher pay grades represent. For example, certified public accounting jobs require a broader range of skills (e.g., knowledge of financial accounting principles and both state and federal tax codes) than do mailroom clerk jobs. Companies often assign trainee positions to the lower, narrower pay grades because trainees generally have limited job-relevant skills. For instance, Grade 1 may contain

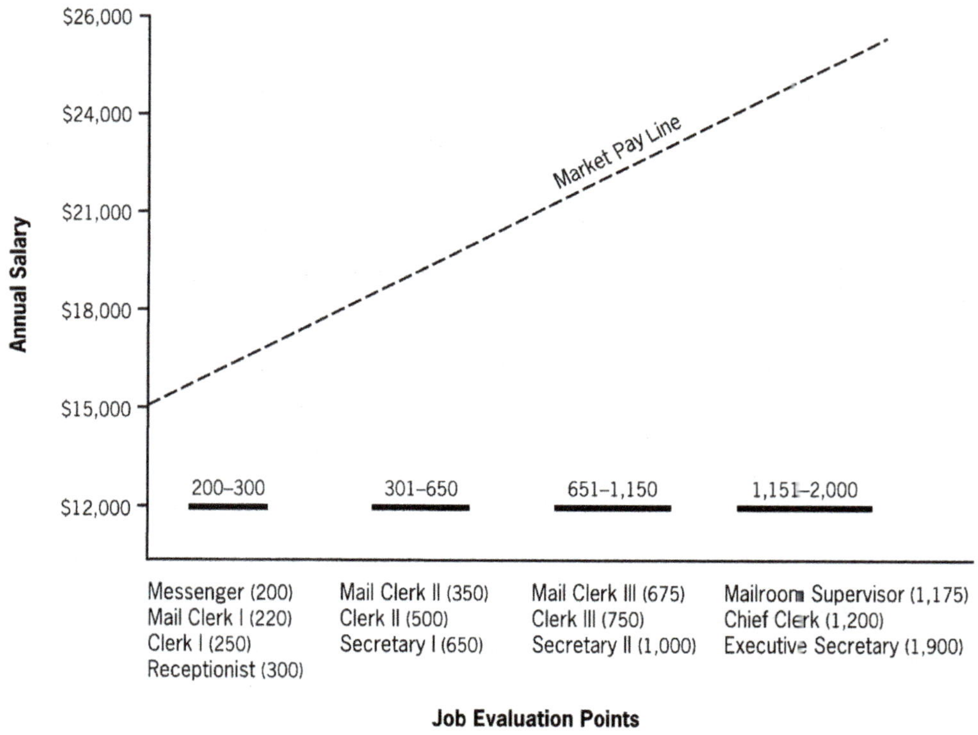

FIGURE 2 **Pay Grade Definitions**

trainee positions with job evaluation scores that range from 1 to 150, Grade 2 may contain basic jobs beyond traineeships with scores of 151–400, and Grade 3 may include advanced jobs with scores of 401–1,000.

Step 4: Calculating Pay Ranges for Each Pay Grade

Pay ranges build upon pay grades. Pay grades represent the horizontal dimension of pay structures (i.e., job evaluation points). **Pay ranges** represent the vertical dimension (pay rates). Pay ranges include midpoint, minimum, and maximum pay rates. The minimum and maximum values denote the acceptable lower and upper bounds of pay for the jobs within particular pay grades. Figure 3 illustrates pay ranges.

Human resource professionals establish midpoints first, followed by minimum and maximum values. The **midpoint pay value** is the halfway mark between the range minimum and maximum rates. Midpoints generally match values along the market pay line, representing the competitive market rate determined by the analysis of compensation survey data. Thus, the midpoint may reflect the market average or median.

A company sets the midpoints for its pay ranges according to its competitive pay policy. If the company wants to lead the market with respect to pay offerings (market lead policy), it sets the midpoint of the ranges higher than the average for similar jobs at other companies. Companies wanting to pay according to the market norm (market match policy) should set midpoints equal to the market average. Companies wanting to lag the market (market lag policy) would set the midpoints below the market average. A company's base-pay policy line graphically connects the midpoints of each pay grade.

How do compensation professionals calculate pay grade minimums and maximums? They may fashion pay grade minimums and maximums after the minimums and maximums for pay grades that their competitors have established. An alternate approach is to set the pay

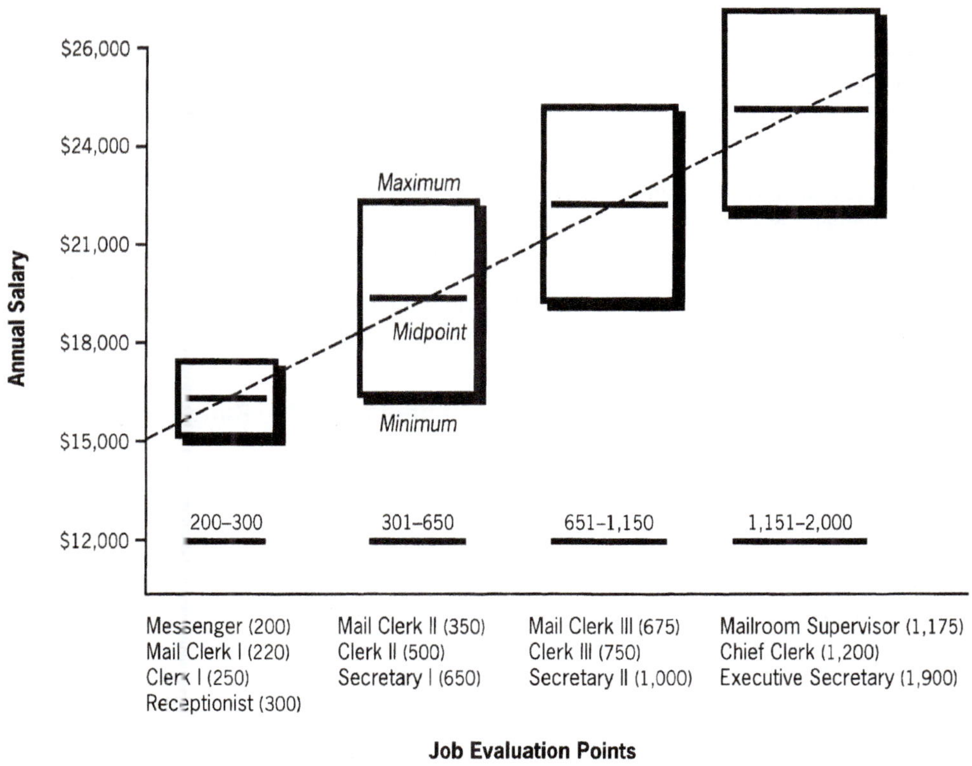

FIGURE 3 **Pay Range Definitions**

Steps

1. Identify the midpoint: $20,000
2. Determine the range spread: 40%
3. Calculate the minimum:

$$\frac{\text{midpoint}}{100\% + (\text{range spread}/2)} = \frac{\$20{,}000}{100\% + (40\%/2)}$$

$$= \$16{,}666.67$$

4. Calculate the maximum:
minimum + (range spread × minimum) = $16,666.67 + (40% × $16,666.67)
= $23,333.33

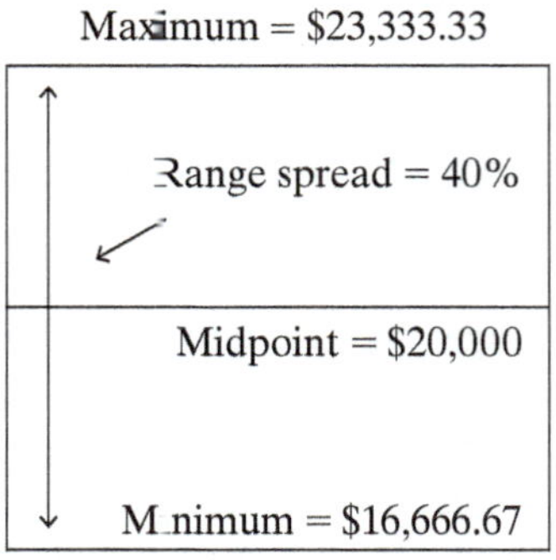

FIGURE 4 Calculation of Range Spread

grade minimums and maximums on the basis of range spread. A **range spread** is the difference between the maximum and minimum pay rates of a given pay grade. It is expressed as a percentage of the difference between the minimum and maximum divided by the minimum.

Companies generally apply different range spreads across pay grades. Most companies apply range spreads that vary typically between 20 percent and 80 percent.[5] They most commonly use progressively higher range spreads for pay grades that contain more valuable jobs in terms of the companies' criteria. Smaller range spreads characterize pay grades that contain relatively narrowly defined jobs that require simple skills with generally low responsibility. Entry-level clerical employees perform limited duties ranging from filing folders alphabetically to preparing file folders and affixing labels. These jobs presumably represent bottom-floor opportunities for employees who will probably advance to higher-level jobs as they acquire the skills needed to perform these jobs proficiently. Advanced clerical employees review and analyze forms and documents to determine the adequacy and acceptability of information.

Higher-level jobs afford employees greater promotion opportunities than entry-level jobs. Employees also tend to remain in higher pay grades longer, and the specialized skills associated with higher pay grade jobs are considered valuable. It therefore makes sense to apply larger range spreads to these pay grades. The following are typical range spreads for different kinds of positions:[6]

- 10–50 percent: hourly employees
- 45–65 percent: salaried (non-executives)
- 45–85 percent: executive

After deciding on range spread, compensation professionals calculate minimum and maximum rates. Figure 4 illustrates the calculation of minimum and maximum rates based on knowledge of the pay grade midpoint (as discussed earlier in Step 1) and the chosen range spread. Table 1

TABLE 1 The Impact of Alternative Range Spreads on Pay Range Minimum and Maximum Values, with Midpoint of $25,000

	Range Spread ($)			
	20%	50%	80%	120%
Minimum: $\frac{\text{midpoint}}{100 + (\text{range spread}/2)}$	$22,727	$20,000	$17,857	$15,625
Maximum: minimum + (range spread × minimum)	$27,272	$30,000	$32,143	$34,375
Difference between maximum and minimum values	$4,545	$10,000	$14,286	$18,750

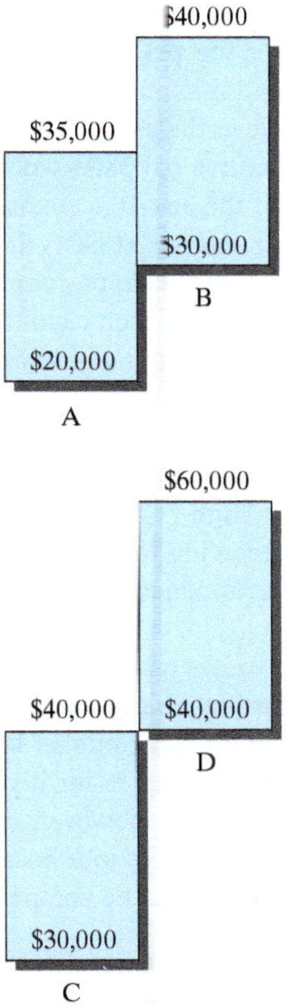

$$100\% \times \frac{(\text{max. rate for A} - \text{min. rate for B})}{(\text{max. rate for A} - \text{min. rate for A})}$$

$$100\% \times \frac{(\$35{,}000 - \$30{,}000)}{(\$35{,}000 - \$20{,}000)}$$

The overlap between range A and range B is 33.33%

$$100\% \times \frac{(\text{max. rate for C} - \text{min. rate for D})}{(\text{max. rate for C} - \text{min. rate for C})}$$

$$100\% \times \frac{(\$40{,}000 - \$40{,}000)}{(\$40{,}000 - \$30{,}000)}$$

The overlap between range C and range D is 0%

FIGURE 5 Calculating Pay Range Overlap

illustrates the impact of alternative range spread values on minimum and maximum values. This approach is typically applied when a company chooses to base the minimum and maximum rates on budgetary constraints, we will discuss budgeting issues later in this chapter. Pay range spread percentage amounts can be calculated with knowledge of a pay range's minimum and maximum values: (maximum rate – minimum rate)/minimum rate.

Adjacent pay ranges usually overlap with other pay ranges so that the highest rate paid in one range is above the lowest rate of the successive pay grade. Figure 5 illustrates how to calculate pay range overlap. Overlapping pay ranges allow companies to promote employees to the next level without adding to their pay. Approximately 36 percent of companies that responded to a large-scale survey indicate that they promote employees to higher pay grades without pay increases.[7] For those that offer pay increases based on job promotions, the average increase was 7.6 percent for nonexempt employees, 8.8 percent for exempt employees, and 10.1 percent for officers/executives. Nonoverlapping pay ranges require pay increases for job promotions. Compensation professionals express overlap as a percentage. In this example, the degree of overlap between pay range A and pay range B is about 33 percent.

PAY COMPRESSION The minimum pay rate for a range usually is the lowest pay rate that the company will pay for jobs that fall within that particular pay grade. In theory, newly hired employees receive pay that is at or near the minimum. In practice, new employees often receive well above minimum pay rates, sometimes only slightly below or even higher than the pay moderately tenured employees receive. **Pay compression** occurs whenever a company's pay spread between newly hired or less qualified employees, and more qualified job incumbents is small.[8]

Two situations result in pay compression. The first is a company's failure to raise pay range minimums and maximums. Companies that retain set range maximums over time limit increase amounts. For example, let's assume that the entry-level starting salaries for newly minted certified public accountants have increased 7 percent annually for the past 5 years. Tax-It, a small accounting firm, did not increase its pay range minimums and maximums for entry-level accountants during the same period because of lackluster profits. Nevertheless, Tax-It hired several new accountants at the midpoint pay rate. Failure to pay competitive pay rates would hinder Tax-It's ability to recruit talented accountants. As a result, many of the Tax-It accountants with 5 or fewer years' experience have lower salaries (or slightly higher salaries at best) than newly hired accountants without work experience. The second situation that results in pay compression is a scarcity of qualified candidates for particular jobs. When the supply of such candidates falls behind companies' demand, wages for newly hired employees rise, reflecting a bidding process among companies for qualified candidates.

Pay compression can threaten companies' competitive advantage. Dysfunctional employee turnover is a likely consequence of pay compression. Dysfunctional turnover represents high-performing employees' voluntary termination of their employment. High-performing employees will probably perceive their pay as inequitable because they are receiving lower pay relative to their positive contributions (i.e., experience and demonstrated performance) than newly hired employees who are receiving similar pay.

How can companies minimize pay compression? Maximum pay rates represent the most that a company is willing to pay an individual for jobs that fall in that particular range. Maximum pay rates should be set close to the maximum paid by other companies in the labor market for similar jobs. Setting competitive maximum rates enables a company to raise pay rates for high-quality employees who may consider employment opportunities with a competitor; however, maximum rates should not exceed maximum rates offered by competitors for comparable jobs because high maximums represent costs to the company over and above what are needed to be competitive.

GREEN CIRCLE PAY RATES Employees sometimes receive below-minimum pay rates for their pay ranges, especially when they assume jobs for which they do not meet every minimum requirement in the worker specification section of the job description. Below-minimum pay range rates are known as **green circle rates**. The pay rates of employees who are paid at green circle rates should be brought within the normal pay range as quickly as possible, which requires that both employer and employee take the necessary steps to eliminate whatever deficiencies in skill or experience that warranted paying below the pay range minimum. In addition, companies should regularly review current employees' pay relative to the starting pay rates for newly hired employees in comparable jobs to plan for necessary pay adjustments before current employees' pay falls below the minimum rates.[9]

RED CIRCLE PAY RATES On occasion, companies must pay certain employees greater than maximum rates for their pay ranges. Known as **red circle rates**, these higher pay rates help retain valued employees who have lucrative job offers from competitors. On the other hand, exemplary employees may receive red circle rates for exceptional job performance, particularly when a promotion to a higher pay grade is not granted. For these exemplary performers, companies may provide lump sum pay awards that are not added to regular base pay.[10] Red circle rates also apply to employees who receive job demotions to pay grades with lower maximum rates than the employees' current pay. Companies usually reduce demoted employees' pay over time until they receive pay that is consistent with their new jobs. In this case, red circle rates allow employees a chance to adjust to pay decreases.

Step 5: Evaluating the Results

After compensation professionals establish pay structures according to the previous steps, they must evaluate the results. They must specifically analyze significant differences between the company's internal values for jobs and the market's values for the same jobs. If discrepancies are evident, the company must reconsider the internal values they have placed on jobs. If their valuation of particular jobs exceeds the market's valuation of the same jobs, they must decide whether higher-than-market pay rates will undermine attainment of competitive advantage. If a company undervalues jobs relative to the market, managers must consider whether these discrepancies will limit the company's ability to recruit and retain highly qualified individuals.

Compensation professionals must also consider each employee's pay level relative to the midpoint of the pay grade. Again, the midpoint represents a company's competitive stance relative to the market. **Compa-ratios** index the relative competitiveness of internal pay rates based on pay range midpoints. Compa-ratios are calculated as follows:

$$\frac{\text{Employee's pay rate}}{\text{Pay range midpoint}}$$

Compa-ratios are interpreted as follows: A compa-ratio of 1 means that the employee's pay rate equals the pay range midpoint. A compa-ratio less than 1 means that the employee's pay rate falls below the competitive pay rate for the job. Companies with market lag policies strive for compa-ratios of less than 1. A compa-ratio that is greater than 1 means that an employee's pay rate exceeds the competitive pay rate for the job.

Human resource professionals also can use compa-ratios to index job groups that fall within a particular pay grade. Compa-ratios specifically may be calculated to index the competitive position of a job—by averaging the pay rates for each job incumbent. Moreover, compa-ratios may be calculated for all jobs that comprise a pay grade, departments, or such functional areas as accounting.

Compa-ratios provide invaluable information about the competitiveness of companies' pay rates. Compensation professionals can use compa-ratios as diagnostic tools to judge the competitiveness of their companies' pay rates. Compa-ratios that exceed 1 tell compensation professionals that pay is highly competitive with the market. Compa-ratios that fall below 1 tell them that pay is not competitive with the market and that they should consider another course of action to increase pay over a reasonable period.

We've reviewed the elements of pay structures and the steps compensation professionals follow to construct them. Next, we will consider three popular pay structures that should be familiar to compensation professionals:

- Merit pay structure
- Sales incentive compensation structure
- Person-focused structure

DESIGNING MERIT PAY SYSTEMS

2. Discuss the components of merit pay systems.

Companies that use merit pay systems must ensure that employees see definite links between pay and performance. We also reviewed the rationale for using merit pay systems, as well as the possible limitations of this kind of pay system. Establishing an effective merit pay program that recognizes employee contributions requires avoiding such pitfalls as ineffective performance appraisal methods and poor communication regarding the link between pay and performance. In addition to these considerations, managers interested in establishing a merit pay system must determine merit increase amounts, timing, and the type of merit pay increase (i.e., permanent or recurring increases versus one-time or nonrecurring additions to base pay). They must also settle on base-pay levels relative to the base pay of functionally similar jobs.[11]

Merit Increase Amounts

Merit pay increases should reflect prior job performance levels and motivate employees to perform their best As managers establish merit increase amounts, they must consider both past performance levels and establish rates that will motivate employees even after the impact of inflation and payroll deductions. Updating compensation survey data should account for increases in consumer prices. Just-meaningful pay increases" refer to the minimum amounts employees will see as making a meaningful change in their compensation.[12] Trivial pay increases for average or better employees will not reinforce their performance or motivate them.

No precise mathematical formula determines the minimum merit increase that will positively affect performance; managers must consider three research findings.[13] First, boosting the merit increase amount will not necessarily improve productivity because research has shown diminishing marginal returns on each additional dollar allocated to merit increases.[14] In other words, each additional merit increase amount was associated with a smaller increase in production.

Second, employees' perceptions of just-meaningful differences in merit increases depend on their cost of living, their attitudes toward the job, and their expectations of rewards from the job. For employees who value pay for meeting economic necessity, a just-meaningful difference in pay increase tends to depend on changes in the cost of living. On the other hand, for employees who value pay as a form of recognition, the size of the expected pay raise (versus cost of living) affects a just-meaningful difference.[15]

Third, for the pay increase to be considered meaningful, the employee must see the size of the increase as substantive in a relative sense as well as in an absolute sense.[16] **Equity theory** suggests that an employee must regard his or her own ratio of merit increase pay to performance as similar to the ratio for other comparably performing people in the company. In practical terms, managers should award the largest merit pay increases to employees with the best performance, and they should award the smallest increases to employees with the lowest acceptable performance. The difference between these merit increases should be approximately equal to the differences in performance.

It is also essential that compensation professionals design plans that reinforce employees' motivation to perform well, with just-meaningful pay increases and merit increase percentages that clearly distinguish among employees based on their performance; however, the best-laid plans don't always lead to the desired results. Well-designed merit pay structures (and others that we discuss shortly) will fail without adequate funding.

Compensation budgets are blueprints that describe the allocation of monetary resources to fund pay structures. Compensation professionals index budget increases that fund merit pay programs in percentage terms. For example, a 10 percent increase for next year's budget means that it will be 10 percent greater than the size of the current year's budget. This value is often an indicator of the average pay increase employees will receive. It is obvious that the greater the increase in the compensation budget, the more flexibility compensation professionals will have in developing innovative systems with substantial motivating potential.

The magnitude of the increases in compensation budgets in recent years has unfortunately been just slightly more than the average increases in cost of living. For example, the average earnings for social workers in the United States increased only 1.6 percent between May 2013 and May 2014.[17] Although this value varies by occupation, industry, and region of the country, it does reflect a trend in the United States of stagnant growth in compensation budgets. The picture becomes less positive because the increase in cost of living for the same period was 2.1 percent.[18] This means that, on average, annual merit pay raises fell below the increase in cost of living by 0.5 percent, taking the motivational value out of pay increases.

Timing

The vast majority of companies allocate merit increases, as well as cost-of-living and other increases, annually. At present, companies typically take one of two approaches in timing these pay raises. Companies may establish a **common review date** or **common review period** so that all employees' performances are evaluated on the same date or during the same period (e.g., the month of June, which immediately follows a company's peak activity period). Best suited for smaller companies, common review dates reduce the administrative burden of the plan by concentrating staff members' efforts to limited periods.

On the other hand, companies may review employee performance and award merit increases on the **employee's anniversary date** (i.e., the day on which the employee began to work for the company). Most employees will thus have different evaluation dates. Although these staggered review dates may not monopolize supervisors' time, this approach can be administratively burdensome because reviews must be conducted regularly throughout the year.

Recurring versus Nonrecurring Merit Pay Increases

Companies have traditionally awarded merit pay increases permanently, and permanent increases are sometimes associated with some undesirable side effects (e.g., placing excessive cost burdens on the employer). In terms of costs, U.S. companies are increasingly concerned with containing costs as just one initiative in their quest to establish and sustain competitive advantage in the marketplace. Companies may advocate **nonrecurring merit increases** (i.e., lump sum bonuses), which lend themselves well to cost containment and have recently begun to gain some favor among unions, including the International Brotherhood of Electrical Workers.[19] Lump sum bonuses strengthen the pay-for-performance link and minimize costs because these increases are not permanent, and subsequent percentage increases are not based on higher base-pay levels.

The Watch It! Video discusses the performance appraisal process at Hautelook. The HR Director discusses that informal performance appraisals may take place multiple times during a year; however, decisions about permanent pay increases, bonuses, and promotions take place annually during the formal performance appraisal process. This video also discusses the company's performance appraisal process and possible limitations.

WATCH IT!

If your professor has assigned this, go to the Assignments section of **mymanagementlab.com** to complete the video exercise titled Hautelook: Appraising.

Present Level of Base Pay

Pay structures specify acceptable pay ranges for jobs within each pay grade. Thus, each job's base-pay level should fall within the minimum and maximum rates for its respective pay grade. In addition, compensation professionals should encourage managers to offer similar base pay to new employees performing similar jobs unless employees' qualifications (i.e., education and relevant work experience) justify pay differences. This practice is consistent with the mandates of several laws such as Title VII of the Civil Rights Act of 1964 and the Equal Pay Act of 1963. Of course, employees' merit pay increases should vary with their performance.

Rewarding Performance: The Merit Pay Grid

Table 2 illustrates a typical merit pay grid that managers use to assign merit increases to employees. Managers determine pay raise amounts by two factors jointly: employees' performance ratings and the position of employees' present base-pay rates within pay ranges. Pay raise amounts are expressed as percentages of base pay. For instance, let's say that two employees will each receive a 5 percent merit pay increase. One employee is paid on an hourly basis, earning $8.50 per hour, and the other is paid on an annual basis, earning $32,000. The employee whose pay is based on an hourly rate (usually nonexempt in accord with the Fair Labor Standards Act; one who must be paid overtime for time worked in excess of 40 hours per week) receives a pay raise of $0.44 per hour, increasing her hourly pay to $8.94. The employee whose pay is based on an annual rate, typically exempt from the Fair Labor Standards Act provisions, receives a pay increase of $1,600, boosting her annual pay to $33,600.

In Table 2, employees whose current annual salary falls in the 2nd quartile of the pay range and whose performance rates an average score receive a 6 percent merit pay increase. Employees whose current annual salary falls in the 1st quartile of the pay range and whose job performance is excellent receive a 12 percent merit pay increase. The term *cell* (as in spreadsheet

TABLE 2 Merit Pay Increase Grid

		Performance Rating				
		Excellent (%)	Above Average (%)	Average (%)	Below Average (%)	Poor (%)
Q4 ⇒	$70,000					
	$65,000	5	3	1	0	0
	$60,000					
Q3 ⇒	$55,000					
	$50,000	7	5	3	0	0
	$45,000					
Q2 ⇒	$40,000					
	$35,000	9	7	6	2	0
	$30,000					
Q1 ⇒	$25,000					
	$20,000	12	10	8	4	0
	$15,000					

software programs such as *Microsoft Excel*) is used to reference the intersection of quartile ranking and performance rating. Table 2 contains 20 cells.

EMPLOYEES' PERFORMANCE RATINGS Merit pay systems use performance appraisals to determine employees' performance. Where merit pay systems are in place, an overall performance rating guides the pay raise decision. In Table 2, an employee receives any one of five performance ratings ranging from "Poor" to "Excellent." As you can see when we hold position in pay range constant, pay raise amounts increase with level of performance. This pattern fits well with the logic underlying pay-for-performance principles—it recognizes higher performance with greater rewards.

EMPLOYEES' POSITIONS WITHIN THE PAY RANGE Employees' positions within the pay range are indexed by quartile ranking, which we described as a measure of dispersion. Again, quartiles allow compensation professionals to describe the distribution of data (i.e., in this case, hourly or annual base-pay amount) based on four groupings known as quartiles. In Table 2, the 1st quartile is the point below which 25 percent of the salary data lie (and above which 75 percent of the salary data are found), which is $25,000. In this example, 25 percent of the salary figures are less than or equal to $25,000 and 75 percent of these figures are greater than $25,000. The 2nd quartile is the point below which 50 percent of the salary data lie (and above which 50 percent of the salary figures are found), which is $40,000 for this example. The 3rd quartile is the point below which 75 percent of the salary figures lie (and above which 25 percent of the salary figures are found), which is $55,000 for this example. The 4th quartile is the point below which all of the salary data lie, which is $70,000. The lower a person's pay falls within its designated pay grade (e.g., the 1st quartile versus the 3rd quartile), the higher the percentage pay raise, all else being equal. Along those lines, the higher a person's pay within its grade, the lower the percentage pay raise, all else being equal.

Holding performance ratings constant, compensation professionals reduce merit pay increase percentages as quartile ranks increase to control employees' progression through their pay ranges. Pay grade minimums and maximums reflect both corporate criteria about the value of various groups of unlike jobs and may be dictated by budgeting. We'll look at the issue of budgeting shortly. Let's take the case of two employees whose performance ratings are identical but whose base pay places them in different quartiles of the pay grade (i.e., one in the 3rd quartile and the other in the 1st quartile). If these employees were to receive the same pay raise percentage, the base-pay rate for the employee in the 3rd quartile likely would exceed the maximum pay rate for the range more quickly than would the base-pay rate for the employee in the 1st quartile.

Merit Pay Increase Budgets

Now that we've considered the design principles for merit pay grids, we'll take a closer look at budgetary considerations. Budgets limit the merit pay increase percentages in each cell. A **merit pay increase budget** is expressed as a percentage of the sum of employees' current base pay. For instance, let's assume that a company's top financial officers and compensation professionals agree to a 5 percent merit pay increase budget. Let's also assume that the sum of all employees' current base pay is $10 million based on an employee population of 350. A 5 percent merit pay increase budget for this example equals $500,000, that is, 5 percent of the sum of all employees' current base pay totaling $10,000,000 (5 percent × $10,000,000). In other words, the company will distribute $500,000 to increase current base pay of its employees. Merit pay increases awarded to individual employees will vary according to performance level and position in the pay range; however, the total of the individual pay increases must not exceed the allotted merit pay increase budget, again, $500,000 in this example. As an aside, the typical merit pay increase budget today ranges between 2 and 3 percent for the small proportion of companies that even have awarded pay increases in the past few years. This range is much lower than the average 4 percent increase in recent past years.

Compensation professionals begin plans for setting the merit increase pay grid within the estimated merit increase pay budget with the following six steps:

1. Compensation professionals ask managers and supervisors to indicate the percentage of employees who they expect will fall in each of the performance categories in the performance appraisal instrument. Managers will often use the actual distribution of employees based on recent past years as an estimate for budget planning. The sample merit pay grid illustrated in Table 2 lists five performance categories. For illustrative purposes, let's assume the following performance distribution for employees:
    - Excellent: 10 percent
    - Above average: 20 percent
    - Average: 40 percent
    - Below average: 25 percent
    - Poor: 5 percent
2. Compensation professionals rely on position in the pay range to determine the percentage of employees whose pay falls into each pay quartile. For example, let's assume the following distribution of employees in each pay quartile:
    - Q4: 20 percent
    - Q3: 25 percent
    - Q2: 40 percent
    - Q1: 15 percent

    In other words, 20 percent of employees earn pay that falls in the range from $55,000 to $70,000 (4th quartile) in Table 2. Similarly, 25 percent of the employees earn pay that falls in the range from $40,000 to $55,000 (3rd quartile). The same rationale applies to the 1st and 2nd quartiles.
3. Compensation professionals combine both sets of information to determine the percentage of employees who fall into each cell. The percentage of employees whose performance rating is excellent and whose base pay falls in the 4th quartile equals 2 percent (10 percent × 20 percent). The sum of the cell percentages totals 100 percent.

	Excellent (%)	Above Average (%)	Average (%)	Below Average (%)	Poor (%)
Q4	10 × 20 = 2	20 × 20 = 4	40 × 20 = 8	25 × 20 = 5	5 × 20 = 1
Q3	10 × 25 = 2.5	20 × 25 = 5	40 × 25 = 10	25 × 25 = 6.25	5 × 25 = 1.25
Q2	10 × 40 = 4	20 × 40 = 8	40 × 40 = 16	25 × 40 = 10	5 × 40 = 2
Q1	10 × 15 = 1.5	20 × 15 = 3	40 × 15 = 6	25 × 15 = 3.75	5 × 15 = 0.75

4. Next, compensation professionals calculate the expected number of employees who fall into each cell. It is important to remember that this is the expected (versus actual) number of employees because managers provide only an estimate of employees' performance distribution. For this example, let's assume that the company employs 350 people. The number of employees whose performance rating is excellent and whose base pay falls in the 4th quartile equals 7 (350 people × 2 percent).

	Excellent	Above Average	Average	Below Average	Poor
Q4	350 × 2% = 7	350 × 4% = 14	350 × 8% = 28	350 × 5% = 17.5	350 × 1% = 3.5
Q3	350 × 2.5% = 8.75	350 × 5% = 17.5	350 × 10% = 35	350 × 6.25% = 21.875	350 × 1.25% = 4.375
Q2	350 × 4% = 14	350 × 8% = 28	350 × 16% = 56	350 × 10% = 35	350 × 2% = 7
Q1	350 × 1.5% = 5.25	350 × 3% = 10.5	350 × 6% = 21	350 × 3.75% = 13.125	350 × 0.75% = 2.625

5. Compensation professionals now distribute the merit increase budget amount ($500,000) to each cell based on the following formula:

Expected number of employees in cell × Desired pay increase for cell %
× Current median pay level for the current quartile

We calculated the expected number of employees in each cell in the previous step. The desired pay increase amount is an estimate that we made (see Table 2). Compensation professionals usually specify these percentage amounts initially on pay-for-performance and equity considerations (i.e., holding performance constant, individuals in higher pay quartiles receive smaller percentage increases than employees in lower pay quartiles). Let's assume for this example that the medians for each quartile are:

- Q4: $65,000
- Q3: $50,000
- Q2: $35,000
- Q1: $20,000

	Excellent	Above Average	Average	Below Average	Poor
Q4	7 × 5% × $65,000 = $22,750	14 × 3% × $65,000 = $27,300	28 × 1% × $65,000 = $18,200	17.5 × 0% × $65,000 = $0	0.5 × 0% × $65,000 = $0
Q3	8.75 × 7% × $50,000 = $30,625	17.5 × 5% × $50,000 = $43,750	35 × 3% × $50,000 = $52,500	21.875 × 0% × $50,000 = $0	4.375 × 0% × $50,000 = $0
Q2	14 × 9% × $35,000 = $44,100	28 × 7% × $35,000 = $68,600	56 × 6% × $35,000 = $117,600	35 × 2% × $35,000 = $24,500	7 × 0% × $35,000 = $0
Q1	5.25 × 12% × $20,000 = $12,600	10.5 × 10% × $20,000 = $21,000	21 × 7% × $20,000 = $29,400	13.125 × 4% × $20,000 = $10,500	2.625 × 0% × $20,000 = $0

The sum of expected merit pay increases equals $523,425.

6. Compensation professionals check whether the expected merit increase total fits within the actual budgeted amount. In this example, the sum of expected increases exceeds the budgeted amount by $23,425 (i.e., $523,425 – $500,000). When the expected increase amount exceeds the budgeted amount, compensation professionals adjust the percentages in the cells with the following considerations in mind: lowering costs, recognizing performance differences, and considering equity.

   Pay structures based on merit differ from sales compensation in at least two key ways. First, whereas sales compensation programs center on incentives that specify rewards an employee will receive for meeting a preestablished—often objective—level of performance, merit pay programs generally base an employee's reward on someone else's (most often the employee's supervisor's) subjective evaluation of the employee's past performance. Second, in most instances, a sales employee's compensation is variable to the extent that it is composed of incentives. Under a merit pay system, an employee earns a base pay appropriate for the job (as discussed earlier in this chapter) that is augmented periodically with permanent pay raises or one-time bonuses.

DESIGNING SALES INCENTIVE COMPENSATION PLANS

3. Summarize the features of sales compensation plan design.

Compensation programs for salespeople rely on incentives.[20] Sales compensation programs can help businesses meet their objectives by aligning the financial self-interest of sales professionals with the company's marketing objectives.[21] By extension, sales compensation programs can help companies achieve strategic objectives by linking sales professionals' compensation to fulfilling customer needs or other marketing objectives (e.g., increasing market share). Thus, sales compensation plans derive their objectives more or less directly from strategic marketing objectives, which, in turn, are derived from company competitive strategy. Particular sales objectives include:[22]

- *Improve sales productivity*: More volume and profit from current investment in sales resources.
  - New-customer sales volume
  - New-product sales volume
  - New balanced product-line sales
  - Reduced "churn" among current customers

- *Improve sales coverage of current customers*: Regardless of industry, customers want flexibility, customization, faster response, and personalized service. To meet these requirements, market-leading companies improve the coverage of their current customers. This often means investments in new ways to interact with customers.
  - Overall account volume
  - Greater share of the account's business
  - Achievement of customer objectives
  - More lines of business sold
  - Account profitability

- *Grow sales overall*: Track the percentage of sales realized from the following:
  - New direct customers
  - New distribution channels
  - New products

Alternative Sales Compensation Plans

Companies usually use one of five kinds of sales incentive plans. The type of plan appropriate for any given company will depend on the company's competitive strategy. The order of presentation roughly represents the degree of risk (from lowest to highest) to employees.

- Salary-only plans
- Salary-plus-bonus plans
- Salary-plus-commission plans
- Commission-plus-draw plans
- Commission-only plans

SALARY-ONLY PLANS Under **salary-only plans**, sales professionals receive fixed base compensation, which does not vary with the level of units sold, increase in market share, or any other indicator of sales performance. From the employees' perspective, salary-only plans are relatively risk-free because they can expect a certain amount of income. From a company's perspective, salary-only plans are burdensome because the company must compensate its sales employees regardless of their achievement levels. Thus, salary-only plans do not fit well with the directive to link pay with performance through at-risk pay. Nevertheless, salary-only plans may be appropriate for such particular kinds of selling situations as:

- Sales of high-priced products and services or technical products with long lead times for sales
- Situations in which sales representatives are primarily responsible for generating demand, but other employees actually close the sales
- Situations in which it is impossible to follow sales results for each salesperson (i.e., where sales are accomplished through team efforts)
- Training and other periods when sales representatives are unlikely to make sales on their own

SALARY-PLUS-BONUS PLANS **Salary-plus-bonus plans** offer a set salary coupled with a bonus. Bonuses usually are single payments that reward employees for achievement of specific, exceptional goals. For a real estate agent, generating in excess of $2 million in residential sales for a 1-year period may mean earning a bonus totaling several thousand dollars.

SALARY-PLUS-COMMISSION PLANS **Commission** is a form of incentive compensation based on a percentage of the selling price of a product or service. **Salary-plus-commission plans** spread the risk of selling between the company and the sales professional. The salary component presumably enhances a company's ability to attract good employees and allows a company to direct its employees' efforts to deter employees from undertaking tasks that do not lead directly to commissions (e.g., participating in further training or servicing accounts). The commission component serves as the employees' share in the gains they generated for the company.

COMMISSION-PLUS-DRAW PLANS **Commission-plus-draw plans** award sales professionals with subsistence pay or draws—money to cover basic living expenses—yet provide them with a strong incentive to excel. This subsistence pay component is known as a **draw**. Unlike salaries, however, companies award draws as advances, which are charged against commissions that sales professionals are expected to earn.

Companies use two types of draws. **Recoverable draws** act as company loans to employees that are carried forward indefinitely until employees sell enough to repay their draws. **Nonrecoverable draws** act as salary because employees are not obligated to repay the loans if they do not sell enough. Nonrecoverable draws clearly represent risks to companies because these expenses are not repaid if employee sales performance is lackluster. Companies that adopt nonrecoverable draws may stipulate that employees cannot continue in the employment of the company if they fail to cover their draw for a specified number of months or sales periods during the year. This arrangement is quite common among car salespeople.

COMMISSION-ONLY PLANS Under **commission-only plans**, salespeople derive their entire income from commissions. Three particular types of commissions warrant mention. **Straight commission** is based on a fixed percentage of the sales price of the product or service. For instance, a 10 percent commission would generate a $10 incentive for a product or service sold that is priced at $100 and $55 for a product or service sold that is priced at $550.

Graduated commissions increase percentage pay rates for progressively higher sales volume. For example, a sales professional may earn a 5 percent commission per unit for sales volume up to 100 units, 8 percent for each unit from 101 to 500 units, and 12 percent for each unit in excess of 500 sold during each sales period.

Finally, **multiple-tiered commissions** are similar to graduated commissions, but with one exception. Employees earn a higher rate of commission for all sales made in a given period if the sales level exceeds a predetermined level. For instance, employees might earn only 8 percent for each item if total sales volume falls short of 1,000 units. If total sales volume exceeds 1,000 units, however, then employees might earn a per-item commission equal to 12 percent for every item sold. Evidence encourages the use of multiple-tiered commissions because a pattern of higher performance was achieved prior to the use of these structures.[23] Commission-only plans are well suited for situations in which:

- The salesperson has substantial influence over the sales.
- Low-to-moderate training or expertise is required.
- The sales cycle—the time between identifying the prospect and closing the sale—is short.

In contrast to salespeople on salary-only plans, commission-only salespeople shoulder all the risk: Employees earn nothing until they sell. Despite this risk, potential rewards are substantial, particularly with graduated and multiple-tiered commission plans.

Although commissions may fit well with cost-cutting measures, these incentives are not always the best tactic for compensating sales professionals. In fact, commission structures probably suffer from many of the same limitations of individual incentive plans. Moreover, some sales experts argue that commissions undermine employees' intrinsic motivation to sell (i.e., their genuine interest for the challenge and enjoyment that selling brings). These experts argue that once salespeople have lost that intrinsic motivation, commissions act essentially as controls to maintain sales professionals' performance levels. Said another way, such professionals may simply go through the motions in order to earn money without regard to quality and customer satisfaction.[24] In addition, the younger generation appears to be more risk averse than older generations, which is making it difficult for companies to fill sales positions because members of the younger generation prefer higher certainty associated with earning base pay.[25]

For any sales compensation plan, it is critical that companies establish realistic total sales targets and individual performance standards. Beyond reasonable limits, it is possible that sales compensation plans will backfire. Consequences of such backfire include lower employee motivation, unprofessional behavior, and compromised profits.

Sales Compensation Plans and Competitive Strategy

Sales plans with salary components are most appropriate for differentiation strategies. Under salary-based sales plans, employees can count on receiving income. By design, salary plans do not require employees to focus on attaining sales volume goals or other volume indicators (e.g., market share). Sales professionals who receive salaries can turn their attention to addressing clients' needs during the presale and servicing phases of the relationship. Salary-based sales compensation applies to the sale and servicing of such technical equipment as computer networks, including the hardware (e.g., the individual computers and network server) and the software (e.g., applications programs such as *Microsoft Excel* or the *Microsoft Windows* operating system).

Commission-oriented sales compensation plans are best suited for lowest-cost strategies because compensation expenditures vary with sales revenue. As a result, only the most productive employees earn the best salaries. Commissions essentially represent rewards for "making the sale." For example, real estate sales agents' earnings depend on two factors: number of houses sold and their selling price. New-car salespersons' earnings similarly depend on the number of cars sold and their selling price. In either situation, customers are likely to have questions and concerns following sales transactions. Many real estate sales companies employ real estate assistants at low salaries who mediate such buyers' queries of the sellers as, "What grade of rock salt is most appropriate for the water softener apparatus?" Real estate assistants are often training to be full-fledged real estate agents, and they view low pay as a necessary trade-off for learning the ropes.

Regardless of competitive strategy, rapidly growing companies, including ones that acquire new businesses, run the risk of undermining competitive advantage. Cisco Systems faced this problem in its sales function because sales approaches and strategies within the company were decentralized. Communication across the businesses was poor and concerns about undermining sales performance increased. Cisco Systems implemented a sales center of excellence (COE) to help remedy this problem.[26] COEs are established to serve as a capability center for a specific area or focus. It allows management to maximize leverage and create alignment and consistency in how systems, methodologies, and business processes are developed and communicated.

Determining Fixed Pay and the Compensation Mix

Managers must balance fixed and incentive pay elements to directly affect employee motivation. The mix depends mainly on three factors:

- Influence of the salesperson on the buying decision
- Competitive pay standards within the industry
- Amount of nonsales activities required

INFLUENCE OF THE SALESPERSON ON THE BUYING DECISION For the most part, the more influence sales professionals have on "buying" decisions, the more the compensation mix will emphasize incentive pay. Salespeople's influence varies greatly with the specific product or service marketed and the way these are sold. Many sales professionals assume an order-taker role, with little influence over purchase decisions. For example, salespeople in such large department stores as Best Buy have little influence over the merchandise for sale because these stores send their buyers to manufacturers to purchase lines of products that will be sold in their stores throughout the United States and beyond. Product display and promotional efforts are determined by store management.

On the other end of the spectrum, some employees serve as consultants to the client. For instance, when a company decides to invest in computerizing its entire worldwide operations, it may approach a computer manufacturer such as Dell to purchase the necessary equipment. Given the technical complexity of computerizing a company's worldwide operations, the client would depend on Dell to translate its networking needs into the appropriate configuration of hardware and software. These Dell sales professionals ultimately influence the purchaser's decision to buy.

COMPETITIVE PAY STANDARDS WITHIN THE INDUSTRY A company's compensation mix must be as enticing as that offered by competitors if the company wants to recruit high-quality sales professionals. Industry norms and the selling situation are among the key determinants of compensation mix. For instance, competitive standards may dictate that the company must give greater weight to either incentive or fixed pay. Incentive (commission) pay weighs heavily in highly competitive retail industries, including furniture, home electronics, and auto sales. Salary represents a significant pay component in such high entry-barrier industries as pharmaceuticals. In the case of pharmaceuticals, barriers to entry include the U.S. Food and Drug Administration regulations on testing new products that significantly extend the time from product conception through testing to marketing for general use. Salary is an appropriate compensation choice because pharmaceutical companies face little risk of new competition.

AMOUNT OF NONSALES ACTIVITIES REQUIRED In general, the more nonsales duties salespeople have, the more their compensation package should tend toward fixed pay. Some companies and products, for instance, require extensive technical training or customer servicing activities. An excellent example is again the pharmaceuticals industry. Sales professionals employed by such companies as Bristol-Myers Squibb, Eli Lilly and Company, and Merck & Company must maintain a comprehensive understanding of their products' chemical compositions, clinical uses, and contraindications.

DESIGNING PERSON-FOCUSED PROGRAMS

4. Describe the essentials of person-focused pay program design.

Merit pay and incentive pay represent job-based approaches to compensating employees. We discussed the importance of person-focused pay that many companies recognize. For this discussion, we use the terms *knowledge* and *skills* interchangeably, as the design features for both structures are virtually the same. In their purest form, person-focused programs reward employees for the acquisition of job-related knowledge (or skills, in the case of skill-based pay plans). In practice, companies are concerned with how much employees' performance improves as a result of their newly acquired knowledge. Our focus in this section is on the latter.

A fundamental issue in person-focused programs is whether investments in training provide measurable payoffs to companies. The American Society for Training and Development, a premier professional organization of training and development professionals, offered some insight. Based on a research study involving approximately 2,500 companies, training investments are positively related to future total stockholder return, gross profit margin, and income per employee.[27] In addition, executives within and outside the training function at IBM maintain that training programs have strategic value for companies.[28]

Establishing Skill Blocks

Skill (knowledge) blocks are sets of skills (knowledge) necessary to perform a specific job (e.g., typing skills versus analytical reasoning) or group of similar jobs (e.g., junior accounting clerk, intermediate accounting clerk, and senior accounting clerk). Table 3 contains an example of a knowledge block—building market-competitive compensation systems—discussed in the accompanying companion casebook *Building Strategic Compensation Systems*.

The number of skill blocks included in a person-focused structure can range from two to several. The appropriate number of blocks depends on the variety of jobs within a company. The development of skill blocks should occur with three considerations in mind.

First, the company must develop job descriptions. Job descriptions should be treated as blueprints for the creation of a person-focused system. Well-crafted job descriptions should facilitate the identification of major skills, the training programs employees need to acquire horizontal and vertical skills, and accurate measures of performance.

Second, individual jobs should be organized into job families, or groups of similar jobs such as clerical, technical, and accounting. The information conveyed within a job description should enable the plan developers to identify skills that are common to all jobs in the family and skills that are unique for individual jobs in the family. Based on these groupings, all tasks necessary to perform the jobs in a job family should be listed to facilitate the identification of the skills necessary to perform the tasks.

Third, skills should be grouped into blocks. There are no hard-and-fast rules compensation professionals can follow to determine skill blocks. A general guideline is that the blocked knowledge should relate to specific job tasks and duties. Referring again to Table 3,

TABLE 3 Knowledge Block: Building Market-Competitive Compensation Systems

I. Strategic analyses
   A. External market environment
   B. Internal capabilities
II. Compensation surveys
   A. Using published compensation survey data
   B. Compensation surveys: Strategic considerations
   C. Compensation survey data: Summary, analysis, and interpretation

knowledge about the external environment and a company's internal capabilities—two distinct sets of knowledge—together form the foundation of strategic analyses.

Transition Matters

A number of initial considerations arise in the transition from using job-based pay exclusively to using person-focused programs as well. These issues include assessment of skills, alignment of pay with the knowledge structure, and access to training.[29]

SKILLS ASSESSMENT The skills assessment issue centers on who should assess whether employees possess skills at levels that justify a pay raise, on what basis assessments should be made, and when assessments should be conducted. Gaining employee trust is critical during the transition period because employees may view new systems as threats to job security. Some combination of peer and self-assessments, as well as input from known "experts" such as supervisors, therefore, might be essential. The important ingredients here are employee input and the expertise of supervisors and managers. In the case of knowledge assessment, paper-and-pencil tests are useful tools.

Having established who should conduct assessments, on what basis should assessments be made? During the transition, companies use conventional performance measures that reflect employees' proficiency in skills use, complemented by employees' self-assessments. The use of both types of data is likely to increase an employee's understanding of the new system as well as build faith in it, particularly when testimony and the more conventional performance measures converge.

A final assessment matter concerns timing. During transition phases, managers should assess employees' performance more frequently to keep employees informed of how well they are doing under the new system. In addition, more frequent assessments should reinforce the key aim of pay for knowledge (i.e., to encourage employees to learn more). Performance feedback is essential for this process.

ALIGNING PAY WITH THE KNOWLEDGE STRUCTURE One of the most difficult tasks that managers face as they guide employees toward a person-focused system is aligning pay with the knowledge structure.[30] This is often the case because most compensation surveys price whole jobs (e.g., surgeons) rather than specific knowledge or skill sets that make up particular jobs, such as jobs that require manual dexterity. (See the article by Judy Canavan listed in endnote 30, which addresses strategies for pricing skills.) Still, upon implementation of pay for knowledge, employees' core compensation must reflect the knowledge or skills they have that the company incorporates into its person-focused structure. If employees' actual earnings are more than what the person-focused system indicates, managers must develop a reasonable course of action so that employees can acquire skills that are commensurate with their current pay. If employees are underpaid, the company must provide pay adjustments as quickly as possible. The length of time required to make these necessary adjustments will depend on two factors: the number of such employees and the extent to which they are underpaid. With limited budgets, companies will obviously require more extended periods as either the number of underpaid employees or the pay deficit increases.

ACCESS TO TRAINING A final transition matter is access to training. Person-focused systems make training necessary, rather than optional, for those employees who are motivated for self-improvement. Companies that adopt pay for knowledge must therefore ensure that all employees have equal access to the needed training for acquiring higher-level skills. They must do so both to meet the intended aim of person-focused programs (i.e., to reward employees for enhancing their skills) and to address legal imperatives. Restricting access to training can lead to a violation of key laws (i.e., Title VII of the Civil Rights Act of 1964 and the Age Discrimination in Employment Act of 1967). Companies must also educate employees about what their training options are and how successful training will lead to increased pay and advancement opportunities within the company. In other words, employers should not assume that employees will necessarily recognize the opportunities that are available to them unless they are clearly communicated. Written memos, e-mails, and informational meetings conducted by HR representatives are effective communication media.

Training and Certification

Successful person-focused programs depend on a company's ability to develop and implement systematic training programs. For many of reasons (i.e., intense domestic and global competition, rapid technological advancement, and educational deficits of new workforce entrants), progressive companies in the United States have adopted a continuous learning philosophy, which, like person-focused pay programs, encourages employees to take responsibility for enhancing their skills and knowledge.[31] Training clearly represents a key venue for continuous learning.

Because employees are required to learn new skills constantly, training becomes an ongoing process. Companies implementing pay for knowledge typically increase the amount of classroom and on-the-job training.[32] When training is well designed, employees should be able to learn the skills needed to increase their pay as well as the skills necessary to teach and coach other employees at lower skill levels. Accurate job descriptions are useful in determining training needs and focusing training efforts.

Employers must make necessary training available to employees so they can progress through the person-focused system. A systematic method for ensuring adequate training coverage involves matching training programs with each skill block. Accessibility does not require that employers develop and deliver training themselves. Training that is developed and delivered by an agency not directly affiliated with the company (e.g., community college, vocational training institute, university, or private consultant) can be just as accessible when the employer integrates the offering of these other sources with its person-focused program.

In-House or Outsourcing Training

The following criteria should be used to determine whether to develop and deliver training within the workplace or to outsource.[33]

Expertise Specialized training topics require greater expertise, and more generic topics require less expertise. Employers generally turn to in-house resources if they can draw on existing expertise. If in-house expertise is lacking, employers often seek an outside provider either to fill the need directly or to train individuals who become instructors. Employers usually rely on in-house expertise for employer- and product-specific training. Such training is governed by employer philosophies and procedures and is, therefore, not readily available in the external market.

Timeliness Employers often seek outside services if the in-house staff does not have adequate time to develop and deliver the program within the time frame requested. For example, Oracle, a business applications software development company, trains its clients on how to use the systems it installs. Over time, client companies experience turnover, which often includes the departure of employees who are well trained to use installed Oracle systems. To maintain effective business operations, client companies require training on demand. PeopleSoft offers training on demand to its clients through different forms of media, including the Internet and DVDs.

Size of the Employee Population to Be Trained Employers typically rely on in-house resources for larger groups of employees. The major impetus behind this decision is economics. If there is a large demand for training, the program is more likely to be delivered more than once, resulting in economies of scale.

Sensitivity or Proprietary Nature of the Subject Matter Sensitive or proprietary training is defined as training used to gain a competitive advantage or training that gives access to proprietary, product, or strategic knowledge. Employers rarely issue security clearances to outside resources to provide training of this nature. If the area of the training is sensitive or proprietary, the training is likely to be done in-house regardless of the other factors just discussed.

CERTIFICATION AND RECERTIFICATION **Certification** ensures that employees possess at least a minimally acceptable level of skill proficiency upon completion of a training unit. If employees do not have an acceptable degree of skill, then the company quite simply wastes any skill-based compensation expenditure. Supervisors and coworkers, who are presumably most familiar with the intricacies of their work, usually certify workers. Certification methods can include work samples, oral questioning, and written tests.

Recertification, under which employees periodically must demonstrate mastery of all the jobs they have learned or risk losing their pay rates, is necessary to maintain the workforce flexibility offered by a person-focused plan.[34] The recertification process typically is handled by retesting employees, retraining employees, or requiring employees to occasionally perform jobs that use their previously acquired skills.

For example, the Society for Human Resource Management (SHRM) offers two types of professional certification: the SHRM-CP (CP: certified professional) and the SHRM-SCP (SCP: senior certified professional). Individuals with at least one year of HR work experience earn certification when they pass a comprehensive examination of knowledge in the HR domain. Because the field of HR knowledge changes over time, individuals with certification must periodically earn continuing education credits to maintain certification. Credits are earned through a wide variety of activities, including course and/or conference attendance, membership in professional organizations, leadership with the association, teaching, speaking, writing, and projects completed on the job. This updating process is known as recertification.

5. Summarize pay structure variations.

PAY STRUCTURE VARIATIONS

The principles of pay structure development apply to the majority of established pay structures in companies throughout the United States. Broadbanding and two-tier pay structures represent variations to those pay structure principles.

Broadbanding

THE BROADBANDING CONCEPT AND ITS ADVANTAGES Companies may choose **broadbanding** to consolidate existing pay grades and ranges into fewer, wider pay grades and broader pay ranges.[35] Figure 6 illustrates a broadbanding structure and its relationship to traditional pay grades and ranges. Broadbanding represents the organizational trend toward flatter, less hierarchical corporate structures that emphasize teamwork over individual contributions alone.[36] Some federal government agencies, including the Navy, the General Accounting Office, and the Central Intelligence Agency, began experimenting with the broadbanding concept in the 1980s to introduce greater flexibility to their pay structures. Some private sector companies began

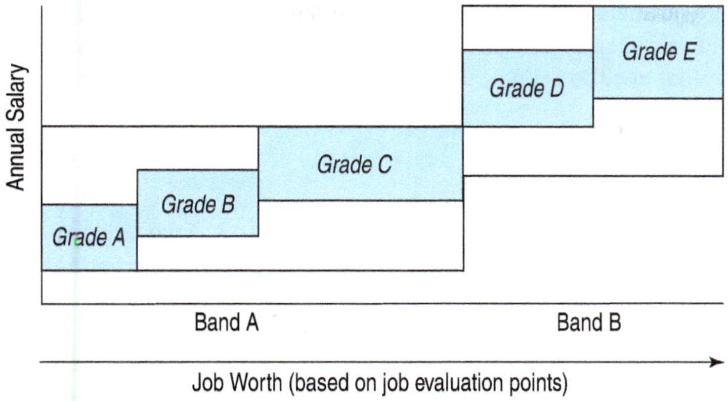

FIGURE 6 Broadbanding Structure and Its Relationship to Traditional Pay Grades and Ranges

using broadbanding in the late 1980s for the same reason. General Electric's former plastics business is a noteworthy adopter of broadbanding.

Broadbanding uses only a few large salary ranges to span levels within the organization previously covered by several pay grades. Thus, HR professionals place jobs that were separated by one or more pay grades in old pay structures into the same band under broadbanding systems. For example, condensing three consecutive grades into a single broadband eliminates the hierarchical differences among the jobs evident in the original, narrower pay grade configuration. Employees holding jobs in a single broadband now have equal pay potential, unlike employees in a multiple pay grade configuration. In addition, elimination of narrow bands broadens employees' job duties and responsibilities.

Some companies establish broadbands for distinct employee groups within the organizational hierarchy (e.g., upper management, middle management, professionals, and staff). This approach reduces management layers dramatically, and it should promote quicker decision-making cycles. Other companies create broadbands on the basis of job families (e.g., clerical, technical, and administrative). Job–family-based bands should give employees broader duties within their job classes. Still others may set broadbands according to functional areas, collapsing across job families. For example, a broadband may be established for all HR specialists (i.e., training, compensation, recruitment, and performance appraisal). These bands should encourage employees to expand their knowledge and skills in several HR functions.

Broadbanding shifts greater responsibility to supervisors and managers for administering each employee's compensation within the confines of the broadbands. Because broadbands include a wider range of jobs than narrowly defined pay grades, supervisors have greater latitude in setting employees' pay according to the tasks and duties they perform. Under traditional pay grades, employees receive pay and pay increases based on a limited set of duties stated in their job descriptions.

LIMITATIONS OF BROADBANDING Notwithstanding the benefits of broadbanding, it does possess some limitations. Broadbanding is not a cure-all for all compensation-related dysfunction within companies. For instance, broadbanding changes how compensation dollars are allocated, but not how much is allocated. Managers often think that flatter organizational structures reduce costs. To the contrary, broadbanding may lead to higher compensation expenses because managers have greater latitude in assigning pay to their employees. In fact, the federal government's limited experience showed that broadbanding structures were associated with more rapid increases in compensation costs than traditional pay structures.[37]

Broadbanding also necessitates a trade-off between the flexibility to reward employees for their unique contributions and a perception among employees that fewer promotional opportunities are available. This transition from multiple narrowly defined pay grades to fewer broadbands reduces organizational hierarchies that support job promotions. Employers and employees alike need to rethink the idea of promotions as a positive step through the job hierarchy.

Two-Tier Pay Structures

THE TWO-TIER PAY SYSTEM CONCEPT AND ITS ADVANTAGES **Two-tier pay structures** reward newly hired employees less than established employees. Under the temporary basis, employees have the opportunity to progress from lower entry-level pay rates to the higher rates enjoyed by more senior employees. Permanent two-tier systems reinforce the pay-rate distinction by retaining separate pay scales: Lower-paying scales apply to newly hired employees, and current employees enjoy higher-paying scales. Although pay progresses within each scale, the maximum rates to which newly hired employees can progress are always lower than more senior employees' pay scales. Table 4 illustrates a typical two-tier wage structure.

Two-tier wage systems are more prevalent in unionized companies. For example, at Ford Motor Company, a two-tier wage structure will compensate new hires substantially less than other employees, including an hourly base rate that is $10 below the previous one.[38]

Labor representatives have reluctantly agreed to two-tier wage plans as a cost-control measure. In exchange for reduced compensation costs, companies have promised to limit layoffs. These plans represent a departure from unions' traditional stance of single base-pay rates for all employees within job classifications.

Two-tier pay structures also enable companies to reward long-service employees while keeping costs down by paying lower rates to newly hired employees who do not have an established performance record within the company. As senior employees terminate their employment (i.e., taking jobs elsewhere or retiring), they are usually replaced by workers who are compensated according to the lower-paying scale.

In 2015, Ford Motor Company's management decided to hire approximately 1,500 new hourly employees because of increased business demand.[39] The collective bargaining agreement between the company and the United Auto workers, set to expire at the end of 2015, limited the number of employees who can be paid at the lower-tier wage to 20 percent of the unionized

TABLE 4 Two-Tier Wage Structures

Typical Base Rate	Assembler ($)	Tool & Die ($)
Base Rate—Contract End	26.86	31.52
COLA Fold-In	1.19	1.19
New Agreement Base	28.05	32.71
Beginning COLA Float	1.06	1.06
Base Rate Plus COLA	29.11	33.77
Lump Sum Examples	**Assembler ($)**	**Tool & Die ($)**
October 2014 Settlement Bonus	3,000	3,000
September 2015 Performance Bonus (3%)	2,171	2,534
September 2016 Performance Bonus (4%)	2,894	3,377
September 2017 Performance Bonus (3%)	2,170	2,533

Note: Based on a standard 2,080-year, plus 10 percent overtime, with projected COLA adjustments based on inflation averaging 2.44 percent.

hourly workforce. As a result, the company has been moving hundreds of workers from lower-tier (entry) wages to a higher pay rate.

LIMITATIONS OF TWO-TIER PAY STRUCTURES A potentially serious limitation of two-tier plans is that the lower pay scale applied to newly hired workers may restrict a company's ability to recruit and retain the most highly qualified individuals. Resentment can build among employees on the lower tier toward their counterparts on the upper tier, which may lead to lower-tier employees' refusal to perform work that extends in any way beyond their job descriptions. Such resentment may lead employees on the upper tier to scale back their willingness to take on additional work to the extent that they perceive pay premiums are not sufficiently large to compensate for extra duties. In addition, opponents of two-tier wage systems contend that pay differentials cause lower employee morale. Finally, conflict between the tiers may lead to excessive turnover. When high performers leave, then the turnover is dysfunctional to the company and can have long-term implications for productivity and quality.

COMPENSATION IN ACTION

As a line manager or HR manager, you will be faced with the challenge of determining which pay structures best suit the employee populations you serve. Regardless of the specifics of the plan (several specific plans are covered in this chapter), there are general guidelines that should be followed to build the link between the pay structure and the successful recognition of employee contributions. As you are educated by compensation specialists, you will provide senior executives with recommendations that appropriately identify correct incentives and produce desired behaviors.

Action checklist for line managers and HR—keeping the focus on employees as structures are built

HR takes the lead

- Assess the organization, and identify factors that will determine the pay structures within the organization (e.g., hourly versus salaried and geographic location). Line managers help in this assessment and provide additional insight to identify the correct factors.
- Partner with compensation specialists to group employees into pay grades that are determined by some similarity in the work they produce; corresponding ranges will also be established for each grade.
- Compensation specialists conduct market analyses to certify that current employees are being compensated at the right levels and that offers are being made to prospective employees that are comparable to the offers made by competitors (retain and attract top talent).

Line managers take the lead

- Communicate with HR regarding behaviors in employee population—HR and line managers work together to ensure that the compensation and benefits incentives are continuing to target the correct behaviors. HR carefully considers subtle changes to the system in face of market pressures or new leadership and direction within the company.
- Employees will continue to progress within the grade in which they have been placed, receiving pay increases (as determined by line manager in consultation with HR) commensurate with their individual performance—compensation specialists will work with HR to ensure that, with these merit increases, equity still exists in the grade and that the percentage increases in pay correspond with superior levels of performance.

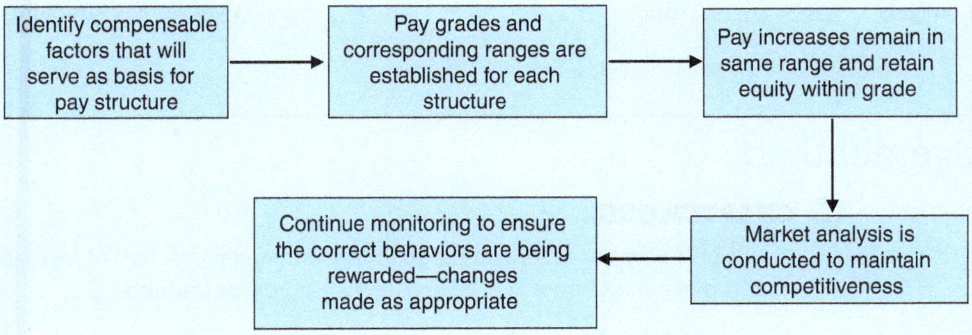

END OF CHAPTER REVIEW

MyManagementLab

Go to **mymanagementlab.com** to complete the problems marked with this icon ✪.

Summary

Learning Objective 1: Pay structures assign different pay rates for jobs of unequal worth and provide the framework for recognizing differences in individual employee contributions. Compensation professionals develop pay structures based on five steps: deciding on a number of pay structures, determining the market pay line, defining pay grades, calculating pay ranges for each pay grade, and evaluating the results.

Learning Objective 2: Merit pay systems reward employees for past performance. The key considerations include merit increase amounts, timing of increases, recurring versus nonrecurring increases, present level of base pay, merit pay grid design, and merit pay increase budget.

Learning Objective 3: The main components of sales incentive compensation plans is the choice of commission, bonus, salary, and the mix of these elements.

Learning Objective 4: Person-focused pay programs require consideration of skill blocks establishment, transition matters from job-based plans, and training and certification.

Learning Objective 5: Two common pay structure variations include broadbanding and two-tier pay structures. Broadbanding consolidates existing pay grades and ranges into fewer, wider pay grades and broader pay ranges. Two-tier pay structures reward newly hired employees less than established employees.

Key Terms

pay structures
pay grades
pay ranges
midpoint pay value
range spread
pay compression
green circle rates
red circle rates
compa-ratios
equity theory
compensation budgets
common review date
common review period
employee's anniversary date
nonrecurring merit increases
merit pay increase budget
salary-only plans
salary-plus-bonus plans
commission
salary-plus-commission plans
commission-plus-draw plans
draw
recoverable draws
nonrecoverable draws
commission-only plans
straight commission
graduated commissions
multiple-tiered commissions
skill (knowledge) blocks
certification
recertification
broadbanding
two-tier pay structures

MyManagementLab

✪ **CHAPTER QUIZ!**

If your professor has assigned this, go to the Assignments section of **mymanagementlab.com** to complete the Chapter Quiz! and see what you've learned.

Discussion Questions

1. Respond to the following statement: "Pay grades limit a company's ability to achieve competitive advantage." Do you agree? Provide a rationale for your position.
2. Two employees perform the same job, and each received exemplary performance ratings. Is it fair to give one employee a smaller percentage merit increase because his pay falls within the 3rd quartile but give a larger percentage merit increase to the other because his pay falls within the 1st quartile? Please explain your answer.
3. Describe some ethical dilemmas sales professionals may encounter. How can sales compensation programs be modified to minimize ethical dilemmas?
4. React to the statement: "Merit pay grids have the potential to undermine employee motivation." Please discuss your views.
5. Compression represents a serious dysfunction of pay structures. Discuss some of the major ramifications of compression. Also, discuss how companies can minimize or avoid these ramifications.

CASE

A New Sales Representative

An additional Supplemental Case can be found on MyMangementLab.

After 10 years in business, John Shurtman has determined that it is time to hire a sales representative. As the founder and president of United Fleet Service (UFS), John has been the main driver of new business sales for the company. However, as UFS has grown, John has found that he must spend more time on planning and administration, leaving little time to generate new sales leads or call on potential customers.

UFS provides maintenance, mechanical repair services, and body repair services to organizations that maintain fleets of large vehicles. UFS customers include mostly school districts that own bus fleets and municipalities that own fleets of fire and police vehicles. While UFS has a strong hold on these public sector organizations, John sees many opportunities for expansion through targeting other potential customers such as utility companies and commercial trucking companies.

UFS has several competitors in its geographic area, but none provide as comprehensive a service as UFS. For example, several competitors provide mechanical repair services, but do not provide body repair services; on the other hand, several competitors provide body repair services, but do not provide mechanical repair services. UFS also has a reputation for high-quality repairs and fast turnaround times on service. With these strengths in mind, John is convinced that an effective sales representative that can take the time to contact and develop relationships with potential customers can help lead the organization to expansion.

John has experienced steady growth over the past 10 years, acquiring just two or three new customers each year. Leads on potential new customers have come primarily through referrals from current customers. John personally called on the leads to secure sales. Once a target was established as a customer, John handed the customer account over to a service advisor. The service advisor's role is to process incoming vehicles and communicate work progress with customers. Service advisors are also encouraged to generate new sales from current customers by suggesting add-on services or establishing ongoing maintenance schedules. Due to increased volume growth, the service advisors have had little time to develop more significant relationships with customers. Because of this, UFS has missed out on many add-on sales opportunities.

Therefore, John plans to hire a new sales representative to both call on new customers and develop better relationships with current customers. Cultivating new customers will require cold-calling on potential customers as well as following up on referrals from current customers. Because most companies that have vehicle fleets establish contractual relationships with mechanical service providers, some new customers may take a long time to acquire. That is, the sales representative may have to interact with a potential new customer over an extended period of time until the company's contract with another service provider expires.

Working with current customers will require significant interaction with the service advisors to understand each customer's past history of services and identify opportunities to increase the number and frequency of services provided. Growing business from current customers will also require spending time developing relationships with each customer.

Before he begins recruiting for this position, John must determine how to compensate the new sales representative. He's researched market rates for sales representatives in his industry and has a targeted salary range, but he wants to make sure that the compensation plan provides enough incentive to both secure new sales and spend time developing relationships with current customers.

Questions:

6. What are the sales objectives for the new sales representative?
7. What role will the compensation design play in motivating the new sales representative?
8. What kind of sales incentive plan do you recommend? Why?

Crunch the Numbers!

Calculating Pay Range Minimums, Maximums, and Pay Range Overlap

An additional Crunch the Numbers! exercise can be found on **mymanagementlab.com**

You have been assigned to calculate the pay range minimum and maximum values for two pay grades as well as the overlap between these two pay ranges.

Questions:

9. *Pay Range A*: For a pay range midpoint equal to $47,500, calculate the minimum and maximum pay values for a 15 percent range spread.
10. *Pay Range B*: For a pay range midpoint equal to $53,750, calculate the minimum and maximum pay rates for a 25 percent range spread.
11. What is the overlap between pay range A and pay range B?

MyManagementLab

Go to **mymanagementlab.com** for Auto-graded writing questions as well as the following Assisted-graded writing questions:

12. How should companies address red circle rates for high performers and low performers, respectively?
13. Briefly discuss designing job-based pay systems (e.g., merit pay, sales incentive pay) and person-focused programs. What considerations arise when making a transition from using a job-based pay system to using a person-focused plan?
14. MyManagementLab Only – comprehensive writing assignment for this chapter.

Endnotes

1. WorldatWork (2015). *Compensation Programs and Practices* (January). Scottsdale, AZ: WorldatWork.
2. WorldatWork and Deloitte Consulting LLP. (2012). *Salary Structure Policies and Practices* (October). Scottsdale, AZ: WorldatWork.
3. WorldatWork and Deloitte Consulting LLP. (2012). *Salary Structure Policies and Practices* (October). Scottsdale, AZ: WorldatWork.

4. WorldatWork and Deloitte Consulting LLP. (2012). *Salary Structure Policies and Practices* (October). Scottsdale, AZ: WorldatWork.
5. WorldatWork and Deloitte Consulting LLP. (2012). *Salary Structure Policies and Practices* (October). Scottsdale, AZ: WorldatWork.
6. WorldatWork (2015). *Compensation Programs and Practices* (January). Scottsdale, AZ: WorldatWork.
7. WorldatWork (2015). *Promotional Guidelines* (January). Scottsdale, AZ: WorldatWork.
8. Ulrich, L. (2008). Money talks: Identifying, preventing and alleviating systemic salary compression issues. *Workspan*, November, pp. 43–46.
9. Manoli, R. (2009). Addressing salary compression in any economy. *Workspan*, December, pp. 54–57.
10. Klein, A. L., McMillan, A., & Reiter, G. (2010). The mixed value of using lump sums in lieu of putting merit pay into base pay. *WorldatWork Journal*, First Quarter, pp. 49–57.
11. Heneman, R. L. (1992). *Merit Pay: Linking Pay Increases to Performance*. Reading, MA: Addison-Wesley.
12. Krefting, L. A., & Mahoney, T. A. (1977). Determining the size of a meaningful pay increase. *Industrial Relations, 16*, pp. 83–93.
13. Heneman, *Merit Pay*.
14. Rambo, W. W., & Pinto, J. N. (1989). Employees' perceptions of pay increases. *Journal of Occupational Psychology, 62*, pp. 135–145.
15. Krefting, L. A., Newman, J. M., & Krzystofiak, F. (1987). What is a meaningful pay increase? In D. B. Balkin & L. R. Gómez-Mejía (Eds.), *New Perspectives on Compensation*. Upper Saddle River, NJ: Prentice Hall.
16. Heneman, *Merit Pay*.
17. U.S. Bureau of Labor Statistics. (2015). *Occupational Earning Statistics*. Available: *www.bls.gov*, accessed June 21, 2015.
18. U.S. Bureau of Labor Statistics. (2015). *Consumer Price Index*. Available: *www.bls.gov*, accessed June 21, 2015.
19. Erickson, C. L., & Ichino, A. C. (1994). Lump-sum bonuses in union contracts. *Advances in Industrial and Labor Relations, 6*, pp. 183–218.
20. Carey, J. F. (1992). *Complete Guide to Sales Force Compensation*. Homewood, IL: Irwin.
21. Kuhlman, D. C. (1994). Implementing business strategy through sales compensation. In W. Keenan Jr. (Ed.), *Commissions, Bonuses, & Beyond*. Chicago, IL: Probus Publishing.
22 Colletti-Fiss, J. A., & Colletti-Fiss, M. S. (2007). Designing sales incentive plans for competitive advantage. In D. Scott (Ed.), *Incentive Pay* (pp. 43–56). Scottsdale, AZ: WorldatWork.
23. Steenburgh, T., & Ahearne, M. (2012). Motivating salespeople: What really works. *Harvard Business Review* (July). Available: *http://www.hbr.org*, accessed February 28, 2015.
24. Keenan, W., Jr. (Ed.). (1994). The case against commissions. In *Commissions, Bonuses, & Beyond*. Chicago, IL: Probus Publishing.
25. Weber, L. (2015). Why it's so hard to fill sales jobs. *The Wall Street Journal* (February 4). Available: *http://www.wsj.com*, accessed March 2, 2015.
26. DiMisa, J., & Jahanbakhsh, P. (2013). How to build a sales compensation center of excellence. *Workspan* (November): 43–46.
27. American Society for Training and Development. (2000). *Profiting from Learning: Do Firms' Investments in Education and Training Pay Off?* Available: *www.astd.org/virtual—community/research/PFLWhitePaper.pdf*, accessed July 7, 2002.
28. American Society for Training and Development. (2006). *C-Level perceptions of the strategic value of learning research report*. January. Available: *www.astd.org/astd/research/research*, accessed June 19, 2007.
29. Dewey, B. J. (1994). Changing to skill-based pay: Disarming the transition landmines. *Compensation & Benefits Review, 26*, pp. 38–43.
30. Canavan, J. (2008). Overcoming the challenge of aligning skill-based pay levels to the external market. *WorldatWork Journal* (First Quarter): 18-25.
31. Rosow, J., & Zager, R. (1988). *Training: The Competitive Edge*. San Francisco, CA: Jossey-Bass.
32. Jenkins, G. D., Jr., & Gupta, N. (1985). The payoffs of paying for knowledge. *National Productivity Review, 4*, pp. 121–130.
33. Noe, R. A. (2010). *Employee Training and Development* (5th ed.). Burr Ridge, IL: McGraw-Hill Higher Education.

34. Jenkins, G. D., Jr., Ledford, G. E., Jr., Gupta, N., & Doty, D. H. (1992). *Skill-Based Pay*. Scottsdale, AZ: American Compensation Association.
35. Dougherty, E. (2010). You want me to talk about *what?* Broadbanding? *Workspan,* March, pp. 69–72.
36. Risher, H. H., & Butler, R. J. (1993–1994). Salary banding: An alternative salary-management concept. *ACA Journal, 2*, pp. 48–57.
37. Schay, B. W., Simons, K. C., Guerra, E., & Caldwell, J. (1992). *Broad-Banding in the Federal Government—Technical Report*. Washington, DC: U.S. Office of Personnel Management.
38. Giancola, F. (2009). Ford Motor Company's 58 years of experience with a cost-of-living allowance plan. *WorldatWork Journal,* Third Quarter, pp. 37–46.
39. Ramsey, M., & Stoll, J. D. (2015). Ford to move hundreds of entry-level workers to higher pay rate. *The Wall Street Journal* (February 4). Available: *http://www.wsj.com*, accessed February 6, 2015.

Glossary

Broadbanding is a pay structure form that leads to the consolidation of existing pay grades and pay ranges into fewer wider pay grades.

Certification ensures that employees possess at least a minimally acceptable level of skill proficiency upon completion of a training unit. Certification methods can include work samples, oral questioning, and written tests.

Commission is a form of incentive compensation, based on a percentage of the product or service selling price and the number of units sold.

Commission-only plans are specific kinds of sales compensation plans. Some salespeople derive their entire income through commissions.

Commission-plus-draw plans award sales professionals commissions and draws.

Common review date is the designated date when all employees receive performance appraisals.

Common review period is the designated period (e.g., the month of June) when all employees receive performance appraisals.

Compa-ratios index the relative competitiveness of internal pay rates based on pay range midpoints.

Compensation budgets are blueprints that describe the allocation of monetary resources to fund pay structures.

Draw is a subsistence pay component (i.e., to cover basic living expenses) in sales compensation plans. Companies usually charge draws against commissions that sales professionals are expected to earn.

Employee's anniversary date represents the date an employee began working for his or her present employer. Employees often receive performance appraisals on their anniversary dates.

Equity theory suggests that an employee must regard his or her own ratio of merit-increase pay to performance, as similar to the ratio for other comparably performing people in the company.

Graduated commissions increase percentage pay rates for progressively higher sales volume in a given period.

Green circle rates represent pay rates for jobs that fall below the designated pay minimums.

Merit pay increase budget limits the amount of pay raises that can be awarded to employees for a specified time period. A merit pay increase budget is expressed as a percentage of the sum of employees' current base pay.

Midpoint pay value is the halfway mark between the range minimum and maximum rates. Midpoints represent the competitive market rate determined by the analysis of compensation survey data.

Multiple-tiered commissions increase percentage pay rates for progressively higher sales volume in a given period only if sales exceed a predetermined level.

Nonrecoverable draws act as salary because sales employees are not obligated to repay the loans if they do not sell enough.

Nonrecurring merit increases or merit bonuses are lump sum monetary awards based on employees' past job performances. Employees do not continue to receive nonrecurring merit increases every year. Employees must instead earn them each time.

Pay compression occurs whenever a company's pay spread between newly hired or less qualified employees and more qualified job incumbents is small.

Pay grades group jobs for pay policy application. Human resource professionals typically group jobs into pay grades based on similar compensable factors and value.

Pay ranges represent the span of possible pay rates for each pay grade. Pay ranges include midpoint, minimum, and maximum pay rates. The minimum and maximum values denote the acceptable lower and upper bounds of pay for the jobs within particular pay grades.

Pay structures represent pay rate differences for jobs of unequal worth and the framework for recognizing differences in employee contributions.

Range spread is the difference between the maximum and the minimum pay rates of a given pay grade.

Recertification ensures that employees periodically demonstrate mastery of all the jobs they have learned.

Recoverable draws act as company loans to employees that are carried forward indefinitely until employees sell enough (i.e., earn a sufficient amount in commissions) to repay their draws.

Red circle rates represent pay rates that are higher than the designated pay range maximums.

Salary-only plans are specific types of sales compensation plans. Sales professionals receive fixed-base compensation, which does not vary with the level of units sold, increase in market share, or any other indicator of sales performance.

Salary-plus-bonus plans are specific types of sales compensation plans. Sales professionals receive fixed base compensation, coupled with a bonus. Bonuses are usually single payments that reward employees for achievement of specific, exceptional goals.

Salary-plus-commission plans are particular types of sales compensation plans. Sales professionals receive fixed base compensation and commission.

Skill (knowledge) blocks are sets of skills (knowledge) necessary to perform a specific job (e.g., typing skills versus analytical reasoning) or group of similar jobs (e.g., junior accounting clerk, intermediate accounting clerk, and senior accounting clerk).

Straight commission is based on a fixed percentage of the sales price of the produce or service.

Two-tier pay structures reward newly hired employees less than established employees on either a temporary or permanent basis.

Compensating Executives

From Chapter 11 of *Strategic Compensation: A Human Resource Management Approach*, Ninth Edition. Joseph J. Martocchio.

Compensating Executives

Learning Objectives

When you finish studying this chapter, you should be able to:

1. Explain the difference between executive pay and pay for nonexecutives.
2. Define executive status.
3. List the components of executive compensation packages.
4. Discuss the principles and processes of setting executive compensation.
5. Summarize the executive compensation disclosure rules and the reasons why they have been established.
6. Briefly explain the executive compensation controversy as it relates to whether U.S. executives are paid too much.

CHAPTER WARM-UP!

If your professor has assigned this, go to the Assignments section of **mymanagementlab.com** to complete the Chapter Warm-Up! and see what you already know. After reading the chapter, you'll have a chance to take the Chapter Quiz! and see what you've learned.

Executive compensation practices in U.S. companies have received substantial attention in the press. Questions about whether executives' compensation packages are tied to company performance is among the major issues. As we will see, executive pay practices have raised concerns that many executives receive lucrative compensation and benefits even when company performance falls below shareholder expectations. Many critics have questioned whether such practices may interfere with some executives' motivation to achieve excellent performance. Other concerns have been voiced by labor unions, which focus on social injustice given the substantial gap in pay between executive and nonexecutive employees, particularly when executive-level management chooses to limit labor through extensive reductions-in-force of nonexecutive employees.

CONTRASTING EXECUTIVE PAY WITH PAY FOR NONEXECUTIVE EMPLOYEES

1 Explain the difference between executive pay and pay for nonexecutives.

From an economic standpoint, the chief executive officer (CEO) is the seller of his or her services, and the compensation committee is the buyer of these services. Under classic economic theory, a reasonable price is obtained through negotiations that are at arm's length between an informed seller and an informed buyer. An awkward situation can result when the CEO hires a professional compensation director or compensation consultant. In this case, the compensation consultant who makes the recommendation to the compensation committee works for the CEO. In theory, the CEO hires the consultant to perform an objective analysis of the company's executive pay package and to make whatever recommendations the consultant feels are appropriate. This relationship has the potential to promote a conflict of interest because of the perceived pressure for the consultant to protect the CEO's financial interests. The irony is that the consultant is often viewed as representing the shareholders' interests. In a sense, the buyers of the CEO's services are the shareholders and their representatives, the compensation committee of the board of directors. They tend to act upon the compensation consultant's recommendation.[1]

It is possible that applying such practices to executives contradicts the main assumptions of performance-based pay. *Successful performance* triggers merit and incentive awards and the *degree of success* determines the amount of award. After all, pay-for-performance applies to most nonexecutive employees in U.S. companies. In some instances, executives are rewarded even after they have not performed well, with multimillion dollar awards contingent on their leaving the company. It is not surprising that those instances are often referred to as *pay-for-nonperformance* or, more harshly, *pay-for-failure*, and have become increasingly more common events in the world of executive compensation.

DEFINING EXECUTIVE STATUS

2 Define executive status.

It is important to define executive status because it is not an arbitrary designation. In fact, the Internal Revenue Code (IRC), which is the tax code of the United States, provides criteria to guide us in the definition of executives as these are key employees and highly compensated employees.

Who Are Executives?

Virtually all the components of executive compensation plans provide favorable tax treatment for both the executive and the company. Who are executives? From a tax regulation perspective, the IRC recognizes two groups of employees who play a major role in a company's policy decisions: highly compensated employees and key employees. The IRC uses "key employees" to determine the necessity of top-heavy provisions in employer-sponsored qualified retirement plans that cover most nonexecutive employees. As an aside, a plan is said to be top-heavy if the accrued benefits or account balances for key employees exceed 60 percent of the accrued benefits or account balances for all employees. For clarity, an accrued benefit is the amount that a participant has earned under the plan's terms at a specified time.

The IRC uses "highly compensated employees" for nondiscrimination rules in employer-sponsored health insurance benefits. Although these two designations were created for federal tax rule applications, employees in both groups typically participate in executive compensation and benefits plans.

Key employees and highly compensated employees hold positions of substantial responsibility. Figure 1 illustrates the placement of key employees in a typical organizational structure. Although titles vary from company to company and in pay structures, CEOs, presidents, executive vice presidents, vice presidents of functional areas (e.g., human resources), and the directors below them usually meet the criteria for key employees.

Key Employees

The term **key employee** means any employee who at any time during the year is:[2]

- An officer having annual pay of more than $170,000, *OR*
- an individual who for 2015 was either of the following:

  a. A 5 percent owner of the employer's business.
  b. A 1 percent owner of the employer's business whose annual pay was more than $150,000.

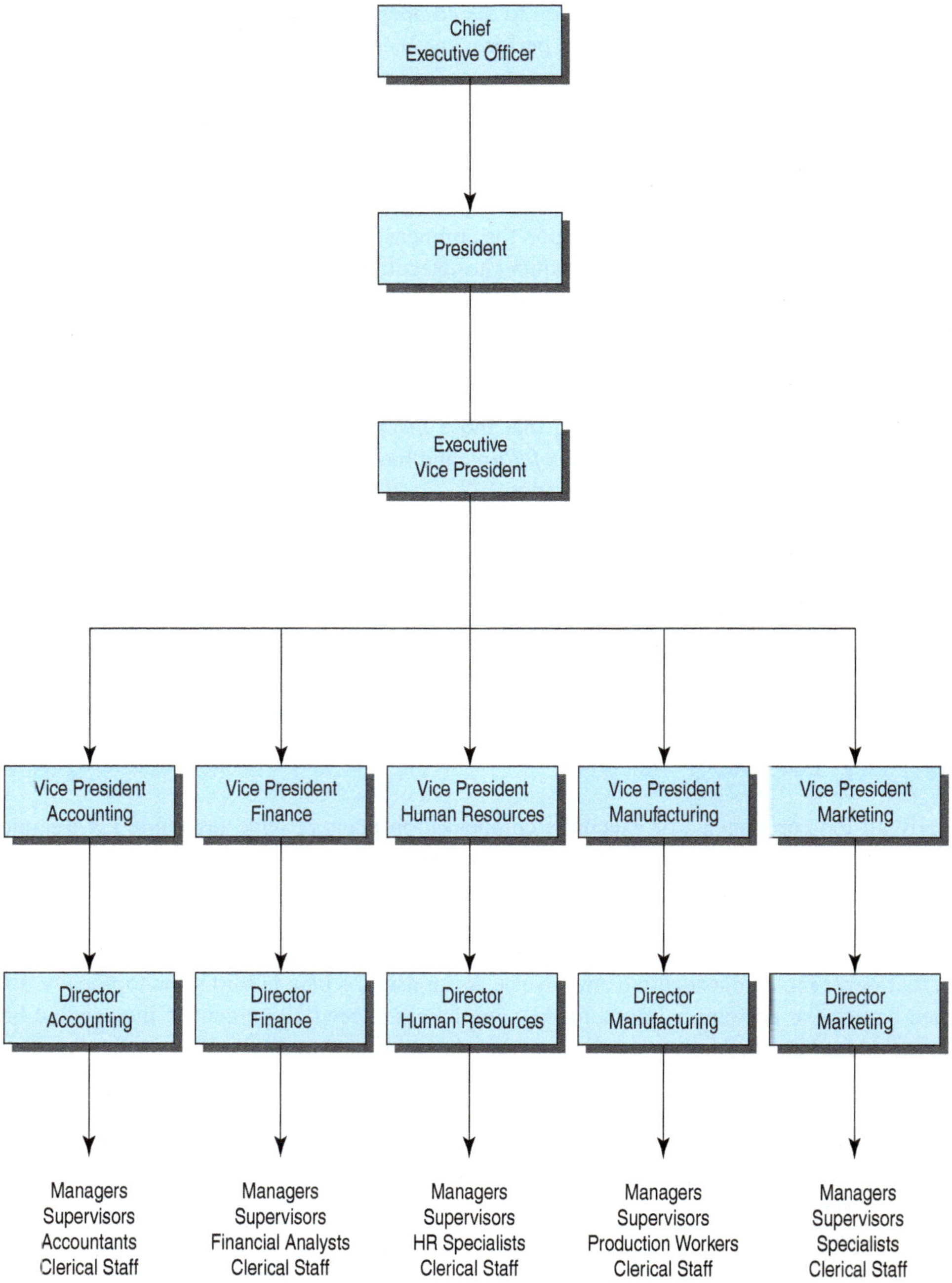

FIGURE 1 Examples of Key Employees

U.S. Treasury Regulations define the term *officer* used in this definition of key employees:[3]

Generally, the term officer means an administrative executive who is in regular and continued service. The term officer implies continuity of service and excludes those employed for a special and single transaction. An employee who merely has the title of an officer but not the authority of an officer is not considered an officer for purposes of the key employee test. Similarly, an employee who does not have the title of an officer but has the authority of an officer is an officer for purposes of the key employee test.

Highly Compensated Employees

The IRC defines a **highly compensated employee** as one of the following during the current year or preceding year:[4]

- A 5 percent owner at any time during the year or the preceding year, *OR*
- for the preceding year,
  - the employee had compensation from the employer in excess of $120,000 in 2015, *AND*
  - if the employer so chooses, the employee was in the top-paid group of employees where top-paid employees are the top 20 percent most highly compensated employees.

We have pointed out to the complexity of defining executive status. It is worth stepping aside for a moment to consider the real-world challenges of executives. In the Watch It! video, you will hear about the challenges that Microsoft's CEO Satya Nadella is facing in changing its direction in software applications to become more competitive with other companies.

WATCH IT!

If your professor has assigned this, go to the Assignments section of **mymanagementlab .com** to complete the video exercise titled Microsoft's Nadella Takes Charge.

EXECUTIVE COMPENSATION PACKAGES

3 List the components of executive compensation packages.

Executive compensation has both core and employee benefits elements, much like compensation packages for other employees; however, one noteworthy feature distinguishes executive compensation packages from nonexecutive compensation packages. Executive compensation packages emphasize long-term or deferred rewards over short-term rewards. The main components of executive compensation include (we describe the components here and defer examples to later in this chapter):

- Current or annual core compensation
- Deferred core compensation: equity agreements
- Deferred core compensation: separation agreements
- Clawback provisions
- Employee benefits: enhanced protection program benefits and perquisites

Components of Current Core Compensation

Executive current core compensation packages contain two components: annual base pay and bonuses.

BASE PAY Base pay is the fixed element of annual cash compensation. Companies that use formal salary structures may have specific pay grades and pay ranges for nonexempt employees and exempt employees, including supervisory, management, professional, and executive jobs, with the exception of the CEO.

Chief executive officer jobs do not fall within formal pay structures for two reasons. First, CEOs' work is highly complex and unpredictable. It is not possible to specify discrete responsibilities and duties. The choice of competitive strategy by CEOs and other executives and the influence of external and internal market factors make it impossible to describe CEOs' jobs. Second, setting CEO compensation differs dramatically from the rational processes compensation professionals use to build market-competitive pay structures. We will discuss agency theory, tournament theory, and social comparison theory later as explanations for setting CEO compensation.

In most cases, annual base pay represents a relatively small part of a CEO's total compensation for two reasons. First, it typically takes years before the fruits of the CEOs' strategic initiatives are realized. Second, the IRS limits the amount of annual salary a company may exclude as a business expense. Only the first $1 million annually for an executive's pay may be excluded from the company's income tax liability as long as the pay is not deemed to be pay-for-performance.[5] Base pay would fall under this rule. This ruling was put into place to keep companies from boosting CEO annual pay to astronomical levels for the purposes of tax savings.

BONUSES Bonuses represent single pay-for-performance payments companies use to reward employees for achievement of specific, exceptional goals. Bonuses also represent a key component of executive compensation packages.

Companies' compensation committees recommend bonus awards to boards of directors for their approval (as we will discuss later in this chapter). Four types of bonuses are common in executive compensation:

- Discretionary bonus
- Performance-contingent bonus
- Predetermined allocation bonus
- Target plan bonus

As the term implies, boards of directors award **discretionary bonuses** to executives on an elective basis. They weigh four factors in determining the amount of discretionary bonus: company profits, the financial condition of the company, business conditions, and prospects for the future. For example, boards of directors may award discretionary bonuses to executives when a company's position in the market is strong.

Executives receive **performance-contingent bonuses** based on the attainment of specific performance criteria. The performance appraisal system for determining bonus awards is often the same appraisal system used for determining merit increases or general performance reviews for salary.

Unlike the previous executive bonuses, the total bonus pool for the **predetermined allocation bonus** is based on a fixed formula. The central factor in determining the size of the total bonus pool and bonus amounts is company profits.

The **target plan bonus** ties bonuses to executives' performance. The bonus amount increases commensurately with performance. Executives do not receive bonuses when their performance falls below minimally acceptable standards. The target plan bonus differs from the predetermined allocation bonus in an important way: Predetermined allocation bonus amounts are fixed, regardless of how well executives perform.

SHORT-TERM INCENTIVES Companies award short-term incentive compensation to executives to recognize their progress toward fulfilling competitive strategy goals. Executives may participate in current profit sharing plans and gain sharing plans. Whereas short-term objectives reward nonexempt and lower-level management employees for achieving major milestone work objectives, short-term incentives applied to executives are designed to reward them for meeting intermediate performance criteria. The performance criteria relate to the performance of a company as dictated by competitive strategy. Change in the company's earnings per share over a 1-year period, growth in profits, and annual cost savings are criteria that may be used in executives' short-term incentive plans.

Short-term incentive compensation programs usually apply to a group of select executives within a company. The plan applies to more than one executive because the synergy that results from the efforts and expertise of top executives influences corporate performance. The board of directors distributes short-term incentive awards to each executive based on rank and compensation levels. Thus, the CEO will receive a larger performance award than will the executive vice president, whose position is lower in the company's structure than the CEO's position.

For example, let's assume that the CEO and executive vice president of a chain of general merchandise retail stores have agreed to lead the corporation as the lowest-cost chain of stores in the general merchandise retail industry. The CEO and executive vice president establish a 5-year plan to meet this lowest-cost competitive strategy. The vice president of compensation recommends that the company adopt a gain sharing program to reward top executives for contributing to the cost reduction objective. After 1 year, the complementary decisions made by the CEO and executive vice president have enabled the corporation to save $10,000,000. The board of directors agrees that the executives' collaborative decisions led to noteworthy progress toward meeting the lowest-cost strategy and award the CEO 2 percent of the annual cost savings ($200,000) and the executive vice president 1 percent ($100,000).

Components of Deferred Core Compensation

Deferred compensation refers to an agreement between an employee and a company to render payments to an executive at a future date. Deferred compensation is a hallmark of executive compensation packages. As an incentive, deferred compensation is supposed to create a sense of ownership, aligning the interests of the executive with those of the owners or shareholders of the company over the long term. The rationale for creating an ownership stake for the executive is explained by agency theory, which we will discuss later in this chapter. Broadly speaking, there are two general types of deferred compensation plans. The first, **equity plans**, provides an executive with ownership stakes in the company through a variety of mechanisms, including various stock option plans and stock purchase plans. The second, **separation agreements**, guarantee that an executive will receive a lucrative compensation package upon employment termination.

The prevalent way in which companies create ownership interests, also known as equity interests, is by making the executive an owner of the company. Company stock ownership or company stock options create an equity interest in the company.

Equity Agreements

Company stock and stock options provide the foundation for equity agreements. **Company stock** represents total equity of the firm. **Company stock shares** represent equity segments of equal value. Equity interest increases positively with the number of stock shares. Stocks are bought and sold every business day in a public stock exchange. The New York Stock Exchange is among the best-known of the stock exchanges. Table 1 lists basic terminology pertaining to stocks.

Companies design executive stock compensation plans to promote an executive's sense of ownership of the company. A sense of ownership should presumably motivate executives to strive for excellent performance. Stock value generally increases with gains in company performance. In particular, a company's stock value rises in response to reports of profit gains; however, factors outside executives' control often influence stock prices despite executives' performance. For example, forecasts of economy-wide recession, increases in the national unemployment rate, and threats to national security or political instability are often associated with declines in stock value.

TABLE 1 Employee Stock Terminology

Stock option. A right granted by a company to an employee to purchase a number of stocks at a designated price within a specified period of time.

Stock grant. A company's offering of stock to an employee.

Exercise of stock grant. An employee's purchase of stock, using stock options.

Disposition. Sale of stock by the stockholder.

Fair market value. The average value between the highest and lowest reported sales price of a stock on the New York Stock Exchange on any given date. The Internal Revenue Service specifies whether an option has a readily ascertainable fair market value at grant. An option has a readily ascertainable fair market value if the option is actively traded on an established stock exchange at the time it is granted.

Five particular forms of deferred (stock) compensation include:

- Stock options
- Restricted stock and restricted stock units
- Stock appreciation rights
- Phantom stock plans
- Employee stock purchase plans

STOCK OPTIONS Broadly, there are two particular types of stock options—incentive stock options and nonstatutory stock options. **Incentive stock options** entitle executives to purchase their companies' stock in the future at a predetermined price. The predetermined price usually equals the stock price at the time an executive is granted the stock option In effect, executives are purchasing the stocks at a discounted price. Executives generally exercise their option to purchase the stock after the price has increased dramatically. An executive receives **capital gains** as the difference between the stock price at the time of purchase and the lower stock price at the time an executive receives the stock option. Executives receive income tax benefits by participating in incentive stock option plans. They are not required to pay tax on the capital gains until they sell their stock shares. The tax rate for such transactions is called the capital gains rate. It is typically substantially lower than the executive's ordinary income tax rate, further adding incentive value to incentive stock options. If stock price at the time of disposition were lower than at the price of the stock option grant, the executive would experience a **capital loss**.

Much like incentive stock options, companies award stock options to executives at discounted prices. In contrast to incentive stock options, **nonstatutory stock options** do not qualify for favorable tax treatment. Executives pay income taxes on the difference between the discounted price and the stock's fair market value at the time of the stock grant, not at the time of disposition, and they do so at their ordinary income tax rate. They do not pay taxes in the future when they choose to exercise their nonstatutory stock options.

Nonstatutory stock options do provide executives an advantage. Executives' tax liability is ultimately lower over the long term: Stock prices generally increase over time. As a result, the capital gains will probably be much greater in the future when executives exercise their options rather than when their companies grant these options.

RESTRICTED STOCK PLANS, RESTRICTED STOCK UNITS, AND PERFORMANCE STOCK AWARDS Under **restricted stock plans**, a company may grant executives with stock options at market value or discounted value, or they may provide stock. Under restricted stock plans, executives do not have any ownership control over the disposition of the stock for a predetermined period, often many years. This predetermined period is known as the vesting period, much like vesting rights associated with employer-sponsored retirement plans. Alternatively, companies may provide executives with restricted stock units. **Restricted stock units** are shares of company stock that are awarded to executives at the end of the restriction period.

Similar to restricted stock plans and restricted stock units in terms of the vesting period, a company may choose to add to the vesting period a performance criterion for determining whether to award stock options or stock units. This type of equity agreement is referred to as a **performance plan**. A company's board of directors determines the performance criteria. For example, a company's earnings per stock share is often used. Coca-Cola Company recently modified its executive-level and top-management equity agreements to follow performance plan standards. These leaders will receive fewer stock shares, but additional performance share units. One of the main reasons for this change is shareholders' dissatisfaction with the company's weak performance in the U.S. market.[6]

STOCK APPRECIATION RIGHTS **Stock appreciation rights** provide executives income at the end of a designated period, much like restricted stock options; however, executives never have to exercise their stock rights to receive income. The company simply awards a bonus payment to executives based on the difference in stock price between the time the company granted the stock rights at fair market value to the end of the designated period, permitting the executives to keep the stock. Executives pay tax on any income, from gains in stock value to when they exercise their stock rights,[7] presumably after retirement when their tax rates are lower.

PHANTOM STOCK PLANS A **phantom stock** plan is a compensation arrangement whereby boards of directors promise to pay a bonus in the form of the equivalent of either the value of company shares or the increase in that value over a period of time. Phantom stock plans are similar to restricted stock plans because executives must meet specific conditions before they can convert these phantom shares into real shares of company stock.[8] There are generally two conditions. First, executives must remain employed for a specified period, usually several years. Second, executives must retire from the company. Upon meeting these conditions, executives receive income equal to the increase in the value of company stock from the date the company granted the phantom stock to the conversion date. Phantom stock plans provide executives with tax advantages. Executives pay taxes on the capital gains after they convert their phantom shares to real shares of company stock during retirement.

EMPLOYEE STOCK PURCHASE PLANS A company may choose to offer a formal employee stock purchase plan that allows participating employees to purchase stock after a designated period of time. In anticipation of making a stock purchase, employees set aside money through payroll deduction for this specific purpose during the offering period, which is the point in time when they may purchase the employer's stock based on the money set aside in their accounts. The span of time over which employees are permitted to contribute to their accounts is referred to as the **offering period**. Companies have the option of setting up employee stock purchase plans as qualified or nonqualified. To qualify for favorable tax treatment, companies' plans must meet several criteria. For example, all full-time employees with 2 or more years of service must be allowed to participate.

Separation Agreements

GOLDEN PARACHUTES Most executives' employment agreements contain a golden parachute clause. **Golden parachutes** provide pay and benefits to executives after a termination that results from a change in ownership or corporate takeover, that is, the merger or combining of two separate companies. Approximately 80 percent of Standard & Poor's 500 companies offer golden parachute packages to CEOs who are replaced due to corporate takeover.[9] For example, Compuware, which developed software for use on mainframe computers, was taken over by a private equity firm Thoma Bravo, LLC. in 2014. The top six executives of the company held golden parachute agreements equaling approximately $23 million in cash, stock, and other benefits.[10] Among these top executives, former CEO Bob Paul's golden parachute was valued at approximately $6.6 million. Boards of directors often include golden parachute clauses for at least three reasons. First, golden parachutes limit executives' risks in the event of these unforeseen events. Second, golden parachutes promote recruitment and retention of talented executives. Third, in the event that a takeover bid would benefit the company, it is possible that a CEO would work against it in order to save his or her job.

Companies benefit from golden parachute payments because they can treat these payments as business expenses. This means that companies can reduce their tax liability by increasing the parachute amount. The total value of golden parachutes came to exceed executives' annual income levels by far. Public outcry led to government-imposed intervention that limited tax benefits to companies. Companies may generally receive tax deductions on golden parachutes.

PLATINUM PARACHUTES In an ideal world, CEOs will perform on an exemplary basis, making decisions to drive up company profits. As you know, we do not live in a perfect world; sometimes, CEOs do not perform their jobs well and companies lose out on profit opportunities. After a period of unsatisfactory performance as determined by shareholders and other company executives, CEOs may often be terminated even before the expiration of their employment contracts. Many companies reach agreements with CEOs to terminate employment, awarding a platinum parachute as an incentive. **Platinum parachutes** are lucrative awards that compensate departing executives with severance pay, continuation of company benefits, and even stock options. Companies typically use platinum parachutes to avoid long legal battles or critical reports in the press, essentially by paying off a CEO to give up his or her post. For example, Louis Chenevert resigned from United Technologies amid growing criticism from investors that he had become disengaged from the business. He left the company with a platinum parachute worth $195 million including approximately $136.3 million in stock options and about $31 million in pension benefits.[11] Apart from this example, it is important to reiterate that golden parachutes became common when hostile corporate takeovers were occurring in large numbers during the 1980s and 1990s. As such activity slowed down, many companies continued to offer golden parachutes, but extended the use for a CEO's termination for other reasons, such as poor performance. For this purpose, it is not uncommon to see the terms golden parachute and platinum parachute used interchangeably.

Clawback Provisions

Clawback provisions in CEO employment contracts allow boards of directors to take back performance-based compensation if they were to subsequently learn that performance goals were not actually achieved, regardless of whether the CEO was responsible for performance falling short of target levels. Increasingly, these provisions are becoming more common because of the increasing scrutiny of CEO compensation packages by the public and shareholders, particularly since the global financial crisis in the late 2000s. For example, Wilmington Trust Corporation rescinded more than $1.8 million in compensation from Chief Executive Donald Foley. As it turns out, Wilmington's purchase of another bank at a price below market value lowered the overall value of the combined company. Government agencies may also follow suit. For instance, Department of Veterans Affairs (VA) Eric Shinseki rescinded a monetary bonus from Sharon Helman, Director of the Phoenix VA system.[12] Shinseki acted on allegations of falsified data on delays in doctor appointments, and the death of some veterans which occurred while awaiting care. More broadly, well-publicized corporate accounting scandals led to tighter accounting standards. Modified corporate tax law put tighter restrictions on deferred compensation payouts to prevent corporate executives from siphoning money out of their corporations. There specifically was a rash of executives withdrawing deferred compensation money before their companies went bankrupt. Perhaps the most well-known scandal occurred at Enron. In response to corporate accounting scandals, the Securities and Exchange Commission (SEC) administered the Sarbanes-Oxley Act of 2002. The Sarbanes-Oxley Act is perhaps the most significant legislation because it imposes rigorous requirements for companies' financial disclosure to limit the chance that covert misuses of corporate funds will occur. In 2002, President George W. Bush strengthened the oversight of the SEC when he signed the **Sarbanes-Oxley Act of 2002** into law. The act mandates a number of reforms to enhance corporate responsibility, enhance financial disclosures, and combat corporate and accounting fraud in response to corporate accounting scandals, such as in Enron, Tyco, and other large U.S. corporations. The act established Public Company Accounting Oversight Board (PCAOB) to oversee the activities of the auditing profession.

Employee Benefits: Enhanced Protection Program Benefits and Perquisites

Executives receive discretionary benefits like other employees; however, executives' discretionary benefits differ in two ways. First, protection programs include supplemental coverage that provides enhanced benefit levels. Second, the services component contains benefits exclusively for executives. These exclusive executive benefits are known as **perquisites** or **perks**.

ENHANCED PROTECTION PROGRAM BENEFITS Supplemental life insurance and supplemental executive retirement plans distinguish protection programs for executive employees from protection programs for other employees. Employer-provided life insurance protects employees' families by paying a specified amount to an employee's beneficiaries upon an employee's death. Most policies pay some multiple of the employee's salary (e.g., benefits paid at twice the employee's annual salary). In addition to regular life insurance, executives receive **supplemental life insurance** protection that pays an additional monetary benefit. Companies design executives' supplemental life insurance protection to meet two objectives.[13] First, supplemental life insurance increases the benefit to designated beneficiaries upon their deaths. Life insurance programs may be designed to provide greater benefits than standard plans usually allow. Second, these programs provide executives with favorable tax treatments.

Supplemental retirement plans are designed to restore benefits restricted under qualified plans. We discussed some of the characteristics of qualified plans. A qualified plan generally entitles employees to favorable tax treatment of the benefits they receive upon their retirement. Any investment income that is generated in the pension program is not taxed until the employee retires.

The IRS limited the annual earnings amount for determining qualified plan benefits to $265,000 in 2015 (indexed for inflation, in increments of $5,000). In general, all annual earnings greater than this level cannot be included in defined benefit plan formulas or the calculation of annual additions to defined contribution plans. In addition, the IRS limits the annual benefit amounts for defined benefit plans to the lesser of $210,000 in 2015, indexed for inflation, or 100 percent of the highest average compensation for 3 consecutive years.[14] For example, an executive's three highest annual salaries are $690,000, $775,000, and $1,100,000. The average of these three highest salaries is $855,000. Of course, $210,000 is less than $855,000; therefore, an executive's retirement income based on the company's qualified pension plan cannot exceed $210,000 adjusted for inflation.

A supplemental retirement plan can make up this difference. For illustrative purposes, let's assume that the annual benefit under a qualified pension plan is 60 percent of the final average salary for the past 15 years of service, which is $400,000. Based on this formula, the executive should receive an annual retirement benefit of $240,000 ($400,000 × 60 percent). This annual benefit exceeds $210,000 (the statutory limit for qualified retirement plans). Because of the statutory limit, companies may offer a supplemental executive retirement plan that provides the difference between the value derived from the pension formula ($240,000) and the statutory limit ($210,000). In this example, the executive would receive a supplemental annual retirement benefit of $30,000.

PERQUISITES Executive perquisites are an integral part of executive compensation. Perquisites cover a broad range of benefits, from free lunches to the free use of corporate jets. Table 2 lists common executive perks. Perquisites serve at least four purposes. First, these benefits recognize executives' attained status. Membership in an exclusive country club reinforces executives' attained social status. Second, executives use perks for personal comfort or as a business tool. For example, a company may own a well-appointed cabin in Vail, Colorado. Executives may use the cabin for rest and relaxation or as a place to court new clients or close a lucrative business deal. Arranging relaxing weekends in Vail benefits executives and their families and provides executives opportunities to develop rapport with prospective clients. Third, the use of corporate aircraft may be considered a security measure for executives who are public figures.[15] The CEOs from a majority of Fortune 100 companies have this perk, with an average annual cost approaching $150,000.[16] Promoting security goes beyond the use of corporate jets. A variety of security measures have cost Fortune 100 companies a median value of $28,618 in 2013. The cost ranged from as low as $284 for Phillips 66 CEO to as high as $1.6 million for Amazon.com's CEO.[17] Fourth, particular perks, such as having a chauffeur or tax and financial

TABLE 2 Common Executive Perks

- Company cars
- Supplemental life insurance
- Legal services (e.g., income tax preparation)
- Recreational facilities (e.g., country club and athletic club memberships)
- Security detail (protection)
- Travel perks (e.g., use of corporate jet)

planning services, permit executives to have fewer distractions, providing for more opportunities to attend to work matters.

Despite the rationale for providing lucrative perks, many companies have begun scaling back offerings. For example, Regeneron Pharmaceuticals decided to reduce perks for its top executives.[18] The company is eliminating perks such as car allowances, credit card fees, and its CEO's golf membership, costing $18,500 per year.

It is possible that companies will provide cash in lieu of perquisites because of stricter reporting requirements by the Securities and Exchange Commission. Particularly after the corporate scandals at Enron and other corporations, company shareholders expect management to display greater accountability for the nonbusiness use of such company property as corporate jets. Since 2008, companies have had to report perks valued at $10,000 or more apiece.

A survey of executive compensation practices in Fortune 500 companies revealed that a significant number of companies, about 85 percent, offer executive perks, but fewer of them than in the past.[19] In particular, between 2008 and 2013, the percentage of companies offering three or more executive perks dropped from 60 percent to 33 percent. In the same time frame, the number of companies that eliminated executive perks altogether jumped from 6 percent to 15 percent. The prevalence of fewer perks offerings may be due to greater economic uncertainties and the recent requirement that companies report perks valued at $10,000, or more, apiece. Greater shareholder scrutiny is also a contributing factor, as more emphasis is given on performance-based rewards.

PRINCIPLES AND PROCESSES FOR SETTING EXECUTIVE COMPENSATION

4 Discuss the principles and processes of setting executive compensation.

Although pay-for-performance is the public rationale for setting executive compensation, reality is often quite different. Three alternative theories explain the principles and processes for setting executive compensation: agency theory, tournament theory, and social comparison theory. We will begin by discussing the key players in setting executive compensation.

The Key Players in Setting Executive Compensation

Different individuals and groups participate in setting executive compensation. They include compensation consultants, compensation committees, and boards of directors. Each plays a different role in setting executive compensation.

EXECUTIVE COMPENSATION CONSULTANTS **Executive compensation consultants** usually propose several recommendations for alternate pay packages. Executive compensation consultants are often employed by large consulting firms that specialize in executive compensation or advise company management on a wide variety of business issues. The regulations involving executive compensation plans are extremely complex. To understand them fully requires expertise often found in leading executive compensation and benefits consulting firms. Some of the leading and most well-respected firms in this area include the following:

- Frederic W. Cook & Company (*www.fwcook.com*)
- The Hay Associates (*www.haygroup.com*)
- Pearl Meyer & Partners (*www.pearlmeyer.com*)
- Towers Watson (*www.towerswatson.com*)
- William M. Mercer (*www.mercer.com*)

Consultants make recommendations about what and how much to include in executive compensation packages based on strategic analyses, which entail an examination of a company's external market context and internal factors. Examples of external market factors include industry profile, information about competitors, and long-term growth prospects. Financial condition is the most pertinent internal factor regarding executive compensation. Strategic analyses permit compensation consultants to see where their client company stands in the market based on external and internal factors. Strong companies should be able to devote more financial resources to fund lucrative executive compensation programs than weaker companies. More often than not, executive compensation consultants find themselves in conflict-of-interest situations:

> Ostensibly, compensation consultants were hired by the CEO to perform an objective analysis of the company's executive pay package and to make whatever recommendations the consultant felt were appropriate. In reality, if those recommendations did not cause the CEO to earn more money than he was earning before the compensation consultant appeared on the scene, the latter was rapidly shown the door.[20]

Executive compensation consultants' professional survival may depend on recommending lucrative compensation packages. Recommending the most lucrative compensation packages will quickly promote a favorable impression of the consultant among CEOs, leading to future consulting engagements.

Since 2008, the Securities and Exchange Commission rulings require companies to include the identity of the consulting firm in public disclosure statements. This ruling has created concerns about possible conflicts of interest for consulting firms that also provide consulting services in other areas (e.g., performance management and change management) for the same client firms. Executive compensation consulting represents just one of many possible areas of management consulting. The conflict potentially arises when a consultant intentionally recommends a more-lucrative-than-warranted executive compensation package in the hope of gaining management favor and additional other management consulting opportunities. Of course, compensation consulting firms are concerned about the public image of possible conflicts of interest and have considered a variety of practices to ensure the integrity of their recommendations to client firms. For example, there has been some speculation that executive consulting practices will be spun off into independent businesses. Many companies are concerned about their own public image and have instituted policies to prevent compensation consultants from conducting other work for management.

BOARD OF DIRECTORS A **board of directors** represents shareholders' interests by weighing the pros and cons of top executives' decisions. Boards of directors have approximately 15 members. These members include CEOs and top executives of other successful companies, distinguished community leaders, well-regarded professionals (e.g., physicians and attorneys), and possibly a few top-level executives of the company.

Boards of directors give final approval of the compensation committee's recommendation. Some critics of executive compensation have argued that CEOs use compensation to coopt board independence.[21] CEOs often nominate candidates for board membership, and their nominations usually lead to candidates' placement on the board. Board members receive compensation for their service to the boards. It's not uncommon for a board member to earn more than $50,000 per year plus a fee ($10,000 or more) for each board meeting attended. Along with monetary and stock compensation, companies are using such benefits as medical insurance, life insurance, and retirement programs to attract top-notch individuals to join boards of directors. In general, board members' failure to cooperate with CEOs may lead either to fewer benefits or their removal.

> The board determines the pay of the CEO. But who determines the pay of the outside directors? Here, a sort of formal Japanese Kabuki has developed. The board of directors determines the pay of the CEO, and for all practical purposes, the CEO determines the pay of the board of directors. Is it any accident, then, that there is a statistical relationship between how highly the CEO is paid and how highly his outside directors are paid?[22]

As we will discuss shortly, recent changes in Securities and Exchange Commission rulings and the passage of the Dodd-Frank Act have increased the transparency of how executives are compensated, as well as board members' accountability for approving sound executive compensation packages—supportive of shareholders' best interests.

COMPENSATION COMMITTEE Board of directors members within and outside the company make up a company's **compensation committee**. Outside board members serve on compensation committees to minimize conflict of interest. Thus, outside directors usually are the committee's membership majority.

Compensation committees perform three duties. First, compensation committees review consultants' alternate recommendations for compensation packages. Second, compensation committee members discuss the assets and liabilities of the recommendations. The complex tax laws require compensation committees to consult compensation experts, legal counsel, and tax advisors. Third, based on these deliberations, the committee recommends the consultant's best proposal to the board of directors for its consideration.

Theoretical Explanations for Setting Executive Compensation

Three prominent theories describe the processes related to setting executive compensation: agency theory, tournament theory, and social comparison theory. The following discussion provides concrete interpretations of these theories. In addition to the works cited throughout this chapter, several excellent scholarly journal articles provide full explanations of these theoretical frames as applied to executive compensation.[23]

AGENCY THEORY Ownership is distributed among many thousands of shareholders in such large companies as Microsoft, General Electric, General Motors, and IBM. For example, owning at least one share of stock in IBM bestows ownership rights in IBM. Each shareholder's ownership is quite small, amounting to far less than 1 percent. Inability to communicate frequently or face to face to address business concerns is a major disadvantage of thousands of shareholders.

Under **agency theory**, shareholders delegate control to top executives to represent their ownership interests; however, top executives usually do not own majority shares of their companies' stocks. As a result, executives usually do not necessarily share the same interests as the collective shareholders. These features make it possible for executives to pursue activities that benefit themselves rather than the shareholders. The actions of executives on behalf of their own self-interest are known as the **agency problem**.[24] Executives may specifically emphasize the attainment of short-term gains (e.g., increasing market share through lower costs) at the expense of long-term objectives (e.g., product differentiation). Boards of directors may be willing to provide executives generous annual bonuses for attaining short-term gains.

Shareholders negotiate executive employment contracts with executives to minimize loss of control. Executive employment contracts define terms of employment pertaining to performance standards and compensation, specifically current and deferred compensation and benefits. The main shareholder objective is to protect the company's competitive interests. Shareholders use compensation to align executives' interests with shareholders' interests. Boards of directors award company stock to align executives' interests with shareholders' interests.

TOURNAMENT THEORY **Tournament theory** casts lucrative executive compensation as the prize in a series of tournaments or contests among middle- and top-level managers who aspire to become CEOs.[25] Winners of the tournament at one level enter the next tournament level. In other words, an employee's promotion to a higher rank signifies a win, and more lucrative compensation (e.g., higher base pay, incentives, enhanced benefits, and perks) represents the prize. The ultimate prize is promotion to CEO and a lucrative executive compensation package. The chance of winning competitions decreases dramatically as employees rise through the ranks: There are fewer positions at higher levels in corporate hierarchical structures. Figure 2 depicts a visual representation of CEO compensation as a tournament.

SOCIAL COMPARISON THEORY According to **social comparison theory**, individuals need to evaluate their accomplishments, and they do so by comparing themselves to similar individuals.[26] Demographic characteristics (e.g., age or race) and occupation are common comparative bases. Individuals tend to select social comparisons who are slightly better than themselves.[27] Researchers have applied social comparison theory to explain the processes for setting executive compensation.[28]

Compensation committees play an important role in setting executive compensation, and compensation committees often include CEOs from other companies of

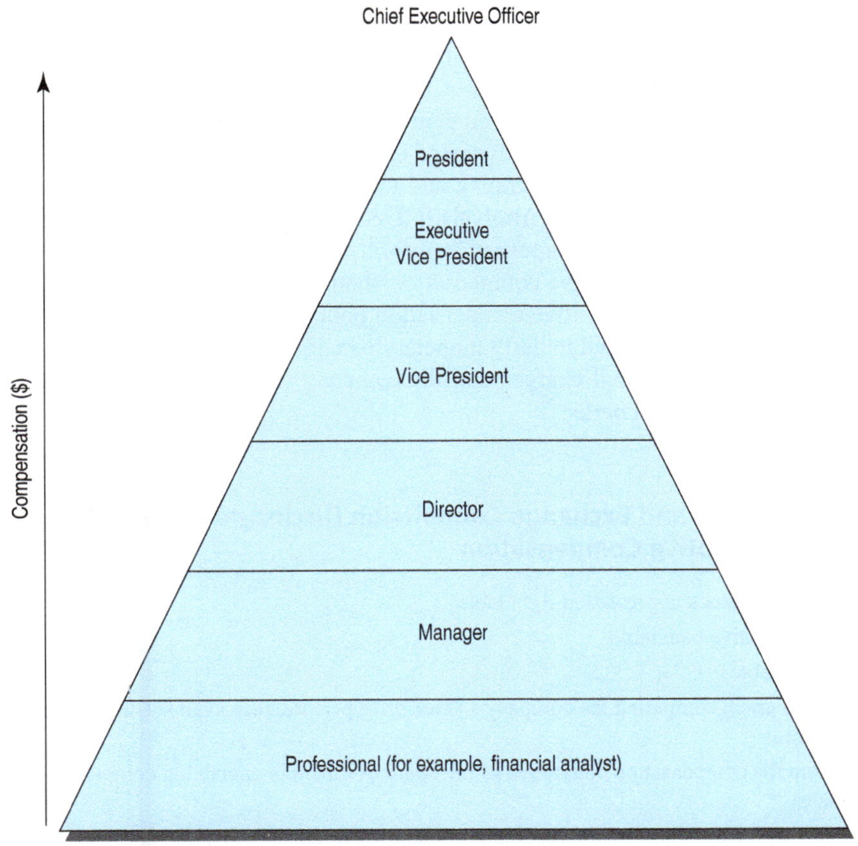

FIGURE 2 CEO Compensation as a Tournament

equal or greater stature. Based on social comparison theory, compensation committee members probably rely on their own compensation packages and the compensation packages of CEOs in companies of equal or greater stature to determine executive compensation.

EXECUTIVE COMPENSATION DISCLOSURE RULES

5 Summarize the executive compensation disclosure rules and the reasons why they have been established.

Disclosure of executive compensation components and engagement of shareholder opinion set executive compensation practices apart from compensating other employee groups. Two laws, in particular, are responsible for these requirements: Securities and Exchange Act of 1934 and the Wall Street Reform and Consumer Protection Act of 2010 (Dodd-Frank Act).

Securities and Exchange Act of 1934

Companies that sell and exchange securities (e.g., company stocks and bonds) on public stock exchanges are required to file a wide variety of information with the **Securities and Exchange Commission (SEC)**, including executive compensation practices. One of the main goals is to help prospective investors understand the financial matters of importance to themselves. The SEC is a nonpartisan, quasi-judicial federal government agency with responsibility for administering federal securities laws. The **Securities Exchange Act of 1934** applies to the disclosure of important company financial information as well as information about executive compensation practices. Each year, companies are required to file a Form 10-K, which contains a detailed picture of a company's business, the risks it faces, and the operating and financial results for the fiscal year. In addition, the 10-K includes management's perspective on their business results and what is influencing them.

Companies are also required to complete a **Definitive Proxy Statement** under Section 14A of the Securities Exchange Act, typically referred to as a DEF 14A. It reveals detailed information about the compensation of the CEO and **Named Executive Officers (NEOs)**, who generally are the four most highly compensated officers after the CEO. Within the DEF 14A, companies must disclose multiple types of information, which are listed in Table 3. The information should be presented in narrative and tabular form. The narrative is referred to as the **Compensation Discussion and Analysis (CD&A)** where it must present an unambiguous explanation of all executive compensation information contained in the tables. Disclosing detailed information about executive compensation should increase the accountability of company boards of directors for executive compensation policies and decisions. Failure to comply with SEC reporting rules can lead to hefty monetary penalties. For example, Polycom Inc. paid the SEC $750,000 to settle civil charges that the company failed to report when a CEO used nearly $200,000 for personal perks.[29]

TABLE 3 Securities and Exchange Commission Disclosure Requirements for Executive Compensation

- Stock option and stock appreciation right tables
- Long-term incentive plan table
- Pension plan table
- Performance graph comparing the company's stock price performance against a market index and a peer group
- Report from the compensation committee of the board of directors explaining compensation levels and policies
- Description of the directors' compensation, disclosing all amounts paid or payable
- Disclosure of certain employment contracts and golden parachutes

TABLE 4 2008 Summary Compensation Table

		Annual Compensation	Long-term Compensation	All Other Compensation ($)
Keith S. Sherin, Vice Chairman and CFO	2008	$1,500,000	$2,550,000	$2,987,493
	2007	$1,354,167	$3,000,000	$3,076,095
	2006	$1,225,000	$2,550,000	$2,808,919
Michael A. Neal, Vice Chairman	2008	$1,650,000	$2,900,000	$3,512,898
	2007	$1,550,000	$3,880,000	$4,212,201
	2006	$1,400,000	$3,300,000	$3,906,929
John G. Rice, Vice Chairman	2008	$1,650,000	$2,700,000	$3,659,090
	2007	$1,550,000	$3,000,000	$4,406,900
	2006	$1,400,000	$2,550,000	$4,122,437
Brackett B. Denniston, Senior Vice President, General Counsel and Secretary	2008	$1,200,000	$1,850,000	$2,284,110
David R. Nissen, Former President & CEO, GE Money	2008	$1,350,000	$1,310,000	$6,777,594
Robert C. Wright, Former Vice Chairman	2008	$916,667	$2,783,000	—
	2007	$2,750,000	$7,590,000	$1,943,665
	2006	$2,500,000	$6,900,000	$2,516,712

Source: Based on Summary Compensation Table: 17 C.F.R 229.402(b), as amended November 29, 1993, effective January 1, 1994.

DEF 14As must be filed each year in advance of the annual meeting of the board of directors and company shareholders. This information is available to the public through a company's annual report, which can be found on its website. Also, the SEC offers a database on its site (*http://www.sec.gov*) referred to as EDGAR, which contains all of the required filings.

There are several tables contained within the DEF 14A, but the most important here is the Summary Compensation Table,[30] which discloses compensation information for the CEO and the four most highly paid executives over a 3-year period. As you can see in Table 3, the Summary Compensation Table for General Electric covers the compensation paid to the named executive officers during the past completed fiscal year and the two preceding fiscal years. The table contains two main subheadings: annual compensation and long-term compensation. Annual compensation includes salary (i.e., base pay), bonus, and other annual compensation. Long-term compensation includes restricted stock awards, stock appreciation rights, and long-term incentive payouts. The last column, "All Other Compensation ($)," is a catchall column to record other forms of compensation. Information in this column must be described in a footnote.

In 2008, the SEC unveiled additional rules for disclosing executive compensation. These rules require that companies reveal how much executives are paid, making such previously hard-to-find information as pension and estimated severance package totals transparent. Although the new rules represent a substantial improvement in pay disclosure, the SEC made a revision that resulted in a less-meaningful disclosure of stock options.

In 2009, the SEC chairperson announced further changes in the disclosure of executive compensation in a company's Summary Compensation Table. The change pertains to the reported value for stock options and stock awards. The SEC disclosure rules show components of compensation previously hidden as well as provide clarity into elements of compensation already disclosed. The most significant changes follow:

Total. The Summary Compensation Table of a company's proxy will now have a column that adds up and displays the total compensation an executive received for the previous year. In the SEC pay database this year, this is labeled SEC Total.

Change in Pension Value and Nonqualified Deferred Compensation. This column in the Summary Compensation Table shows the increase in actuarial value to the executive officer of all defined benefit pension plans and earnings on nonqualified deferred compensation plans.

All Other. This column captures compensation that does not fit in any other column of the Summary Compensation Table, including perquisites and other personal items (e.g., aircraft usage, car service, and club memberships). Each item of compensation included in All Other that exceeds $10,000 will now be separately identified and quantified in a footnote.

Pension Benefits. The new rules require companies to disclose the present value of accumulated pension benefits, showing the total lump sum amount of money an executive would receive in retirement.

Severance Benefits. Companies must disclose any termination or change-in-control agreements with executives. They must disclose the specific circumstances that will trigger payment and the estimated total payments and benefits provided for each circumstance.

The following table describes each component of the All Other Compensation column.

2008 All Other Compensation Table

We provide our named executives with additional benefits, reflected in the table below for 2008, that we believe are reasonable, competitive, and consistent with the company's overall executive compensation program. The costs of these benefits constitute only a small percentage of each named executive's total compensation.

Name of Executive	Other Benefits[a] ($)	Tax Payments[b] ($)	Value of Supplemental Life Insurance Premiums[c] ($)	Payments Relating to Employee Savings Plan[d] ($)	Total ($)
Immelt	212,293	0	152,476	8,050	372,819
Sherin	178,522	14,403	87,743	8,050	288,718
Neal	185,253	0	150,741	8,050	344,044
Rice	130,547	12,915	109,561	8,050	261,073
Denniston	74,943	21,000	146,864	8,050	250,857
Nissen	34,695	4,923	142,758	8,050	190,426
Wright	1,274,024	13,195	784,789	8,050	2,080,058

[a] See the 2008 Other Benefits Table for additional information.
[b] This column reports amounts reimbursed for the payment of taxes with respect to financial counseling, tax preparation services, and the personal use of car service. Starting in 2009, the company will no longer reimburse named executives for the payment of these taxes. See the 2008 Other Benefits Table for the incremental costs associated with providing these services.
[c] This column reports taxable payments made to the named executives to cover premiums for universal life insurance policies owned by the executives. These policies include: (1) Executive Life, which provides universal life insurance policies for the named executives totaling $3 million in coverage at the time of enrollment, increased 4 percent annually thereafter, and (2) Leadership Life, which provides universal life insurance policies for the named executives with coverage of two times their salary plus 100 percent of their latest bonus payments. The amount for Mr. Wright also includes Supplemental Life, the predecessor plan to Executive Life.
[d] This column reports company matching contributions to the named executives' 401(k) savings accounts of 3.5 percent of pay up to the limitations imposed under IRS rules.

The following table describes other benefits and the cost to the company of providing them. The total amount of these other benefits is included in the All Other Compensation Table for each named executive.

2008 Other Benefits

The following table describes other benefits and the incremental cost to the company of providing them in 2008. The total amount of these other benefits is included in the 2008 All Other Compensation Table above for each named executive.

Name of Executive	Use of Aircraft[a] ($)	Leased Cars[b] ($)	Financial Counseling and Tax Preparation[c] ($)	Other[d] ($)	Total ($)
Immelt	189,449	0	0	22,844	212,293
Sherin	116,673	31,170	20,575	10,104	178,522
Neal	175,060	0	0	10,193	185,253
Rice	69,484	18,534	18,450	24,079	130,547
Denniston	9,713	28,620	30,000	6,610	74,943
Nissen	0	21,040	7,033	6,622	34,695
Wright	244,083	8,832	12,790	1,008,319	1,274,024

[a] The calculation of incremental cost for personal use of company aircraft includes the variable costs incurred as a result of personal flight activity: a portion of ongoing maintenance and repairs, aircraft fuel, satellite communications, and any travel expenses for the flight crew. It excludes nonvariable costs, such as exterior paint, interior refurbishment, and regularly scheduled inspections, which would have been incurred regardless of whether there was any personal use of the aircraft.
[b] Includes expenses associated with the leased cars program, such as leasing and management fees, administrative costs, and gas allowance.
[c] Includes expenses associated with the use of advisors for financial, estate, and tax preparation and planning, as well as investment analysis and advice.
[d] This column reports the total amount of other benefits provided, none of which individually exceeded the greater of $25,000 or 10 percent of the total amount of these benefits for the named executive. These other benefits included: (1) car service fees, (2) home alarm and generator installation, maintenance, and monitoring, (3) costs relating to company-sponsored events at board meetings for the executives' spouses, (4) participation in the Executive Products and Lighting Program pursuant to which executives can receive GE appliances or other products with incremental cost calculated based on the fair market value of the products received, and (5) an annual physical examination. For Mr. Wright, the amount includes contributions aggregating $1 million made by the company to charitable organizations upon Mr. Wright's retirement as a director.

Wall Street Reform and Consumer Protection Act of 2010 (Dodd-Frank Act)

President Barack Obama signed the **Wall Street Reform and Consumer Protection Act of 2010** to further enhance the transparency of executive compensation practices. Also commonly referred to as the **Dodd-Frank Act**, the act requires the companies that trade stock on public exchanges to comply with four major provisions. The first provision requires **say on pay**. Say on pay gives company shareholders the right to vote yes or no on executive compensation proposals that are contained in proxy statements, including current and deferred components and golden parachute agreements. The frequency is determined by shareholder vote. Although the say on pay provision guarantees shareholders the right to vote on executive compensation proposals, the vote is nonbinding. That is, the outcome of shareholders' voting does not overrule any compensation decision made by the company's board of directors. The nonbinding vote advises the company's board of directors of possible concerns about the structure of executive compensation packages, including excessive perks and the lack of clarity between compensation and business results. In 2013, shareholder support for executive compensation programs exceeded 90 percent, and only 2 percent of companies failed the vote based on receiving fewer than 50 percent support.[31]

The second provision details independence requirements for compensation committee members and their advisors, such as compensation consultants and legal counsel. Members of compensation committees typically receive compensation for their services, and this practice is considered to be acceptable. However, possible violations of the Dodd-Frank independence requirement may arise when at least one committee member also receives compensation as a company employee. For example, a compensation committee member who also serves as the company's executive vice president may be considered violating the independence requirement. On the other hand, a compensation committee member who does not receive compensation from the company as an employee or external consultant would not violate the independence requirement.

Similarly, the Dodd-Frank Act specifies independence requirements for advisors to the compensation committee such as compensation consultants and legal counsel. A company's compensation committee must consider whether the fees charged by advisors exceed reasonable limits based on the amount of the fees as a percentage of the company's total revenue. Another consideration is whether an advisor has a business or personal relationship with committee members.

The third provision requires that companies disclose the circumstances under which an executive would benefit from a golden parachute arrangement. Specifically, disclosure is required of all agreements and understandings that the acquiring and target companies have with the executive officers of both companies.

The fourth provision requires that companies report the ratio of CEO compensation to the median compensation of its employees in SEC filings that require executive compensation disclosure. This disclosure will help inform shareholders when taking a "say on pay" vote. The SEC adopted this rule in August 2015, with which companies must comply for their first fiscal year beginning on or after January 1, 2017. The rule provides companies with flexibility in calculating this pay ratio. For instance, a company may choose the methodology for identifying its median employee and that employee's compensation. Statistical sampling of its employee population is considered to be an acceptable method.

EXECUTIVE COMPENSATION: ARE U.S. EXECUTIVES PAID TOO MUCH?

6 Briefly explain the executive compensation controversy as it relates to whether U.S. executives are paid too much.

Are U.S. executives paid too much? Popular press and newspaper accounts generally suggest that executives are overpaid. Of course, you should form your own opinion based on the following pertinent information:

- Comparison between executive compensation and other worker groups
- Strategic questions: Is pay for performance?
- Ethical considerations: Is executive compensation fair?
- International competitiveness

Comparison between Executive Compensation and Compensation for Other Worker Groups

The median annual earnings for all civilian workers was $47,230 in May 2014.[32] Among the nonexecutive employees, fast food cooks earned the least ($19,480) and anesthesiologists earned the most ($246,320).[33] The U.S. Bureau of Labor Statistics reports that the median annual salary for top executives was $180,200.[34] However, other surveys provide substantially higher estimates. For example, the *Wall Street Journal*/Hay Group survey reports that average annual total compensation amounts to approximately $11.4 million, of which $1.2 million is annual salary, $2.3 is annual incentives, and $7.9 million is based on long-term incentives. The difference in reported amounts for CEO pay is staggering, but closer consideration of sample characteristics helps to explain some of this gap. The U.S. Bureau of Labor Statistics conducts a nationwide survey of a representative sample of companies in the private and public sectors, by different ownership types, and company size. The *Wall Street Journal*/Hay Group study is based on the 300 largest firms based on an analysis of proxy statements filed with the SEC.[35]

Strategic Questions: Is Pay for Performance?

There are several measures of corporate performance (Table 5). Are CEOs compensated commensurately with their companies' performance? It is difficult to answer just *yes* or *no* because the evidence is mixed based on decades of academic research and the compensation of executives relative to company performance; therefore, a simple statement cannot be made about the relationship between CEO pay and company performance. Shareholder returns most often describe company performance, but there are complex forces beyond the control of CEOs that may influence shareholder returns. For example, in the pharmaceutical industry, substantial investments in research to identify promising medicines require trial and error before a promising outcome occurs in the laboratory. Then lengthy clinical trials that span multiple years may show that the new medication does not cure an illness for which it was created. Such public failures often result in lower confidence in the company, which often translates into lower shareholder returns. In the intervening time, the company hires a new CEO who was not involved in the decision to pursue the failed initiative, raising the question whether she should receive lower compensation following a decline in shareholder returns.

TABLE 5 Corporate Performance Measures

Size
- Sales
- Assets
- Profits
- Market value
- Number of employees

Growth
- Sales
- Assets
- Profits
- Market value
- Number of employees

Profitability
- Profit margin
- Return on assets (ROA)
- Return on equity (ROE)

Capital Markets
- Dividend yield
- Total return to shareholders
- Price–earnings ratio
- Payout

Liquidity
- Current ratio
- Quick ratio
- Working capital from operations
- Cash flow from operations

Leverage
- Debt-to-equity ratio
- Short-term vs. long-term debt
- Cash flow vs. interest payments

Nevertheless, some companies do reduce CEO pay when company performance does not meet a preestablished standard. For example, Credit Suisse cut its CEO's incentive pay in 2014 by more than 1 million Swiss francs when the company reported a 19 percent decline in profits because of costly legal battles in which the company has been involved.[36] Canadian aircraft manufacturer Bombardier cut its former CEO's pay drastically in 2014 from $6.02 million the year before to $5.16 million when the company failed to meet its deadline for a new product launch.[37]

Ethical Considerations: Is Executive Compensation Fair?

Is executive compensation fair? Three considerations drive this question: companies' abilities to attract and retain top executives, income disparities between executives and other employees, and layoffs of thousands of nonexecutive employees.

ATTRACT AND RETAIN TOP EXECUTIVES Many compensation professionals and board of directors members argue that the trends in executive compensation are absolutely necessary for attracting and retaining top executives. Even though most CEOs are promoted from within, it is often the case that companies that hire new CEOs from other companies pay them substantially more than individuals who are promoted to CEO from within the company ranks. For example, median total pay for internal promotions was $7.76 million while nearly 42 percent higher for external hires, amounting to $10.99 million.[38] However, regardless of source, the typical percentage of total compensation awarded in equity plans was approximately 50 percent.

INCOME DISPARITIES Table 6 illustrates the marked income disparity between annual pay for various nonexecutive jobs and pay for CEOs. The typical annual earnings for the lowest-paid occupation (fast food cooks) amounted to a mere 0.55 percent (yes, about one-half of 1 percent) of the average annual CEO salary and bonus. The ratio of highest-paid occupation (anesthesiologiests) to the average annual CEO salary and bonus was not much better (i.e., 7.0 percent). Said differently, the typical CEO's annual salary plus bonus was nearly 180 times greater than the typical fast food cook's annual pay and approximately 15 times greater than the typical anesthesiologist's annual pay!

Labor unions continually argue that substantial pay discrepancies between CEOs and non-CEOs are socially unjust and promote economic inequality. The AFL-CIO indicates that the CEO-to-minimum wage pay ratio was 774:1.[39] In addition, they maintain that the full-time

TABLE 6 Selected Median Annual Nonexecutive Earnings, May 2014

Occupation	Annual Earnings ($)
Anesthesiologists	246,320
Lawyers	133,470
General and operations managers	117,200
Registered nurses	69,700
Construction and equipment operators	47,340
Office clerks	30,820
Teacher assistants	26,000
Fast-food cooks	19,480

Source: U.S. Bureau of Labor Statistics. (2015). *Occupational Employment Wages—May 2014* (USDL: 15-0479). Available: *www.bls.gov*, accessed April 7, 2015.

minimum wage earners would work 1,372 hours to earn one hour of former CEO Michael Duke's (Walmart) pay.

LAYOFFS BORNE BY WORKERS BUT NOT EXECUTIVES Millions of workers have been laid off since 1990. Between late 2008 and mid-2009 alone, more than 2 million employees lost their jobs.[40] Top management typically advances several reasons that necessitate these layoffs (e.g., global competition, reductions in product demand, technological advances that perform many jobs more efficiently than employees, mergers and acquisitions, establishing production operations in foreign countries with lower labor costs, and the steep economic downturn following the recession). A scant few executives lost their jobs, but millions of workers lost theirs in the years following the start of the 2008 economic recession.

International Competitiveness

Increased global competition has forced companies in the United States to become more productive. Excessive expenditures on compensation can threaten competitive advantage. Compensation expenditures are excessive when they outpace the quality and quantity of employees' contributions. In addition, compensation expenditures may be excessive when they are substantially higher than competitors' compensation outlays. Concerns about U.S. companies' competitiveness in global markets are common because of the vast differences in compensation levels between the CEOs of U.S. and foreign companies.

INTERNATIONAL COMPENSATION COMPARISONS The SEC rules require the disclosure of executive compensation in U.S. companies; however, comparable rules do not exist in many foreign countries. As a result, it is difficult to make detailed comparisons between U.S. and foreign executive compensation. Nevertheless, recent research has studied the levels and composition of CEO compensation in the U.S. and in other countries where disclosure laws necessitate reporting of CEO pay. Prior to and since this scientific study, surveys indicated that U.S. CEOs make upwards of 300 percent more than their counterparts in other countries. However, while this study demonstrates that CEOs make more than their counterparts, the gap is far more modest. Specifically, the average pay premium was only 26 percent after controlling for relevant characteristics such as company size, ownership and board of directors structure, and CEO characteristics such as source of CEO (internal or external hire), age, and past industry experience.[41] This study found that non-U.S. CEOs earned an annual median total compensation of $1.6 million and U.S. CEOs earned $3.3 million. The levels varied tremendously among non-U.S. CEOs, ranging from $0.9 million in Belgium to $2.7 million in Italy. Composition also varied. For instance, the typical Canadian CEO earned only 33 percent of total compensation in salary while the typical Swedish CEO earned 62 percent of total compensation in salary.

UNDERMINING U.S. COMPANIES' ABILITY TO COMPETE At present, there is no evidence showing that U.S. executive compensation pay practices have undermined U.S. companies' ability to compete with other companies in the global marketplace. Might executive compensation practices undermine U.S. companies' competitiveness in the future?

On one hand, it is reasonable to predict that CEO pay will not undermine U.S. companies' ability to compete because CEO pay increased as company profits increased. On the other hand, the current wave of widespread layoffs may hinder U.S. companies' competitiveness. The U.S. companies use layoffs to maintain profits and cut costs, heightening workers' job insecurities. The remaining workers may lose their faith in pay-for-performance systems and their trust in their employers as colleagues lose their jobs and CEOs continue to receive higher compensation. Workers may not feel that working hard will lead to higher pay or job security; therefore, they may choose not to work proficiently. As a result, reduced individual performance and destabilized workforces may make it difficult for U.S. companies to compete against foreign companies.

COMPENSATION IN ACTION

Executive compensation, long under the watchful eye of the public and politicians, has been under a microscopic lens during the recent global economic crisis. Executive compensation decisions are approved in the end by the board of directors (in response to recommendations provided to them by the compensation committee of the board and external executive compensation consultants); however, line managers and HR should seek to understand the principles being applied and the compensation plans being employed. This knowledge will help as employees raise questions about executive compensation, and it will make you more aware of practices that are fair and successful versus practices that are blatantly contrary to law, thus being able to protect the company and its employees. Perhaps if line managers and HR managers had been more vigilant about these processes, the tragedies at Enron and Tyco would never have occurred.

Action checklist for line managers and HR—assessing executive compensation in your company

HR takes the lead

- Conduct an analysis of the company's culture, ideals, values, and history. Does the executive compensation plan align with those factors?
- Is the executive compensation plan balanced with regards to cash versus equity, reward versus risk, short-term versus long-term performance? An overemphasis on any one side could result in behaviors that help executives but hurt the shareholders and the company in the end.
- What severance plans are being offered? Do the platinum parachutes in your company essentially minimize all risks for executives? Will the financial windfall be so large that an executive has little reason to avoid failure?
- If you believe the practices of your organizations are not in accordance with the disclosure regulations of the SEC or the requirements outlined explicitly under the Sarbanes-Oxley Act, it may be necessary for you to bring this to the attention of line managers. Together you can take these concerns to the proper people inside or outside the company.

Line managers take the lead

- What are the objectives by which the executives in your company are being measured? Are these similar to the objectives by which you are measured?
- What are the long-term incentives? Is this completely tied to stock price? Ideally, the long-term plan should include multiyear stock and a cash plan. With the plan too tied to stock price (through stock options), the wrong behaviors are encouraged and shareholders suffer in the long term. (Note: At the start of 2000, 90 percent of long-term incentives were in the form of stock options; now it is closer to 50 percent.)

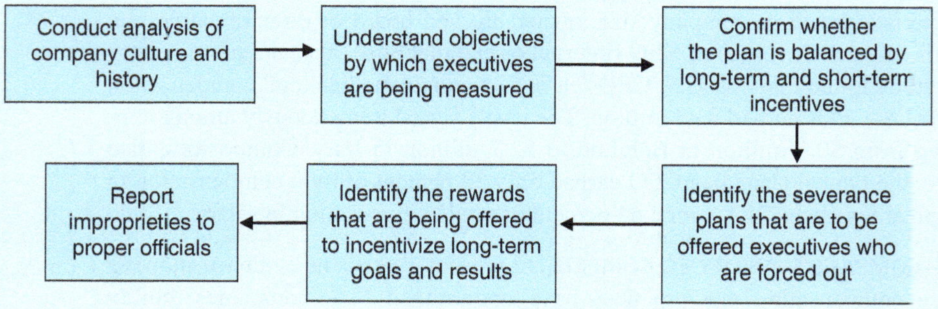

END OF CHAPTER REVIEW

MyManagementLab

Go to **mymanagementlab.com** to complete the problems marked with this icon ✪.

Summary

Learning Objective 1: Executive compensation is determined by a company's board of directors who are usually high-level executives, either within and outside the company, as well as prominent community members, such as lawyers. The recommendation for executive compensation comes from a compensation consultant, who is often hired by the CEO. Compensation for nonexecutive employees is typically based on market rates or from the negotiations between union and management, and is adjusted according to performance or acquisition of new knowledge or skills.

Learning Objective 2: The Internal Revenue Code defines two group of employees—key employees and highly compensated employees—who are deemed to have executive status. Although the criteria differ somewhat between these two groups, both criteria are generally based on salary level and ownership stake in the company.

Learning Objective 3: The components of executive compensation packages include four main components: (1) current or annual core compensation, various types of deferred compensation, including (2) stock-based compensation, and (3) separation agreements such as golden parachutes and platinum parachutes, (4) enhanced employee benefits and perquisites, and (5) clawback provisions.

Learning Objective 4: The principles and processes for setting executive compensation are based on three theories. These include agency theory, tournament theory, and social comparison theory.

Learning Objective 5: Executive compensation disclosure rules were established to protect the interests of potential and current investors (or, shareholders) of companies. Both the Securities and Exchange Act of 1934 and the Wall Street Reform and Consumer Protection Act of 2010 (Dodd-Frank Act) require extensive reporting of executive compensation amounts and the rationale for these amounts for the CEO and named executive offers, and shareholder engagement through nonbinding votes on proposed executive compensation packages.

Learning Objective 6: There is ongoing public controversy regarding whether executives are excessively highly compensated. The debate draws on various data and principles, such as international competitiveness, fairness, and social justice. There is not a straightforward solution to this controversy based on differences in data presented to support each side's arguments as well as differences in ideology.

Key Terms

key employee
highly compensated employee
discretionary bonuses
performance-contingent bonuses
predetermined allocation bonus
target plan bonus
equity plans
separation agreements
deferred compensation
company stock
company stock shares
incentive stock options
capital gains
capital loss
nonstatutory stock options
restricted stock plans
restricted stock units
performance plan
stock appreciation rights
phantom stock
offering period
golden parachutes
platinum parachutes
clawback provisions
Sarbanes-Oxley Act of 2002
perquisites
perks
supplemental life insurance
supplemental retirement plans
executive compensation consultants
board of directors
compensation committee
agency theory
agency problem
tournament theory
social comparison theory
Securities and Exchange Commission (SEC)
Securities Exchange Act of 1934
Definitive Proxy Statement [DEF 14(A)]
Named Executive Officers (NEO)
Compensation Discussion and Analysis (CD&A)
Wall Street Reform and Consumer Protection Act of 2010
Dodd-Frank Act
say on pay

MyManagementLab

CHAPTER QUIZ!

If your professor has assigned this, go to the Assignments section of **mymanagementlab.com** complete to the Chapter Quiz! and see what you've learned.

Discussion Questions

1. What can be done to make the function of compensation committees consistent with shareholders' interests? Explain your answer.
2. Which component of compensation is most essential to motivate executives to lead companies toward competitive advantage? Discuss your rationale.
3. Discuss your position on executive compensation. Is executive compensation universally excessive or appropriate?
4. Discuss the differences between enhanced benefits and perquisites.
5. Consult a recent news article about a company's executive pay. Summarize the main issues detailed within the article.

CASE
CEO Pay in the News

An additional Supplemental Case can be found on MyManagementLab.

A recent campaign by organized labor unions has brought the issue of executive compensation into the public eye. Media coverage of executive compensation concerns has been extensive over the past few weeks with articles in national publications and a featured story on a television special, in addition to stories on local news stations. This extensive coverage has highlighted public concerns of the high level of pay that top executives receive. The union promotes an executive compensation awareness campaign every year as a strategy to build awareness of perceived inequities between the pay of CEOs and frontline employees. Such awareness often prompts employees to consider forming a union, resulting in the growth of national unions.

The publicity has caused some turmoil at Oakwood Lawns. For the first time, the company's CEO pay is featured as an example of perceived excess in the executive suite. Several field managers have been in touch with Don Henry, the director of human resources, to report that employees are outraged at the rate of pay of the company CEO and other top executives. In addition to the company's desire to remain union-free, Don also knows that such outrage could lead to low morale and other problems at Oakwood.

The union targeted Oakwood because it is a big company that has faced some financial challenges. The landscaping company has more than 15,000 employees in offices throughout the Midwest, and most of its employees are frontline laborers. The media coverage has been extensive in the area, and many company employees who viewed the story were surprised to learn the CEO is among the highest paid in the United States. The news was especially difficult to hear as the company recently announced that employees would not receive an annual pay increase due to the financial challenges the company is facing.

Oakwood CEO's annual salary is $975,000. Add in a bonus, stock awards, retirement benefits, and other benefits, and his total compensation is close to $10 million a year. The average landscaping technician is paid $28,000 annually. The disparity is clear, and Don must now plan a response to address the employees' concerns.

Questions:

6. What additional information about the CEO's pay package should Don identify to potentially share with the employees?
7. How can Don explain the pay disparity to the employees to ease their concerns about the fairness of the CEO's pay?

Crunch the Numbers!

Comparison of Pay within and Across Industries

An additional Crunch the Numbers! exercise can be found on **mymanagementlab.com.**

As a newly hired compensation analyst, you have been asked to conduct analyses to determine differences in pay for similar jobs between two industries, the ratio of pay for similar jobs within two industries, and the ratio of pay for different jobs within an industry. The data represent annual base wages and exclude incentives or employee benefits. These data were extracted from the U.S. Bureau of Labor Statistics Occupational Employment Statistics Query System (*www.bls.gov*) for May, 2014.

	Industry	
	Oil and Gas Extraction	Retail
Occupation	Annual median wage ($)	Annual median wage ($)
Chief Executives	187,199	180,360
Human Resources Managers	118,730	95,020
Accountants and Auditors	71,780	64,920
File Clerks	30,700	23,430

Questions:

8. By what percent does annual median pay differ between the oil and gas extraction industry and the retail trade industry for (a) chief executives, (b) human resources managers, (c) accountants and auditors, and (d) file clerks?
9. In the oil and gas extraction industry relative to the retail trade industry, what are the pay ratios between (a) chief executives, (b) human resources managers, (c) accountants and auditors, and (d) file clerks, respectively?
10. In the oil and gas extraction industry, what are the pay ratios for the chief executives job to (a) human resources managers, (b) accountants and auditors, and (c) file clerks? In the retail trade industry, what is the ratio of pay for chief executives to (d) human resources managers, (e) accountants and auditors, and (f) file clerks, respectively?

MyManagementLab

Go to **mymanagementlab.com** for Auto-graded writing questions as well as the following Assisted-graded writing questions:

11. Summarize three forms of deferred (stock) compensation.
12. What are the objectives of the say-on-pay rule? Do you think that shareholders should be limited to taking an advisory vote or should shareholders be able to determine an executive's compensation?
13. MyManagementLab Only—comprehensive writing assignment for this chapter.

Endnotes

1. Walters, B., Hardin, T., & Schick, J. (1995). Top executive compensation: Equity or excess? Implications for regaining American competitiveness. *Journal of Business Ethics, 14*, pp. 227–234.
2. Internal Revenue Code, §416 (i).
3. Treas. Reg. §1.416–1, Q13.

4. Internal Revenue Code, §414 (q).
5. §162(m)
6. Esterl, M., & Lublin, J. S. (2014). Coke scales back executive equity compensation, bowing to pressure. *The Wall Street Journal* (October 1). Available: *www.wsj.com*, accessed February 15, 2015.
7. Internal Revenue Code 61, 83, 162, 451; *Treasury Regulations* 1.83.
8. Internal Revenue Code 61, 83, 162; *Treasury Regulations* 1.83.
9. Joshi, P. (2013). Golden parachutes are still very much in style. *The New York Times (June 29)*. Available: *www.nytimes.com*, accessed March 31, 2015.
10. Reindl, J. C. (2014). Compuware execs could get millions in golden parachutes. *The Detroit Free Press* (November 7). Available: *www.freep.com*, accessed April 4, 2015.
11. Mann, T. (2015). A $195 million exit for United Technologies CEO. *The Wall Street Journal* (February 5). Available: *www.wsj.com*, accessed February 10, 2015.
12. Wagner, D. (2014). Phoenix VA chief's bonus rescinded among controversy. *The Arizona Republic* (May 22). Available: *www.azcentral.com*, accessed April 7, 2015.
13. Martocchio, J. J. (2011). *Employee Benefits: A Primer for Human Resource Professionals*. Burr Ridge, IL: McGraw-Hill.
14. I.R.C. §415 (b)(1)(A).
15. Holloway, S. (2015). Executive Perquisites. *Workspan* (March). Available: *www.worldatwork.org*, accessed April 7, 2015.
16. Hodgson, P. (2015). Come fly with them: These CEOs spend the most on the corporate jet. *Fortune* (January 27). Available: *www.fortune.com*, accessed March 5, 2015.
17. Zillman, C. (2015). Which Fortune 100 CEO has the biggest security budget? *Fortune* (January 7). Available: *www.fortune.com*, accessed April 2, 2015.
18. Walker, J. (2015). Fore! Regeneron CEO must pay for his own golf club membership. *The Wall Street Journal* (March 20). Available: *www.wsj.com*, accessed March 22, 2015.
19. Ahmed, M. (2013). Despite the scrutiny, perks remain a key component of executive rewards. *Executive Compensation Bulletin* (July 31). Available: *www.towerswatson.com*, accessed April 3, 2015.
20. Crystal, G. S. (1991). Why CEO compensation is so high. *California Management Review, 34*, pp. 9–29.
21. Ibid.
22. Ibid.
23. Eisenhardt, K. M. (1989). Agency theory: An assessment and review. *Academy of Management Review, 14*, pp. 57–74; Jensen, M., & Meckling, W. H. (1976). Theory of the firm: Managerial behavior, agency costs, and ownership structure. *Journal of Financial Economics, 3*, pp. 305–360; Tosi, H. L., Jr., & Gomez-Mejia, L. R. (1989). The decoupling of CEO pay and performance: An agency theory perspective. *Administrative Science Quarterly, 34*, pp. 169–189; Goodman, P. S. (1974). An examination of referents used in the evaluation of pay. *Organizational Behavior and Human Performance, 12*, pp. 170–195; Lazear, E., & Rosen, S. (1981). Rank-order tournaments as optimum labor contracts. *Journal of Political Economy, 89*, pp. 841–864; O'Reilly, C. A., III, Main, B. G., & Crystal, G. S. (1988). CEO compensation as tournament and social comparison: A tale of two theories. *Administrative Science Quarterly, 33*, pp. 257–274.
24. Jensen, M. C., & Meckling, W. H. (1976). Theory of the firm: Managerial behavior, agency costs, and ownership structure. *Journal of Financial Economics, 3*, pp. 305–360.
25. Lazear, E., & Rosen, S. (1981). Rank-order tournaments as optimum labor contracts. *Journal of Political Economy, 89*, pp. 841–864.
26. Festinger, L. (1954). A theory of social comparison processes. *Human Relations, 7*, pp. 117–140.
27. Tversky, A., & Kahneman, D. (1974). Judgment and uncertainty: Heuristics and biases. *Science, 185*, pp. 1124–1131.
28. O'Reilly, C. A., III, Main, B. G., & Crystal, G. S. (1988). CEO compensation as tournament and social comparison: A tale of two theories. *Administrative Science Quarterly, 33*, pp. 257–274.
29. Stynes, T. (2015). Polycom Inc. agrees to pay $750,000 to settle SEC civil charges. *The Wall Street Journal* (March 31). Available: *www.wsj.com*, accessed April 1, 2015.
30. Summary Compensation Table: 17 C.F.R 229.402(b), as amended November 29, 1993, effective January 1, 1994.
31. Slutsky, S. (2014). Say on pay: The shareholder's voice emerges. *Workspan* (April): pp. 21–25.

32. U.S. Bureau of Labor Statistics. (2015). *Occupational Employment Wages—May 2014* (USDL: 15-0479). Available: *www.bls.gov*, accessed April 7, 2015.
33. Ibid.
34. Ibid.
35. Hay Group. *The Wall Street Journal/Hay Group CEO compensation survey 2013* (news release). Available: *www.haygroup.com*, accessed April 7, 2015.
36. Letzing, J. (2015). Credit Suisse cuts CEO Brady Dougan's pay. *The Wall Street Journal* (March 20). Available: *www.wsj.com*, accessed April 1, 2015.
37. Vieira, P. (2015). Bombardier cut former CEO Beaudoin's pay. *The Wall Street Journal* (March 31). Available: *http://www.wsj.com*, accessed April 2, 2015.
38. Equilar, Inc. (2015). *In With the New – Compensation of Newly Hired Chief Executive Officers* (February 7). Available: *www.equilar.com*, accessed March 30, 2015.
39. AFL-CIO (2014). *Executive Paywatch: High Paid CEOs and the Low Wage Economy.* Available: *www.aflcio.org*, accessed April 1, 2015.
40. U.S. Bureau of Labor Statistics, *Mass Layoffs*; U.S. Bureau of Labor Statistics, *Extended Mass Layoffs*.
41. Fernandes, N., Ferreira, M., Matos, P., & Murphy, K. (2013). Are U.S. CEOs paid more? New international evidence. *Review of Financial Statistics, 26*: pp. 323–367.

Glossary

Agency problem describes an executive's behavior that promotes his or her self-interests rather than the interests of the company owners or shareholders.

Agency theory provides an explanation of executive compensation determination based on the relationship between company owners (shareholders) and agents (executives).

Board of directors represents shareholders' interests by weighing the pros and cons of top executives' decisions. Members include chief executive officers and top executives of other successful companies, distinguished community leaders, well-regarded professionals (e.g., physicians and attorneys), and a few of the company's top-level executives.

Capital gains refers to the difference between the company stock price at the time of purchase and the lower stock price at the time an executive receives the stock options when the stock price at disposition is higher.

Capital losses refers to the difference between the company stock price at the time of purchase and the lower stock price at the time an executive receives the stock options when the stock price at disposition is lower.

Clawback provisions are provisions in CEO employment contracts that allow boards of directors to take back performance-based compensation if they were to subsequently learn that performance goals were not actually achieved, regardless of whether the CEO was responsible for performance falling short of target levels.

Company stock represents the total equity or worth of the company.

Company stock shares represent equity segments of equal value. Equity interest increases with the number of stock shares held.

Compensation committees contain board of director members within and outside a company. Compensation committees review executive compensation consultants' alternate recommendations for compensation packages, discuss the assets and liabilities of the recommendations, and recommend the consultant's best proposal to the board of directors for its consideration.

Compensation Discussion & Analysis (CD&A) contained within the definitive proxy statement (DEF 14A), must present an unambiguous explanation of all executive compensation information contained in the tables.

Deferred compensation refers to an agreement between an employee and a company to render payments to an employee at a future date. Deferred compensation is a hallmark of executive compensation packages.

Definitive proxy statement must file this statement under Section 14a of the Securities Exchange Act. This statement is typically referred to as a **DEF 14A**, revealing detailed information about the compensation of the chief executive officer (CEO) and **named executive officers (NEOs)**, who are the four most highly compensated executives after the CEO. Within the DEF 14A, companies must disclose multiple types of information about compensation. This information should be presented in narrative and tabular form. The narrative is referred to as the Compensation Discussion & Analysis (CD&A) and it must present an unambiguous explanation of all executive compensation information contained in the tables.

Discretionary bonuses are awarded to executives on an elective basis by boards of directors. Boards of directors weigh four factors in determining discretionary bonus amounts: company profits, the financial condition of the company, business conditions, and prospects for the future.

Dodd-Frank Act See also *Wall Street Reform and Consumer Protection Act of 2010.*

Equity plans refers to a type of deferred compensation that is designed to provide an executive with an ownership stake in the company through a variety of mechanisms, including stock plans.

Executive compensation consultants propose recommendations to chief executive officers and board of director members for alternate executive compensation packages.

Golden parachutes a kind of executive deferred compensation, provide pay and benefits to executives following their termination resulting from a change in ownership or corporate takeover.

Highly compensated employees are defined by the Internal Revenue Service as an officer. The term key 'employee' means any employee who at any time during the year is an officer having annual pay of more than $170,000, *OR* an individual who for 2015 was either of the following: a 5 percent owner of the employer's business or a 1 percent owner of the employer's business whose annual pay was more than $150,000.

Incentive stock options entitle executives to purchase their companies' stock in the future at a predetermined price. The predetermined price usually equals the stock price at the time an executive receives the stock options. Incentive stock options entitle executives to favorable tax treatment.

Key employees as defined by the Internal Revenue Service (IRS), include any employee who during the current year is an officer of the employer having an annual pay of more than $170,000, *or* an individual who for 2015 was either of the following: a 5 percent owner of the employer's business or a 1 percent owner of the employer's business whose annual pay was more than $150,000. These dollar amounts are indexed for inflation in increments of $5,000.

Named executive officers (NEOs) are the four most highly compensated after the CEO, and detailed information about their compensation must be disclosed in the definitive proxy statement DEF 14A.

Nonstatutory stock options a kind of executive deferred compensation, entitle executives to purchase their companies' stock in the future at a predetermined price. The predetermined price usually equals the stock price at the time an executive receives the stock options. Nonstatutory stock options do not entitle executives to favorable tax treatment.

Offering period refers to the span in time over which employees, including executives, may purchase the employer's stock based on the money set aside in their accounts established through payroll deduction.

Performance-contingent bonuses awarded to executives, are based on the attainment of such specific performance criteria as market share.

Performance plan refers to a type of equity agreement whereby a company's board of directors establishes performance criteria that an executive must meet before receiving a reward of stocks or stock options.

Perks See also *perquisites*.

Perquisites are benefits offered exclusively to executives (e.g., country club memberships).

Phantom stock a type of executive deferred compensation, is an arrangement whereby boards of directors compensate executives with hypothetical company stock rather than actual shares of company stock. Phantom stock plans are similar to restricted stock plans because executives must meet specific conditions before they can convert these phantom shares into real shares of company stock.

Platinum parachutes are lucrative awards that compensate departing executives with severance pay, continuation of company benefits, and even stock options.

Predetermined allocation bonuses awarded to executives, are based on a fixed formula. Company profits are often the main determinant of the bonus amounts.

Restricted stock plans a company may grant executives with stock options at market value or discounted value, or they may provide stock instead. Under restricted stock plans, executives do not have any ownership control over the disposition of the stock for a predetermined period, often many years. This predetermined period is known as the vesting period, much like vesting rights associated with employer-sponsored retirement plans.

Restricted stock units are shares of company stock that are awarded to executives at the end of the restriction period.

Sarbanes-Oxley Act of 2002 mandated a number of reforms to enhance corporate responsibility, enhance financial disclosures, and combat corporate and accounting fraud in response to corporate accounting scandals in Enron, Tyco, and other large U.S. corporations. The act established Public Company Accounting Oversight Board (PCAOB) to oversee the activities of the auditing profession.

Say on pay gives company shareholders the right to vote yes or no on executive compensation proposals, including current and deferred components, including golden parachute agreements, at least once every 3 years. Although the say on pay provision guarantees shareholders the right to vote on executive compensation proposals, the vote is nonbinding.

Securities and Exchange Commission (SEC) is a nonpartisan, quasi-judicial federal government agency with responsibility for administering federal securities laws.

Securities Exchange Act of 1934 applies to the disclosure of executive compensation.

Separation agreements refer to a type of deferred compensation which guarantees that an executive will receive a lucrative compensation package upon employment termination.

Social comparison theory provides an explanation for executive compensation determination based on the tendency for the board of directors to offer executive compensation packages that are similar to those in peer companies.

Stock appreciation rights a type of executive deferred compensation, provide executives income at the end of a designated period, much like restricted stock options; however, executives never have to exercise their stock rights to receive income. The company simply awards payment to executives based on the difference in stock price between the time the company granted the stock rights at fair market value to the end of the designated period, permitting the executives to keep the stock.

Supplemental life insurance protection represents additional life insurance offered exclusively to executives. Companies design executives' supplemental life insurance protection to increase the value of executives' estates, bequeathed to designated beneficiaries (usually family members) upon their death, and to provide greater benefits than standard plans usually allow.

Supplemental retirement plans offered to executives, are designed to restore benefits restricted under qualified plans.

Target plan bonuses awarded to executives, are based on executives' performance. Executives do not receive bonuses unless their performance exceeds minimally acceptable standards.

Tournament theory provides an explanation for executive compensation determination based on substantially greater competition for high-ranking jobs. Lucrative chief executive compensation packages represent the prize to those who win the competition by becoming chief executives.

Wall Street Reform and Consumer Protection Act of 2010 enhances the transparency of executive compensation practices. Also commonly referred to as the Dodd-Frank Act.

Index